담화표상이론

이 장 송

한국문화사

머리말

언어의 의미는 언어의 표상성을 중심으로 하는 유심주의적 전통과 언어의 대상성을 중심으로 하는 객관주의적 전통에서 주로 연구되어 왔다. 유심주의적 전통에서의 의미 연구는 언어 표현의 의미를 그 표현으로부터 도출 가능한 어떤 심적 표상과 동일시하며 이에 반해 객관주의 의미 연구는 언어 표현의 의미를 이 표현이 참되게 기술할 수 있는 세계의 모습과 동일시한다. 이 두 가지의 의미 연구 전통은 언어 의미의 기술과 설명에 상호 보충적 특성을 지님에도 불구하고 상호 대립적 관계를 이루어 언어 의미 현상에 대한 포괄적 설명을 어렵게 만들어 왔다. 담화표상이론은 이 두 가지 관점을 다 받아들일 수 있는 통합적 의미론 모형을 제공한다.

이 책의 제 1부는 담화표상이론의 이론적 배경 및 그 기본 구조에 대한 입문서적인 성격을 지닌다. 여기에서는 언어 표현으로부터 의미표상을 도출하는 방법과 이 의미표상이 세상의 모습을 참되게 반영하고 있는지를 확인해 보는 절차를 다룬다. 제 2부는 자연 언어의 다양한 양화표현의 의미를 담화표상이론의 기본적 전제를 유지하면서 일관되게 설명할 수 있는 방법을 모색해 본다.

담화표상이론은 이기용 교수님 등에 의해서 우리 나라에 이미 오래 전에 소개되어 많은 분들이 관심을 가지고 연구해 오고 있다. 그러나 아직이 이론에 대한 적절한 소개서가 없어 저자가 만용에 가까운 용기를 내어이 책을 집필하게 되었다. 원래는 담화표상이론의 기본 구조에 대한 설명

4

에 뒤이어 양화 문제, 시제 및 양상 문제, 명제적 태도 등을 차례로 다루고자 하였는데 여러 가지의 제약으로 이 정도로 그치고 말았다.

여러 가지로 부족한 사람을 깊은 애정을 가지고 지도해 주신 고려대학교의 이기용 교수님과 미국 일리노이대 Morgan 교수님께 감사한다. 누가 되지 않는다면 이 작은 결실을 이 분들께 바치고 싶다. 연구를 지원해 준 육군사관학교 화랑대 연구소에 감사한다. 어려운 상황에서도 이 책의 출판을 흔쾌히 맡아 주신 한국 문화사 김진수 사장님께 감사한다.

1999년 5월

저자

차 례

제2부 담화표상이론의 확장

8

제1부

담화표상이론의 기초

제 1 장 담화표상이론이란 무엇인가?

담화표상이론(Discourse Representation Theory; 이하에서 DRT)은 Hans Kamp의 논문 "A Theory of Truth and Semantic Representation"과 Irene R. Heim의 박사 학위 논문 The Semantics of Definite and Indefinite Noun Phrase 의 접근 방법을 따르는 자연언어의 의미에 관한 이론을 일컫는다.

언어 표현의 의미는 주로 두 가지의 관점에서 연구되어 왔다. 첫 번째 견해는 언어 표현의 의미는 그 표현이 참이 되는 조건을 명시함으로써 얻어질 수 있다는 것이다. 예를 들어 "철수가 용감하다"라는 문장의 의미는 이 문장이 진실 되게 기술할 수 있는 대상 세계가 어떠한 것인가를 명시함으로써 접근할 수 있다. 이 문장이 참되게 사용되기 위해서는 기술하는 세계가 "철수"라 불리는 어떤 개체를 포함하고 있어야 하며 이 개체가 "용감하다"라는 말로 표현되는 어떤 속성을 가지고 있어야 한다. 다시 말하면 이 문장의 의미는 이 문장으로 참되게 기술해 낼 수 있는 세상의 모습들 (state of affairs)이다. 따라서, 어떤 문장의 의미를 알기 위해서는 그 문장이 참이 될 수 있는 조건을 이해하면 된다. 이러한 견해는 논리학 등에 바탕을 둔 논리적 의미론(logico-semantics) 또는 형식 의미론(formal semantics)의 전통을 형성하여 진리조건적 의미론(truth-conditional semantics), 모형이론적 의미론(model-theoretic semantics) 등의 모습으로 나타나게 되었다.

진리조건적 의미론은 언어의 대상성(aboutness)을 강조한다. 언어는 우리들로 하여금 세상에 대하여 이야기할 수 있게 하며 우리 자신과 주변 환경에 대하여 정보를 교환할 수 있게 한다. 이 견해에 따르면 언어 표현의 의미는 표현과 세계와의 관계에서 포착되며 이 관계는 언어 사용자와 무

관하게 이루어지는 과정이다. Chierchia and McConnell-Ginet은 언어의 대상성을 언어의 정보적 의미(the informational significance of language)라 부른다.

언어의 정보적 의미로 인하여 두 대화자간 의사 소통이 가능하게 된다면 한 언어 표현이 나타내는 대상은 두 대화자에게 동일한 것이 되어야 할 것이다. 따라서, 한 표현과 그것이 기술하는 대상 사이에는 규칙적이고 체계적인 어떤 관계가 형성되어 있어야 할 것이며 이 체계적 관계는 그 언어를 쓰는 사람들이 공유하고 있어야 한다. 만약, 한 사람이 "황소"라고 부르는 동물을 다른 사람은 "돼지"라고 부른다면 성공적인 의사 소통이 불가능할 것이기 때문이다.

언어는 기표(signifier)와 기의(signified)로 구성된 기호(sign)의 체계이다. 한 기표는 상당한 시간 동안 한 특정 기의와 결합하는 안정적 구조를 가지게 된다. 예를 들어, 한국어의 "연필"이라는 언어 표현(기표)은 흑연 심이 나무로 둘러 쌓여 있는 글을 쓸 때 사용하는 도구라는 기의와 연관되어 있으며, 이 연관 관계는 한국어를 사용하는 화자들에 의해 상당 기간 유지된다. 이런 관계가 유지되는 이유에 관하여 크게 나누어 두 가지의 주장이 제기되어 오랫동안 많은 논란이 계속되었다. 첫 번째 주장은 기표와 기의간에 속성상의 밀접한 관계가 존재하기 때문이라는 것이다. 어떤 새가 "뻐꾸기"라고 불리는 것은 그 새가 가지고 있는 어떤 본래적 속성(여기서는 그 울음소리)과 "뻐꾸기"라는 (음성적) 언어 표현과 밀접한 관계가 있기 때문이라는 것이다. 두 번째의 주장은 언어적 기표와 기의간의 관계는 약정적(conventional)이라는 주장이다. 위에서 언급한 글쓰는 도구를 "연필"이라 부르고 한 특정한 새를 "뻐꾸기"라 부르는 것은 그 언어를 사용하는 언어 사회 구성원들이 그렇게 부르자고 약속했기 때문이며 언어 표현과 기의간에 어떤 필연적 관계가 존재하지 않는다는 주장이다. 이 논의는 "Nature vs. Nurture Controversy"로 알려지고 있다.

모든 언어 표현의 의미가 표현과 대상 세계의 모습과의 관계에서 파악될 수 있는 것은 아니다. 다시 말하여 두 표현의 진리 조건이 동일하다고

해서 같은 의미를 가진다고 하기에는 꺼림칙한 점이 있다. 모든 여자가 어머니인 어떤 세계를 가정해 보자. 이 세계에서 (1)의 문장이 참이 되는 조건하에서 (2)의 문장도 반드시 참이 된다. 즉, 두 문장은 가정된 세계에서 진리 조건이 같다. 그렇다고 이 두 문장의 의미가 같다고 할 수는 없다.

(1) 모든 어머니는 아이가 있다.
(2) 모든 여자는 아이가 있다.

Gotlob Frege(1897)는 언어 표현의 의미는 표현과 대상물과의 관계를 나타내는 지시(reference)와 표현의 개념 또는 속성을 나타내는 의의(sense)의 두 가지 양상을 지니고 있으며 지시적 의미는 의의를 통하여 결정된다고 한다. (1), (2)의 예에서, "어머니"와 "여자"는 지시적 의미는 동일하지만 그 의의가 다르다. 즉, "어머니"는 아이가 있다라는 속성을 가지는데 반해, "여자"는 이러한 속성이 없을 수도 있기 때문이다. Carnap(1947), Kripke(1972), Montague(1974) 등은 의의의 유심적(mentalistic) 성격을 제거하고 객관주의적 접근 방법에 따라 언어 의미를 기술하기 위하여 Frege의 지시와 의의를 외연(extension)과 내포(intension)라는 개념을 도입하여 형식화한다. Montague에 따르면 내포는 가능세계(possible world)와 시점(point of time)으로 구성된 지표(index)로부터 외연으로 가는 함수로 정의된다. 위의 예에서 "어머니"와 "여자"는 한 지표(즉, 가정된 세계)에서의 외연은 동일하지만 내포가 다르기 때문에 (즉, 두 표현의 외연이 다른 지표가 존재할 수 있으므로) 의미적으로 동일하지 않다. 다시 말하여, (1), (2)의 문장은 대상 세계의 기술 잠재력에서 차이가 나므로 그 진리 조건이 동일하지 않다고 할 수 있다.

그러나 (3)과 (4) 같은 문장은 어떠한 지표에서도 참이 되기 때문에 두 표현의 진리조건은 동일하다. 그러나, 두 문장에 대한 직관적 의미는 다르다고 해야 할 것이다. 이러한 예는 문장의 의미는 진리조건 뿐 아니라, 문장에 의해서 명제가 표상 되는 방식에도 관련되어 있음을 보여 준다.

   (3) 삼각형의 내각의 합은 180도이다.
   (4) 모든 어머니는 여자이다.

   언어 표현의 의미에 대한 두 번째 견해는 언어의 의미적 표상성 (semantic representation)을 강조한다. 이 견해에 따르면, 언어 표현의 의미는 언어 사용자가 자신이 듣거나 읽은 표현을 이해했을 때 머리 속에 떠올리는 어떤 심상(image), 개념(concept), 생각(thought) 등을 뜻한다. 언어적 입력에 대한 반응으로 생성되는 표상의 구조를 명시하는 것에 관심이 있는 전산 언어학자, 심리언어학자, 언어학자 등이 이러한 접근방법을 추구하고 있다. Chierchia and McConnell-Ginet은 언어의 표상성을 언어의 인지적 의미(cognitive significance)라 부른다.

   표상(representation)이란 어떤 대상을 일정한 구도(scheme)나 규칙(rule)에 맞추어 어떤 표현 수단을 사용하여 나타낸 것이라 할 수 있다. 예를 들어, 지도는 3차원의 대상을 등고선 등 다양한 부호를 사용하여 어떤 정해진 방식에 따라 2차원의 도형(configuration)으로 표현해 놓은 것이다. 이와 비슷하게 (5)의 영어 문장은 흔히 (6)과 같은 도형으로 표상된다. 통사 표상 (6)에서 "John"이라는 소리는 영어 알파벳, j, o, h, n으로 표상되어 있으며, "John"이라는 소리의 연쇄(sequence of sounds)가 "loves"라는 소리연쇄보다 먼저 발음된다는 사실은 John이라는 부호가 loves라는 부호의 왼쪽에 놓음으로써 표상되고 있다. 영어 알파벳이 결합하여 만들어진 부호 John은 N으로 표시된 범주에 속하며, VP로 표상된 범주는 각각 V, NP로 표상된 범주로 구성되었다고 하는 정보 등을 나타내고 있다. (5)의 문장을 (6)과 같이 표상하는 것은 위에서 언급한 소리연쇄들의 선형성(linearity), 구성성 (constituency), 계층성(hierarchy) 등의 표상 방법에 대한 어떤 구도를 따르고 있기 때문이다.

(5) John loves Mary.

(6)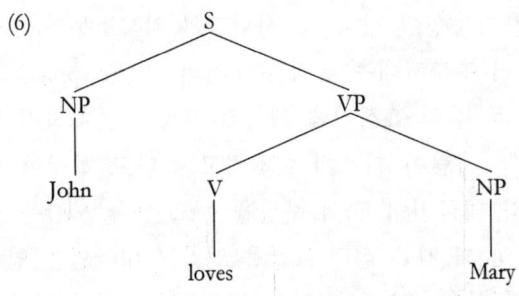

(5)의 문장은 표상방법을 다르게 함으로써 다양하게 표상될 수 있다. 예를 들어, (7)과 같이 [,]를 사용하여 표상할 수도 있고 HPSG(Head-driven Phrase Structure Grammar)의 규약을 따라 매우 다른 모습으로 표상할 수도 있을 것이기 때문이다.

(7) [s[NPJohn] [vp[vloves][NPMary]]]

이제 언어 표현의 의미를 이 표현을 입력으로 하여 얻어진 어떤 심적 표상(mental representation)이라고 한다면 이 표상은 어떤 지형을 표상하는 지도나 어떤 표현의 통사 구조를 표상하는 (6)과는 다른 것이 될 것이다. 왜냐하면 심적 표상은 대상과 표상간에 어떤 인과 관계가 있을 것이기 때문이다. 다시 말하면, 지도 등과 같이 어떤 약속된 부호나 표상 방법에 따라 대상을 표상하는 것이 아니라 한 개인에 내재된 어떤 규칙에 따라 뇌의 어떤 부분에 물리적 변화를 초래하여 입력된 대상을 표상할 것이기 때문이다. 우리는 아직 이와 같은 역할을 하는 뇌의 한 부분의 구조와 활동을 명확히 파악할 수 없으므로 언어 입력으로부터 심적 표상을 추출하는 어떤 연산 방식(algorithm)이 존재하는 것으로 단순히 가정하고자 한다.

언어의 대상성(the aboutness of language)이 언어 표현과 외부 대상 세계와의 관계를 말한다고 하면, 언어의 표상성은 언어 표현과 마음의 내적 상태와의 관계이다. 따라서, 같은 언어 표현을 입력으로 하여 각 사람마다 다른 심적 표상을 만들어낼 가능성이 있다. 두 사람간의 의사소통의 성공 여부는 한 언어 표현으로부터 추출해내는 심적 표상들의 사상(mapping) 가 능성에 달려 있다. 만약 이 두 심적 표상간에 체계적 사상이 존재하지 않 는다면 이 표현의 의미를 두 사람이 다르게 이해하고 있다고 하여야 할 것이다. 예를 들어, 한국인과 미국인이 (5)의 문장을 듣고 한국 사람은 한 국어와 같은 구조를 가지는 (8)과 같은 심적 표상을 얻었고 미국인은 영어 와 같은 구조를 가지는 (9)와 같은 표상을 얻었으며 한국어와 영어 사이에 어떤 사상(mapping)이 존재한다면 이 두 사람은 문장 (5)를 같은 의미로 이 해한다고 할 수 있을 것이다.

(8) 존이라고 불리는 사람이 있다.
메리라고 불리는 사람이 있다.
존이라고 불리는 사람은 메리라고 불리는 사람과 사랑하는 관계에 있다.

(9) There is a person called John.
There is a person called Mary.
The person called John is in the loving relation with the person called Mary.

Chierchia and McConnell-Ginet(1990)이 지적하듯이, 의미의 표상성을 주창 하는 사람들은 대체로 화자의 인지적 상태나 과정 (즉 화자의 심적 의미 표상)에 관하여 청자가 무엇을 어떻게 추론해내는가 하는 문제를 집중적 으로 연구하는 반면 사람들이 매우 일관되게 문장과 그것이 표현하는 대 상 세계의 상황들간의 관계를 판단할 수 있는 능력을 지니고 있음을 간과 한다. Ullmann(1957)은 언어 표현의 의미를 결정하는 데 필요한 대상 세계 사물의 속성은 그 사물로부터 추상되어져서 개념에 표상되기 때문에 대상 세계의 지시물은 의미론자의 직접적 관심의 대상이 될 수 없다는 견해를 피력한다.

언어의 대상성과 표상성은 언어 표현의 의미의 두 구성 요소이다. 위에서 보았듯이, 한 측면만을 강조해서는 언어 의미의 전체적 모습을 파악하기 어렵다. Kamp(1981)는 지금까지 추구해온 의미의 연구가 이 두 가지 의미 양상 중 하나만을 강조해 옴으로써 의미론의 발전에 장애가 되어왔다고 주장하며 담화표상이론(Discourse Representation Theory: DRT)으로 알려진, 언어 의미론에 대한 종합적 접근 방법을 제안한다.

Kamp 이론의 전반적 구조는 매우 단순하다. 언어 사용자는 듣거나 읽은 언어 입력으로부터 심적 표상(mental representation)을 구성한다(이렇게 구성된 표상을 Kamp는 담화표상(discourse representation: DR)이라 부른다). 담화표상은 일종의 부분 모형(partial model)으로 간주된다. 이 표상이 어떤 세상(또는 모형)의 모습을 참되게 기술하고 있는가는 기술하는 세상(또는 모형)으로 이 표상이 사상(mapping)될 수 있는가에 달려 있다. 즉 이 표상이 어떤 모형화된 세계에 내포될(embedded) 수 있다면 이 표상은 세상의 일부분의 모습을 참되게 기술하고 있다고 여겨진다.

한 담화 표상은 술어논리에 있어서 변수(variable)와 같은 역할을 하는 담화 지시체(discourse referent)들의 집합과 이 담화 지시체가 만족하여야 할 조건(condition)으로 구성된다. 담화표상 (10)은 x라는 담화 지시체와 이 지시체에 대한 조건 "x is a student"와 "x is brave"라는 조건으로 구성되어 있다.

(12)

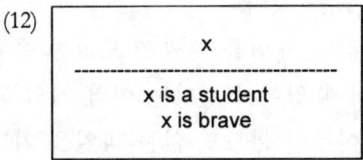

이제 다음과 같은 모형 M=<U, F>를 가정하자. (U는 모형에 존재하는 개체들의 집합이며, F는 기본 표현에 의미값을 부여하는 해석함수이다.)

U={a, b, c}
F(John)=a, F(Mary)=b, F(Bill)=c
F(is-a-student)={a, b}
F(is-brave)={a, c}
F(loves)={<a, b>, <b, c>}

담화표상 (10)의 담화 지시체 "x"가 모형 M의 개체 "a"로 사상된다면 담화표상 (10)은 모형 M에 비추어 참이 된다. 왜냐하면 "x"가 사상된 개체 "a"는 "is-student"와 "is-brave"라는 표현에 의해 기술되는 속성들을 가지고 있기 때문이다.

담화표상에서 중요한 역할을 하는 담화 지시체(discourse referent)는 담화표상 상의 개체이다. 이것은 담화표상의 세계에서 모형의 개체와 비슷한 역할을 한다. 이것은 언어표현으로 지시되며, 어떤 속성을 지니는 것으로 묘사되며, 다른 담화 지시체와 특정한 관계를 유지하기도 한다. 담화 지시체는 모형(또는 대상세계)의 개체에 사상된다. 즉, 어떤 함수에 의해 모형의 개체를 그 값으로 가질 수 있다. 이러한 측면에서 담화 지시체는 술어논리언어(predicate logical language)의 변수(variable)와 비슷하다. 따라서, 한 담화 지시체는 사상의 방식에 따라 한 모형의 상이한 개체를 그 값으로 취할 수 있다. 예를 들어, 담화표상 (10)에서 담화 지시체 x는 내포함수(embedding function) f_1에 의해 모형의 개체 a를 그 값으로 가지며 또다른 함수 f_2에 의해 개체 b에 연결될 수도 있을 것이다.

Heim(1982)은 Kamp의 담화지시체와 같은 개념을 파일 카드라는 은유를 사용하여 표현한다. 그녀에 의하면 대화에 있어서 청자는 여러 개의 파일을 정리하는 비서와 흡사하다. 청자가 아무런 카드도 없는 파일을 가지고 대화를 시작했다고 하자. 이제 청자가 (11)의 문장을 들었다면 그는 서랍에서 두 개의 빈 카드를 꺼내어 파일에 철하고 여기에 1과 2라는 지표를 붙인 다음 각각의 카드에 (12)와 같은 정보를 기록한다.

(11) A woman was beaten by a dog.

(12)

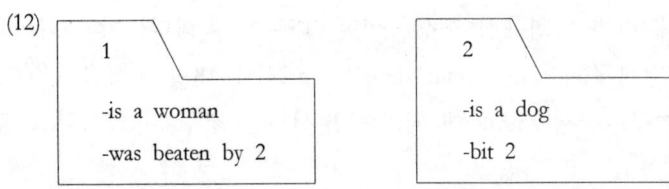

문장 (11)에 이어 (13)의 문장을 들었을 때, 청자는 대명사 she는 1번 카드, 즉 지표 1에 해당하고 대명사 it는 2번 카드 즉 지표 2에 해당한다고 결정하고 (14)와 같이 각 카드에 새로운 정보를 기입한다.

(13) She hit it.

(14)

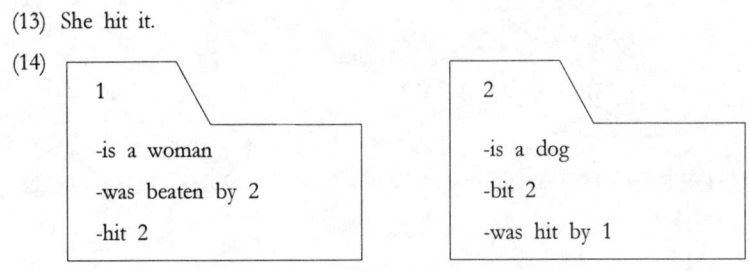

Heim의 파일은 언어입력을 처리하여 도출한 심적 표상으로 Kamp의 담화표상과 동일하며 파일 카드는 담화지시체와 같은 역할을 한다. 즉 파일 카드는 한 모형의 어떤 개체에 대한 표상이다. Heim은 파일과 파일 카드라는 개념을 사용하여 하나 또는 그 이상의 문장으로 구성된 담화 (discourse)를 표상하고 이 표상을 대상 모형에 비추어 평가하는 File-changing Semantics를 구성하였다. 이 이론은 이상에서 살펴 본 바와 같이 Kamp의 담화표상 이론과 담화에 대한 접근 방법과 이론적 가정들을 공유하고 있다. 이 책의 나머지 부분에서 편의상 Kamp의 방식을 따르겠다.

Kamp의 담화표상이론에서 문장에 대한 표상은 그 문장의 통사 구조에 어떤 규칙이 적용되어 도출된다. 이 규칙을 담화표상 구성 규칙(Discourse

Representation Construction Rules)이라 한다. 따라서 문장의 통사 구조를 명시하는 방법에 따라 담화표상 구성 규칙은 다르게 정의되어야 한다. 예를 들어 비한정 명사구(indefinite noun phrase) "an N"에 대한 구성규칙은 통사 구조를 구구절구조규칙(PS-rule)에 의하여 명시하는 경우 다음과 같이 정의된다.

(15) 통사구조가 (a) 또는 (b)일 경우, (가) 담화표상에 새로운 담화지시체 α를 도입하고, (나) 해당 비한정 명사구를 이 담화지시체로 대체한 구조와 N(α)를 담화표상의 조건으로 도입한다.

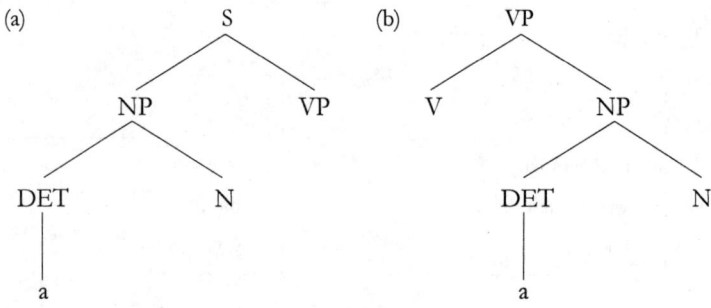

담화표상구성규칙 (15)에 의해 (15a)의 구조는 (16)으로 표상 된다.

(16)

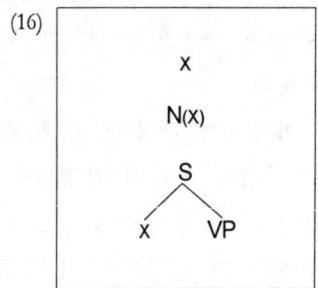

이상에서 살펴 본대로 담화표상이론은 문장의 통사분석부문, 분석된 통사구조로부터 담화표상을 도출하는 담화표상구성규칙과 담화표상을 모형에로 사상시켜 표상의 참과 거짓을 결정하는 의미부문으로 구성된다.

담화의 표상은 담화를 구성하는 문장들을 순서대로 처리하여 이루어진다. 즉, 담화의 최초 문장을 처리하여 어떤 표상을 얻은 후, 이를 바탕으로 두 번째 문장을 처리하여 두 번째 정보를 포함하도록 최초의 표상을 확장하고 담화의 마지막 문장을 처리하여 담화에 대한 최종 표상을 도출하게 된다. 위의 (11), (13)의 문장으로 이루어진 담화는 (11)을 처리하여 (17)의 담화표상을 도출하고 다시 (13)을 처리하여 (18)의 최종 담화표상을 얻는다.

(17)
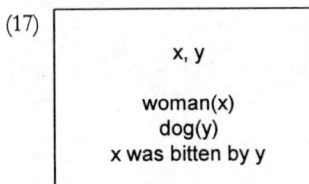

(18)
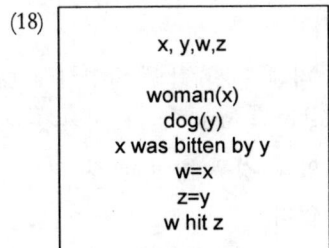

담화표상이론은 언어표현의 대상성(aboutness)과 표상성(representation)을 포착할 수 있다는 장점과 함께 문장의 범위를 벗어나는 담화 차원의 현상을 설명할 수 있는 방법을 제공한다. 한 단어는 그 자체로서의 완전한 의

미를 가지는 것이 아니고 자신이 포함되어 있는 문장에 의하여 표현되는 명제의 내용에 공헌하는 바에 따라 결정된다. 즉 단어의 의미는 문장 내에서의 쓰임에 의해 결정된다. 이와 마찬가지로, 문장의 의미도 그 문장이 쓰이는 담화의 맥락에 의해 결정된다. 다시 말하여, 담화 내의 문장들은 순차적으로 대상 세계를 표상하는데 기여한다. 문장 범위 밖의 표현과 조응하는 담화 조응어는 담화 내 문장들의 이러한 성격에 의하여 그 의미를 부여받게 된다. 그러므로, 담화를 정확히 이해하기 위해서는 표현과 세계와의 수직적 관계 뿐 아니라, 문장들이 서로 연결되어 복잡한 명제 구조를 표현하는 방식에 대한 이해도 필요하게 된다.

한 표현이 문장의 범위를 넘어 다른 표현의 의미를 결정할 수 있는 잠재력은 표현에 따라 다르게 나타난다. "John"이나 "Mary" 같은 고유명사는 (19)에서와 같이 매우 자유롭게 다음 문장내의 대명사의 선행사가 될 수 있다.

(19) (a) John$_i$ loves his$_i$ mother.

　　 (a) Mary loves John$_i$. He$_i$ likes music.

　　 (b) A woman loves John$_i$. He$_i$ likes music.

　　 (c) Every woman loves John$_i$. He$_i$ likes music.

"a man" 같은 비한정 명사구는 고유명사에 비해 문장 밖의 대명사에 대한 통제력에서 제한되어 있다. (20)의 예에서 보이는 바와 같이 비한정 명사구가 전칭 양화 표현 "every"의 범위 안에 있을 경우 이 비한정 명사구는 다음 문장 내의 대명사의 선행사가 될 수 없다.

(20) (a) [A man]$_i$ loves his$_i$ mother.

　　 (b) Mary loves [a man]$_i$. He$_i$ likes music.

　　 (c) A woman loves [a man]$_i$. He$_i$ likes music.

　　 (d) Every woman loves [a man]$_i$. *He$_i$ likes music.

"every man"과 같은 전칭 양화 명사구는 문장 밖의 대명사를 통제할 수 있는 역동성의 측면에서 매우 제한되어 있다. (21)에서처럼, 전칭 양화 명사구는 문장 범위 내에서만 단수 대명사를 통제할 수 있다.

(21) (a) [Every man]$_i$ loves his$_i$ mother.

(b) Mary loves [every man]$_i$. *He$_i$ likes music.

(c) A woman loves [every man]$_i$. *He$_i$ likes music.

(d) Every woman loves [every man]$_i$. *He$_i$ likes music.

영어 한정사 "a"와 "every"를 일차술어논리 언어(first-order predicate logical language)의 존재 양화사(또는 특칭 양화사) ∃와 전칭 양화사 ∀로 간주하는 전통적 형식의미론은 (19)와 (21)의 자료들을 잘 설명할 수 있다. 즉, 고유명사는 지시표현이며 (19)의 대명사는 공지시 대명사(coreferential pronoun)이기 때문에 (19)의 조응관계는 적형하다. (21)의 경우, 양화사 "every"는 일차술어논리 언어의 전칭 양화사가 그러하듯이 문장을 양화 범위(quantificational scope)로 가지게 되어 구속변수(bound variable)의 역할을 하는 대명사가 자신의 양화 범위 내에 있을 때 이를 통제할 수 있다. 즉, (21b, c, d)에서 대명사 "he"가 "every man"을 선행사로 가질 수 없는 것은 "every"의 전칭 양화사적 특성으로 인한 것이라고 설명할 수 있다.

만약, 영어 한정사 "a"가 일차술어논리 언어의 존재 양화사와 같은 것이고 대명사가 구속변수와 같다면 "a"를 한정사로 갖는 비한정 명사구는 같은 문장내의 대명사와만 조응관계를 가질 수 있을 것이고, (20b, c, d)의 조응관계는 성립될 수 없을 것이다. 그러나, (20b, c, d)에서의 조응관계는 적형한 것으로 모국어 화자들에 의해 받아들여진다. 즉, "a"를 존재양화사와 동일시하는 접근방법에는 문제가 있다.

Kamp(1981)는 "every"는 양화사이나 "a"는 양화사가 아니다라는 태도를 취한다. "a+명사"는 이 표현으로 지칭되는 대상이 화자와 청자 모두에게 친숙한 것은 아니다라는 정보를 제공하며 술어 논리 언어의 구속변수와 같은 역할을 한다. 위에 제시한 대명사의 조응관계는 다음과 같은 방식으로 설명된다.

(22) 담화표상이론에서의 조응관계

    (a) 고유명사는 언제나 주담화표상(main discourse representation)에 담화 지시체를 도입한다.

    (b) "a+명사"는 처리되고 있는 순간의 해당 담화표상에 담화 지시체를 도입한다.

    (c) "every+명사"는 두 개의 담화표상으로 구성된 복합조건을 담화표상에 도입하며 두 개의 담화표상 중 첫 번째 담화표상에 담화 지시체를 도입한다.

    (d) 대명사는 처리되고 있는 순간의 담화표상에 담화 지시체를 도입하며 접근 가능한 다른 담화 지시체와 반드시 연결되어야 한다.

    (e) 같은 담화표상 내의 담화 지시체들은 서로 접근 가능하며, 주담화표상의 담화지시체들은 내포된 담화표상의 담화지시체로부터 접근가능하나 내포된 담화표상의 지시체들은 주담화표상의 담화지시체로부터 접근할 수 없다.

이제 (19b)의 첫 번째 문장은 (22a)에 의해 (23)과 같이 표상된다.

(23)

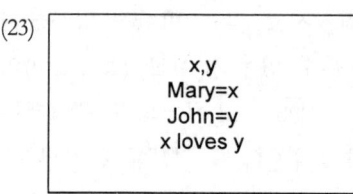

```
        x,y
      Mary=x
      John=y
      x loves y
```

(19b)의 두 번째 문장은 (22d)에 의해 담화표상 (23)을 (24)와 같이 확장한다. 대명사 "he"에 의해 도입된 담화지시체 z는 같은 담화표상내의 담화지

시체 y에 접근 가능하여 이 담화지시체와 연결이 가능하다.

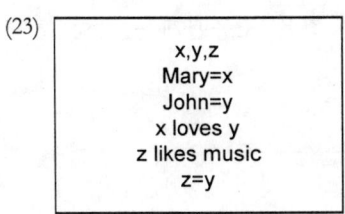

문장 (21a)는 (22c)에 의해 (25)와 같이 표상 된다. "every" 구문은 주담화표상에 담화지시체를 도입하지 않고 두 개의 담화표상과 양화사로 구성된 복합조건을 도입한다. 두 번째 담화표상에 대명사 "his"에 의하여 도입된 담화지시체 y는 첫 번째 담화표상에 도입된 담화지시체 x에 접근 가능하여 y는 x를 선행사로 취할 수 있다.

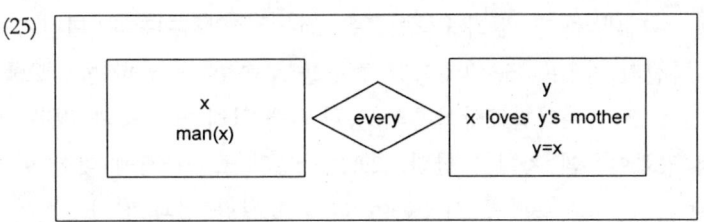

담화표상 (25)의 복합조건은 어떤 개체가 남자라면 그 개체는 자신의 어머니를 사랑한다는 의미를 표상하고 있다. 즉 이 복합조건은 (26)과 같은 일차술어논리 표현과 그 진리조건이 동일하다. (26)은 (27)과 같은 표현이다.

(26) $\forall x[man(x) \rightarrow \exists y[x \text{ loves } x\text{'s mother } \& y=x]]$

(27) $\forall[man(x) \rightarrow x \text{ loves } x\text{'s mother}]$

(21b)의 담화는 (28)과 같이 표상 된다. (21b)의 두 번째 문장의 대명사 "he"
에 의해 주담화표상에 도입된 담화지시체 z는 복합조건 안의 담화지시체
y에 접근 불가능하다. 따라서 (21b)에서와 같은 조응관계는 성립할 수 없
다.

(28)

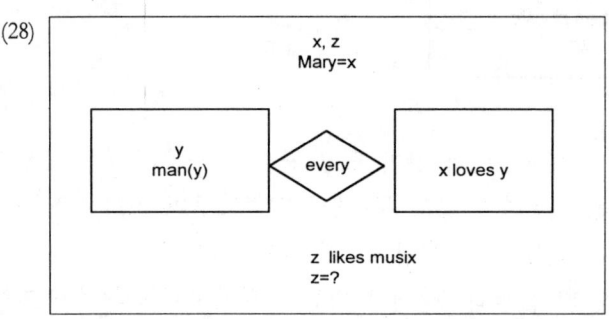

x, z
Mary=x

y
man(y)

every

x loves y

z likes musix
z=?

    (22)에 제시된 조응관계의 처리는 담화표상이론의 양화현상에 대한 접
근 방법을 나타내 준다. 담화표상이론은 전통적 양화이론과 마찬가지로
양화사는 자신의 범위(scope)내에서만 변수를 구속할 수 있다는 태도를 견
지하고 있다. 그러나 담화표상이론의 양화문제 처리는 다음과 같은 점에
서 전통적 양화이론과 차이가 난다. (29)는 (22)의 조응관계에 대한 설명을
일차술어논리 언어적 용어를 사용하여 다시 표현한 것과 같다.

    (29) 담화표상이론에서의 양화 문제
      (a) 대명사는 구속 변수(bound variable)이다.
      (b) 비한정 명사구 "a (or some) + CN"은 양화 표현이 아니고 단순히 구
         속 변수로 작용한다.
      (c) 양화사는 자신의 Scope 안에 있는 하나 이상의 변수를 묶을 수 있다
         (unselective binding)
      (d) 존재 양화사(existential quantifier)는 어떤 구조(담화, 양화사의 핵범위
         등)에 default로 주어진다(existential closure).

이 가정에 따라 문장 (30a), (31a)는 일차술어논리 언어로 (30b), (31b)와 같이 번역된다. (30b)는 (30c)의 구조로부터 existential closure에 의해 존재 양화 의미를 부여받게 된다.

(30) (a) A student came in.

    (b) $\exists[\text{student}(x) \ \& \ \text{came-in}(x)]$

    (c) $\text{student}(x) \ \& \ \text{came-in}(x)$

(31) (a) Every student came in.

    (b) $\forall[\text{student}(x) \rightarrow \text{came-in}(x)]$

(30b)와 (31b)에서 양화사들은 자신의 범위내의 변수 (여기서는 x)를 구속하고 있다. 따라서, (30b)와 (31b)는 (32)와 (33)과 같은 일차술어논리 언어 표현과 상응한다.

(32) $\exists x[\text{student}(x) \ \& \ \text{came-in}(x)]$

(33) $\forall x[\text{student}(x) \rightarrow \text{came-in}(x)]$

이제 많은 논란의 대상이 되어왔던 소위 "당나귀 문장(donkey-sentences)"의 양화문제와 조응관계가 담화표상이론에서 어떻게 설명되는지를 살펴보자. 당나귀 문장은 (34)처럼 "every"를 한정사로 가지는 명사구를 선행사로 하는 관계절에 "a(n)" 명사구가 내포되어 있고 이 비한정 명사구가 주절의 대명사와 조응하는 구조를 가진 문장을 말한다.

(34) Every farmer who owns [a donkey]ᵢ beats itᵢ.

만약 "a"가 존재양화사와 같은 양화표현이라면 이 양화사는 문장을 그 범위로 가져야 하고 이 범위밖에 있는 대명사 "it"를 구속할 수 없어야 한다.

그러나 (34)의 조응 관계는 모국어 화자에 의해 적형한 문장으로 받아들여
진다. (35)는 (34)를 일차술어논리 언어로 번역한 것이다.

(35) $\forall x[[farmer(x) \ \& \ \exists y[donkey(y) \ \& \ x \ owns \ y]] \rightarrow x \ beats \ y]$

(35)는 (34)의 적절한 번역이라고 할 수 없다. 왜냐하면 "x beats y"의 "y"가
자유변수로 남아 있어 (34)와는 다른 의미를 가지기 때문이다. 모국어 화
자의 직관을 충실히 반영한 번역은 (36)과 같다. (36)은 대략 당나귀를 가
지고 있는 모든 농부는 자신이 가지고 있는 모든 당나귀를 때린다라는 의
미를 표현하고 있다.

(36) $\forall x \forall y[[farmer(x) \ \& \ donkey(y) \ \& \ x \ owns \ y] \rightarrow x \ beats \ y]$

"every"와 "a(n)"을 일차술어논리 언어의 양화사 $\forall$와 $\exists$로 간주하는 의미
이론은 당나귀 문장이 보이는 양화의 범위 문제와 "a(n)"을 한정사로 가지
는 명사구가 그 사용 환경에 따라 존재양화 의미와 전칭양화 의미를 지닌
다는 사실을 적절히 설명할 수 없다. (29)의 가정을 받아들이는 담화표상
이론에 따르면 당나귀 문장 (34)는 다음과 같은 표현으로 번역된다.

(37) $\forall[[farmer(x) \ \& \ donkey \ (y) \ \& \ x \ owns \ y] \rightarrow \exists[x \ beats \ y]]$

(37)에서 문장의 핵범위에 주어진 존재양화사는 자신이 묶을 수 있는 적절
한 변수가 없는 공허한 양화사이다. 이제 (37)은 (29c)에 의해 (38)과 같은
양화 효과를 가지게 되며 이는 모국어 화자들의 당나귀 문장 (34)에 대한
직관적 의미인 (36)과 일치한다.

(38) $\forall x, y[[farmer(x) \ \& \ donkey \ (y) \ \& \ x \ owns \ y] \rightarrow x \ beats \ y]$

이상에서 Kamp(1981), Heim(1982) 등에 기원하는 담화표상이론의 개요를 살펴보았다. 담화표상이론은 언어의 표상성과 대상성을 동시에 포착하는 일종의 종합적 의미론으로 언어 입력을 처리하여 어떤 심적 표상을 만드는 기재(mechanism)를 설정하며 이 기재를 통하여 생성된 표상이 어떤 세상의 일부분의 모습을 참되게 나타낼 때 이 표상의 입력이 되었던 언어 표현은 그 세상에 비추어 참이다라고 말할 수 있게 된다. 이 이론은 또한 문장 뿐 아니라 문장들로 구성된 담화 차원의 언어 현상을 연구할 수 있는 방법을 제시해 주며 자연 언어의 양화 문제, 조응 현상 등의 구체적 문제에 대한 해답을 제공한다. 이 이론은 명제적 태도(propositional attitudes), 시간 및 사건, 지시 표현(deictic expressions) 등의 의미 탐구에 대한 유용한 틀로서 사용되고 있으며, 인공 지능 등 자연언어의 전산 처리에 필요한 지식 표상의 모형으로서도 널리 연구되고 있다.

이 책은 1부와 2부로 구성된다. 제1부에서는 위에서 개략적으로 밝힌 담화표상 이론의 구조를 보다 자세히 알아보도록 하겠다. 제2장은 담화표상 생성의 입력이 되는 문장의 구조 분석을 다루며 제3장은 담화표상 구성 규칙에 관한 것이며 제4장은 담화표상이론의 의미론을 다룬다. 제2부에서 필자는 제1부에서 밝힌 담화표상이론의 체계를 자연언어의 다양한 양화 표현들에 비추어 비판적으로 분석한 후 이러한 양화 표현들의 의미와 조응 관계를 포착할 수 있도록 담화표상 이론의 체계에 대한 수정을 시도해 보고자 한다.

제 2 장 통사분석

　제1장에서 개략적으로 살펴 본 것과 같이 담화표상이론은 문장의 통사 구조에 담화표상 구성규칙이 적용되어 담화표상을 추출하고 이 담화표상을 주어진 모형과 양립 가능한가를 살펴어 문장의 진리값을 결정한다. 따라서 문장의 통사 구조에 대한 분석에 따라 담화표상 구성규칙이 다른 모습으로 정의된다.

　통사 분석은 통사 규칙을 통하여 이루어지며, 통사 규칙은 한 언어의 모든 적형한 표현(well-formed expressions)을 생성할 수 있어야 하고 또 오직 적형한 표현만을 생성하여야 한다. 만약 어떤 통사 규칙의 집합이 위의 조건을 만족한다고 가정하면 적형한 구조란 어떤 통사규칙에 의하여 생성될 수 있는, 즉 그 통사 규칙에 의하여 인허되는(licensed) 구조를 말한다.

　이 책은 근본적으로 통사론에 관한 것이 아니고 통사 구조와 의미 구조 사이의 체계성을 보이는 데 그 목적이 있다. 그러므로, 이 장에서는 영어의 모든 적형한 문장의 구조가 아니라 앞으로 다루고자 하는 영어의 한 단편(fragment of English)의 의미 구조의 설명에 필요한 만큼의 통사 구조를 다루고자 한다.

2.1. 통사 구조에 포함해야 할 정보

　한 언어(또는 그 언어의 단편)의 통사 구조를 분석하는 것은 그 언어의 어휘 목록(list of lexical items), 어휘들의 통사 범주(lexical category), 어휘들의 집합에 부여되는 통사 범주(phrasal category), 통사 범주들간의 선형적 순서(linear order), 통사 범주의 구성 요소(constituency), 통사 범주들의 계층 구조(hierarchical structure) 등을 명시하는 것이다. 따라서, 한 문장의 통사 분석은 그 문장을 이루는 어휘와 그 어휘들의 범주, 비어휘 범주들의 구성 성분, 범주들간의 선형적 순서 및 계층 구조에 관한 정보를 포함하여야 한다.

문장 (1)을 구구조 수형도(phrase-structure tree)로 표상한 통사 분석 (2)에서 위의 정보가 어떻게 표현되고 있는가를 살펴 보자.

(1) The child is happy.

(2)

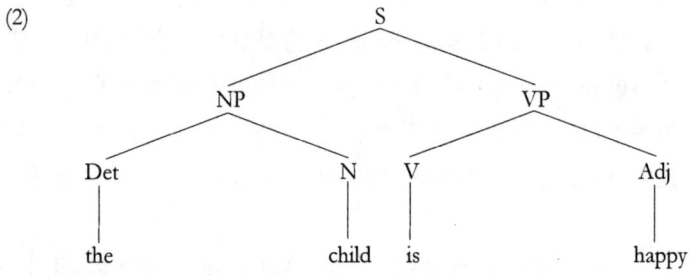

수형도 (2)는 문장 (1)이 "Det"으로 표상된 어휘 범주인 한정사의 한 요소 "the", "N"으로 표상된 보통명사 "child", "V"로 표상된 동사 "is", "Adj"로 표상된 형용사 "happy"로 이루어졌음을 나타낸다. 수형도 (2)는 또한 명사구는 한정사와 보통명사로, 동사구는 동사와 형용사로, 문장은 명사구와 동사구로 이루어졌음(constituency)을 표상하며, 명사구와 동사구는 문장의 딸이고 한정사는 문장의 손녀이며 동시에 동사구의 질녀(niece)임 (hierarchical structure)을 나타낸다. 구성성분 관계는 수형도에서 실선으로 표상되며 계층구조는 나무가지 모양으로 표상된다.

수형도 (2)에 표시된 나무구조는 (3)에 표시된 여러 가지 나무구조들의

합으로 구성되었다. (3)에 표시된 것과 같이 어미-딸의 관계만을 표시하는
나무구조를 국지적 나무구조(local tree)라 한다. 모든 국지적 나무 구조는
국지적 구구조규칙(local phrase-structure rules)에 의해 인허되어야 한다. 즉,
국지적 나무구조를 생성할 구구조규칙이 규정되어야 한다.

(3)
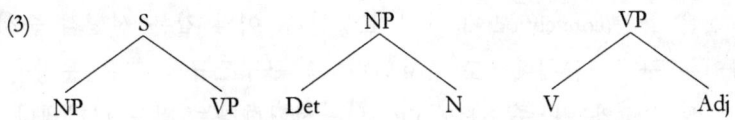

(3)의 국지적 나무구조는 (4)의 국지적 구구조규칙에 의해 인허된다.

(4) S   → NP VP

   NP → Det N

   VP → V Adj

어휘 범주와 특정 어휘가 연결되어 있는 (5)의 국지적 나무구조는 (6)과
같은 어휘 삽입 규칙(lexical insertion rules)에 의해 인허된다. 따라서, 모든
국지적 나무구조는 국지적 구구조규칙이나 어휘 삽입 규칙에 의해 인허되
어야 한다.

(5)
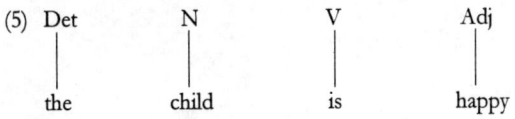

(6) Det → the, ...

   N → child, ...

   V → is, ...

   Adj → happy, ...

문장 (1)을 발화할 때 단어 "the"가 먼저 발화되고 단어 "child"가 나중에 발화된다는 정보를 수형도 (2)에서 단어 "the"를 단어 "child" 보다 왼쪽에 씀으로서 표현한다. 즉, 구구조수형도는 선형적 순서를 표기의 방향성 (즉, 먼저 발화되는 표현을 보다 왼 쪽에 표기)으로 표현한다. 수형도 (2)는 단어 차원의 선형적 순서 뿐 아니라 (2)에 나타나는 모든 범주들간의 선형적 순서도 같은 규약(convention)에 따라 표상한다. 이와 같은 선형적 순서에 대한 규약은 구구조규칙에서도 유효하다. 즉 구구조규칙 (7)은 문장을 이루는 두 범주 NP와 VP 중 NP가 VP 보다 선행한다는 것을 나타낸다.

(7) S → NP VP

일반구구조문법(Generalized Phrase Structure Grammar: GPSG) 등에서는 문법 범주들간의 상대적 순서가 결정되어 있다는 점을 주목하여 구구조규칙에 선형적 순서를 표현하지 않고 선형관계는 규칙에 대한 일반적 제약으로 제시한다. 영어의 적형한 구조를 인허하는 다음과 같은 일련의 구구조규칙들에서 명사구는 자매관계에 있는 동사구를 항상 선행하고 조동사는 명사구 또는 동사구를 선행하며 동사는 명사구 또는 동사구를 선행한다 (Gazdar, Klein, Pullum and Sag (1985), pp44-50, 이하에서 GKPS).

(8) S → NP VP

S → AUX NP VP

VP → AUX VP

VP → V NP

VP → V VP

VP → V NP VP

선형적 순서관계를 ≤로 표시하면 선형관계는 다음과 같은 속성을 지니게 된다.

(9) (a) For any x, y, if x≤y and y≤x, then x=y. (antisymmetry)

    (b) For any x, y, z, if x≤y and y≤z, then x≤z. (transivity)

이제 (8)에서 포착되는 범주들간의 선형관계는 (10)과 같이 표현될 수 있다.

(10) (a) AUX≤NP

    (b) V≤NP

    (c) NP≤VP

이러한 선형 관계에 대한 규정을 선형 순서 진술(Linear Precedence (LP) Statement)이라 한다. (10)의 선형 순서 진술을 상정하면 (8)의 구구조규칙은 직접 지배 관계(Immediate Dominance) 만을 언급하는 (11)의 직접 지배 규칙으로 다시 쓸 수 있다. 직접 지배 규칙은 선형관계가 배제되고 한 범주가 어떤 구성 성분으로 이루어졌는가를 명시하는 규칙으로 (12a)는 (12b)와 동일하다.

(11) S → NP, VP

    S → AUX, NP, VP

    VP → AUX, VP

    VP → V, NP

    VP → V, VP

    VP → V, NP, VP

(12) (a) S → AUX, NP, VP

    (b) S → VP, NP, AUX

GPSG처럼 직접 지배 규칙과 선형 순서 진술을 상정하면 한 국지적 구구조 수형도는 직접 지배 규칙과 선형 순서 진술에 의해 인허받아야 한다. 즉 수형도에 표상된 범주간 순서 관계는 선형 순서 진술의 규정에 일치하여야 하고 구성성분은 직접 지배 규칙 중 하나에 의해 포착되어야 한다. 수형도 (13)은 직접지배규칙 S → NP, VP에 의해, 그리고 선형 순서 진술 NP≤VP에 의해 인허된다.

(13)
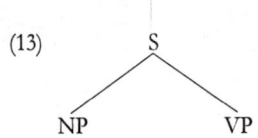

이 책은 Kamp and Reyle(1991)를 따라 GKPS의 통사 기술 모형을 통사 분석의 모형으로 취한다. 그러나, 선형 관계의 잉여성을 인정하면서 구구조규칙에 선형관계를 포함하는 (8)과 같은 전통적 구구조규칙을 계속 사용하고자 한다.

2.2. 단층 통사 분석

2.2.1. 상위규칙(metarules)

Chomsky의 통사 분석은 심층구조(또는 D-structure), 표면구조(또는 S-structure), 논리형태(Logical Form) 등의 여러 층위로 구성된 분석 방법으로 특징지워진다. Chomsky(1965)에서 제시된 표준이론에 의하면 심층구조는 표현의 의미에 영향을 미치지 않는 변형규칙(transformational rules)에 의해 표면구조로 사상(mapping) 된다. 생성된 구조와 변형에 의하여 도출된 구조간의 관계는 확대표준이론, 수정확대표준이론, 소형이론(minimalist program) 등을 통하면서 수정이 가해져 왔지만 두 층위의 구조를 변형규칙

에 의해 연결하는 이론의 틀은 변하지 않은 채 유지되고 있다. 이러한 다
층위이론(multistratal theory)으로 어떤 문장의 통사적 적형성(well-formedness)
를 결정하기 위해서는 이 문장의 표면구조의 적형성을 결정해야 한다. 표
면구조의 적형성은 이 문장의 심층구조라 여겨지는 구조가 구구조규칙에
의해 인허되었는가를 검토하여야 하고 심층구조에서 표면구조로의 사상
이 이 언어가 지니고 있는 변형규칙에 부합되는가를 살펴야 한다. 문장
(14)의 적형성을 결정하기 위해서는 심층구조 (15)를 인허하는 구구조규칙
이 있는가를 검토하여야 하고 (15)에서 (16)을 도출하는 변형규칙 (17)이 영
어에서 용인가능한 규칙임이 전제되어야 한다.

(14) Mary, John likes.

(15)

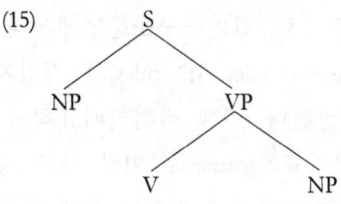

(16) SD: NP V X NP Y
           1 2 3 4 5
    SC: 4 1 2 3 ϕ 5

수정확대표준이론(Revised Extended Standard Theory)에서 처럼, 변형규칙
을 이동 규칙 하나로 제한하고(Move-α) 이동규칙에 의해 이동된 요소는
자신의 자리에 "보이지 않는" 흔적(trace)를 남긴다면 표면구조는 심층구조
의 모든 구조적 정보를 그대로 유지하게 된다. 어떤 문장의 적형성을 판
단하기 위해서는 그 문장의 구조 분석이 이 언어의 구구조규칙에 의해 인
허되고 흔적에 대한 어떤 조건을 만족시키면 된다. 즉, 한 문장의 적형성
을 살피기 위해서는 두 층위의 구조와 이를 연결하는 변형규칙을 모두 고

려할 필요 없이 그 문장의 표면구조의 적형성만 점검하면 된다.

수정확대이론 및 그 이후의 Chomsky 통사 이론은 Move-α의 힘을 극대화하여 모든 요소를 어느 곳으로나 이동시킬 수 있게 규정함으로써 역설적으로 그 힘을 최소화한다. 즉, 문장의 적형성은 어떤 변형규칙이 적형한 구조에 규칙이 규정하고 있는 방식으로 적용되고 있는가에 의하여 결정되는 것이 아니라 변형규칙의 적용 결과로 생긴 흔적의 적형성을 일련의 제약에 비추어 살펴 봄으로써 결정된다.

일반구구조문법은 통사 구조의 층위를 하나만 설정하는 단층 통사 이론(monostratal theory)이다. 이 이론에서의 통사 구조는 수정확대이론에서의 표면구조가 포함하는 모든 정보를 포함한다. 이 이론은 이동규칙 등의 변형규칙을 인정하지 않으므로 흔적 등과 같은 공범주(empty categories)는 구구조규칙에 의해 직접 도입된다. 구체적으로, 일반구구조문법에서의 구구조규칙은 직접지배규칙(immediate dominance rules: ID rules)과 직접지배규칙으로부터 도출된 구구조규칙으로 구성된다. 이때 직접지배규칙에 적용되어 구구조규칙을 확장하는 규칙을 상위규칙(metarules)이라 한다. 공범주는 공범주를 도출하는 상위규칙이 직접지배규칙에 적용되어 통사 구조상에 도입된다. 상위규칙은 그 역할에 있어 변형규칙과 비슷하나 규칙에 적용되어 새로운 규칙을 만든다는 점에서 한 구조에 적용되어 다른 구조를 도출하는 변형규칙과 다르다.

상위규칙이 새로운 구구조규칙을 만드는 과정을 수동태 문장을 예로 하여 보다 자세히 살펴 보자. GKPS를 따라 영어의 다음과 같은 직접 지배 규칙을 가정하자. VP[PAS]는 머리 동사가 과거분사형인 "loved by Mary", "given a book" 등을 나타내며 이 동사구의 통사 자질 [PAS]을 머리자질 중의 하나라 하고 수형도 상의 어미 마디(mother node)의 머리 자질은 머리가 되는 딸(head daughter) 마디의 머리 자질과 일치해야 된다는 모녀 마디가 지니는 자질들 간의 제약을 인정하자. H[1], H[2], … 등은 해당 직접지배 규칙의 적용을 받을 수 있는 머리 범주들의 유형을 나타낸다.

(17) 직접지배규칙

   (a) S → NP VP

   (b) VP → H[1]

   (c) VP → H[2] NP

   (d) VP → H[3] NP PP

   (e) VP → H[4] NP NP

   (f) VP → H[5] NP S

   (g) VP → H VP[PAS]

이제 수동태 문장 (18)의 적형성을 검토해 보자. 문장 (18)은 (19)와 같은 구조로 분석된다.

(18) Mary is loved by John.

(19)

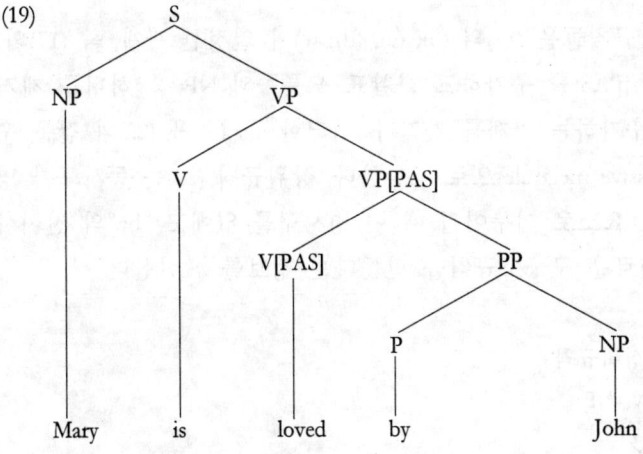

한 구구조 수형도가 적형한 것이 되기 위해서는 그 수형도를 이루는 모든 국지적 구구조 수형도(local phrase structure tree)가 적형한 것이어야 하고 한 국지적 수형도가 적형한 것이 되기 위해서는 구구조규칙에 의해 인허되어야 한다. 수형도 (19)의 가장 상위의 국지적 수형도는 구구조규칙

(a)에 의해 인허된다. 두 번째 국지적 수형도는 구구조규칙 (g)에 의해 인
허된다. 세 번째 국지 수형도는 (17)의 규칙에 의해 인허되지 못한다. 이를
인허하기 위해서 (20)과 같은 구구조규칙을 추가하여야 한다.

(20) VP[PAS] → V[2'] PP

그러나 (17)의 (c), (d), (e)에 의하여 인허받는 동사구 또한 수동화될 수 있
으므로 (21)과 같은 구구조규칙이 필요해 진다.

(21) (a) VP[PAS] → V[3'] PP PP
     (b) VP[PAS] → V[4'] NP PP
     (c) VP[PAS] → V[5'] S PP

(20)과 (21)의 규칙들은 (17)의 (b), (c), (d), (e)와 일정한 관계, 즉 (17)의 규
칙들에서 VP에 [PAS]를 추가하고 화살표 오른쪽의 NP 중 하나를 제거하
는 대신 PP를 추가하는 관계를 가진다. 이러한 규칙성을 (22)와 같은 수동
태 상위규칙(passive metarule)으로 포착한다. 상위규칙 (22)는 동사구가 명사
구와 다른 어떤 요소로 이루어질 때 이 명사구를 없애고 "by"의 전치사구
를 추가하는 새로운 구구조규칙을 만든다는 정보를 표현한다.

(22) 수동태 상위규칙
     VP → W, NP
        ⇩
     VP[PAS]   W, (PP[by])

(22)의 상위규칙을 둠으로서 (17)의 규칙 체계를 (20)과 (21)의 규칙을 포함
하도록 확장하는 효과를 가져온다.

다음으로 공범주를 도입하는 상위규칙을 살펴 보자. GKPS는 구성 성분

중 일부를 상실한 구 범주(phrasal category)를 표현하기 위해 SLASH라는 자질을 통사기술에 도입한다. 예를 들어 VP[SLASH NP]는 NP가 없는 VP를 표현하며 간단히 VP/NP로 표기하기도 한다. GKPS는 Chomsky 이론의 PRO를 공범주로 인정하지 않고 흔적(trace)에 해당하는 공범주만을 설정한다. 따라서 공범주 "e"는 XP/XP를 말한다. SLASH 자질은 다른 자질과 마찬가지로 자질들이 발현될 수 있는 조건을 충족하면 어떤 범주에도 발현될 수 있다. GKPS는 SLASH 자질을 발자질(foot feature)로 규정하고 발자질에 대한 제약으로서 딸 범주의 발자질 값은 어미 범주의 발자질 값과 같아야 한다고 규정한다. 머리자질의 경우 어미 마디의 머리자질 값은 머리딸(head daughter)의 머리자질 값과 같아야 되는데 반해 발자질의 경우는 발자질을 가지고 있는 어떤 딸의 자질값과 어미 마디의 발자질값이 같아야 한다는 점에서 차이가 난다. 이제 (14)의 주제 구문의 적형성을 검토해 보자. (14)는 (23)과 같이 표상된다.

(14) Mary, John likes.

(23)

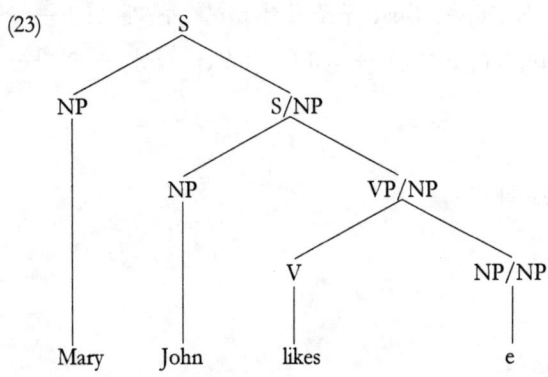

GKPS는 (23)의 최상위 국지 수형도를 인허하기 위하여 (24)의 구구조규칙을 도입한다. (24)는 문장은 어떤 품사의 구와 그 구가 없는 문장으로 구성된다는 것을 뜻한다.

(24) S → XP H/XP

(23)의 두 번째와 세 번째 국지 수형도는 이를 인허하는 구구조규칙이 있고 SLASH 자질에 대한 조건을 만족하므로 적형하다. 그러나 (25)의 국지 수형도는 모녀 관계에 있는 두 요소간에 발자질의 조건이 충족되지 못하고 있다.

(25) NP/NP
  |
  e

따라서, SLASH 자질의 발현이 어디에서 끝나는가를 명시해 주어야 한다. 이를 위하여 [+NULL]이라는 자질을 도입하고 이 자질을 가진 범주가 어미 마디가 될 때, 어미와 딸간에 SLASH 값이 일치하지 않아도 되도록 규정한다. [+NULL] 자질은 (26)의 SLASH 종결 상위규칙(slash termination metarule)에 의해 도입된다. (26)은 X-bar 구조에서 bar를 두 개 가지는 어떠한 범주도 (예를 들어 NP, VP, PP 등) [+NULL] 자질을 가질 수 있다는 것을 뜻한다.

(26) SLASH 종결 상위규칙

$$X \rightarrow W, X^2$$
$$\Downarrow$$
$$X \rightarrow W, X^2[+NULL]$$

이제 구구조규칙 (17c)에 SLASH 종결 상위규칙이 적용되어 (27)의 새로운 구구조규칙을 생성한다.

(27) VP → V NP[+NULL]

(27)의 규칙에 의해 (25)의 구조는 (28)과 같이 되어 적형한 구조를 이룬다. 이제 (23)의 모든 국지적 수형도는 적형하고, 따라서 수형도 (23)은 적형한 구조가 된다.

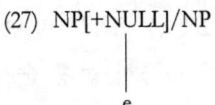

(27) NP[+NULL]/NP

   |

   e

이상에서 변형문법의 변형규칙의 역할을 단층 통사이론에서 수행하는 상위규칙의 작용에 대해 알아 보았다. 일반구구조문법은 위에서 언급한 수동태 상위규칙과 SLASH 종결 상위규칙이외에도 주어-조동사 도치 상위규칙(Subject-Aux Inversion Metarule), 외치 상위규칙(Extraposition Metarule) 등 몇 가지의 상위규칙을 설정하고 있다.

2.2.2. 구구조규칙으로부터 나무구조에로의 투사

구구조규칙은 어떤 투사함수(projection function)에 의해 구조 수형도로 투사된다. 투사된 나무구조(tree)는 구구조규칙이 포함하는 모든 정보를 포함하여야 하고 해당 규칙에 명시되지 않은 여러 가지 자질들을 추가로 포함할 수 있다. 즉, 어떤 구구조규칙에서 투사된 나무구조는 구구조규칙에 명시되지 않은 정보를 포함할 수 있다. 이 관계는 그림 (28)에 표시되어 있다(Sells 1985, p.100). (28)의 나무구조에서의 마디 C_n^+는 구구조규칙의 범주 C_n에서 투사되었으나 C_n에 명시된 것 보다 많은 정보를 포함한다는 것을 나타낸다.

(28) 구구조규칙　　　　투사함수　　　　　　나무구조

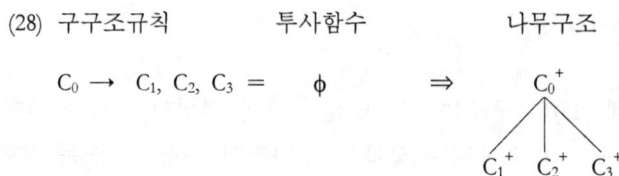

$$C_0 \rightarrow C_1, C_2, C_3 = \phi \Rightarrow$$

투사함수 ϕ는 구구조규칙을 용인 가능한(admissible) 나무구조로 투사시킨다. 즉 투사함수는 나무구조가 용인 가능하게 되는 조건을 규정한다. 나무구조가 용인 가능하기 위해서는 나무구조의 마디들이 가능한 선형 순서를 유지하여야 하고 각 범주에 추가된 자질들이 어떤 관계를 유지하여야 한다. 예를 들어 C_1^+가 한정 동사(finite verb)라면 어미 범주인 C_0^+도 한정 동사구가 되어야 한다. 범주의 자질들 간의 관계는 용인가능한 자질들 간의 관계를 규정하는 다음과 같은 5가지 원칙으로 표현된다. 자질들은 어미 범주와 머리딸 범주와의 관계에서 자질들간의 제약이 결정되는 머리자질(head features)과 어미 범주와 모든 딸 범주와의 관계에서 자질들간의 제약이 결정되는 발자질(foot features), 어미 범주와 상호작용하지 않는 자질들(non-propagating features)로 구분된다.

● Feature Cooccurrence Restrictions (FCR): 한 언어의 가능한 범주를 규정한다. 예를 들어 영어에서 시제 자질을 포함하는 범주는 한정 동사구이어야 한다. GKPS는 이를 [PAST] ⊃ [FIN, -SUBJ]로 나타낸다.

● Feature Specification Default (FSD): 한 자질의 무표적(unmarked) 자질값을 결정한다. 만약 명시적 규칙에 의해 자질값이 주어지지 않는다면 그 자질은 무표적으로 주어진 자질값을 갖는다. 예를 들어 자질 [NULL]은 SLASH 종결 상위규칙에 의해 그 값이 +로 주어지지 않는 모든 경우에서 -를 그 값으로 가진다. GKPS는 이를 ~[NULL]로 표현한다.

● Head Feature Convention (HFC): 머리자질을 가지는 마디들 간의 관계를 규정한다. HFC는 한 국지적 나무구조에서 어미 범주의 머리자질들 (엄밀히 말하여, 자질과 자질값의 순서쌍의 집합. 예: {<N, ->, <V, +>, <BAR, 2>, ...})과 머리딸의 머리자질들이 일치해야 할 것을 규정한다.

● Foot Feature Principle (FFP): 발자질을 가지는 범주들 간의 관계를 규정한다. FFC에 따르면 한 국지적 나무구조에서 어미마디의 발자질들 중 구구조규칙에 명시되지 않은 발자질들은 이 어미마디의 모든 딸마디들의 발자질들 중 구구조규칙에 명시되지 않은 모든 발자질들의 합과 같아야 한다.

● Control Agreement Principle (CAP): 통제하는 마디의 일치 자질은 통제를 받는 마디의 일치 자질 (AGR)과 동일해야 한다. 통제 관계는 의미론적으로 정의된다. 즉, 어떤 표현 (또는 마디) A가 어떤 술어 B의 논항이 되어 문장을 형성한다면 논항이 되는 마디는 술어가 되는 마디를 통제한다. 구체적으로 주어 명사구는 논항이 되고 동사구는 술어가 되어 문장을 형성하므로 (즉 동사구의 의미값에 주어 명사구의 의미값이 적용되어 명제를 결정하므로) 주어 명사구는 동사구를 통제한다. 또한 다음의 구조에서 VP3는 의미적으로 NP2를 논항으로 취하는 술어의 역할을 하여 "Susi flatters herself"의 의미값이 되는 명제를 표현하므로 NP2는 VP3를 통제한다. VP3와 같이 국지적 나무구조에서 적당한 통제자를 발견하지 못할 경우 그 다음 마디로 AGR 자질값이 계승되며 적절한 통제자가 있는 국지적 나무구조까지 이러한 과정이 계속된다. 결과적으로 국지적 나무구조에서 CAP가 적용될 수 있게 된다. 수형도 (29)에서 CAP에 의하여 통제자 NP2 − 3rd person female singular NP − 와 통제를 받는 마디 VP3의 AGR 자질값이 같아지도록 규제 받는다.

(29)

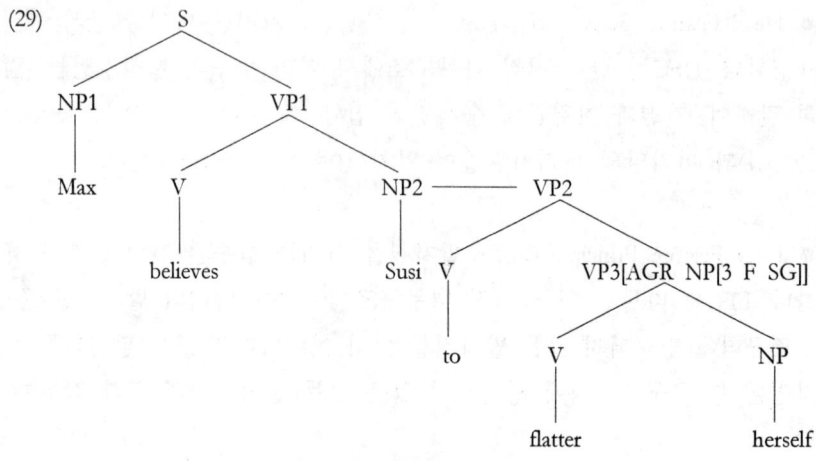

이상에서 개략적으로 살펴 본 바와 같이 일반 구구조 문법은 성분구조 (constituency)를 명시하는 구구조규칙과 성분들간의 선형적 순서를 결정하는 선형 순서 진술(LP statement), 직접 지배 규칙이 투사된 나무구조에서 마디들의 자질들간의 적형성 조건(HFC, FFP, CAP, FCR, FCD 등)으로 구성된다. 구구조규칙은 다시 어미 범주와 딸 범주들간의 직접 지배 관계를 표시하는 직접 지배 규칙과 직접 지배 규칙에 작용하여 기존의 규칙을 확장하는 상위규칙으로 구성된다. 한 국지적 나무구조는 구구조규칙, 선형 순서 진술, 자질들에 대한 제약들에 의해 인허될 때 적형하다. 전체 나무구조는 이를 구성하는 모든 국지적 나무구조가 적형하면 적형하다.

2.3. 담화표상이론에서의 통사분석

담화표상이론은 언어 표현의 의미에 대한 이론이며 표현의 의미는 표현의 통사 분석을 처리하여 얻어진다. 즉, 통사 구조와 의미 구조간의 상응 관계(corespondency)를 상정하고 있으며, 이러한 상응 관계를 명시적으로 보여주는 것이 이 이론의 주된 관심사이다. 따라서 이하에서는 담화표상이론이 통사 구조와 의미 구조간의 관계를 밝히고자 하는 영어의 한 단편을 정의하고 정의된 범위내의 문장의 통사 분석을 다루어 보고자 한다.

2.3.1. 영어의 단편

담화표상이론은 Kamp(1981)과 Heim(1982)에서 대명사와 그 선행사간의 다양한 조응관계를 설명하기 위한 한 대안으로서 최초 제시되었다. 특히 "당나귀 문장"에서의 조응관계의 설명은 담화표상이론의 형성에 결정적 영향을 미쳤다. 초기에는 단수 대명사와 단수 선행사간의 조응관계만을 설명하고자 하였으며 이를 바탕으로 담화표상이론의 틀을 구성하였다. 이 모형은 단수 대명사의 조응관계이외의 다른 언어현상을 설명하기 위해 점차적으로 확장되어 Kamp and Reyle(1990)에서 종합 정리되었다.

담화표상이론의 전체적 모습을 파악하기 위해, 최초 분석의 대상이 되었던 단수 대명사의 조응관계가 포착되는 언어 현상을 먼저 다루고 이를 점차 확장해 가는 방법을 택하고자 한다. Kamp(1981)은 고유명사와 이를 선행사로 취하는 대명사를 포함하는 (30)과 같은 문장들, 비한정 명사구를 포함하는 (31)과 같은 문장들, 전칭 양화명사구를 포함하는 (32)와 같은 문장들, 그리고 (33)과 같은 조건문을 다룬다.

(30) Pedro owns Chiquita. He beats her.

(31) Pedro owns a donkey. He beats her.

(32) Every widow admires Pedro.

Every widow admires a farmer.

Every farmer who owns a donkey beats it.

Every farmer courts a widow who admires him.

(33) If Pedro owns a donkey he beats it.

If Pedro likes a woman who owns a donkey he feeds it.

2.3.2. 회기적 정의에 의한 통사 분석

Kamp(1981)는 Montague(1970, 1973) 등을 따라 통사부를 회귀적 방식 (recursion)으로 정의한다. 회기적 방식으로 정의된 통사부는 기저부(base), 회기적 구성 규칙(recursive formation rule) 그리고 배제 진술(exclusive statement)로 나뉜다. 기저부는 통사 범주(syntactic categories)와 각 범주에 속하는 기본 표현들(basic expressions; 어휘 항목)로 구성되며, 구성 규칙은 기본 표현들을 결합하여 큰 표현들을 도출한다. 배제 진술은 기본 표현과 구성 규칙에 의하여 도출된 표현 이외에는 적형한 표현이 아님을 규정한다. 예를 들어 모든 표현이 범주 X에 속하고 각 표현은 기본 표현 a와 b로만 구성되어 있는 a, b, aa, bb, ab, ba, aaa, bbb, aab, abb, ... 등을 생성하기 위하여 문법을 다음과 같이 회기적으로 정의할 수 있다.

(34) 기저: $a \in X$ and $b \in X$.

형성 규칙: If $\alpha \in X$ and $\beta \in X$, then $\alpha\beta \in X$.

배제 진술: Nothing is a member of X except as required by the base and the recursive formation rule.

Kamp는 (30)-(33)의 문장을 생성하기 위하여 다음과 같이 통사부를 정의한다.

(35) 회기적 정의에 의한 통사부

(A) 통사 범주 및 기본 표현들

1) T (Term)   : Pedro, Chiqita, John, Mary, Bill, ...; he, she, it

2) CN (Common Noun Phrase) : farmer, donkey, widow, man, woman, ...

3) IV (Intransitive Verb Phrase) : thrives, ...

4) TV (Transitive Verb Phrase) : owns, beats, loves, admires, courts, likes, feeds, loathes, ...

5) S (Sentence)   : ---

6) RC (Relative Clause)   : ---

(B) 형성 규칙들

FR 1. If $\alpha \in$ TV and $\beta \in \beta$T then $\alpha\beta' \in$ IV where β'=him if β=he, β'=her if β=she and β'=β otherwise.

FR 2. If $\alpha \in$ IV and $\beta \in$ T then $\beta\alpha \in$ S.

FR 3. If $\alpha \in$ CN then (i) *a(n)* α, and (ii) *every* α are in T.

FR 4. If $\phi \in$ S and the k-th word of ϕ is a pronoun then $\beta\phi' \in$ RC, where ϕ' is the result of eliminating the k-th word from ϕ and β is who, whom, which, according as the pronoun is he or she, him or her, or it, respectively.

FR 5. If α is a basic CN and $\beta \in$ RC then $\alpha\beta \in$ CN.

FR 6. If ϕ, $\Psi \in$ S then *if ϕ*, Ψ and *if ϕ then $\Psi \in$* S.

(C) 배제 진술: 이 이외의 것은 적형한 표현이 아니다.

구성 규칙 1 (FR 1)은 타동사 다음에 명사구가 결합되어 자동사를 구성한다는 것을 나타내며 이때 명사구가 he나 she이면 이 명사구는 him이나 her로 바뀐다는 것을 규정한다. 구성 규칙 1에서 보는 것과 같이 이 문법에서 격(case)은 구성 규칙에 의해 직접적으로 설명된다. 구성 규칙 2는 자동사 앞에 명사구가 결합하여 문장을 이룸을 표현하며 구성 규칙 3은 a(n)이나 every가 보통명사와 결합하여 명사구를 이룬다는 것을 나타낸다. a(n)이나 every는 통사범주가 주어진 기본 표현이 아니라 규칙에 의하여 직접 도입된다(syncategorematically introduced). 구성 규칙 4는 관계대명사에 의하여 유도되는 관계절의 구성 규칙이다. 어떤 문장의 k번째 단어가 대명사 he나 she, him이나 her, 또는 it일 경우 이들을 제거하고 문두에 각각 who, whom, which를 결합하면 관계절이 된다. 구성 규칙 5는 보통명사와 관계절이 결합하면 별개의 보통명사가 도출됨을 나타낸다. 구성 규칙 6은 조건절 형성에 관한 것으로 If S, S나 If S then S가 문장이라는 것을 규정한다.

(35)의 문법에 의하여 (36)의 문장이 도출되는 과정을 살펴보자. (36)의 문장을 도출하기 위해서는 구성 규칙 6을 제외한 모든 규칙을 동원하여야 한다.

(36) Every farmer who owns a donkey beats it.

먼저 관계절 who owns a donkey를 구성해 보자. 구성 규칙 3에 의해 보통명사 donkey는 a와 결합하여 명사구(term)를 이룬다. 이 명사구는 타동사 ows와 결합하여 자동사 owns a donkey를 형성한다 (구성 규칙 1). 이 자동사는 명사구 he와 결합 he owns a donkey라는 문장을 형성한다 (구성 규칙 2). 구성 규칙 4에 의해 이 문장의 첫 번째 대명사 he를 삭제하고 who와 결합 who owns a donkey를 형성한다. 이 과정을 요약하면 다음과 같다.

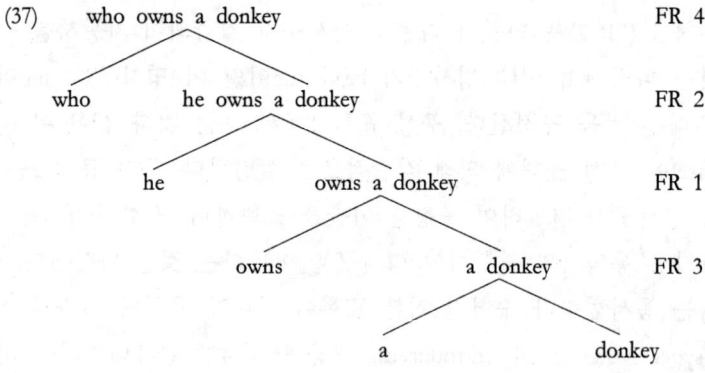

(37)

관계절 who owns a donkey는 구성 규칙 5에 의해 보통명사 farmer와 결합

새로운 보통명사 farmer who owns a donkey를 구성하고 여기에 구성 규칙 3, 2, 1 등이 작용하여 (36)의 문장을 형성한다.

(35)에 의하여 정의된 문법은 비문법적 문장을 생성할 수 있다. 구성 규칙 4는 대명사를 포함하는 모든 문장에 작용하여 관계절을 생성할 수 있다. 이 규칙에 의하면 (38)의 문장은 대명사를 포함함으로 (39)와 같이 관계절이 될 수 있다.

(38) Every farmer who owns it beats a donkey.
(39) Which every farmer who owns beats a donkey

이 문제는 생성 문법에서 섬 제약(island condition)으로 알려진 현상으로 (39)와 같은 관계절의 생성을 막을 수 있는 방법이 제시되었다. Kamp는 어떤 한 문장이 구성 규칙 4의 적용을 받아 관계절이 되면 나머지 대명사들은 유표적(marked)인 것이 되어 더 이상 구성 규칙 4의 적용을 받을 수 없도록 구성 규칙을 수정하는 방안을 제시한다. 이 방법을 정교히 하여 문법을 수정할 수 있으나 이 책의 목적이 통사 분석과 의미와의 관계를 밝히는 것이므로 이 문제는 더 이상 다루지 않겠다.

(35)의 문법은 (30)-(33)의 문장을 통사적으로 분석하기 위하여 제시되었다. 이 문장들을 분석하는 데 있어 선행사와 대명사 간의 조응 관계가 매우 중요하다. 그러나 (35)의 문법은 변수나 지표가 붙여진 대명사를 사용하지 않아 선행사와 대명사간의 조응 관계가 통사 분석에서 드러나지 않는다. 즉, 조응 관계는 통사 분석 이외의 부분에서 다루어진다. Kamp의 담화 표상 이론에서 조응 관계는 통사 분석을 기반으로 하여 형성되는 담화 표상 체계에서 포착된다.

2.3.3. 구 구조 규칙에 의한 통사 분석

Kamp and Reyle(1991)은 담화표상의 추출에 대한 입력으로 구 구조 규칙에만 의존하는 단층 통사분석을 사용한다. 이와 같은 통사분석은 GB 통사론 등에서 채택하는 다층 통사 분석(multi-stratal analysis of syntax)과는 다르게 두 개의 층위를 이어 주는 변형규칙 같은 사상규칙(mapping rules)을 상정하지 않는다. 구 구조 규칙에만 의지하는 통사분석은 2.1.에서 다룬 단층 통사 분석의 가정과 방법을 상당 부분 공유한다. Kamp and Reyle(1990)는 어미 마디와 딸 마디간의 자질 값의 상호관계를 단순히 구 구조 규칙에서 규정하게 하는 것이 다르다. 문장 요소들의 선형 관계도 구 구조 규칙에 포함시켜서 표현한다. 따라서 어떤 국지적 구조 수형도(local tree)의 적형성은 오직 구 구조 규칙에 의해서만 인허된다.

예를 들어 주어 명사구와 동사의 수가 일치해야 한다는 사실은 GPSG에서는 Control Agreement Principle(CAP)에 의하여 포착된다. (한 술어가 논항을 취하여 문장을 형성할 때, 술어의 일치 자질(agreement feature)의 값은 논항의 일치 자질 값과 동일해야 한다.) Kamp and Reyle의 통사 분석 체계에 있어서는 이 사실을 다음과 같은 구 구조 규칙을 설정하여 구조의 적형성을 포착한다. 이하에서 Num은 수, Gen은 성, Case는 격, Fin은 동사의 한정성(finiteness: 시제의 유무), Trans는 타동성(Trans=+는 타동사), nom은 주격(nominative case)을 나타낸다.

(40) (a) S[Num=α] $\rightarrow$ NP[Num=α] VP[Num=α]
　　　(b) VP[Num=α] $\rightarrow$ V[Num=α] NP[Num=β]

규칙 (40a)는 주어 명사구의 수는 동사구의 수와 일치해야 함을 표시하여 CAP의 역할을 구 구조 규칙에 통합하고 있으며 문장의 수와 동사구의 수가 일치하게 함으로서 Head Feature Convention (HFC)의 효과를 포착한다.

(40b)는 동사구는 그의 머리딸인 동사와 머리자질인 Num의 자질값이 일치해야하며 머리딸이 아닌 명사구의 머리자질 값과는 일치할 필요가 없음을 나타낸다. (40)의 규칙은 딸 범주들의 선형관계를 규칙의 일부로 표현하고 있음을 주의해야 한다. 즉, (40a)는 (41)의 규칙과는 선형관계의 표현에서 다르다.

(41) S[Num=α] → VP[Num=α] NP[Num=α]

GPSG의 Foot Feature Principle (FFP)의 효과도 구 구조 규칙에 의해 직접 포착된다. 구 구조 규칙 (42)는 딸 범주인 명사구의 발자질인 Gap (GPSG에서의 SLASH)의 자질값과 어미 범주의 Gap의 자질값이 동일해야 함을 표현하고 있다.

(42) VP[Gap=NP[Num=α]] → V NP[Gap=NP[Num=α]]

어떤 범주의 Gap 자질의 자질값이 그 자신과 같을 때는 공범주 "e"가 어휘 항목으로 선택된다는 (43)과 같은 어휘 삽입 규칙을 설정하여 (44) 구조의 적형성을 인허하게 한다.

(43) NP[Num=α, Gap=NP[Num=α]] → e

(44)

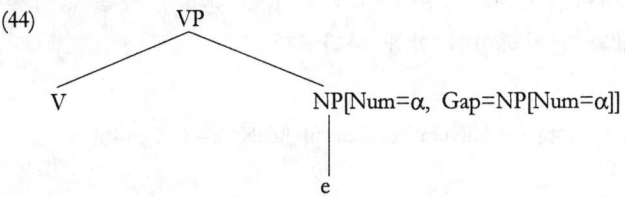

문장 (45)는 당나귀 문장의 대표적 경우로 담화표상이론에서 중요하게

다루어지는 현상이다. (45)의 문장을 통사적으로 분석하기 위해서는 관계
절에 대한 처리를 규정하여야 한다. 관계절을 내포하는 표현의 구조는
(46)과 같이 관계절을 NP의 자매로 처리하기도 하고 (47)과 같이 N의 자매
로 간주하기도 한다. 두 접근 방법 모두 나름대로의 이유와 근거를 가지
고 있지만 더 이상의 논의 없이 (47)의 구조를 따르기로 한다. (47)의 구조
는 GPSG와 Kamp and Reyle에서 채택되고 있으며 관계절이 자매가 되는
명사의 의미(개체들의 집합)를 제한하는 의미론적 역할을 직접적으로 포
착하고 있다. RC는 관계절(relative clause)을 뜻한다.

(45) Every farmer who owns a donkey beats it.

(46)

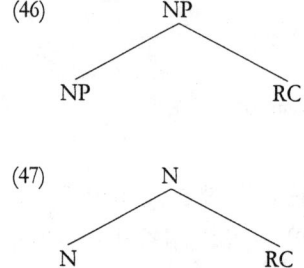

(47)

Kamp and Reyle는 (47)의 구조를 인허하기 위해 (48)의 규칙을 설정한다.
규칙 (49)는 관계절의 성(性)과 수(數) 자질에 대한 자질 값은 관계 대명사
의 자질 값과 일치하며 관계 대명사의 자질 값은 Gap의 자질 값이 되는
명사구의 자질 값과 일치하여야 함을 나타낸다.

(48) N[Num=α, Gen=β] → N[Num=α, Gen=β] RC[Num=α, Gen=β]

(49) RC[Num=α, Gen=β] → RPRO[Num=α, Gen=β] S[Num=γ, Gap=NP[Num=α]]

이제 문장 (45)의 farmer who owns a donkey는 이들 구 구조 규칙에 의해
(50)의 구조를 부여받게 된다.

(50)

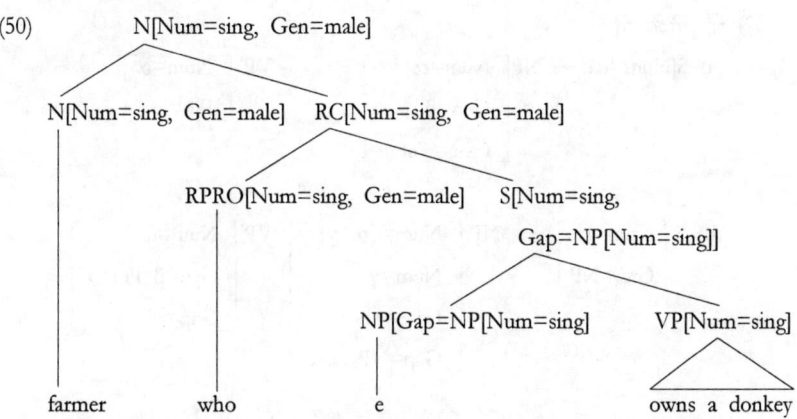

(50)의 구조는 GPSG에서는 용인 불가능한 구조임에 주목해야 한다.
GPSG에서 공범주 "e"가 나타나기 위해서는 SLASH 종결 상위 규칙의 적
용을 받아야 하는데 이 상위 규칙은 주어 명사구에 적용될 수 없기 때문
이다. 이 점에서 Kamp and Reyle의 통사 분석은 GPSG와 차이가 있다. 여
기에서는 Kamp and Reyle의 체계를 따르기로 하겠다.

구 구조 규칙은 어휘 삽입 규칙(lexical insertion rule)으로 보강된다. 어휘
삽입 규칙은 나무 구조의 최종 마디에 특정 어휘 항목을 삽입하는 역할을
한다. 예를 들어 [Num=sing, Gen=fem, Case=-nom]의 자질 명세를 갖는 대
명사는 규칙 (51)에 의해 her로 실현된다.

(51) PRO[Num=sing, Gen=fem, Case=-nom] → her

다음은 앞으로의 논의에 필요한 문장들을 생성하기 위한 구 구조 규칙
과 어휘 삽입 규칙을 정리 한 것이다. VP'는 조동사를 포함하는 동사구를

표상하기 위하여 설정한 범주로 동사의 최대 투사(maximal projection)이다. 조동사가 없을 때, VP'는 VP와 동일하다. (Reyle 1991, pp.47-50 참조)

(52) 구 구조 규칙

(a) $S[Num=\alpha] \rightarrow NP \begin{bmatrix} Num=\alpha \\ Gen=\beta \\ Case=+nom \end{bmatrix}$ $VP' \begin{bmatrix} Num=\alpha \\ Fin=+ \end{bmatrix}$

(b) $S \begin{bmatrix} Num=\alpha \\ Gap=NP \end{bmatrix} \rightarrow NP \begin{bmatrix} Num=\{\alpha, \gamma\} \\ Num=\gamma \\ Case=+nom \\ Gap=NP_{Num=\gamma} \end{bmatrix}$ $VP' \begin{bmatrix} Num=\alpha \\ Gen=\beta \; Fin=+ \\ Gap=- \end{bmatrix}$

(c) $S \begin{bmatrix} Num=\alpha \\ Gap=NP_{Num=\gamma} \end{bmatrix} \rightarrow NP \begin{bmatrix} Num=\alpha \\ Gen=\beta \\ Case=+nom \\ Gap=- \end{bmatrix}$ $VP' \begin{bmatrix} Num=\alpha \\ Fin=+ \\ Gap=NP_{Num=\gamma} \end{bmatrix}$

(d) $VP' \begin{bmatrix} Num=\alpha \\ Fin=\beta \\ Gap=\gamma \end{bmatrix} \rightarrow AUX \begin{bmatrix} Num=\alpha \\ Fin=\beta \end{bmatrix}$ not $VP \begin{bmatrix} Num=\delta \\ Fin=- \\ Gap=\gamma \end{bmatrix}$

(e) $VP' \begin{bmatrix} Num=\alpha \\ Fin=+ \\ Gap=\gamma \end{bmatrix} \rightarrow VP \begin{bmatrix} Num=\alpha \\ Fin=+ \\ Gap=\gamma \end{bmatrix}$

(f) $VP \begin{bmatrix} Num=\alpha \\ Fin=\beta \\ Gap=NP_{Num=\gamma} \end{bmatrix} \rightarrow V \begin{bmatrix} Num=\alpha \\ Fin=\beta \\ Trans=+ \end{bmatrix}$ $NP \begin{bmatrix} Num=\gamma \\ Gen=\delta \\ Case=-nom \\ Gap=NP_{Num=\gamma} \end{bmatrix}$

(g) $VP \begin{bmatrix} Num=\alpha \\ Fin=\beta \end{bmatrix} \rightarrow V \begin{bmatrix} Num=\alpha \\ Fin=\beta \\ Trans=- \end{bmatrix}$

(h) $NP \begin{bmatrix} Num=\alpha \\ Gen= \\ Case= \\ Gap=NP_{Num=\gamma} \end{bmatrix} \rightarrow \varnothing$

(i) $NP \begin{bmatrix} Num=\alpha \\ Gen=\beta \\ Case=\gamma \end{bmatrix} \rightarrow DET_{Num=\alpha} \quad N \begin{bmatrix} Num=\alpha \\ Gen=\beta \end{bmatrix}$

(j) $NP \begin{bmatrix} Num=\alpha \\ Gen=\beta \\ Case=\gamma \end{bmatrix} \rightarrow PN \begin{bmatrix} Num=\alpha \\ Gen=\beta \end{bmatrix}$

(PN: proper noun)

(k) $NP \begin{bmatrix} Num=\alpha \\ Gen=\beta \\ Case=\gamma \end{bmatrix} \rightarrow PRO \begin{bmatrix} Num=\alpha \\ Gen=\beta \\ Case=\gamma \end{bmatrix}$

(l) $N \begin{bmatrix} Num=\alpha \\ Gen=\beta \end{bmatrix} \rightarrow N \begin{bmatrix} Num=\alpha \\ Gen=\beta \end{bmatrix} \quad RC \begin{bmatrix} Num=\alpha \\ Gen=\beta \end{bmatrix}$ (RC: relative clause)

(m) $RC \begin{bmatrix} Num=\alpha \\ Gen=\beta \end{bmatrix} \rightarrow RPRO \begin{bmatrix} Num=\alpha \\ Gen=\beta \end{bmatrix} \quad S \begin{bmatrix} Num=\gamma \\ Gap=NP_{Num=\gamma} \end{bmatrix}$

(RPRO: relative pronoun)

(53) 어휘 삽입 규칙

(a) $DET_{Num=sing}$ → a, every, the, some

(b) PRO $\begin{bmatrix} Num=sing \\ Gen=male \\ Case=+nom \end{bmatrix}$ → he

(c) PRO $\begin{bmatrix} Num=sing \\ Gen=male \\ Case=-nom \end{bmatrix}$ → him

(d) PRO $\begin{bmatrix} Num=sing \\ Gen=fem \\ Case=+nom \end{bmatrix}$ → she

(e) PRO $\begin{bmatrix} Num=sing \\ Gen=fem \\ Case=-nom \end{bmatrix}$ → her

(f) PRO $\begin{bmatrix} Num=sing \\ Gen=-hum \\ Case=+/-nom \end{bmatrix}$ → it

(g) PN $\begin{bmatrix} Num=sing \\ Gen=male \end{bmatrix}$ → John, Bill, Smith, ...

(h) PN $\begin{bmatrix} Num=sing \\ Gen=fem \end{bmatrix}$ → Mary, Susan, ...

(i) N $\begin{bmatrix} \text{Num=sing} \\ \text{Gen=male} \end{bmatrix}$ → man, husband, student, farmer, ...

(j) N $\begin{bmatrix} \text{Num=sing} \\ \text{Gen=fem} \end{bmatrix}$ → man, husband, student, farmer, ...

(k) N $\begin{bmatrix} \text{Num=sing} \\ \text{Gen=-hum} \end{bmatrix}$ → dog, cat, donkey, book, ...

(l) AUX $\begin{bmatrix} \text{Num=sing} \\ \text{Fin=+} \end{bmatrix}$ → does

(m) AUX $\begin{bmatrix} \text{Num=sing} \\ \text{Fin=-} \end{bmatrix}$ → to (infinitive marker as in to go)

(n) AUX $\begin{bmatrix} \text{Num=plur} \\ \text{Fin=+} \end{bmatrix}$ → do

(o) V $\begin{bmatrix} \text{Num=sing/plur} \\ \text{Trans=+} \\ \text{Fin=-} \end{bmatrix}$ → like, own, love, ...

(p) V $\begin{bmatrix} \text{Num=sing/plur} \\ \text{Trans=-} \\ \text{Fin=-} \end{bmatrix}$ → sing, come-in, rotate, ...

(q) V $\begin{bmatrix} \text{Num=sing} \\ \text{Trans=}\beta \\ \text{Fin=+} \end{bmatrix}$ → <Pres, sing3rd>(α), where $\alpha \in$ V $\begin{bmatrix} \text{Num=sing/plur} \\ \text{Trans=}\beta \\ \text{Fin=-} \end{bmatrix}$

(r) RPRO $\begin{bmatrix} \text{Num=sing/plur} \\ \text{Gen=male/fem} \end{bmatrix}$ → who

(s) RPRO $\begin{bmatrix} \text{Num=sing/plur} \\ \text{Gen=-hum} \end{bmatrix}$ → which

2.4. 요약

이상에서 담화표상 이론에서 채택하고 있는 통사 분석 체계를 살펴보았다. 통사 구조는 단어, 구 등의 표현들 간의 선형 관계(linearity), 비어휘 요소들의 구성성(constituency), 구 구조에서의 계층성(hierarchy) 등을 명시하여야 한다. 이러한 조건을 만족하는 통사 기술 방법은 다양하다. Kamp (1981)은 회기적 구성 규칙을 사용하는 방법을 사용하여 통사 구조를 분석하였으며 Kamp and Reyle(1990)은 단층 통사 이론인 GPSG의 기술 방법을 사용한다. 이 장에서는 앞으로 논의 될 영어의 한 단편을 회기적 구성 규칙에 의한 통사 이론과 단층 통사 이론에서 어떻게 분석하는가를 개략적으로 다루었다.

제 3 장 담화표상 구성규칙

3.1. 담화표상 구성규칙

담화표상이론에서 담화(discourse)의 진리값은 주어진 담화의 표상을 모형에 비추어 결정하며 담화표상은 담화의 통사 분석으로부터 추출한다. 담화표상 구성규칙은 담화의 통사 분석으로부터 담화표상을 도출해 내는 규칙을 말한다. 따라서 담화표상 구성규칙은 통사 분석을 담화표상으로 사상(mapping)하는 규칙을 일컫는다. 담화표상은 담화 지시체(discourse referent)들의 집합과 이 담화 지시체들에 대한 조건들(conditions)로 구성되므로 담화표상 구성 규칙은 통사 분석을 담화 지시체와 이들에 대한 조건들로 변환시키는 규칙이다. (담화 지시체에 대한 조건을 담화표상 조건 (DRS-conditions)이라 부르기로 하자. 담화 지시체의 집합을 Kamp를 따라 담화 표상의 universe라 부르겠다.)

담화표상은 담화 지시체들의 집합과 이들에 대한 담화표상 조건들의 집합으로 이루어지므로 순서쌍의 개념을 사용하여 (1)과 같이 나타낼 수도 있고 우리에게 이미 친숙해진 사각형을 사용하여 (2)와 같이 표상할 수도 있다. Kamp 등을 따라 사각형의 위 부분에 담화 지시체를 표기하고 아래 부분에 담화표상 조건을 표기하도록 하겠으며 필요시 두 부분을 점선을 사용하여 구분하고자 한다.

(1) 담화표상=<{담화지시체들}, {담화표상 조건들}>

(2)
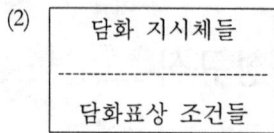

담화표상은 주어진 담화표상을 확대해 가는 방식으로 구축된다. 우리는 아무런 담화 지시체도 없고 담화표상 조건도 주어지지 않은 최초의 담화표상 (3)을 생각해 볼 수 있다. 이러한 담화 표상을 Kamp and Reyle는 공담화표상(empty discourse representation)이라 정의한다.

(3) DRS1=<∅, ∅>

이제 담화표상의 universe에 새로운 담화 지시체 x가 도입되고 x에 대한 담화표상 조건 condition 1이 정해지면 담화표상 (3)은 담화표상 (4)로 확대되며 이는 사각형 도식 (5)로 표상 된다.

(4) DRS2=<{x}, {condition 1}>

(5)
```
+------------------+
|        x         |
|------------------|
|   condition 1    |
+------------------+
```

담화는 문장들로 구성되며 문장들의 순서가 중요한 역할을 한다. 두 개의 문장으로 이루어진 (6)의 담화 1은 이 두 개의 문장의 순서가 바뀐 담화 2와 그 의미가 다르다. 담화 1에서 대명사 He는 /John/이라 불리는 어떤 개체를 지칭할 수 있으나 담화 2에서 대명사 He는 John이라 불리는 개체와는 다른, 어떤 개체를 지칭하기 때문이다.

(6) 담화 1: John is brave. He is a soldier.

(7) 담화 2: He is a soldier. John is brave.

따라서, 담화는 순서가 유지되는 문장들의 집합, 즉 문장들의 순서쌍으로 정의될 수 있다.

(8) 담화=<문장 1, 문장 2, ..., 문장 n>

어떤 담화의 담화표상은 공담화표상으로부터 시작하여 각 문장이 이를 확대함으로써 얻어진다. 다시 말하여 각 문장은 그것이 일부를 이루는 담화의 담화표상의 구축에 일정 부분 공헌하게 되는 것이다. (9)의 담화에서 각 문장이 어떠한 방식으로 담화의 담화표상에 공헌하는지를 살펴보자.

(9) John is brave. Mary is smart.

(9)의 첫 번째 문장은 공담화표상을 확장한다. 이 문장은 /jaːn/이라 불리는 어떤 개체가 용감하다는 속성을 가지고 있다라는 의미를 가진다. 즉 어떤 개체 x가 주어진 모형 (또는 대상 세계)에서 /jaːn/이라 불리는 조건과 용감하다는 조건을 만족시키면 모형의 일부분을 참되게 기술했다고 여겨진다. 따라서 이 문장은 최초의 공담화표상을 (10)과 같이 확장하는데 공헌하고 있다.

(10)
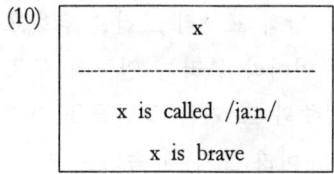

이와 비슷한 방식으로 (9)의 두 번째 문장은 담화표상 (10)을 확장하여 (11)

의 담화표상을 만드는 데 공헌한다.

(11)
```
            x, y
    -------------------------
        x is called /jaːn/
        x is brave
        y is called /mɛəri/
        y is smart
```

이제 "x is called /jaːn/"과 같은 조건을 간단히 John(x)로 표기하기로 하면 (11)의 담화표상은 (12)와 같이 표상 된다.

(12)
```
            x, y
    -------------------------
            John(x)
        x is brave
            Mary(y)
        y is smart
```

"x is brave"라는 담화조건은 x가 is-brave라는 술어의 논항이라는 통사 정보를 나타낸다. 즉, 이 조건은 통사적 구조를 갖는다. 통사구조에서 각 표현은 명사구, 동사구 등의 통사 범주를 가진다. 담화 표상의 조건을 담화표상 언어의 한 표현으로 생각하고 이 담화표상 언어라 불리는 언어의 구조를 살펴보자. 이 언어는 영어와 동일한 통사 범주와 그 기본 표현들을 가지며 여기에 덧붙여 담화 지시체라는 통사 범주 (dr이라 표기)에 속하는 기본 표현들과 John(x)와 같은 도출 표현들을 갖는다. 이제 "x is brave"라는 담화조건은 담화표상 언어의 한 문장으로 (13)의 통사 구조를 가지게 된다.

(13)

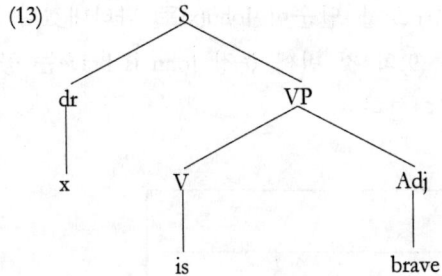

Kamp and Reyle는 dr이라는 통사 범주를 수형도 상에 표기하지 않는다. 즉 (14)의 통사 구조는 실제로는 (13)의 통사 구조와 동일하다. 이하에서 필자는 Kamp and Reyle의 표기 규약을 따르겠다.

(14)

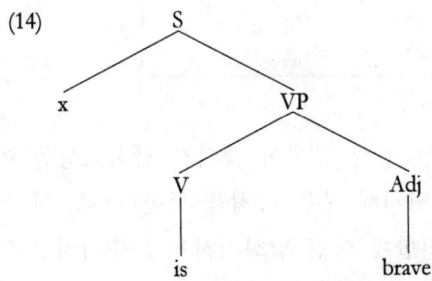

"John(x)"와 같은 표현은 문장의 한 경우로 간주한다. 이 표현은 (15)와 같은 구조를 가지는 것으로 생각될 수 있다. (,), = 등은 어떤 통사 범주 MISC의 표현들이라 하자.

(15)

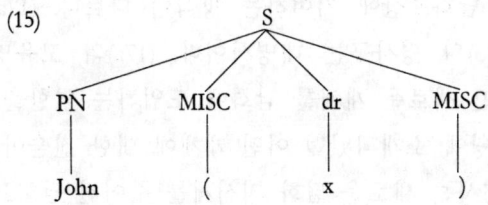

이하에서 이러한 표현들의 통사 구조를 단순히 John(x)로 나타내겠다. 위에서 논의한 방식을 따르면 담화 (9)의 첫 번째 문장 John is brave는 공담화표상을 (16)의 담화표상으로 확대한다.

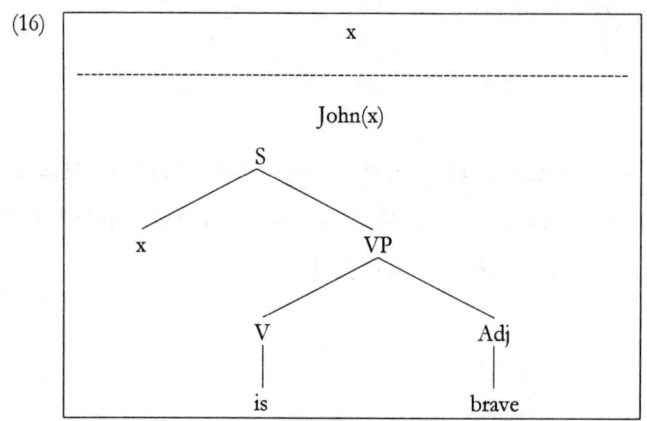

(16)

담화표상 구성규칙은 어떤 특정 통사 분석이 주어진 담화표상을 어떠한 방식으로 확장하게 되는가를 명시해 주는 규칙을 말한다. 즉, 한 통사 분석이 기존의 담화지시체들의 집합에 어떤 담화지시체를 추가하고 담화표상 조건들의 집합에 어떤 담화표상 조건을 새로이 추가하는가를 밝혀 주는 규칙인 것이다. 따라서, 담화표상 구성규칙은 입력(input)이 되는 통사 구조(triggering configuration)와 이 규칙이 주어진 입력 구조에 작용하는 방식(modus operandi)으로 정의된다.

입력 구조는 국지 구조(local structure)만으로 정의되지 않는다. (17)의 두 문장에서 각각의 명사구가 담화표상에 기여하는 방식이 다르다. (17a)의 명사구는 고유명사이며 (17b)의 명사구는 대명사이다. (17a)의 고유명사 John은 John이라 불리는 어떤 새로운 개체를 담화에 도입하는 역할을 하나, (17b)의 대명사 He는 기왕에 소개되었던 어떤 개체에 대한 진술이 계속됨을 나타낸다. 즉, 고유명사는 새로운 담화 지시체를 주어진 담화표상에 도입하나 대명사는 기존의 담화지시체 중 어떤 특정한 담화지시체와 동일시되어야만 하는 담화 지시체를 도입하게 된다.

(17) (a) John sings.

    (b) He sings.

따라서 (17a)의 고유명사를 처리하기 위한 담화표상 구성규칙의 입력 구조는 NP의 지배를 받는 구성소의 범주까지를 언급해 주어야 하므로 (18a)가 아니라 (18b)의 구조가 되어야 한다.

(18) (a)

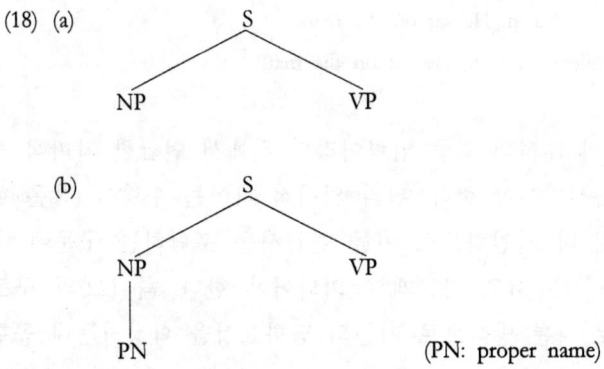

    (b)

(PN: proper name)

   때로 담화표상 구성규칙은 어휘 항목(lexical item)에 의하여 결정되기도 한다. 예를 들어 영어 양화사 a(n)과 every는 같은 통사범주에 속하지만 담화 표상에 공헌하는 바는 매우 다르다. (19a)는 학생 중 대머리가 한 명 이상이라는 것을 뜻하고 (19b)는 학생이라면 모두 대머리라는 것을 나타낸다. 이러한 관계는 (20)으로 도식할 수 있다.

(19) (a) A student is bold.

    (b) Every student is bold.

(20) (a)

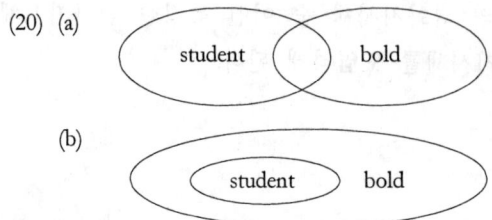

(b)

조응 관계(anaphoric relation)에 있어서도 이 둘은 다르게 작용한다. (21a)에서 대명사 He는 그 선행사로 A student를 취할 수 있지만 (21b)에서 대명사 He는 Every student를 선행사로 취할 수 없다.

(21) (a) A student came in. He sat on the mat.
    (b) Every student came in. He sat on the mat.

담화 표상이 의미 해석의 최종 입력이라면 위에서 언급한 의미적 차이가 담화 표상에 명시되어야 한다. 위의 의미적 차이는 수량사 (혹은 한정사) a(n)과 every로부터 기인하므로 이들 한정사를 포함하는 구문에 대한 담화표상 구성 규칙은 서로 다르게 정의되어야 한다. 즉 (22)의 구조와 (23)의 구조는 서로 다른 방식으로 기존의 담화표상을 확장하는데 공헌하게 된다.

(22)

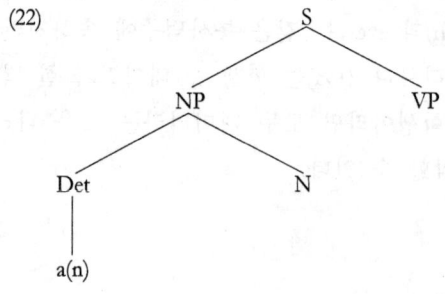

(23)

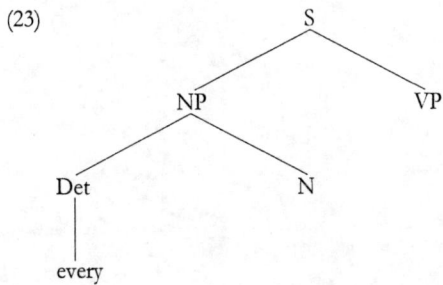

담화표상 구성규칙은 입력이 되는 통사구조와 이에 작용하여 새로운 담화표상 조건을 만들어내는 방식으로 구성된다. 새로운 담화조건은 통사구조의 의미적 성격에 입각하여 도입되는 담화표상조건과 입력 통사구조의 일부를 적절한 담화지시체로 대체하여 만들어지는 담화표상 조건으로 대별할 수 있다. (17a)의 문장은 (24)와 같은 구조로 분석되어지며 어떤 개체가 John이라 불린다는 정보와 이 개체가 노래한다라는 속성이 있다는 정보를 기존의 담화에 추가한다.

(24)

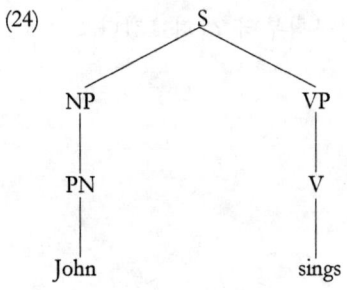

즉 (24)의 통사 분석에 어떤 규칙이 작용하여 차후 의미해석 부분에서 이들 두 가지 정보를 얻을 수 있도록 기존의 담화표상을 확대하여야 한다. 어떤 개체 x가 John이라 불린다는 정보는 John(x)라 담화표상에 표상되고 이 개체가 노래한다는 속성을 가졌다는 정보는 (25)와 같이 표상된다.

(25)

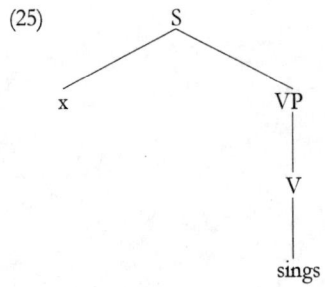

(25)의 구조는 (24)의 구조 중 [NP[PN John]]을 x로 대체함으로써 얻어진다. 이와 같이 어떤 구조의 일부를 담화지시체로 대체하는 과정을 어떤 구조를 다른 구조로 "간략히 한다(reduce)"라고 표현한다.

3.2. 고유명사의 담화표상 구성규칙

이상의 논의를 바탕으로 몇 가지 구체적 담화표상 구성규칙을 정의해 보도록 하자. 먼저 고유명사에 대한 구성규칙부터 살펴보겠다.

(26) 고유명사에 대한 담화표상 구성규칙

(i) 입력 구조(triggering configuration)

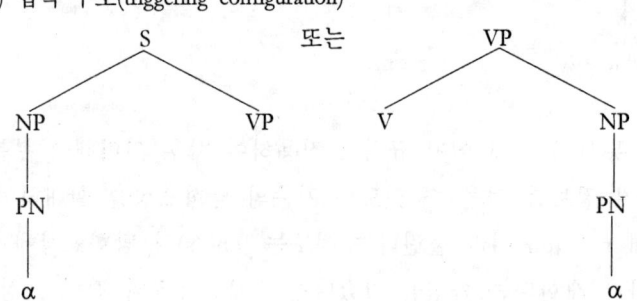

(ii) 규칙 작용 방식 (modus operandi)

  (1) 새로운 담화지시체 x를 담화표상의 담화지시체의 집합(universe)에 추가한다.

  (2) 새로운 담화조건 α(x)를 담화표상 조건들의 집합에 추가한다.

  (3) 입력 구조 중 [NP[PN α]]를 x로 대체한다.

담화표상 구성규칙 (26)이 어떻게 기존의 담화표상을 확장하는지를 문장 (17a)를 예로 들어 살펴보자. 문장 (17a)가 어떤 담화를 시작하는 첫 번째 문장이라 가정하자. 이 문장은 (27)과 같은 공담화표상을 우선 (28)의 담화 표상으로 확대한다.

(27)

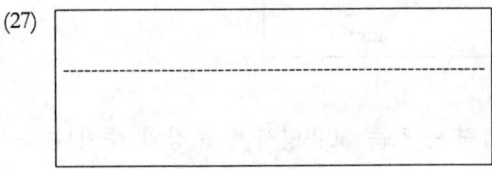

(28)

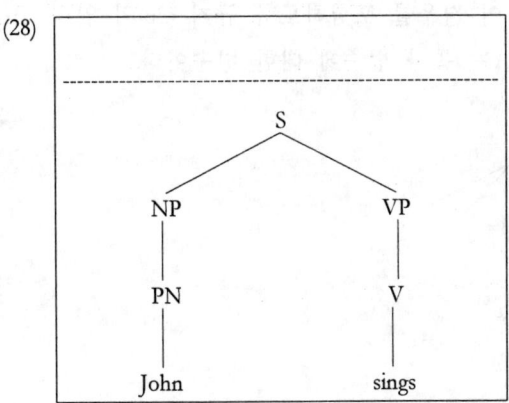

(28)의 담화표상은 담화표상 구성규칙 (26)을 작동시킬 구조를 지닌 담화 표상 조건을 포함하고 있으므로 이 조건에 규칙 (26)이 작용하여 (29)의 담

화표상을 도출한다.

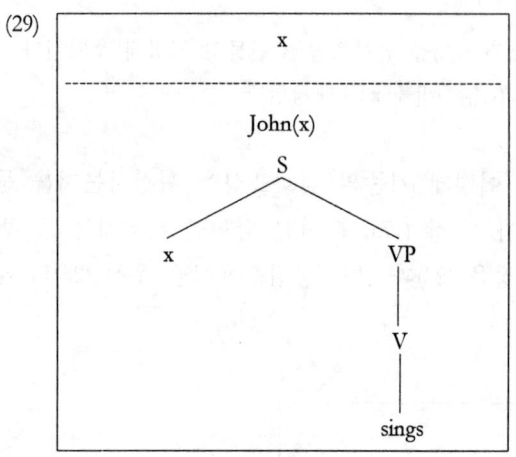

담화표상 구성규칙 (26)의 입력 구조는 고유명사가 문장의 주어나 동사의
목적어로 쓰이는 경우만을 언급하고 있으나 고유명사는 전치사 등의 목적
어로도 쓰일 수 있으므로 이 경우를 포함하도록 규칙 (26)의 입력 구조를
(30)처럼 확장할 수 있다. A는 통사 범주에 대한 변수이다.

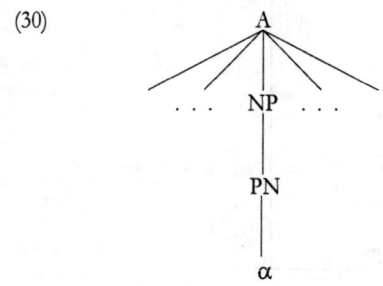

3.3. 대명사의 담화표상 구성규칙

대명사에 대한 담화표상 구성규칙을 살펴보자. 대명사는 크게 지시적 대명사(deictic pronoun)와 조응적 대명사(anaphoric pronoun)로 구분된다. 지시적 대명사는 손가락으로 특정 지시물을 가리키거나 고개를 끄덕이거나 하는 것과 같은 지시적 행동과 수반하여 쓰이는 대명사이다. 어떤 화자가 여러 사람 중 한 명을 손가락으로 가리키면서 he is my brother라 했다면 대명사 he는 손가락으로 가리켜진 바로 그 사람을 지칭하게 된다. 이러한 지시적 대명사의 의미는 발화 현장의 상황에 의하여 즉각적으로 결정되나 글로 표현된 담화에서 이 대명사의 지시체를 파악하기는 매우 곤란하다. 이와 같은 이유로 여기에서는 지시적 대명사는 다루지 않기로 하겠다. 조응적 대명사(혹은 조응 대명사)는 이 대명사 이전의 담화에서 사용된 표현의 지시체를 그 지시체로 가지게 된다. 즉, 조응대명사는 그 선행사와 지시체를 공유한다. (31)의 담화에서 대명사 He는 그 선행사 John이 지칭하는 개체를 의미값으로 한다.

(31) John came in. He sat on the mat.

조응 대명사에 대한 연구는 주로 (특히 생성문법의 전통 속에서) 대명사와 선행사간의 통사적 제약에 초점을 맞추어 진행되었다. 대명사와 선행사에 대한 통사적 분석은 이러한 표현들이 만족시켜야 할 통사적 조건들을 탐구하는 데에 주어졌다. 대표적 통사 제약으로 선행사는 대명사를 성분통어(c-command) 해서는 안된다는 것이다. 예를 들어 문장 (32)에서 대명사 him이 John을 그 선행사로 취할 수 없는 것은 (33)의 구조에서처럼 John이라는 표현이 him이라는 표현을 성분통어하기 때문이다.

(32) John loves him.

(33)

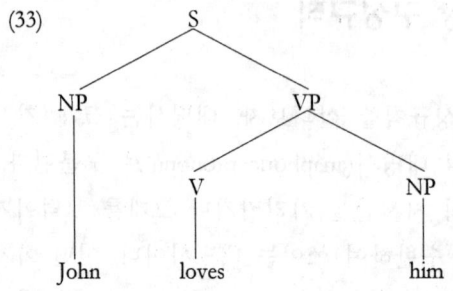

성분통어로 대명사와 선행사의 관계를 포착하려는 시도는 많은 예외적 자료에 부딪쳐 대안을 모색하지 않으면 안되게 되었다 (자세한 내용은 Pullun and Sag 1990 참조). 담화표상이론은 따라 대명사와 선행사의 관계를 이러한 표현들이 도입하는 담화지시체들 간의 관계로 규정하고 이 담화지시체들이 준수해야할 조건을 탐구한다.

조응대명사는 새로운 담화 지시체를 담화표상에 도입하는 것이 아니라 기 도입된 담화지시체 중 하나를 선택하여 자신의 담화 지시체로 삼는다. 바꾸어 말하면 조응 대명사가 도입하는 담화지시체는 기존의 담화지시체 중 하나와 동일시되어야 한다. 이 관계는 다음과 같이 표상된다. u는 대명사에 의하여 도입된 담화 지시체이며 y는 u가 담화표상에 도입되기 전에 존재하던 담화 지시체이다.

(34) u=y

(34)는 담화표상 조건 중의 하나로 의미해석 규칙에 의해 u의 지시체와 y의 지시체가 동일하게 되어야 한다.

조응 대명사에 대한 담화표상 구성규칙은 (35)와 같이 정의된다. 규칙 (35)의 입력구조는 대명사가 문장의 주어 또는 목적어로 기능 하는 경우만을 다루고 있음을 나타낸다. 그러나 고유명사와 마찬가지로 대명사는 전치사 등의 목적어로도 쓰이기 때문에 (30)의 구조와 비슷하게 일반화할 수 있다.

(35) 조응대명사에 대한 담화표상 구성규칙

(i) 입력구조:

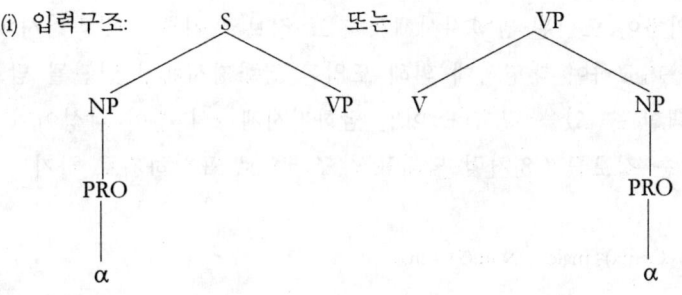

(ii) 규칙 작용 방식
(1) 새로운 담화지시체 u를 담화지시체의 집합(universe)에 추가한다.
(2) 새로운 담화조건 u=y를 담화표상 조건들의 집합에 추가한다.
(3) 입력구조의 [NP[PRO α]]를 u로 대체한다.

대명사에 의해 도입된 담화지시체는 기 도입된 담화지시체 중의 하나와 동일시되어야 한다. 두 개 이상의 기 도입된 담화지시체 중 어떤 것과 동일시되어야 하느냐 하는 것은 매우 까다로운 문제이다. 우선 대명사의 성과 수는 선행사의 그것과 일치하여야 한다. 담화 (36)에서 대명사 He는 John을 선행사로 취할 수 있으나 Mary를 선행사로 취할 수 없다. 일상적 명명 규약을 따라 John은 남자이며 Mary는 여자라 하면 John만이 대명사와 성에 있어서 일치하기 때문이다.

(36) John loves Mary. He is a student.

담화 (37)에서 대명사 He는 선행사로서 John을 택할 수 있으나 the teachers를 택할 수 없다.

(37) John loves the teachers. He is a student.

성과 수와 같은 지표(index)는 통사 정보이므로 대명사와 선행사간에는 구조적 제약이 존재한다. 이러한 지표 정보를 담화표상에 포함시켜 대명사에 의하여 도입된 담화지시체의 지표 정보와 기존의 담화지시체의 지표 정보를 비교하여 대명사에 의해 도입된 담화지시체가 연관될 담화지시체를 선택할 수 있을 것이다. 어떤 담화지시체 x의 성이 남성이며 그 수가 단수라는 정보를 (38)처럼 담화표상 조건으로 표상하기로 하자.

(38) Gen(x)=male, Num(x)=sing

성, 수에 대한 정보는 통사 분석에 포함되므로 담화표상 구성규칙의 입력구조에 지표 정보를 명시하여 이 정보에 준하여 (38)과 같은 담화표상 조건을 도출하도록 구성규칙을 정의하여야 한다.

성, 수 등의 지표 정보 이외의 다른 제약이 대명사와 그 선행사간에 존재한다. 담화 (39a)에서 비한정 명사구 a donkey는 대명사 it의 선행사가 될 수 있으나 담화 (39b)에서는 이러한 관계가 성립하지 않는다.

(39) (a) John owns a donkey. Bill beats it.
    (b) Every farmer owns a donkey. Bill beats it.

담화 (39a, b)에서의 조응 관계의 차이는 고유명사 John과 양화 명사구 (quantificational NP) Every farmer가 기존의 담화표상을 확장하는 방식의 차이에 기인한다. 위에서 언급하였듯이 고유명사는 담화표상의 universe에 새로운 담화지시체를 도입하며 담화표상 조건들의 집합에 규칙 (26)에서 명시한 조건들을 도입한다. 반면에 양화 명사구 every farmer는 기존의 담화표상에 새로운 담화 지시체를 도입하는 대신에 (40)과 같이 양화사로 연결되어진 두 개의 담화표상으로 구성된 복합 담화표상 조건을 도입한다. (*every* 명사구의 담화표상 구성규칙은 아래에서 다루기로 하겠다.) 비한정 명사구 a donkey는 새로운 담화지시체 y와 담화표상 조건 donkey(y)와 이 비한정 명사구를 담화지시체 y로 대체한 담화표상 조건(그 통사구조를 명시하지 않고 단순히 x owns y로 표기하였다. 한 담화표상 조건의 구조를 명시할 필요가 없을 때에는 이와 같은 간단한 표기법을 사용하겠다)을 도입하는 것으로 처리하였다.

(40)

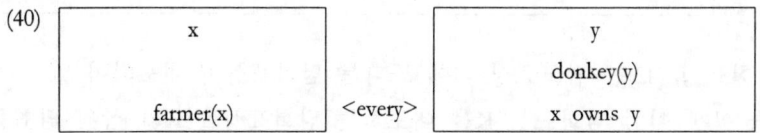

이제 담화 (39a)는 (41)과 같이 표상 된다. 대명사에 의해 도입된 담화 지시체 u는 비한정 명사구 a donkey에 의해 도입된 담화지시체 y와 동일시되어 (39a)의 조응관계를 잘 나타내고 있다.

(41)

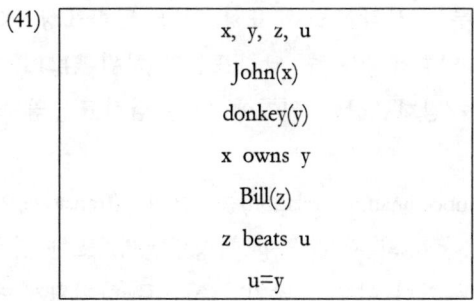

반면 담화 (39b)는 (42)와 같이 표상 된다. 대명사에 의해 도입된 담화 지시체가 기존의 어떤 담화 지시체와도 연결되지 못하고 있다.

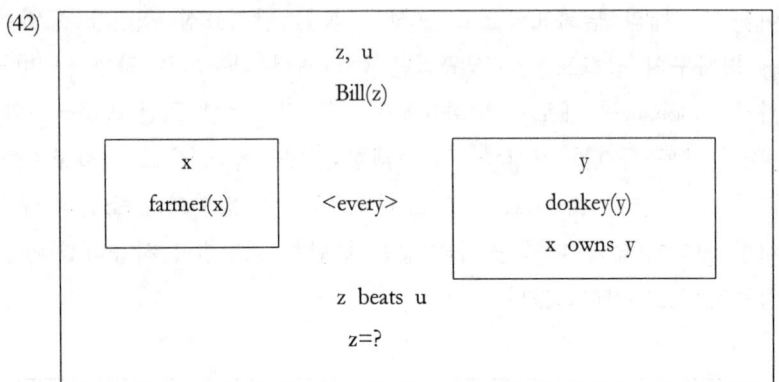

담화표상 (42)는 담화표상 내에 또다른 담화표상이 내포되어 있는 경우이다. 이제 어떤 담화표상 K를 내포하는 담화표상을 K의 상위 담화표상(supraordinate DR), K에 내포되어 있는 담화표상을 K의 하위 담화표상(subordinate DR)이라 부르고 한 담화표상은 그 자신의 하위 담화표상 중의 하나라 하고 그 관계를 ≤로 표시한다. 따라서 담화표상 K_2가 담화표상 K_1의 하위 담화표상인 관계는 $K_2 \leq K_1$으로 표시된다. 최상위의 담화표상(the most supraordinate DR)을 주 담화표상(principal DR)이라 부르기로 하자. 주 담화표상은 최 외곽을 이루는 사각형으로 표상 된다. 담화표상 (42)에서 양화사 every로 연결된 두 담화표상은 주 담화표상의 하위 담화표상들로서 양화사의 오른쪽에 있는 담화표상이 왼쪽에 있는 담화표상의 하위 담화표상이다.

담화표상 간의 하위관계(subordination relation)는 전이적(transitive)이다. 즉, $K_3 \leq K_2$이고 $K_2 \leq K_1$이면 $K_3 \leq K_1$의 관계가 항상 성립한다. 또한 임의의 두 담화표상은 하위관계를 이루거나 이루지 않거나 하므로 하위관계는 비연결적(non-connected)이며, 임의의 두 담화표상 K_1과 K_2가 $K_1 \leq K_2$이면서 $K_2 \leq K_1$의 관계를 이루는 것은 K_1과 K_2가 동일한 담화표상일 경우에 한정되므로 하위관계는 대칭적이 아니다(non-symmetric). 따라서 하위관계는 약한 순서관계(weak ordering relation)이다.

한 담화는 단일한 담화표상에 의해 표상되는 것이 아니라 하위관계에 따라 구성된 담화표상들, 즉 담화표상체계(Discourse Representation System; DRS)로 표상된다. 담화표상체계는 Kamp and Reyle(1991)를 따라 (43) 등과 같이 사각형 안에 다른 사각형이 내포되어 있는 도식으로 표시한다.

(43)
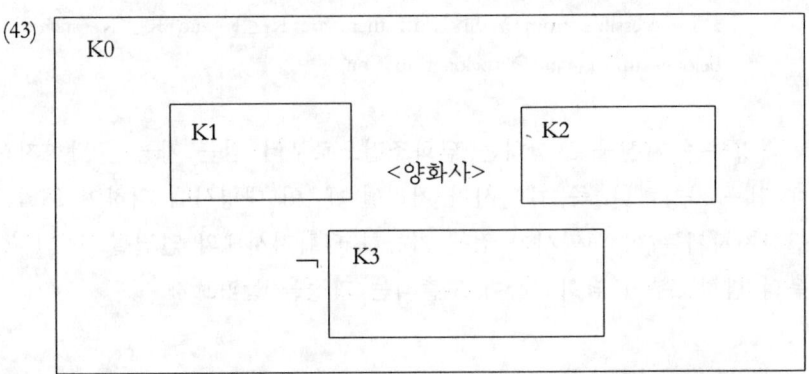

다음으로 접근가능성(accessibility)이라는 개념을 정의해 보자. 이 개념은 대명사와 그 선행사간의 조응 관계를 규정하기 위하여 필요하다. 위에서 밝힌 바대로 담화표상이론에서 조응관계는 대명사에 의하여 도입된 담화 지시체와 담화표상에 기 도입된 담화 지시체와의 관계이다. 그러나 대명 사에 의해 도입된 담화 지시체는 (39)의 예에서 보는 바와 같이 모든 기존 의 담화 지시체와 연관될 수 없고 담화표상 상의 어떤 구조적 조건을 만 족하는 담화 지시체와만 연관되어질 수 있다. 이 구조적 조건을 접근가능 성이라는 개념을 통하여 표현한다.

접근가능성은 담화 지시체와 담화표상조건 간의 관계이다. 상위 담화표 상에 도입된 담화지시체는 하위 담화표상의 담화표상조건으로부터 접근 가능하다. Kamp and Reyle는 접근가능성을 다음과 같이 정의한다.

(44) 접근가능성

K, x, Y를 각각 담화표상, 담화지시체, 담화조건이라 하자. $K_1 \leq K$, $K_2 \leq K_1$ 이며 x는 K_1의 universe에 속해 있고 (즉 $x \in U_{K1}$), Y는 K_2의 한 담화조건일 때 (즉 $Y \in Con_{K2}$), x는 K안에서 Y로부터 접근 가능하다.

Let K be a DRS, x a discourse referent and Y a DRS condition. We say that x is accessible from Y in K iff there are $K_1 \leq K$ and $K_2 \leq K_1$ such that x belongs to U_{K1} and Y belongs to Con_{K2}.

대명사는 자신을 포함하는 담화조건으로부터 접근 가능한 담화지시체에 접근 가능하다. 즉, 대명사가 처리될 때, 이 대명사에 의하여 도입되는 담화지시체는 이 대명사가 접근 가능한 담화지시체와 연결될 수 있다. 다음의 담화로부터 담화표상이 도출되는 과정을 살펴보자.

(45) John is brave. Every girl loves him.

(45)의 첫 번째 문장으로부터 (46)의 담화표상이 도출된다.

(46)

x
John(x)
x is brave

여기에 (45)의 두 번째 문장이 담화조건으로 추가되어 (47)로 확대된다.

(47)

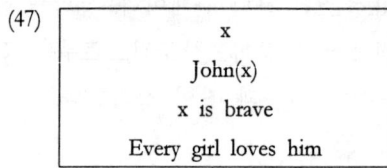

x
John(x)
x is brave
Every girl loves him

추가된 조건 중 every girl이 먼저 처리되어 (48)을 도출한다.

(48)

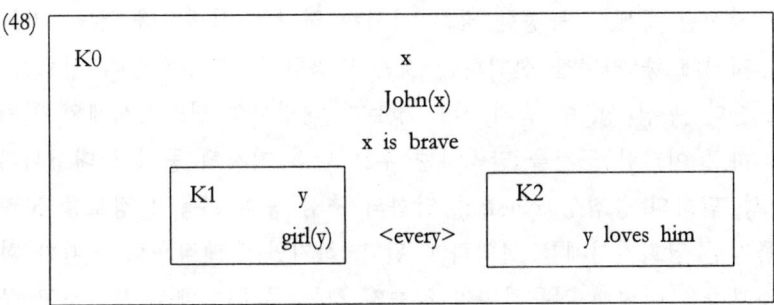

K2의 담화표상 조건 y loves him은 K2의 상위 담화표상인 K1과 K0의 담화지시체 x와 y에 접근 가능하므로 이 조건의 일부를 이루는 him도 x와 y에 접근 가능하다. 따라서 대명사의 담화표상 구성규칙에 준하여 him이 처리되어 최종 담화표상 (49)를 도출한다.

(49)

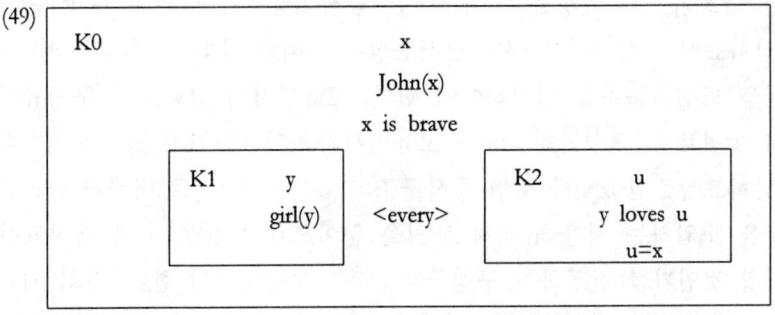

담화표상 (49)에서 담화지시체 u로부터 접근 가능한 담화지시체 y가 선택되지 않은 것은 y의 지표 정보가 u의 지표 정보와 다르기 때문이다. 담화표상 (49)에 명시되지는 않았지만 담화 지시체 x, y, u는 각각 Gen(x)=male, Gen(y)=female, Gen(u)=male이라는 담화표상 조건을 가진다. 즉 x와 u만 성(gender)이 일치하기 때문이다.

담화표상이론에서 대명사의 선행사와의 공지시관계는 담화표상에서 포착된다. 대명사에 의해 도입된 담화 지시체는 자신으로부터 접근 가능한 담화 지시체 중에서 특정한 담화 지시체 하나를 선택한다. 접근 가능한 담화 지시체 중 하나를 선택하는 것은 다양한 통사적, 화용적 정보를 필요로 한다. 우선 성, 수 등의 지표 정보가 대명사의 담화지시체와 일치하여야 하고 이러한 조건을 만족하는 후보 담화 지시체 중에서 대명사와의 근접성, 담화의 응집성(cohesion), 담화의 초점 등의 화용적 정보를 고려하여 특정한 담화지시체를 선택하게 된다. 하지만 구체적으로 어떠한 화용적 정보들을 어떻게 적용하여야 하는지 하는 문제는 매우 복잡하고 우리들의 논의와 큰 관계가 없으므로 여기에서는 더 이상 다루지 않겠다.

3.4. 고유명사의 담화표상 구성규칙(수정)

한 담화가 담화표상들로 이루어진 담화표상체계에 의해 표상 됨으로 각 담화표상 구성규칙은 어떤 담화표상에 어떠한 담화 지시체와 담화표상 조건을 도입하는지를 명시하여야 한다. 고유명사의 담화표상 구성규칙을 다시 살펴보자. 구성규칙 (26)은 고유명사가 α일 때, 새로운 담화지시체 x와 담화표상조건 $\alpha(x)$와 입력 통사구조의 $[_{NP}[_{PN}\ \alpha]]$를 x로 대체한 담화표상 조건을 도입하는 것을 규정하고 있을 뿐이므로 이들을 어떤 담화표상에 도입할 것인가를 결정하여 구성규칙 (26)을 수정하여야 한다. 담화 지시체를 도입할 담화표상을 정하기 위하여 고유명사가 대명사와 조응관계를 형성하는 방식을 살펴보아야 한다.

조응관계에 있어서의 고유명사의 특징은 비한정 명사구와 비교할 때 잘 드러난다. (45)의 경우는 이 두 명사구가 차이가 없다.

(45) (a) John$_i$ loves his$_i$ mother.

(b) [A student]$_i$ loves his$_i$ mother.

(c) John$_i$ loves his mother. He$_i$ gave her a book.

(d) [A student]$_i$ loves his mother. He$_i$ gave her a book.

그러나 (46)에서는 차이를 보인다. (46b)의 첫 문장이 각 선생님이 좋아하는 학생이 최소한 한 명이 있다라는 의미를 가질 때 a student는 후속하는 대명사 He의 선행사가 될 수 없다. (46d)의 첫 문장이 어떤 특정한 자동차를 가정하지 않고 John은 자동차가 없다라는 의미로 쓰일 때는 표시된 것과 같은 조응관계가 성립하지 않는다.

(46) (a) Every teacher loves John$_i$. He$_i$ studies well.

(b) Every teacher loves [a student]$_i$. *He$_i$ studies well.

(c) Mary doesn't love John$_i$. He$_i$ studies well.

(d) Mary doesn't own [a car]$_i$. *It$_i$ is expensive.

(45), (46)의 예문들에서 보는 바와 같이 고유명사는 비한정 명사구와 달리 후속하는 대명사의 선행사가 될 수 있다. 실제로 고유명사는 어떤 통사 구조 속에서 쓰이더라도 후속하는 대명사의 선행사로 간주될 수 있다. 담화표상이론의 용어로 표현하면 고유명사가 도입하는 담화 지시체는 후속하는 대명사 (성과 수에서 일치하는)로부터 접근 가능하여야 한다. 다시 말하면 고유명사는 주 담화표상에 그 담화 지시체를 도입하여야 한다. 고유명사 α가 도입하는 담화표상조건 중 $\alpha(x)$는 담화 지시체 x와 같은 담화표상에 도입하여야 하고 고유명사 α를 지배하는 NP를 x로 대체한 담화표상조건은 그 문장이 처리되고 있는 당시의 담화표상(current DR)에 도입하여야 한다. 따라서 고유명사에 대한 담화표상 구성규칙 (26)은 (47)로 수정되어야 한다.

(47) 고유명사에 대한 담화표상 구성규칙 (수정)

    (i) 입력 구조: (26)의 입력 구조와 동일
    (ii) 규칙 작용 방식
      (1) 새로운 담화지시체 x를 주 담화표상의 담화지시체의 집합(universe)
         에 추가한다.
      (2) 새로운 담화조건 $\alpha(x)$를 주 담화표상의 담화조건들의 집합에 추가
         한다.
      (3) 입력 구조 중 $[_{NP}[_{PN}\ \alpha]]$를 x로 대체한다.

3.5. 비한정 명사구의 담화표상 구성규칙

비한정 명사구 a(n)+보통명사(common noun: CN)는 담화표상이론에서 양화표현이 아닌 단순한 변수(variable)로 간주된다. 즉, 그 자체로서 양화력(quantificational force)를 가지지 않기 때문에 어떤 양화 표현의 양화범위에 속할 때 그 양화 표현에 구속되거나 담화에 독립적으로 부여되는 존재 양화사에 구속되기도 한다. 이러한 비한정 명사구의 특징으로 인해 (45)와 (46)에서 보인 것과 같은 조응 관계를 형성한다. 담화 (45d)는 그 자체에 양화 표현을 포함하지 않으므로 우선 (48)과 같이 1차 술어논리 언어로 번역된다. 여기서 비한정 명사구 a student는 새로운 변수 x와 이 변수가 의미 해석부에서 학생이라는 속성을 가져야 한다는 것을 나타내는 조건 student(x)로 번역되며 이 명사구와 같은 지표를 가지는 대명사도 변수 x로 번역된다.

    (48) $student(x) \wedge love(x, x's\ mother) \wedge book(y) \wedge gave(x, x's\ mother, y)$

(48)에 존재하는 자유 변수(free variable)들 x, y는 담화 전체에 주어지는 존재 양화사에 의하여 구속되게 된다. (49)는 전통적인 1차술어논리 언어 표

현 (50)과 동일하다. (50)은 자유 변수가 존재하지 않으므로 적형한 구조가
된다.

(49) ∃[student(x) ∧ love(x, x's mother) ∧ book(y) ∧ gave(x, x's mother, y)]

(50) ∃ₓ∃ᵧ[student(x) ∧ love(x, x's mother) ∧ book(y) ∧ gave(x, x's mother, y)]

(46b)는 우선 (51)과 같이 번역된다. a student 및 이와 같은 지표를 가지
는 대명사 He는 같은 변수로 번역되어야 한다. 담화 전체에 존재 양화사
가 부여되면 (52)가 되는데 여기에서 비한정 명사구 a student에 의해 도입
되는 변수 y는 전칭 양화사에 의해 구속되고 대명사에 의하여 도입된 변
수 y는 존재 양화사에 구속되어 실제로 (52)는 (53)의 표기적 변형(notational
variant)에 불과하게 된다. 즉, a student는 He의 선행사가 될 수 없다.

(51) ∀[teacher(x) ∧ student(y) ∧ love(x, y)] ∧ studies-well(y)

(52) ∃[∀[teacher(x) ∧ student(y) ∧ love(x, y)] ∧ studies-well(y)]

(53) ∃z[∀ₓ, ᵧ[teacher(x) ∧ student(y) ∧ love(x, y)] ∧ studies-well(z)]

요약하면, 비한정 명사구가 같은 문장 내에서 양화 표현이나 부정 표현
(negational expression) 등과 함께 쓰이게 되었을 때, 이러한 범위 유발 표현
(scope bearing expression)이 나타내는 범위 내에서 변수로 작용하게 된다.
　사각형들의 조합으로 담화를 표상하는 표상 체계에서 실제로 각 사각
형은 양화사나 연산자들의 작용 범위를 나타내게 된다. 즉 담화표상 (54)
는 1차술어논리 언어 표현 (55)와 동일하며 담화표상 (56)은 (57)과 동일하
다. (양화사나 연산자가 주어지지 않은 담화표상은 담화 전체에 주어지는
존재 양화사 ∃가 있는 것으로 간주한다.)

(54)

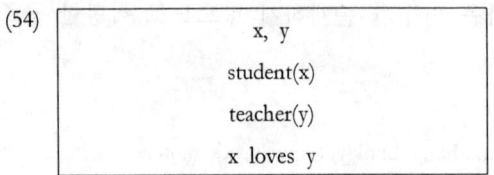

x, y

student(x)

teacher(y)

x loves y

(55) ∃x∃y[student(x) ∧ teacher(y) ∧ loves(x, y)]

(56)

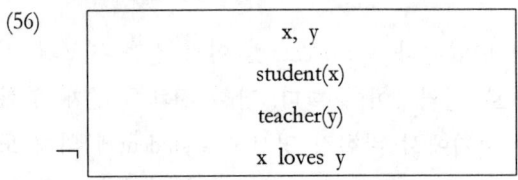

x, y

student(x)

teacher(y)

x loves y

(57) ¬ [∃ₓ∃ᵧ[student(x) ∧ teacher(y) ∧ loves(x, y)]]

따라서 비한정 명사구의 의미적, 조응적 특징을 포착하기 위해서는 비한정 명사구는 자신을 지배하는 양화사 또는 연산자의 범위가 되는 담화표상에 담화지시체를 도입하여야 하며 비한정 명사구에 대한 담화표상 구성규칙은 이를 보장해 줄 수 있어야 한다. Kamp and Reyle는 비한정 명사구가 처리되고 있는 바로 그 담화표상에 담화지시체를 도입하게 하는 구성규칙 (58)로 이 문제를 해결한다.

(58) 비한정 명사구에 대한 담화표상 구성규칙

(i) 입력 구조:

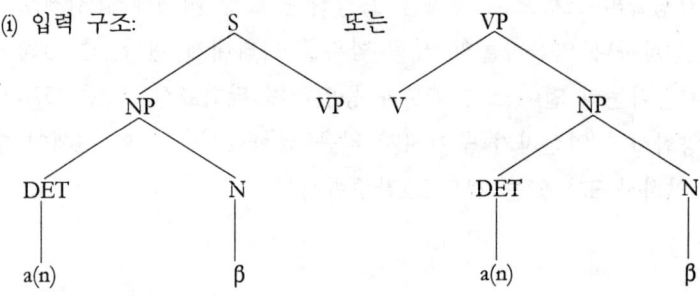

(ii) 규칙 작용 방식

    (a) 새로운 담화지시체 u를 입력 구조가 처리되고 있는 담화표상(current DR)의 담화지시체들의 집합(universe of DR K: UK)에 도입한다.

    (b) 새로운 담화표상 조건 β(u)를 Con$_K$에 도입한다.

    (c) [$_{NP}$[$_{DET}$ a(n)][$_N$ β]]를 u로 대체한다.

이제 문장 (59)가 (60)의 DRS 중 DR K1에서 처리된다고 하고 구성 규칙 (58)이 어떻게 작용하는가를 살펴보자.

(59) A student came in.

(60)
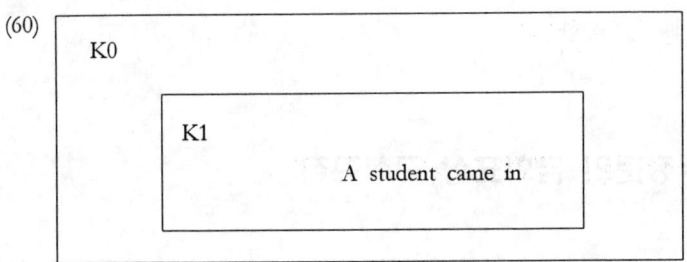

(59)에 의해 비한정 명사구 a student는 처리되고 있는 담화표상 K1에 담화 지시체 x와 담화표상 조건 student(x)를 도입하고 문장의 통사분석에서 비 한정 명사구를 x로 대체하여 (61)을 얻는다.

(61)
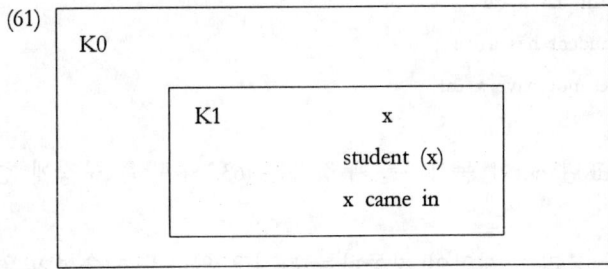

K1의 담화표상 조건 x came in은 (62)의 통사 구조를 간략히 표시한 것이다.

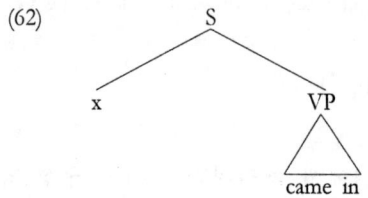

(62)

구성 규칙 (58)은 비한정 명사구는 자신이 처리되고 있는 담화표상에 담화지시체와 담화표상 조건들을 도입한다는 점에서 고유명사와의 의미적 및 조응적 차이를 포착한다.

3.6. 부정문의 담화표상 구성규칙

다음으로 부정문(negation)에 대하여 살펴보자. 부정 표현은 (63)에서와 같이 다양한 형태로 나타날 수 있다. (63a)는 부정 한정사 no가 명사를 부정하며, (63b)는 부정 표현 not이 한정사 a를 부정하고 있으며, (63c)는 부정 표현 not이 동사구를 부정하는 경우이다.

(63) (a) No student has a car.

(b) Not a student has a car.

(c) John does not have a car.

여기에서는 부정 표현 not이 동사구를 부정하는 (63c)와 같은 문장에 한정하고자 한다.

(63c)는 John이라 불리는 개인이 자동차를 가지고 있다라는 속성이 없음을 나타낸다. 즉, (63c)의 문장이 참이 되기 위해서는 John이라는 개인이

자동차를 가지고 있다라는 조건을 만족시키는 상황이 전혀 없는 경우이다. 이러한 의미 관계는 (64)와 같이 일차 술어 논리언어 표현으로 나타내어진다.

(64) ¬∃x[car(x) ∧ have(j, x)]

위에서 언급한 고유명사에 대한 담화표상 구성 규칙에 따르면 (64)는 (65)와 같다. (65)는 John이라 불리는 어떤 개체가 존재하는데 이 개체가 자동차를 가지고 있는 경우가 전혀 없을 때 이 문장은 참이 됨을 나타낸다.

(65) ∃x[John(x) ∧ ¬∃y[car(y) ∧ have(x, y)]]

(65)에서 변수 y를 구속하는 양화사는 부정 연산자 ¬의 범위 안에 있으며 이는 다시 x를 묶어 주는 양화사의 범위에 내포되고 있다. 이 관계는 사각형의 표기 규약에 따라 (66)으로 표상할 수 있다.

(66)
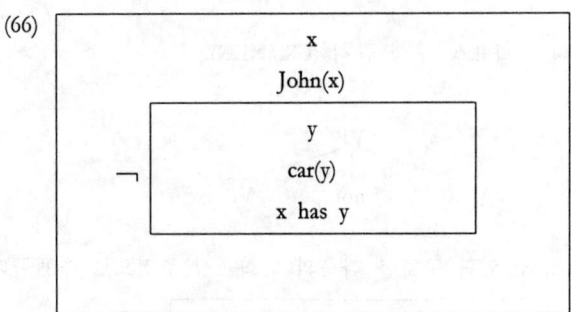

문장 (63c)의 비한정 명사구 a car는 (67)에서와 같이 후속하는 문장의 대명사 it의 선행사가 될 수 없다. 이러한 조응 관계는 담화표상 (68)에 의하여 잘 나타내어진다.

(67) John does not have [a car]i. Iti runs fast.

(68)

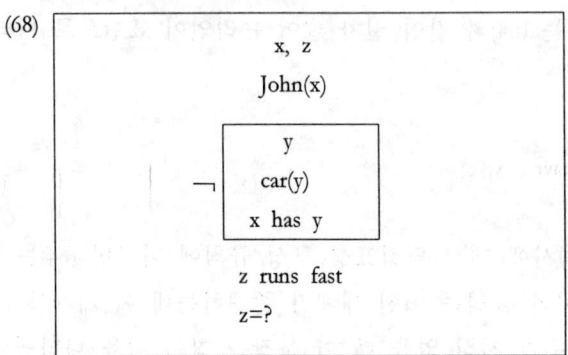

위에서 설명한 부정 표현 not의 통사 의미적 기능을 담화표상에서 포착하기 위하여서는 (69)의 담화표상 구성규칙이 필요하다. (69)의 구성규칙은 입력 구조가 처리되고 있는 담화표상에 입력 구조의 조동사 do와 not을 없앤 구조를 담화표상 조건으로 하는 새로운 담화표상을 도입함을 나타낸다. (조동사가 can, may, will 등인 경우는 이 구성규칙을 약간 수정하여 적용할 수 있을 것이다.)

(69) 부정 표현 not의 담화표상 구성 규칙 (CR. NEG)
  (i) 입력 구조:

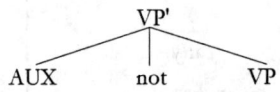

  (ii) 규칙 작용 방식: 입력 구조를 다음의 담화표상 조건으로 대체한다.

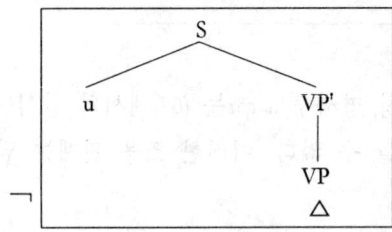

3.7. 관계사절의 담화표상 구성규칙

다음으로 관계사절의 수식을 받는 보통 명사에 대한 담화표상 구성규칙을 살펴보겠다. 먼저 관계사 절이 문장의 의미에 기여하는 바를 알아보자. 문장 (70)은 학생이면서 Mary를 사랑하는 한 개체가 부자라는 것을 뜻한다. 즉, 학생이면서 Mary를 사랑하며 부자인 개체가 최소한 하나는 존재함을 나타내는 (71)의 표현과 같은 의미를 가진다.

(70) A student who loves Mary is rich.

(71) $\exists x[student(x) \wedge x \text{ loves Mary} \wedge x \text{ is rich}]$

(71)은 담화표상 (72)와 동일한 정보를 표시한다.

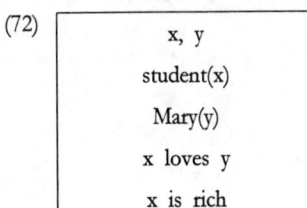

(72)
$$
\begin{array}{|c|}
\hline
x, y \\
student(x) \\
Mary(y) \\
x \text{ loves } y \\
x \text{ is rich} \\
\hline
\end{array}
$$

그런데, 문장 (70)은 우선 비한정 명사구에 대한 담화표상 구성 규칙의 적용을 받아 (73)으로 처리된다. 여기서 student who loves Mary는 하나의 보통명사 (CN)으로 여겨진다.

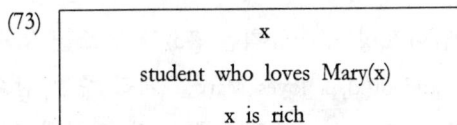

(73)
$$
\begin{array}{|c|}
\hline
x \\
student \text{ who loves } Mary(x) \\
x \text{ is rich} \\
\hline
\end{array}
$$

표현 student who loves Mary는 명사로서 다음과 같은 구조를 갖는다.

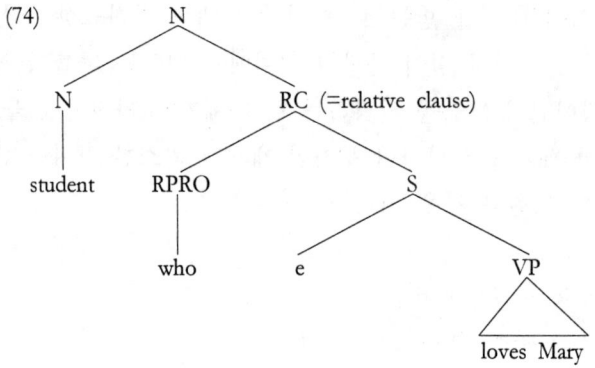

이제 담화표상 조건 student who loves Mary(x)의 구조를 (75)로 표기하기로 하겠다. (75)의 구조는 (74)의 최상위 마디에 (x)가 병기된 것이다.

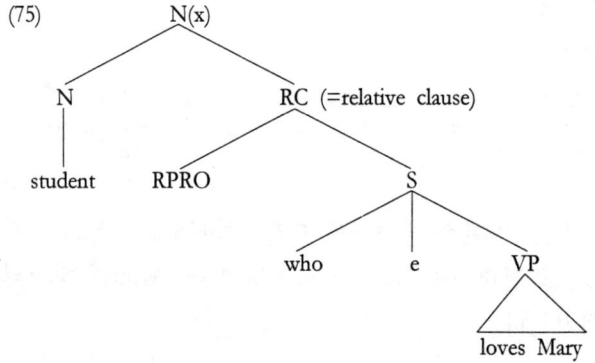

따라서, 관계대명사절에 대한 담화표상 구성규칙은 (75)의 구조를 입력으로 하여 새로운 담화표상 조건 student(x), x loves Mary를 처리 중인 담화표상에 도입하도록 정의되어야 한다. Kamp and Reyle를 따라 관계대명사절에 대한 담화표상 구성규칙을 (76)과 같이 정의한다.

(76) 관계대명사절에 대한 담화표상 구성규칙 (CR. NRC)

(i) 입력구조:

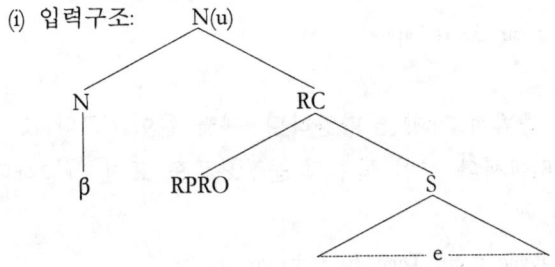

(ii) 규칙적용방식

(i) 새로운 담화표상조건 β(u)를 처리되고 있는 담화표상에 도입한다.

(ii) 입력구조를 S로 대체한다.

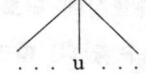

(76)의 규칙적용방식 (ii)는 관계대명사에 의하여 유도되는 문장 S에 있는 공범주 e를 주어진 담화 지시체로 대체하고 이 문장이 전체 입력구조를 대체함을 나타낸다. 이제 구조 (75)는 (76i)에 의하여 student(x)로, (76ii)에 의하여 [s x loves Mary]로 바뀌게 된다.

3.8. 조건문의 담화표상 구성규칙

다음으로 조건문(conditionals)의 처리에 대하여 알아보겠다. 어떤 진술을 만족하는 조건하에 다른 진술의 진위를 파악할 수 있는 문장을 조건문이라 한다. 예를 들어 두 개의 하위 문장으로 구성된 (77)의 문장은 첫 번째 문장으로 표현된 조건이 만족되는 상황하에서만 두 번째 문장의 진실 여부를 파악해 볼 수 있다. 다시 말하여 첫 번째 문장이 참이 되는 각 상황에서 두 번째 문장이 참이 된다면 전체 문장은 참이 된다.

(77) If John owns a car, he is happy.

조건을 나타내는 문법적 장치는 다양하다. 예를 들어 (77)의 첫 문장이 나타내는 조건은 (78)에서와 같이 독립적 문장으로도 표현 가능하다.

(78) Suppose John owns a car. Then, he is happy.

여기에서는 (77)에서 처럼 if S, (then) S의 구조를 가지는 문장만을 다루기로 한다. 조건문에서의 조응 관계는 복잡한 양상을 띤다. 고유명사를 다루면서 언급한 대로 고유명사는 항상 주 담화표상에 담화 지시체를 도입하므로 후속하는 대명사의 선행사로 작용할 수 있다. 따라서 (77)에서 대명사 he는 John을 그 선행사로 취할 수 있다. 또한 (79)에서 처럼 조건문 밖의 대명사도 조건문 내의 고유명사를 그 선행사로 취할 수 있다.

(79) If John$_i$ owns a car, Mary has a bike. He$_i$ is rich.

비한정 명사구가 if-절(또는 선행절; antecedent clause) 안에 있고 대명사가 주절(또는 결과절; consequent clause)에 있는 경우에는 (80)에서와 같이 이 두 표현간에 조응 관계가 성립될 수 있다. 그러나 비한정 명사구가 결과절에 있고 대명사가 선행절에 있는 경우에는 (81)에서와 같이 조응 관계가 성립 불가능하다. 또한, 대명사가 (82), (83)에서처럼 조건문밖에 있을 때는 조응 관계가 불가능하다.

(80) If John owns [a car]$_i$, it$_i$ is a Sonata.
(81) *If it$_i$ runs fast, John buys [a car]$_i$.

(82) If John owns [a car]ᵢ, Mary has a bike. *Itᵢ is a Sonata.

(83) If John owns car, Mary has [a bike]ᵢ. She loves itᵢ.

비한정 명사구는 자신이 처리되는 담화표상에 담화 지시체를 도입하며 대명사에 의해 도입되는 담화 지시체는 접근 가능한 담화지시체와 연결될 수 있으므로 (80)~(83)의 현상을 설명하기 위해서는 (i) 조건문은 주 담화표상에서 접근 불가능한 담화표상을 도입해야 한다. 즉 조건문에 의하여 도입되는 담화표상은 주 담화표상의 하위 담화표상이 되어야 하며 (ii) 조건문의 선행절에 있는 담화지시체는 조건문의 결과절에 있는 담화지시체로부터 접근 가능해야 하며 (iii) 조건문의 결과절에 있는 담화지시체는 선행절의 담화지시체로부터 접근 불가능해야 한다.

Kamp and Reyle는 조건문은 선행절에 의하여 도입되는 담화표상과 결과절에 의하여 도입되는 담화표상으로 분리된 복합 담화표상(split discourse representation)으로 처리한다. (84)는 조건문에 대한 담화표상 구성 규칙이다.

(84) 조건문의 담화표상 구성 규칙

(i) 입력 구조:

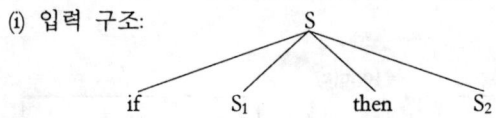

(ii) 규칙적용 방식: 입력 구조를 다음의 구조로 대체한다.

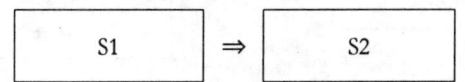

규칙 (84)에 의하여 문장 (80)은 우선 (85)로 처리된다.

(85)

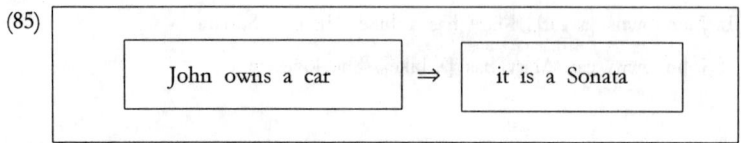

담화표상 (85)는 고유명사, 비한정 명사구, 대명사의 담화표상 구성 규칙에
준해 (86)으로 변환된다.

(86)

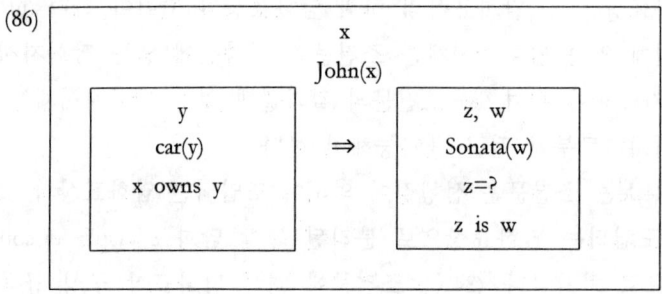

z는 y에 접근 가능하므로 z는 y를 선행사로 가질 수 있어 최종적으로 (87)
과 같이 처리된다.

(87)

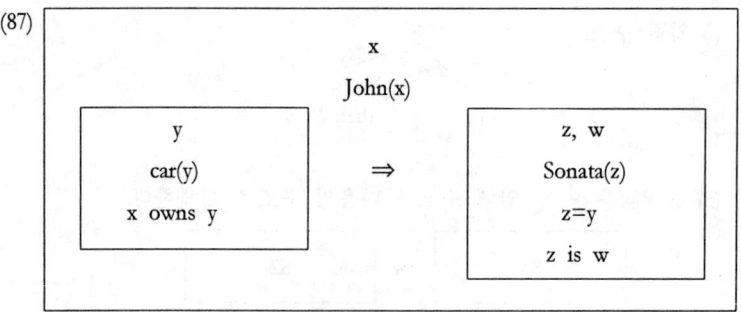

(81)~(83)의 조응관계도 비슷한 방식으로 설명된다. 그러나 대명사가 선
행절에 있고 고유명사가 결과절에 있는 (88)의 조응 관계는 (84)의 구성 규

칙만으로는 설명이 되지 않는다. 한 문장의 통사분석구조는 위에서부터 아래로 왼쪽에서부터 오른쪽으로 처리되어 담화표상구조를 도출하기 때문에 선행절의 대명사를 처리하는 순간에 결과절의 고유명사는 아직 처리되지 않는 상태에 있게 된다. (88)은 (89)로 통사분석되어 담화표상이론의 담화 처리 규약에 의해 S1이 먼저 처리되어 (90)의 담화표상을 이룬다. (90)에서 대명사에 의해 도입된 담화지시체 x는 현 상태에서 접근 가능한 담화지시체가 없는 상태이다.

(88) If he$_i$ is rich, John$_i$ owns a Sonata.

(89)

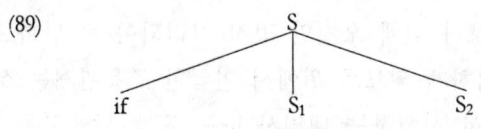

if   S$_1$ S$_2$

he is rich   John owns a Sonata

(90)

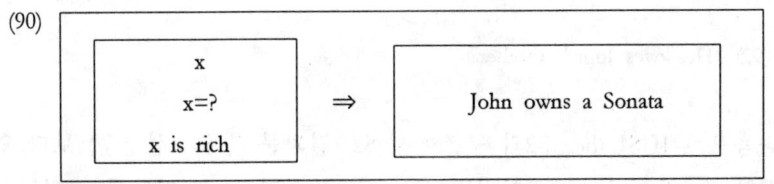

(90)의 복합 담화조건은 (91)로 다시 처리되어 담화지시체 x는 고유명사 John에 의하여 주 담화표상에 도입된 담화지시체 y에 접근 가능하게 된다. 그러나 x가 y에 연결되기 위해서는 그 처리 방향이 바뀌어야하는 문제가 있다.

(91)

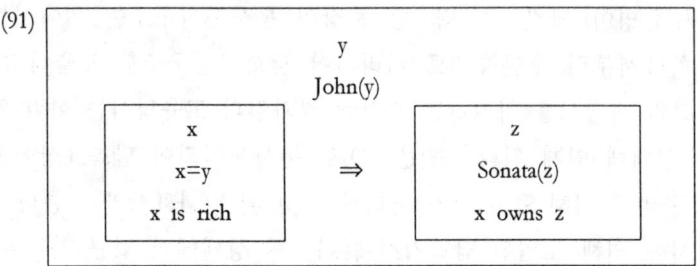

   대안으로 한 문장의 모든 고유 명사는 다른 요소에 앞서 처리하는 예외 규정을 두는 방법을 고려할 수 있다. 이렇게 하면 문장 (88)에서 고유 명사 John이 비록 조응 대명사 he보다 뒤에 오지만 먼저 처리되어 주 담화표상에 자신의 담화지시체를 도입하게 되므로 위에서 언급한 조응관계는 설명이 된다. 그러나 (92)에 있어서 선행하는 대명사 he는 후행하는 고유명사 John과 공지시 관계를 가질 수 없다. 따라서, 한 문장을 담화표상으로 처리할 때 모든 고유명사를 먼저 처리하는 방식은 타당하지 않다.

   (92) *He; loves John;'s mother.

   다음으로 If S1 then S2의 구조에서 S2 (결과문)를 S1 (선행문) 보다 먼저 처리할 수 있거나 두 개의 문장을 동시에 처리할 수 있도록 담화표상의 처리 규약을 완화하는 방법을 생각해 볼 수 있다. 이 방법은 Kamp and Reyle와 Reyle에 의하여 제시되었다. 이 방법에 따르면 결과절의 처리가 선행절보다 먼저이거나 동시에 일어나기 때문에 선행절의 대명사가 처리될 때에 결과절의 고유명사에 의하여 도입된 담화지시체가 주담화표상에 존재하게 되어 (88)의 조응관계는 설명된다.

   If S1 then S2의 구조를 가지는 조건문은 S1이 참이 되는 경우에 S2가 참이 되어야만 전체 문장이 참이 된다. 즉, S1을 참이 되게 하는 상황 또는 세계를 S2가 참이 되는 세계로 확장할 수 있는 경우에만 참이 된다. 다시 말하여 If S1 then S2는 If S1 then S1 and S2의 구조와 같은 의미를 지니게 된다. 이러한 관계가 성립하도록 의미부를 정의하여야 한다.

3.9. 전칭 양화 명사구의 담화표상 구성규칙

전칭 양화 명사구(universal quantificational NP)는 전칭 양화사 ∀에 대응 하는 자연 언어 표현 every, each, all 등을 한정사로 가지는 명사구를 말한 다. 전칭 양화 명사구를 포함하는 (93)의 문장은 학생이라는 속성을 지니 는 모든 개체는 책을 가지고 있다는 속성을 또한 지니고 있음을 뜻한다.

> (93) (a) Every student has a book.
>   (b) Each student has a book.
>   (c) All students have a book.

문장 (93a)와 문장 (93b)에서 전칭 양화 명사구 every student와 each student 는 통사적으로 단수이며 (94)에서와 같이 같은 문장 내에서 단수 대명사의 선행사가 된다.

> (94) (a) Every student loves his (or her) mother.
>   (b) Each student loves his (or her) mother.

반면, (93c)의 전칭 양화 명사구 all students는 통사적 복수이며 (95)에서와 같이 문장 내에서 복수 대명사의 선행사가 된다.

> (95) All students love their mother.

또한 every, each에 의해 유도되는 명사구는 항상 배분적 술어(distributive predicate)에 의해 서술되며 집합적 술어(collective predicate)와 함께 쓰일 수 없으나 all에 의해 유도되는 명사구는 두 가지 종류의 술어를 다 택할 수 있다.

(96) (a) Every student lifted a piano individually.

(b) Each student lifted a piano individually.

(c) All students lifted a piano individually.

(d) *Every student lifted a piano together.

(e) *Each student lifted a piano together.

(f) All students lifted a piano together.

여기에서는 통사적 단수이며 배분적 술어만을 취하는 전칭 양화 명사구 중 every를 한정사로 하는 명사구만을 대상으로 하겠다. 이하에서 전칭 양화 명사구는 every-명사구를 지칭한다.

전칭 양화 명사구는 단수 대명사의 선행사가 된다. 이는 이 명사구가 단수 담화지시체를 도입함을 뜻한다. 전칭 양화 구문에서의 조응관계는 비한정 명사구 구문과 비교하여 특이한 성질을 보인다. 우선 전칭 양화 명사구는 한 문장 내에서 후행하는 단수 대명사의 선행사가 된다. 이는 비한정 명사구와 비슷하다. 그러나 비한정 명사구와 다르게 전칭 양화 명사구는 문장 경계를 벗어난 단수 대명사의 선행사가 될 수 없다.

(97) (a) [Every student]$_i$ loves his$_i$ mother.

(b) [A student]$_i$ loves his$_i$ mother.

(c) [Every student]$_i$ came in. *He$_i$ sat on the mat.

(d) [A student]$_i$ came in. He$_i$ sat on the mat.

(97)의 자료들은 전칭 양화사 every의 양화 범위가 문장에 국한되고 있음을

시사한다. (조응 대명사를 양화 논리 언어의 변수로 간주한다.) 담화 표상 이론의 용어로 표시하면 전칭 양화 명사구는 해당 문장이 처리되는 담화 표상 내에 담화지시체를 도입하여야 함을 뜻한다.

의미적으로 볼 때, 전칭 명사구 every student는 학생의 속성을 가지고 있는 각 개체가 어떤 속성을 가지고 있는가 하는 것을 나타낸다. 즉, (93a)의 문장은 학생이라는 속성을 가지는 각 개체가 책을 소유하고 있다는 것을 뜻한다. 이 문장의 진위를 결정하기 위해서는 어떤 세계 (또는 모형)에서 학생인 개체를 임의적으로 하나를 선택한 후 이 개체가 책을 가지고 있는지를 파악해야 하고 만약 책을 가지고 있다면 이 이외의 학생하나를 선택하여 같은 작업을 하여야 한다. 이렇게 하여 학생의 속성을 지닌 모든 개체가 책을 가지고 있다는 것이 판명되면 이 문장은 이 세계 (또는 모형)에 비추어 참이 되고 만약 한 학생이라도 책을 가지고 있지 않다면 거짓이 된다. 이러한 의미적 속성은 조건문의 그것과 비슷하다.

명사구는 동사구를 취하여 문장을 이루는 통사 범주이다. 동사구는 의미적으로 개체들의 집합을 그 의미값으로 가진다. 즉 $<e, t>$의 통사 유형이다. 그러면 명사구의 의미 유형은 동사구의 의미값을 취하여 참과 거짓을 결정하는 함수를 그 의미 유형으로 가지게 된다. 명사구는 통사상 한정사(determiner)와 보통명사가 결합된 형태이므로 한정사의 의미 유형은 보통명사의 의미값을 취하여 명사구의 의미값을 결정하는 함수의 유이 된다. 한정사의 통사적 역할을 다른 각도에서 보면 보통명사와 동사구의 두 개의 표현을 취하여 문장을 이루는 기능을 담당한다. 즉, $<<<e, t>, <e, t>>, t>$의 통사 유형이다. 이러한 한정사에 대한 견해를 일반 양화사 이론(Generalized Quantifier Theory: GQT)에서 채택하여 다양한 한정사의 의미적 역할을 연구한다. 도식화한 문장 (98)은 술어논리언어 표현 (99)로 번역된다.

(98) Det p q.   (Det: 한정사, p: 보통명사, q: 동사구)

(99) Det'(p', q')   (Det', p', q': Det, p, q의 번역)

(99)는 p'과 q'이 Det'의 관계에 있음을 뜻한다. 다시 말하면 p'으로 표시된 속성을 지니는 개체들의 집합과 이 개체들 중 q'으로 표시된 속성을 아울러 지니는 개체들의 집합 사이에는 Det'로 표기된 數的 관계가 있음을 나타낸다. (이를 한정사의 보수성(conservativity)이라 한다.) 예를 들어 Most students sing이라는 문장의 번역 (100)은 학생들의 집합과 노래부르는 학생들의 집합간에는 most'로 표시된 수적 관계가 있음을 나타낸다. 즉 노래하는 학생의 수가 전체 학생 수의 과반이 되면 이 문장은 참이다. 따라서 (100)은 (101)과 같은 진리조건을 가진다.

(100) most'(student', sing')
(101) most'(student', student' $\land$ sing')

담화표상이론에서 (99)는 한정사에 의하여 연결된 두 개의 담화표상으로 표현된 하나의 복합 담화표상 조건 (102)로 나타내어진다. (102)는 실제로 (103)과 같은 의미관계를 표현하도록 그 의미해석 규칙이 정의되어야 한다.

(102)

| x <br> p(x) | < Det > | x q |

(103)

| x

 p(x) | < Det > | p(x)
 x q |

담화표상 (104)에서 양화사(특히 전칭양화사 every)에 의해 유도되는 복합 담화표상조건의 선행 담화표상 K1은 후행 담화표상 K2에 접근가능하나 그 역은 성립하지 않는다. 마찬가지로 이 복합 담화표상조건을 내포하는 주 담화표상 K0는 K1과 K2에 접근 가능하다. 즉, K1의 담화지시체는 K2의 대명사의 선행사가 될 수 있으며 K0의 담화지시체는 K1과 K2에 접근가능하나 그 역은 성립하지 않는다.

(104)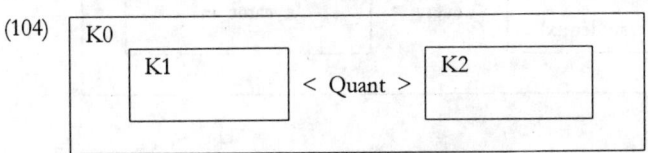

이제 (97a)와 (97c)의 조응관계를 담화표상이론의 틀 안에서 설명이 가능하다. (97a)는 우선 (105)로 처리된다.

(105)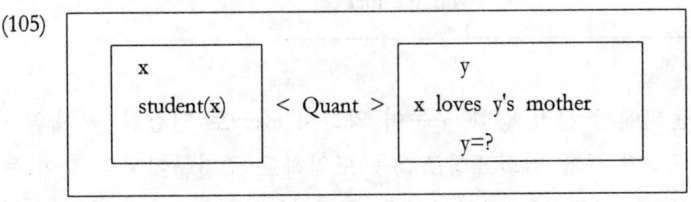

담화지시체 x는 y에 접근 가능하므로 y는 x를 그 선행사로 취할 수 있어 (106)으로 처리된다.

(106)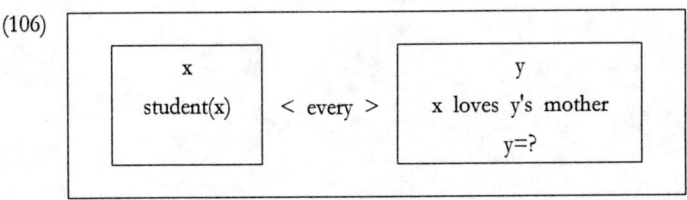

반면에 (97c)의 첫 번째 문장은 주담화표상의 한 담화조건으로 처리되어
(107)을 이루고 두 번째 문장의 대명사는 주담화표상에 담화지시체를 도입
하여 (107)을 (108)로 확대한다. (108)에서 담화지시체 x는 y에 접근 불가능
하여 (97c)에서의 조응관계가 불가능함을 잘 포착한다.

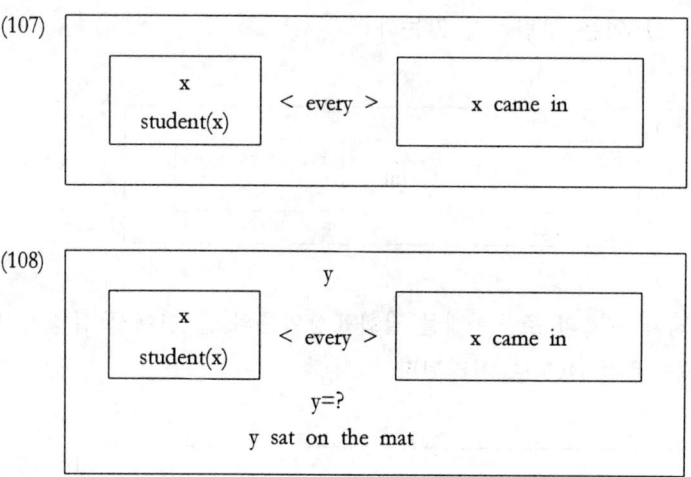

(107)

| x
student(x) | < every > | x came in |

(108)

y

| x
student(x) | < every > | x came in |

y=?
y sat on the mat

이상의 논의에서 전칭 양화 구문이 양화사 every로 연결된 두 개의 담화
표상으로 구성된 복합 담화표상조건을 도입하고 조건문에서와 같이 두 개
의 담화표상 중 선행하는 담화표상은 후행하는 담화표상에 접근가능하나
그 역은 성립하지 않는 관계는 전칭 양화 구문의 조응관계와 의미해석을
올바르게 포착한다는 것을 입증하였다. 따라서 전칭 양화 구분에 대한 담
화표상 구성규칙을 (109)와 같이 정의할 수 있다.

(109) 전칭 양화 구문의 담화표상 구성규칙

(i) 입력구조

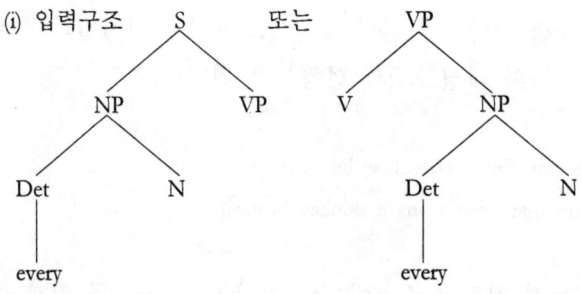

(ii) 규칙적용방식

(i) 새로운 복합 담화표상 조건 K1 <every> K2를 입력구조가 처리되고 있는 담화 표상에 도입한다. K1과 K2는 담화지시체의 집합과 담화표상조건의 집합이 공집합인 공담화표상이다.

(ii) 새로운 담화지시체 u를 K1의 담화지시체들의 집합에 도입한다.

(iii) 새로운 담화표상조건 N(u)를 K1의 담화표상조건들의 집합에 도입한다.

(iv) 입력구조의 하위 구조인 [NP [Det every] [N...]]을 담화지시체 u로 대체한다.

영어의 한정사는 전칭 양화사 every, 존재 양화사 a(n) 이외에도 most, many, few, a few, some, at least five, at most five 등 다양하다. 이들에 대한 의미 및 담화표상 구성규칙은 제 2부에서 자세히 다루도록 하겠다.

3.10. 당나귀 문장 (Donkey Sentences)

당나귀 문장이란 (i) if-절이나 관계사절 안에 비한정 명사구를 포함하고, (ii) if-절이나 관계사절밖에 조응대명사를 포함하며 (iii) 이 대명사가 if-절

또는 관계사절 안의 비한정 명사구와 조응관계를 형성하는 문장들을 일컫는다. 문장 (110a)에서 if-절 내의 비한정 명사구 a man과 a donkey는 주절의 대명사 he와 it의 선행사가 된다. 문장 (110b)에서 관계절의 비한정 명사구 a donkey는 주절의 대명사 it의 선행사가 된다.

> (110) (a) If a man owns a donkey, he beats it.
>
>   (b) Every man who owns a donkey beats it.

이러한 문장은 원래 희랍의 스토아 철학자인 Chrysippos에 의해 최초로 논의되었기 때문에 그 이름을 따서 Chrysippos-문장이라 부르기도 한다. 이 문장은 1962년 미국 코넬 대학의 철학 교수 Geach가 그의 저서 Reference and Generality에서 다시 논의하면서 유명해졌는데, (110)의 문장에서처럼 그 예문에 비한정 명사구 a donkey를 사용함으로써 당나귀 문장(donkey sentences)이란 이름을 얻게 되었다.

당나귀 문장은 최소한 두 가지 측면에서 전통적 명사구 의미론에 의문을 제기한다. 첫째, 전통적으로 비한정 명사구는 존재 양화 명사구로 간주되었고 부정관사 a(n)은 존재 양화사로서 자신을 포함하는 최소의 문장을 그 양화 범위로 가진다. 또한 조응 대명사는 술어논리언어의 변수와 같이 여겨져서 적절한 양화사의 범위 안에서 구속되어야(bound) 한다. 그러나 (110)의 예문에서 대명사들은 자신을 포함하는 최소의 문장 경계밖에 있는 비한정 명사구를 그 선행사로 취하고 있다. (110)의 문장들을 전통적 일차 술어논리 언어로 번역하면 (111)과 같다.

> (111) (a) $[\exists x \exists y[man(x) \land donkey(y) \land x \ owns \ y]] \rightarrow x \ beats \ y$
>
>   (b) $[\forall x[man(x) \land \exists y[donkey(y) \land x \ owns \ y]] \rightarrow x \ beats \ y]$

(111a)에서 x beats y의 두 변수 x, y는 존재 양화사의 범위밖에 있으며, (111b)에서 x beats y의 y가 존재 양화사의 범위밖에 있어 자유 변수가 되

어 (110)의 문장의 의미를 제대로 반영하지 못한다. 두 번째의 문제는 (110) 문장의 비한정 명사구가 영어의 모국어 화자에 의해 전칭 양화 의미를 지니는 것으로 이해된다는 것이다. (110)의 두 문장에 대한 모국어 화자의 직관을 잘 표현하는 번역은 (112)와 같다.

(112) $\forall x \forall y[[man(x) \wedge donkey(y) \wedge x \text{ owns } y] \rightarrow x \text{ beats } y]$

부정관사 a(n)을 존재 양화사로 간주하는 접근 방법에서 이 두 문제는 매우 설명하기 어려운 문제이며 이 문제를 풀기 위한 몇 가지의 시도가 있었으나 그리 성공적이지는 못하였다. (부정관사 a(n)을 존재 양화사로 간주하고 당나귀 문장의 조응관계 및 의미를 설명하려고 했던 시도들에 대한 비판은 Heim(1982)를 참조) 이제 위에서 언급한 담화표상 구성규칙으로 당나귀 문장의 조응관계와 의미가 어떻게 설명되는가를 보이도록 하겠다. (110a)의 문장은 우선 조건문의 담화표상 구성 규칙에 의해 (113)으로 처리된다.

(113)

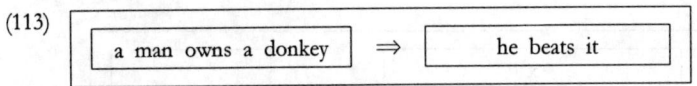

(113)은 다시 비한정 명사구의 담화표상 구성규칙에 의해 (114)로 처리된다.

(114)

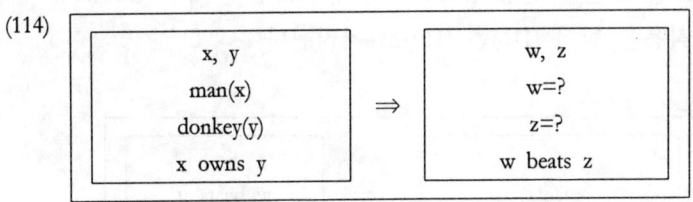

담화표상 (114)의 복합 담화표상 조건의 선행 담화표상의 두 담화지시체

x, y는 후행 담화표상의 두 담화지시체 w, z에 접근 가능하여 w와 x가, z와 y가 연결될 수 있어 (115)의 담화표상의 도출이 가능해 진다.

(115)

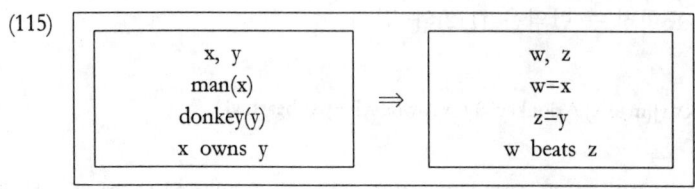

(115)는 두 개의 조응대명사 he와 it가 a man과 a donkey를 선행사로 취할 수 있음을 보여 주며 의미해석 규칙에 의해 당나귀를 가지고 있는 모든 사람은 자신이 가지고 있는 모든 당나귀를 때린다고 하는 의미를 부여받게 되어 모국어 화자의 언어 직관을 잘 포착하게 된다. 의미에 대한 자세한 설명은 다음 장에서 다루겠다.

(110b)의 문장은 우선 전칭 양화 구문의 담화표상 구성규칙 (109)의 적용을 받아 (116)으로 변환된다.

(116)

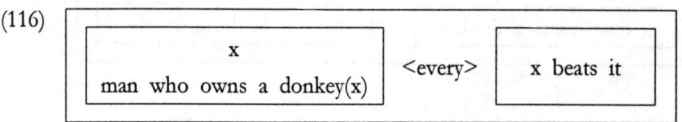

복합 담화표상 조건의 선행 담화표상은 관계사절에 대한 담화표상 구성규칙 (76)의 적용을 받아 (116)은 (117)로 처리된다.

(117)

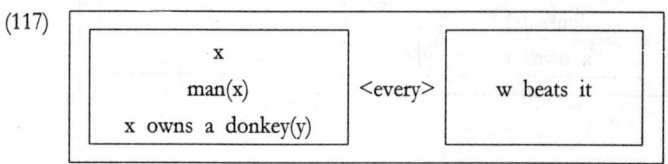

(117)은 다시 비한정 명사구의 담화표상 구성규칙, 조응대명사의 담화표상 구성규칙 등의 적용을 받아 최종적으로 (118)로 처리된다. (115)에서와 마찬가지로 후행 담화표상의 담화지시체 w는 선행 담화표상의 담화지시체 y에 접근 가능하다.

(118)
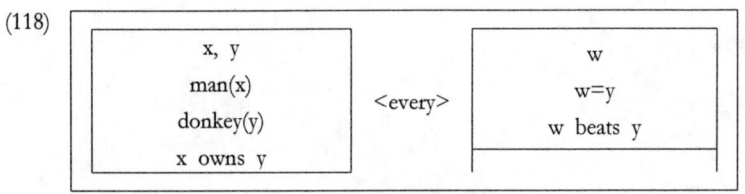

담화표상 (118)은 (115)와 동일한 의미해석을 받게되어 당나귀를 소유한 모든 사람은 자신이 소유한 모든 당나귀를 때린다라는 의미를 정확히 표현한다.

3.11. 요약

담화표상 구성규칙은 문장의 통사분석으로부터 담화표상을 이끌어내는 일종의 사상 규칙(mapping rules)이다. 담화표상 구성규칙은 이 규칙이 적용되는 입력구조와 규칙이 적용되는 방식으로 정의된다. 입력구조는 통사범주 뿐 아니라 특정 어휘 항목도 명시하여야 한다. 예를 들어 같은 명사구라 하여도 전칭 양화 명사구와 비한정 명사구, 고유명사 등에 작용하는 담화표상 구성 규칙이 다르기 때문이다.

한 자연언어의 표현들을 담화표상으로 전환하기 위해서는 이 장에서 언급하지 않은 많은 담화표상 구성규칙이 필요하다. 이 책의 제 2부에서 복수 명사구의 의미를 다루면서 새로운 담화표상 구성규칙들을 소개하고 이 장에서 다룬 담화표상 구성 규칙들이 추가적인 언어 자료를 설명하기 위해 어떻게 수정되어야 하는지를 다루도록 하겠다.

제 4 장   의미부

의미론이란 언어 표현과 언어 이외의 어떤 대상과의 관계를 다룬다. 이 대상을 무엇이라고 생각하느냐에 따라 다양한 의미이론이 가능해진다. 제 1장에서 논의한대로 지금까지 의미론은 언어의 의미란 언어 표현과 그 표현이 우리의 마음속에 불러일으키는 어떤 이미지 또는 영상과의 관계라는 주장과 언어 표현과 실제 세계의 모습과의 관계에서 파악되어진다고 하는 두 가지의 견해가 주 패러다임을 형성하며 발전하여왔다. 담화표상이론은 이 두 가지 경향을 종합하려는 의도 속에서 연구되기 시작하였다. 담화표상이론의 의미에 대한 접근 방법은 어떤 화자가 한 표현을 접했을 때 이 표현으로부터 어떠한 의미적 표상을 추출해내며 이 의미적 표상이 주어진 세계의 모습과 양립가능(compatible)한가를 따져보는 것이다. 제3장에서 다룬 담화표상 구성규칙이 담화로부터 심리적 표상을 추출해내는 과정이라 할 수 있을 것이다. 이 장에서는 이렇게 추출된 담화표상이 어떤 대상 세계와 양립가능한가를 따져 주어진 담화의 참과 거짓을 결정하는 방법을 살펴보고자 한다.

4.1. 모형(model)

객관주의 언어 의미이론은 한 표현이 대상 세계를 참되게 기술하고 있는가에 관심을 갖는다. Tarski의 유명한 예문 "Snow is white"라는 문장은 이 문장이 어떤 세계의 모습을 바르게 기술할 때 그 세계에서 참이 된다.

즉 어떤 세계 W에서 "snow"라고 불리는 어떤 것이 "white"라 불리는 속성
을 가지고 있을 때 이 문장은 참이 된다. 따라서 한 문장의 의미를 파악하
기 위해서는 그 문장이 기술하고 있는 세계의 모습을 자세히 살피지 않으
면 안된다. 그러나 실제 세계는 너무 크고 복잡하기 때문에 세상과 비슷
하게 어떤 대상물들이 언어로 표현된 관계를 맺고 있는 보다 간단하고 명
확히 정의된 추상적 구조를 설정하고 이 구조에 비추어 문장의 의미를 연
구하고 문장들 간의 의미 관계를 추적해 보는 방법을 취한다. 이 추상적
구조를 모형(model)이라 하며 모형에 입각하여 언어 표현의 의미를 연구하
는 의미론을 모형이론적 의미론(model-theoretic semantics)이라 한다.

모형은 개체들의 집합과 언어 표현이 지칭하는 것이 무엇인가를 명시
해 주는 함수로 정의된다. 개체들의 집합을 모형의 universe라 하고 언어
표현에 그 의미값 즉, 그 표현이 지칭하는 것이 무엇인가를 정해 주는 함
수를 의미값 할당함수(value assignment function)라 한다. (1)은 모형에 대한
일반적 정의이다.

(1) 한 언어의 모형 M은 이 모형 내의 모든 개체들(individuals)의 집합(the
    universe of M: U_M)과 의미값 할당 함수(value assignment function: F_M)의 순서
    쌍(ordered pair)이다.
    $M = <U_M, F_M>$

이제 a, b라는 두 개체로 구성된 작은 모형 M1을 생각해 보자. 이 모형 속
에서 a는 "John"라 불리고 b는 "Bill"이라 불리는 사람이며 a와 b는 "is-bold"
라 불리는 속성을 가지고 있고 b는 "is-brave"라고 불리는 속성을 가지고 있
으며 이 두 개체는 서로 "hates"라 이름지어진 관계에 있다고 하자. 이 모
형은 다음과 같이 정의된다.

(2) M1=<U$_{M1}$, F$_{M1}$>

　　　단, U$_{M1}$={a, b}

　　　F$_{M1}$(John)=a, F$_{M1}$(Bill)=b,

　　　F$_{M1}$(is-bold)={a, b}

　　　F$_{M1}$(is-brave)={a}

　　　F$_{M1}$(hates)={<a, b>, <b, a>}

의미값 할당함수를 (1)과 같이 명시적으로 정의하지 않고 표현의 의미
값을 직접 명시하는 방법도 있다. 이 방법은 표현과 표현의 의미값을 순
서쌍으로 표시한다. 예를 들어 <John, a>는 표현 John이 그 의미값으로 개
체 a를 갖는다라는 것을 나타낸다. (3)은 이와 같은 방법으로 모형을 정의
한 것이다.

(3) 한 언어 L의 모형 M은 다음과 같이 세 요소로 구성된 순서 지워진 집합
　　　(ordered set)이다.

　　　　　M=<U$_M$, Name$_M$, Pred$_M$>

　　　　　단, U$_M$은 모형 내의 개체들의 집합 (the universe of M)

　　　　　　　Name$_M$은 언어 L의 각 고유명사 A와 이 이름을 지니고 있는 모형
　　　　　　　　　M 내의 한 개체 i$_A$로 구성된 순서쌍 <A, i$_A$>들의 집합

　　　　　　　Pred$_M$은 언어 L의 각 술어 P와 M에서 P의 의미값 (또는 외연
　　　　　　　　　(extension)) P$_M$으로 구성된 순서쌍 <P, P$_M$>들의 집합

이 정의에 따르면 (2)에 제시된 모형 M1은 (4)와 같이 정의된다.

(4) M1=<U$_{M1}$, Name$_{M1}$, Pred$_{M1}$>

　　　단, U$_{M1}$={a, b}

　　　Name$_{M1}$={<John, a>, <Bill, b>}

　　　Pred$_{M1}$={<is-bold, {a, b}>, <is-brave, b>, <hates, {<a, b>, <b, a>}>}

이 두 가지 표기 방법은 표기적 변이형(notational variant)에 불과하므로 이하에서 (1)의 방법을 주로 하고 필요시 (3)의 방법을 병행 사용하겠다.

(2)에 제시된 모형에서 문장 "John is bold"는 참이다. 왜냐하면, "John"이라 불리는 개체 a는 is-bold라 이름지어진 속성을 지니고 있는 개체 중 하나임을 이 모형이 정의하고 있기 때문이다. 일반적으로 어떤 고유 명사 x와 어떤 술어 P가 결합하여 xP라는 문장을 형성할 때 이 문장의 진리값은 (5)와 같이 결정된다.

> (5) 문장 xP는 어떤 모형 M의 의미값 할당함수를 F라 할 때 $F(x)$가 $F(P)$의 한 요소일 경우에 한하여 참이 된다. (A sentence xP, where x is a proper noun and P is a (one-place) predicate, is true if and only if $F(x) \in F(P)$.)

이제 두 개의 모형 M1과 M2를 살펴보자. M1은 (2)에서 정의된 것과 같고 M2는 (6)과 같이 정의된다고 하자. M2는 M1의 모든 개체들을 포함하고 M2의 의미값 할당함수 F2는 M1의 개체들에 대해서는 F1과 동일하며 M1에는 속해 있지 않고 M2에만 존재하는 개체들의 속성과 관계를 규정해 준다.

> (6) 모형 M2는 개체들의 집합 U_{M2}와 의미값 할당함수 F_{M2}의 순서쌍 $<U_{M2}, F_{M2}>$이다. 단 $U_{M2}=\{a, b, c\}$이며 $F_{M2}(John)=a$, $F_{M2}(Bill)=b$, $F_{M2}(Susan)=c$, F_{M2}(is-bold)=$\{a, b\}$, F_{M2}(is-brave)=$\{b, c\}$, F_{M2}(hates)=$\{<a, b>, <b, a>, <a, c>\}$이다.

이러한 관계에 있는 두 모형 M1과 M2에 대하여 'M2가 M1을 확장한다'(M2 extends M1)라고 한다. 이와 같은 확장 관계는 (7)과 같이 정의된다.

> (7) 어떤 언어 L의 두 모형 M1과 M2가 다음과 같은 관계에 있을 때, M2가 M1을 확장한다라고 하며 M1⊑M2와 같이 표기한다.

(i) $U_{M1} \subseteq U_{M2}$

(ii) 어떤 표현 α에 대하여 UM1에 속한 개체들만이 관련되는 한 $F_{M2}(\alpha)$ $=F_{M1}(\alpha)$.

이 정의에 따라 모형 M2는 (2)에서 정의한 모형 M1을 확장한다. M2의 개체들의 집합 U_{M2}는 M1의 개체들의 집합 UM1의 모든 개체들을 포함하며 M2의 의미값 할당함수 F_{M2}는 UM1에 속해 있는 개체들에 한하여 F_{M1}과 동일하기 때문이다. 그러나 (8)에 정의된 모형 M3는 모형 M1을 확장한 것이 아니다. 비록 M1의 개체들의 집합이 M3의 개체들의 집합의 부분 집합일지라도 F_{M3}는 U_{M1}에 속해 있는 개체들에 관하여 F_{M1}과 다른 값을 부여하고 있기 때문이다. 개체들 a, b에 관하여 F_{M3}(is-bold)의 값이 F_{M1}(is-bold)의 값과 다름에 주목하라.

(8) M3=$<U_{M3}, F_{M3}>$

단, U_{M3}={a, b, c}

F_{M3}(John)=a

F_{M3}(Bill)=b

F_{M3}(Susan)=c

F_{M3}(is-bold)={a, c}

F_{M3}(is-brave)={b, c}

F_{M3}(hates)={<a, b>, <b, a>, <a, c>}

이상에서 정의한 확장(extension)의 개념은 담화표상의 의미론에 있어 중요한 역할을 담당한다.

4.2. 함수(Function)

4.2.1. 순서쌍(Ordered Pair)

집합(set)을 이루는 원소(element)들은 집합 내에서 순서가 지워져 있지 않다. 즉, 두 집합 A, B가 각 집합을 구성하는 원소들이 동일하면 이 두 집합은 동일하다. 따라서, (9)에 명시된 두 집합 A, B는 동일하다.

(9) A={a, b, c}
    B={c, b, a}

순서쌍은 순서가 지워진 두 개의 요소로 구성된다. (순서쌍은 집합이 아니므로 순서쌍의 구성 요소를 원소와 구별하여 "첫 번째 또는 두 번째 요소"라는 용어를 사용하겠다. 영어의 first (or second) member of an ordered pair 또는 first (or second) coordinate of an ordered pair가 이에 해당한다) 여기에서 순서는 중요한 역할을 하므로 두 순서쌍 <a, b>와 <b, a>는 서로 다르다. 순서쌍은 집합의 개념을 사용하여 다음과 같이 정의된다. 즉, 순서쌍의 첫 번째 요소로 구성된 단원소집합(singleton)과 순서쌍의 두 요소로 구성된 집합을 원소로 가지는 집합으로 정의한다. (11)의 집합은 물론 (12)의 집합과 동일하다. 정의에 의해 (11)이나 (12)의 집합에서 단원소집합의 원소를 순서쌍의 첫 번째 원소로, 두 원소로 구성된 집합의 원소 중 단원소집합의 원소이외의 원소를 순서쌍의 두 번째 요소로 이해하게 된다. 따라서, (11)과 (12)는 동일한 순서쌍을 나타낸다.

(10) <a, b> =def {{a}, {a, b}}
(11) {{a}, {a, b}}
(12) {{a, b}, {a}}

두 집합 A, B에서 A의 원소를 첫 번째 원소로 하고 B의 원소를 두 번째 원소로 하는 순서쌍을 만들 수 있다. 이 때 집합 A에 속한 각 원소가 B의 각 원소를 취하여 만들어 내는 모든 순서쌍들의 집합을 카테시안 積 (Cartesian Product)이라 한다. 카테시안 적은 A x B 등과 같이 표기하며 (13) 처럼 정의된다.

(13) A x B = {<x, y>| x∈A and y∈B}

정의에 따라 두 집합 A={a, b, c}, B={1, 2}로부터 얻어지는 카테시안 적은 (14)와 같다.

(14) A x B = {<a, 1>, <a, 2>, <b, 1>, <b, 2>, <c, 1>, <c, 2>}

4.2.2. 관계(Relation)

순서쌍들의 집합 (15)를 살펴보자. (15)의 구성 원소를 이루는 순서쌍들의 첫 번째 요소로 이루어진 집합은 {a, b, c}이고 두 번째 요소로 구성된 집합은 {1, 2}이다. 이 때 집합 {a, b, c}를 "집합 C의 첫 번째 요소로의 투사(the projection of the set C onto the first coordinate)"라 하고 집합 {1, 2}를 "집합 C의 두 번째 요소로의 투사"라 부른다.

(15) C = {<a, 1>, <a, 2>, <b, 1>, <c, 2>}

집합 C는 집합 {a, b, c}와 집합 {1, 2}의 카테시안 적의 부분집합이다. 집합 C는 두 집합 A와 B가 어떤 관계에 있음을 뜻한다. 이 관계를 R이라 하면 집합 C는 집합 A의 원소 a와 집합 B의 원소 1, a와 2, b와 1, c와 2가 R의 관계에 있음을 나타낸다. 예를 들어 R을 "~보다 키가 크다"라는 관계라고 한다면 집합 C는 a가 1, 2보다, b가 1보다, c가 2보다 키가 큼을 나타낸다.

어떤 대상 a, b가 R의 관계에 있을 때 이를 Rab 또는 aRb로 표기한다. 또한 R은 두 집합의 카테시안 적의 부분집합이므로 R⊂A × B(또는 R: A → B)로도 표기한다. R을 이루는 순서쌍들의 첫 번째 요소들의 집합(또는 R의 첫 번째 요소로의 투사)을 관계 R의 영역(domain)이라 하고 이러한 순서쌍들의 두 번째 요소들의 집합(또는 R의 두 번째 요소로의 투사)을 R의 치역(range)이라 한다. 관계 R은 두 집합의 요소들을 화살표로 연결한 (16)과 같은 도식으로 표시하기도 한다. 왼쪽의 집합이 영역을, 오른쪽의 집합이 치역을 이룬다.

(16)

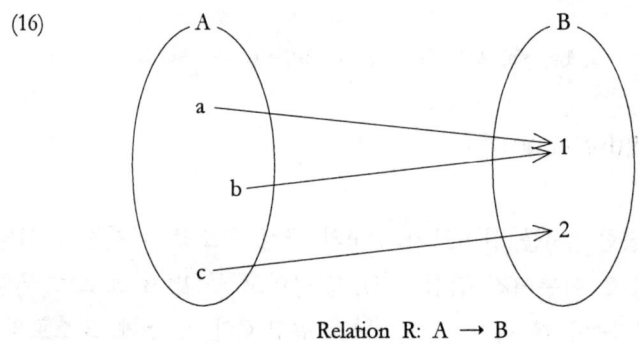

Relation R: A → B

4.2.3. 함수(Function)

함수(function)는 관계(relation)의 특수한 경우이다. 함수는 (17)과 같이 정의된다.

(17) 관계 R: A → B는 다음의 조건을 만족할 때 함수이다.
   (i) R의 영역에 있는 각 원소는 치역에 있는 단 하나의 원소와 순서쌍을 이룬다.
   (ii) R의 영역은 집합 A와 동일하다.

(17-i)의 조건에 의해 (18)의 관계는 함수가 되지 못한다. 집합 A의 한 원소 b가 치역의 두 원소와 연결되어 있기 때문이다.

(18)

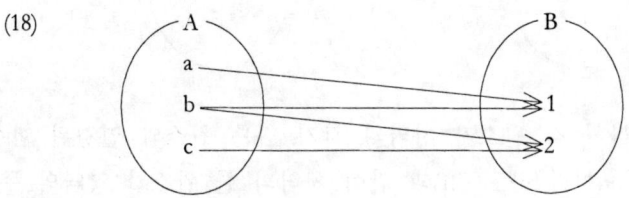

또한 (17-ii)의 조건에 의해 (19)의 관계도 함수가 아니다. 집합 A의 한 원소 c가 이 관계의 영역에 포함되지 않기 때문이다. 즉, 집합 B의 어떤 원소와도 연결되지 않은 집합 A의 원소가 최소한 하나는 존재하기 때문이다.

(19)

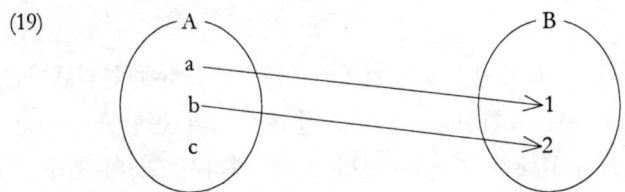

반면, 관계 (20)과 (21)은 (17)의 조건을 모두 만족하는 관계이므로 이들은 함수이다.

(20)

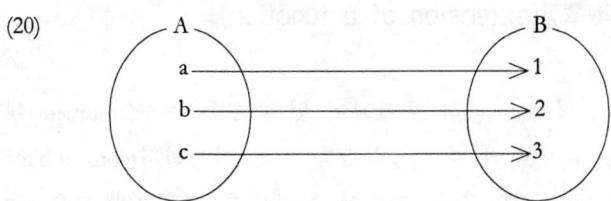

(21)

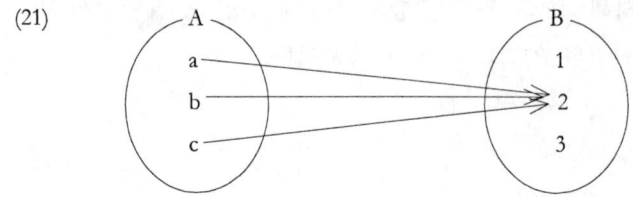

(20)과 같이 영역의 각 원소가 치역의 각기 다른 원소와 연결된 함수를 one-to-one function이라 하고 (21)과 같이 치역의 한 원소가 영역의 두 개 또는 그 이상의 원소와 연결된 경우가 있는 함수를 many-to-one function이라 한다. 또한 집합 A에서 B로 가는 어떤 함수 f에서 f의 치역이 집합 B와 동일할 때 이 함수를 onto function이라 하고 f의 치역이 집합 B의 부분집합일 경우 이 함수를 into function이라 한다. 집합 A는 그 자신의 부분집합 (A⊆A)이므로 onto function은 into function의 한 특수한 경우가 된다. 특별히 one-to-one onto function을 일대일 대응(one-to-one correspondence)이라 한다.

어떤 함수 f에서 영역의 원소 a가 치역의 어떤 원소 b에 연결된다는 점을 일반적으로 f(a)=b로 표기한다. 이 때, a를 함수 f의 논항(argument)이라 하고 b를 함수 f의 a에 대한 값(value)이라 한다. 따라서 (20)의 함수는 (22) 와 같이 나타내어질 수 있다.

(22) f(a)=1,   f(b)=2,   f(c)=3

4.2.4. 함수의 확장(extension of a function)

두 함수 f와 g의 영역에 공히 포함되어 있는 모든 논항(argument)에 두 함수가 같은 값을 부여할 때 이 두 함수를 양립 가능하다(compatible)라고 한다. 예를 들어 (23)에 정의된 두 함수를 살펴보자. 함수 f와 함수 g는 그 영역(domain)에 공통의 원소로 a와 b를 가지고 있으며 이 원소들은 1과 2

라는 원소에 연결되어 있다. 즉 f(a)=g(a)=1이며 f(b)=g(b)=2이다. 따라서 두
함수 f와 g는 양립 가능한 함수들이다.

(23) f: A → B　　　　　　　　　　g: C → D

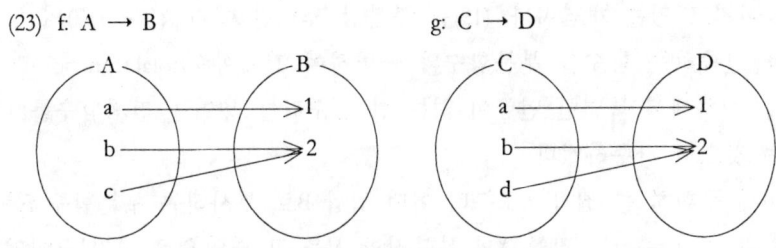

　두 함수 f, g가 양립가능하고 f의 영역이 g의 영역에 포함될 때 즉 f의
영역이 g의 영역의 부분집합일 때, g는 f를 확장한다(g extends f), 또는 g는
f의 확장(extension)이라 하며 f⊑g로 표기한다. 이 정의에 따라 (23)의 두 함
수는 확장 관계에 있지 않다. 왜냐하면 f의 영역 (집합 A)과 g의 영역(집합
C)은 서로에게 포함되지 않기 때문이다. 이제 (24)에 정의된 두 함수 f와 g
를 살펴보자. 이 두 함수는 공통의 논항에 동일한 값을 부여하므로 양립
가능하다. 또한 함수 f의 영역 {a, b}는 함수 g의 영역 {a, b, c}의 부분집합
이다. 따라서 g는 f를 확장한다.

(24) f: A → B　　　　　　　　　　g: C → D

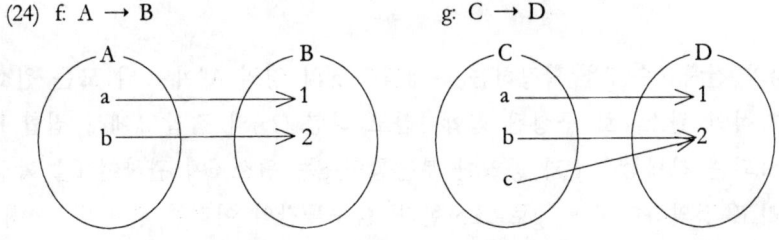

　함수의 확장과 관련하여 부분함수(partial function)를 정의해 보기로 하
자. (17)에서 밝혔듯이 함수 f: A → B의 논항은 반드시 하나만의 값을 부여
받아야 하며 그 영역은 집합 A와 동일해야 한다. 부분함수란 함수의 논항

은 반드시 하나만의 값을 가지나 그 영역이 집합 A의 부분집합을 이루는
함수를 말한다. 따라서 엄밀히 말하여 부분함수는 함수가 아니다. 그러나
부분함수는 의미론의 중요한 수단이 될 수 있으므로 의미론에서 널리 받
아들여지고 있는 개념이다. (19)는 부분함수의 한 예가 된다. (17)의 두 조
건을 만족하는 함수를 부분함수와 구별하여 전체함수(total function)라 부
른다. 이하에서 특별한 언급이 없는 한 함수라는 용어는 전체함수를 나타
내는 것으로 간주하겠다.

　이제 무한히 큰 집합 A로부터 어떤 집합 B로 투사하는 부분함수 f를 상
정하자. 이 함수 f는 집합 A의 부분집합 A'을 그 영역으로 가지는 어떤 전
체함수 f과 동일하다. 이는 다음과 같이 도식된다.

(25) 부분함수 f: A → B　　　전체함수 f: A' → B

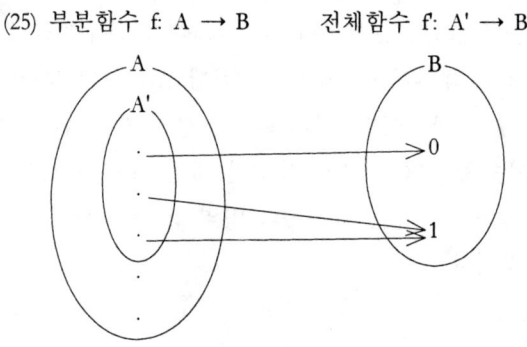

(25)의 전체함수 f을 확장하는 전체함수 g'의 영역 A"이 A'의 모든 원소와
추가적인 원소 c로 구성된 집합이라고 하면 (25)의 집합 A에서 집합 B로
투사되는 전체함수 g'과 동일한 부분함수 g는 원소 c에 관하여 f를 확장한
다라고 정의하며 f ~$_c$ g로 표시한다. 함수들간의 이러한 관계가 (26)에 도
식화되어 있다.

(26)

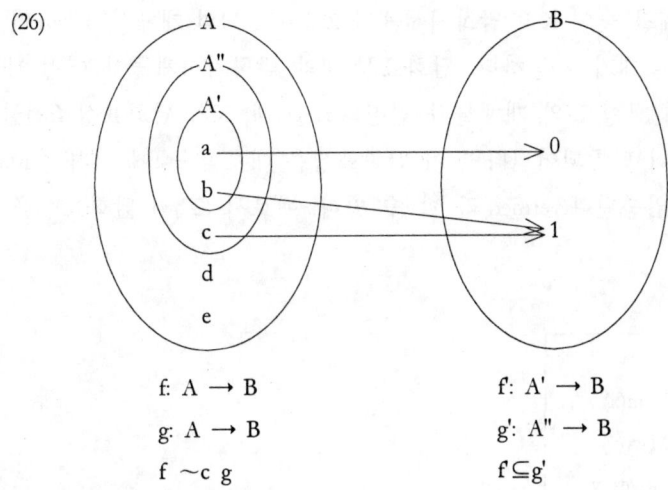

$$f: A \rightarrow B \qquad f': A' \rightarrow B$$
$$g: A \rightarrow B \qquad g': A'' \rightarrow B$$
$$f \sim_c g \qquad f \subseteq g'$$

4.3. 담화표상의 진리조건

담화표상 K는 담화 지시체들의 집합(universe of K)과 이 담화 지시체에 대한 담화표상 조건들의 집합으로 이루어진 순서쌍으로 정의된다. 담화 지시체는 Karttunen(1976)이 도입한 용어로 어떤 표상상의 실체(entity)로 모형이나 실제 세계의 실체와는 다르다. 담화지시체는 어떤 함수에 의해 모형이나 실제 세계의 실체와 연결되는 것으로 술어논리 언어의 변수 (variable)와 같은 역할을 한다. 따라서 모형의 실체와 연결해 주는 함수(내포 함수: embedding function)에 따라 하나의 담화 지시체가 여러 개의 실체 (또는 개체)와 연결되기도 한다. 즉 내포함수 f1은 담화지시체 x를 모형의 개체 a와 연관시키고 또다른 내포함수 f2는 b에 연관시킬 수 있다. 그리고, 두 개 또는 그 이상의 상이한 담화지시체가 어떤 모형의 동일한 개체와 연결될 수도 있다.

어떤 담화표상 K를 주어진 모형 M에 내포시키는 함수는 여러 개가 있

을 수 있다. 예를 들어 K의 담화지시체가 2개이고 M의 개체가 3개라면 내
포함수는 2x3=6개가 가능하다. 담화표상 K의 담화지시체들이 어떤 내포
함수 f에 의해 모형 M의 개체들과 연결되었을 때, K의 담화표상조건들이
그 모형 내에서 만족되어진다면 이 담화표상은 내포함수 f에 의하여 M 안
에서 참임이 입증된다(verified)라 할 수 있다. 예로서 (27)의 담화표상을 살
펴보자.

(27)

$$
\boxed{
\begin{array}{c}
\text{x, y} \\
\text{John(x)} \\
\text{Mary(y)} \\
\text{x loves y}
\end{array}
}
$$

진리 판단의 준거가 되는 모형 M을 (28)이라 하자.

(28) M=<A, F>
　　　A={a, b, c}
　　　F(John)=a, F(Mary)=b, F(Bill)=c
　　　F(loves)={<a, b>, <b, c>, <c, b>}

담화표상 (27)을 모형 M으로 내포시키는 한 내포함수 f1을 (29)로 정의하자.

(29) f1(x) = a, fi(y) = b

내포함수 f1이 주어졌을 때, 담화표상 (27)의 담화표상조건들 John(x),
Mary(y), x loves y가 (28)의 모형 내에서 만족되는지를 살펴보기 위해서는
내포함수 f1이 각 조건을 참이 되도록 입증하는 조건들을 명시하여야 한
다. f1이 John(x)를 참이라 입증하기 위해서는 f1이 담화지시체 x와 연결시

키는 모형 M의 개체가 모형 M의 표현 John에 부여하는 개체와 동일하여야 한다. 즉 f1(x)가 모형 M에서 John이라 불리는 개체일 경우에만 f1은 담화표상조건 John(x)를 참이라 입증한다. 이 관계는 (30)으로 일반화할 수 있다.

(30) f verifies $\pi(x)$ in M iff $f(x)=F(\pi)$, where π is a name.

모형 M은 (30)을 만족하므로 내포함수 f1은 M 안에서 (또는 M에 비추어) 담화표상조건 John(x)가 참임을 입증한다. 마찬가지로 f1(y)=F(Mary)=b이므로 f1은 M에 비추어 담화표상조건 Mary(y)가 참임을 입증한다.

(27)의 세 번째 담화표상조건 x loves y는 f1이 x에 부여하는 M의 개체가 f1이 y에 부여하는 M의 개체가 모형 M에서 loves가 나타내는 관계에 있어야 한다. 즉, <f1(x), f1(y)>가 F(loves)의 한 원소가 되어야 한다. 이 조건은 (31)로 일반화 할 수 있다.

(31) f verifies $x \xi y$ in M iff $<f(x), f(y)>\in F(\xi)$, where ξ is a two-place predicate.

(31)에 의하여 <f1(x), f1(y)>, 즉 <a, b>는 F(loves)의 원소이므로 (27)의 담화표상조건 x loves y는 모형 M 안에서 내포함수 f1에 의하여 입증된다. 따라서 f1은 주어진 모형 M 안에서 담화표상 (27)의 모든 담화표상조건이 참임을 입증하므로 담화표상 (27)이 M에 비추어 참임을 입증한다.

한 담화표상이 주어진 모형 안에서 참임을 입증하는 내포함수가 존재한다는 것은 이 담화표상이 주어진 모형의 일부를 올바로 표상함을 뜻한다. 즉, 어떤 담화표상의 모든 담화표상조건이 주어진 모형 안에서 참임을 입증하는 내포함수가 최소한 하나가 존재할 때 이 담화표상은 주어진 모형에 비추어 참이라 할 수 있다. 어떤 담화표상 K의 진리조건은 (32)와 같이 정의된다.

(32) A DRS K is true in M iff there is at least one embedding function f from the universe of K into the universe of M such that f verifies K in M.

위에서 우리는 담화표상의 어휘는 모형의 어휘에 담화지시체를 추가한 것을 전제로 하였다. 즉, 담화지시체를 제외한 일반 어휘는 담화표상과 모형에서 동일한 언어의 그것임을 받아 들였다. 만약 담화표상의 언어가 한국어 비슷하고 모형의 언어 표현이 영어의 그것이라면 한 언어를 다른 언어로 번역하는 과정을 거쳐야 할 것이다. 예를 들어 모형 (28)에 비추어 담화표상 (33)의 진리값을 구하기 위해서는 담화표상조건의 입증조건 (verification condition) (30), (31)을 (34), (35)로 수정하여야 할 것이다. L1을 담화표상이 근거하는 언어라 하고 L2를 모형이 근거하는 언어라 하자.

(33)

| x, y |
| 존(x) |
| 메어리(y) |
| x가 y를 사랑한다 |

(34) f verifies $\pi(x)$ in M iff $f(x)=F(\pi')$, where π is a name in L1 and π' is the translation of π into L2.

(35) f verifies x가 y를 ξ in M iff $<f(x), f(y)> \in F(\xi')$, where ξ is a two-place predicate in L1 and ξ' is the translation of ξ into L2.

이러한 번역과정은 담화표상의 의미를 연구하는데 중요하지 않으므로 앞으로는 담화표상의 기본 어휘는 모형의 기본 어휘와 담화지시체에 한정된 것으로 하겠다. 이하에서 담화표상조건들을 형식적으로 보다 엄밀히 정의하고 각 담화표상조건들에 대한 입증조건을 살펴보겠다.

4.3.1. 담화표상조건들의 입증조건

담화표상 K는 담화지시체들의 집합과 담화표상조건들의 집합으로 구성된 순서쌍이다. 담화표상조건들은 문장의 통사분석에 담화표상 구성규칙이 작용하여 얻어진다. 한 문장의 통사분석은 분석 수형도의 위에서부터 아래로, 왼쪽에서 오른쪽으로 처리된다. 따라서 한 문장의 통사분석이 완전히 처리되기까지는 여러 번 담화표상 구성규칙이 적용됨으로 완전하게 처리된(fully reduced or fully processed) 담화표상을 얻기까지는 여러 중간단계를 거치게 된다. 그러나 의미해석을 받는 담화표상은 완전히 처리된 담화표상이므로 이러한 담화표상의 담화표상조건을 유형화하는 것은 담화표상조건들의 입증조건을 명시하는 데 있어 필수적이다.

담화표상조건은 담화지시체와 근거하는 언어 표현 그리고 다른 통사범주와 함께 도입되는(syncategorematically introduced) 표현들(=, (,), 등) 만으로 구성된 단순 담화표상조건(simple or atomic DRS conditions)과 ㄱK 등과 같이 담화표상을 그 구성 요소로 가지는 복합 담화표상조건(complex DRS conditions)으로 나뉘어진다. 제 3장에서 소개된 담화표상 구성규칙들에 의하여 도출될 수 있는 담화표상조건들을 포함하는 담화표상은 (36)과 같이 정의된다(Reyle 1991, pp.104-105 참조). V는 모형과 담화표상이 근거하는 언어의 모든 어휘들의 집합, R은 모든 담화지시체들의 집합을 뜻한다.

(36) 담화표상의 정의
   (i) V와 R에 한정된 담화표상 K는 R의 부분집합인 U_K (the universe of K)와, V와 R에 한정된 담화표상들의 집합 Con_K로 구성된 순서쌍 <U_K, Con_K>이다.
   (ii) V와 R에 한정된 담화표상조건은 다음의 유형 중 하나의 표현이다:
      (a) x=y, 단 x, y는 담화지시체
      (b) π(x), 단 x는 담화지시체, π는 V의 고유명사
      (c) η(x), 단 x는 담화지시체, η는 V의 보통명사에 해당하는 일항 술어

(d) xζ, 단 x는 담화지시체, ζ는 V의 자동사에 해당하는 일항 술어

(e) xξy, 단 x, y는 담화지시체, ξ는 V의 타동사에 해당하는 이항 술어

(f) ─K, 단 K는 V와 R에 한정된 담화표상

(g) K1⇒K2, 단 K1, K2는 V와 R에 한정된 담화표상

(h) K1<every>K2, 단 K1, K2는 V와 R에 한정된 담화표상

4.3.1.1. 단순 담화표상조건의 입증조건

어떤 내포함수 f가 (36-ii)로 유형화된 단순 담화표상조건을 V에 한정된 모형 M=<A, F>에 비추어 참이 되게 하는 조건들을 살펴보자. x=y 형태의 담화표상조건은 내포함수 f가 x와 y를 A의 동일한 원소에 내포시킬 때, f에 의하여 참으로 입증된다. π(x) 형태의 담화표상조건은 f(x)의 값이 모형 M에서 π라 불리는 개체일 때, 그리고 η(x) 형태의 담화표상조건은 f(x)가 모형 M에서 표현 η의 의미값 즉 F(η)의 한 원소일 때 f에 의하여 참으로 입증된다. xζ 형태의 담화표상조건은 내포함수 f가 담화지시체 x에 부여하는 M의 개체가 표현 ζ의 M에서의 의미값 F(ζ)에 포함되어 있는 경우에 그리고 xξy의 담화표상조건은 f(x)와 f(y)가 M에서 ξ로 표현된 관계에 놓여 있으면 즉 <f(x), f(y)>∈F(ξ)이면 f가 M에서 이들을 입증한다. 따라서 단순 담화표상조건의 입증조건은 (37)과 같이 정리된다.

(37) 단순 담화표상조건의 입증조건 (Reyle 1991, p.106)

(K를 V와 R에 한정된 담화 표상, γ를 담화표상조건, f를 R에서 M으로 가는 내포함수라 하자.)

(i) f verifies the DRS K in M iff f verifies each of the conditions belonging to Con_K in M.

(ii) f verifies the condition γ in M iff

(a) γ is of the form x=y and f(x)=f(y).

(b) γ is of the form π(x) and f(x) is the bearer of the name π.

(c) γ is of the form η(x) and f(x)∈F(η).

(d) γ is of the form xζ and f(x)∈F(ζ).

(e) γ is of the form xξy and <f(x), f(y)>∈F(ξ).

4.3.1.2. 복합 담화표상조건의 입증조건

(36-ii)의 f, g, h의 세 가지 복합 담화표상조건은 그 안에 하위 담화표상을 포함한다. 먼저 ￢K 형식의 부정 담화표상조건을 살펴보자. 문장 (38)은 고유명사, not을 포함하는 부정문, 비한정 명사구에 대한 담화표상 구성규칙의 적용을 받아 최종적으로 (39)와 같이 처리된다.

(38) John does not have a book.

(39)

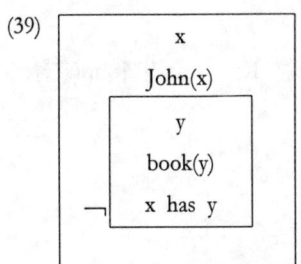

(39)의 주담화표상을 K0라 하고 부정 연산자 ￢의 지배를 받는 하위 담화표상을 K1이라 하자. 주담화표상 K0를 주어진 모형 M에서 참이라 입증하는 내포함수 f는 하위 담화표상 K1을 이 모형 내에서 참으로 입증해 주는 어떠한 내포함수와도 양립 불가능해야 한다. 즉, f를 확장하는 함수로 K1을 M에 내포시키는 함수가 없어야 한다. 즉, 문장 (38)은 John이라 불리는 개체가 존재하고 이 개체와 책이라는 속성을 지닌 어떤 개체가 has라는 표현으로 나타내어진 소유의 관계에 있는 경우가 전혀 없을 때 참이 된다. ￢K에 대한 입증조건은 (40)과 같이 표현할 수 있다.

(40) An embedding function f verifies the condition $\neg K$ in M iff there is no embedding function g from R into M which extends f and verifies K in M.

이제 모형 M을 (41)로 정의하고 이 모형 내에서 (39)의 담화표상이 참인지를 알아보자. 담화표상 (39)가 참이 되기 위해서는 K0를 M에 내포하는 함수 f가 최소한 하나는 존재해야 한다. 그리고 이 내포함수 f는 (i)조건 John(x)를 입증하고, (ii)K1을 내포시킬 수 있게 확장될 수가 없어야 한다.

(41) M=<A, F>

A={a, b, c, d}

F(John)=a, F(book)={b, c}, F(car)={d}

F(loves)={<a, b>, <a, c>}, F(has)={<a, d>}

K0의 한 내포함수 f가 다음과 같다고 하자. f는 K0의 조건 John(x)를 입증한다. (f(x)=F(John)).

(42) f(x)=a

담화지시체 y를 포함하도록 f를 확장시키는 함수 g는 (43)과 같이 4개가 있을 수 있다.

(43) g1: g1(x)=a, g1(y)=a

g2: g2(x)=a, g2(y)=b

g3: g3(x)=a, g3(y)=c

g4: g4(x)=a, g4(y)=d

g1은 K1의 조건 book(y)를 입증하지 못한다. book(y)를 입증하는 내포함수는 g2와 g3 뿐이다. 그러나 g3는 조건 x has y를 M 내에서 입증하지 못한

다(<f(x), f(y)>∉F(has)). g4도 마찬가지로 조건 x has y를 입증하지 못한다. 즉, 이 모형 내에서 K1을 참이라 입증하도록 f를 확장하는 내포함수는 존재하지 않으므로 f는 K0의 모든 담화표상조건 John(x)와 ㄱK1을 참이라 입증한다. 따라서 이 모형 내에서 담화표상 (39)를 참으로 입증하는 내포함수가 최소한 하나는 존재하게 되어 이 담화표상은 (41)의 모형 M 내에서 참이다.

다음으로 K1 ⇒ K2 형식의 담화표상조건의 입증조건을 살펴보자. 이 담화표상조건은 (44)와 같은 조건문으로부터 도출된다.

(44) If Mary likes a man then he owns a car.

조건문의 의미는 매우 복잡한 양상을 지니고 있기 때문에 그 진리조건을 간단히 포착하기는 힘들다. 보다 자세한 조건문의 의미에 대한 논의는 Kratzer 등을 참고하기로 하고 여기서는 조건문의 의미가 일차술어논리 언어의 material implication과 동일한 진리조건을 갖는다고 전제하고 여기에 맞추어 K1 ⇒ K2의 입증조건을 찾아보도록 하겠다.

일차술어논리 언어 표현 P→Q의 진리 조건은 (45)와 같이 정리된다. 표 (45)에 따르면 P가 참일 때 Q가 거짓인 경우를 제외하고 모든 경우에서 참이 된다. 즉, P→Q가 참이 되기 위해서는 P가 참일 경우 항상 Q가 참이 되는가를 살피기만 하면 이 표현의 진리값을 알 수 있다.

(45) P의 진리값	Q의 진리값	P→Q의 진리값
참	참	참
참	거짓	거짓
거짓	참	참
거짓	거짓	참

담화표상의 내포함수에 준하여 조건문의 진리조건을 살펴보자. 담화표상

조건 K1⇒K2는 K1이 참이 되는 모든 경우에 있어 K2가 참이 되어야 한다. 즉, K1을 주어진 모형 M에 내포시키는 모든 내포함수 각각은 K2를 M에 내포시키도록 확장될 수 있어야 한다. 다시 말하면 M 내에서 K1을 내포시키는 모든 내포함수 g에 대하여 K2를 M에 내포시키도록 f를 확장하는 h가 최소한 하나는 존재할 때에 이 복합 담화표상조건은 참이 된다. 그런데, K1⇒K2는 상위 담화표상의 한 담화표상조건이므로 K1을 M에 내포시키는 모든 g는 상위 담화표상의 내포함수 f를 확장하는 것이어야 한다. 이 입증조건은 (46)으로 표현된다.

(46) f verifies K1⇒K2 in M iff for every extension g of f such that Dom(g) =Dom(f) ∪ U_{K1} which verifies K1 in M there is an extension h of g such that Dom(h)=Dom(g) ∪ U_{K2} and h verifies K2 in M.

Dom(f)는 내포함수 f의 영역 (domain)을 뜻한다. 따라서 Dom(g)=Dom(f) ∪ U_{K1}은 g의 영역이 f의 영역에 있는 담화지시체들과 K1의 담화지시체들의 합임을 나타낸다. 즉 함수 g는 함수 f의 영역에 있어서는 f와 동일하며 f의 영역에 있지 않은 담화지시체들에게만 새로운 값을 부여함을 뜻한다.

조건문 (44)는 (47)의 담화표상으로 최종 처리된다. (48)은 (47)의 담화표상이 내포될 모형이다.

(47)

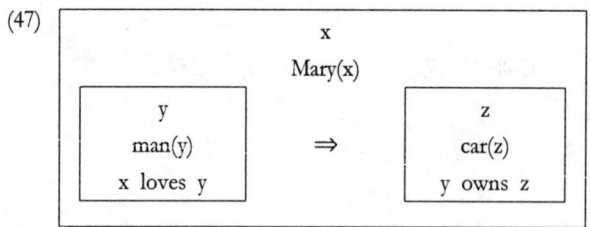

(48) M=<A, F>

　　A={a, b, c, d}

　　F(Mary)=a, F(man)={b, c}, F(car)={d}

　　F(loves)={<a, b>, <a, c>},　F(owns)={<b, d>}

주담화표상 K0를 M에 내포시키는 한 함수를 f라 하고 f(x)=a라 하자. 이 함수는 주담화표상 조건 Mary(x)를 M 내에서 참으로 입증하는 유일한 내포함수이다. (47)의 복합 담화표상조건을 K1⇒K2로 표시하기로 하면 f를 확장하면서 K1을 M에 내포시키는 함수 g는 다음의 두 경우가 된다.

(49)　g1: g1(x)=a, g1(y)=b

　　　g2: g2(x)=a, g2(y)=c

g1을 확장하면서 K2를 M에 내포시키는 함수 h는 (50) 하나가 존재한다.

(50)　h: h(x)=a, h(y)=b, h(z)=d

그러나 g2를 확장하면서 K2를 M에 내포시키는 함수는 존재하지 않는다. 왜냐하면 z에 대하여 g2를 확장하는 함수는 (51) 뿐인데 이 함수는 y owns z를 참으로 입증해 주지 못하기 때문이다 (<h(y), h(z)>∉F(owns)).

(51)　h: h(x)=a, h(y)=c, h(z)=d

즉, K1을 M에 내포시키도록 f를 확장하는 모든 g가 다 K2를 M에 내포시키도록 확장될 수 있는 것은 아니다. 따라서 f는 (47)의 담화표상을 M에 비추어 참으로 입증해 주지 못한다. 그런데, f가 주담화표상 조건 Mary(x)를 M에 내포시킬 수 있는 유일한 함수이므로 (47)의 담화표상을 M에 비추어 참으로 입증해줄 내포함수가 존재하지 않게 되어 이 담화표상은 M

내에서 거짓이 된다. 즉, 담화표상 (47)은 M의 모습을 진실되게 표상하지 못한다.

마지막으로 전칭 양화 구문에서 비롯한 복합 담화표상조건 K1<every> K2의 입증조건을 알아보자. 전칭 양화 구문 (52)는 의미 면에서 조건문 (53)과 매우 유사하다. 문장 (52)는 농부라는 속성을 지니는 모든 개체는 자동차를 가지고 있다는 의미를 표현하고 문장 (53)은 어떤 개체가 농부이기만 하면 그 개체는 자동차를 가지고 있다는 의미를 표현하고 있기 때문이다. 즉, (52)와 (53)의 문장이 참이 될 조건은 동일하다.

> (52) Every farmer owns a car.
>
> (53) If an individual is a farmer then he owns a car.

일반적으로 (52)의 문장은 (54)와 같은 일차 술어논리 언어 표현으로 번역되어진다고 받아들인다. (54)의 번역에서 (52)의 전칭 양화 문장과 조건문의 의미적 연관성이 드러나 있다.

> (54) $\forall x[\text{farmer}(x) \rightarrow \exists y[\text{car}(y) \land x \text{ owns } y]]$

표현 (54)는 농부인 모든 개체는 자동차를 최소한 한 대는 가지고 있는 경우에 참이 된다. 변수 x와 y에 개체를 그 값으로 부여하는 치할당함수를 부분함수(partial function)로 정의하고 위에서 논의한 확장의 개념을 원용하면 (54)의 진리 조건은 "어떤 모형 M에서 변수 x에 농부인 개체를 연결하는 모든 함수가 x에는 같은 값을 부여하고 y에 자동차인 개체를 부여하여 x의 값인 개체가 y의 값인 개체와 owns로 표현된 소유의 관계에 있도록 값을 부여하는 함수로 확장될 수 있는 방법이 최소한 하나 이상 있을 때 이 표현은 M 내에서 참이 된다"라고 명시할 수 있다. 이제 모형을 (55)와 같이 정의하자.

(55) M=<A, F>

　　A={a, b, c, d, e}

　　F(farmer)={a, b, c}, F(car)={d, e}

　　F(owns)={<a, d>, <a, e>, <b, d>, <c, e>}

(54)의 x에 농부인 개체를 부여하는 함수는 다음의 셋이 가능하다.

(56) g1(x)=a, g2(x)=b, g3(x)=c

(56)의 각 함수는 y에 자동차인 개체를 부여하는 함수로 다음과 같이 확장될 수 있다.

(57) (i) g1의 확장 함수 h1: h1(x)=a, h1(y)=d

　　(ii) g1의 확장 함수 h1': h1'(x)=a, h1'(y)=e

　　(iii) g2의 확장 함수 h2: h2(x)=b, h2(y)=d

　　(iv) g2의 확장 함수 h2': h2'(x)=b, h2'(y)=e

　　(v) g3의 확장 함수 h3: h3(x)=c, h3(y)=d

　　(vi) g3의 확장 함수 h3': h3'(x)=c, h3'(y)=e

(57)의 g의 확장 함수 중에서 x의 값과 y의 값이 owns의 관계에 있는 함수는 h1, h1', h2, h3'의 네 개이다. 즉, g1은 h1과 h1'으로, g2는 h2로, g3는 h3'으로 확장되므로 x에 농부인 개체를 부여하는 모든 부분함수는 y에 x의 값인 개체가 소유하는 자동차를 연결하는 함수로 확장될 수 있는 방법이 최소한 하나는 존재하게 된다. 따라서 표현 (54)는 모형 (55)에서 참이 된다.

　　치할당함수를 전체 함수로 정의하면 표현 (54)의 진리 조건을 전칭 양화 표현과 존재 양화 표현에 대한 진리 조건 (58)과 (59)를 사용하여 표현할 수 있다. 구체적으로 어떤 절차를 따라 표현 (54)가 모형 (55)안에서 참이 되는지를 파악할 수 있는지는 독자에게 맡기도록 하겠다.

(58) ∀u[φ] is true with respect to a model M and a value assignment function g iff for every value assignment function g' such that g' is exactly like g except possibly for the individual assigned to u by g', [φ] is true with respect to M and g'.

(59) ∃u[φ] is true with respect to a model M and a value assignment function g iff for some value assignment function g' such that g' is exactly like g except possibly for the individual assigned to u by g', [φ] is true with respect to M and g'.

양화 표현 ∀u[φ], ∃u[φ]가 주어진 모형 M과 (58)과 (59)를 만족하는 모든 치할당함수 g에 비추어 참이라면 이 표현들은 모형 M에서 참이다.

문장 (54)는 every-명사구와 비한정 명사구에 대한 담화표상 구성 규칙의 적용을 받아 (60)의 담화표상으로 처리된다.

(60)
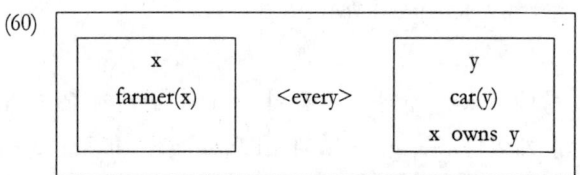

(60)의 담화표상에 있는 복합 담화표상조건은 어떤 모형에서 모든 농부가 최소한 차 한 대를 가지고 있을 때 참이 된다. 이 조건은 담화표상을 모형으로 내포시키는 내포함수를 이용하여 "담화지시체 x를 모형 내의 농부 중 하나에 사상하는 모든 내포함수가 (i) 담화지시체 y에 자동차 중의 하나를 부여하고 (ii) x의 값인 개체가 y값인 개체를 소유하는 관계에 있도록 확장될 수 있을 때 참이 된다"라고 다시 표현할 수 있다. 두 개의 담화표

상을 every라는 양화사로 연결한 복합 담화표상조건은 결국 조건문에서 도출된 복합 담화표상조건 K1⇒K2와 그 입증 조건이 같게 된다. 즉, K1<every>K2의 담화표상조건에 대한 입증조건은 (61)로 주어진다.

(61) f verifies K1<every>K2 in M iff for every extension g of f such that Dom(g)=Dom(f) ∪ UK1 which verifies K1 in M there is an extension h of g such that Dom(h)=Dom(g) ∪ U_{K2} and h verifies K2 in M.

입증 조건 (61)은 결국 치할당함수를 부분함수로 정의할 때의 일차술어논리 언어 표현 $\forall u[[\phi] \rightarrow \exists v[\Psi]]$의 진리 조건과 동일하다.

자연언어에는 일차술어논리 언어의 전칭 또는 존재 양화사로 번역될 수 없는 많은 양화사(예를 들어, most, many, some, few, at least five 등)들이 존재한다. Barwise and Cooper 등이 주창한 일반 양화사 이론(Generalized Quantifier Theory)은 자연언어의 모든 한정사(determiner)는 양화 표현으로 두 개의 속성간의 관계를 나타낸다고 일반화한다. D를 한정사, P와 Q를 속성(또는 개체들의 집합)을 나타내는 표현들이라 하면 표현 (62)는 P의 의미값과 Q의 의미값으로 이루어진 순서쌍이 D의 의미값의 한 원소일 때 즉 (63)의 조건을 만족할 때 참이 된다.

(62) DPQ

(63) DPQ is true in M=<A, F> iff <F(P), F(Q)>∈F(D)

예를 들어 (64)의 문장에서 D는 every이며, P와 Q는 각각 student, sings이다. 문장 (64)는 student로 표현된 개체들의 집합 F(student)가 sings로 표현된 개체들의 집합 F(sings)의 부분집합일 경우 참이다. 따라서, 한정사 every의 의미값은 포함관계에 있는 속성들의 순서쌍의 집합 {<r, s>|r⊆s, r과 s는 속성}으로 정의된다. 따라서 (64)는 (65) 또는 (66)을 만족할 경우 M에서 참이 된다.

(64) Every student sings.

(65) <F(student), F(sings)>∈{<r, s>|r⊆s, r과 s는 속성}

(66) F(student)⊆F(sings)

한정사 D는 또한 두 속성간의 수적 관계를 표시한다. 즉 표현 DPQ는 P로 표현된 속성을 지니는 개체들의 숫자와 P로 표현된 속성을 지니며 동시에 Q로 표현된 속성도 지니는 개체들의 숫자간에 D로 표현된 수적 관계가 있음을 나타낸다. (64)가 참이 되기 위해서는 학생의 수가 학생이면서 노래를 부르는 개체들의 수가 같아야 한다. 어떤 속성 p를 지니는 개체들의 수를 |p|라 하면 Every P Q는 |F(P)|=|F(P)∩F(Q)|일 때 참이 된다. 반면, (67)의 문장은 학생 과반수가 노래를 부르면 참이 된다. 즉 Most P Q는 |F(P)|≥2|F(P)∩F(Q)|일 때 참이 된다.

(67) Most students sing.

Kamp and Reyle는 양화사의 의미를 두 속성간의 관계에서 파악하는 일반 양화사 이론을 받아 들여 DPQ의 통사 표현을 복합 담화표상조건 K1<D>K2로 표상한다. 즉, 문장 (67)은 (68)로 표상 된다.

(68)
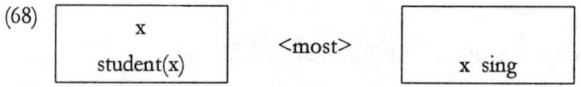

Kamp and Reyle가 전칭 양화 구문과 조건문의 진리 조건이 동일하다는 것을 받아들이면서도 서로 다르게 표상한 이유는 양화사 구문을 일관되게 표현하기 위함이다. 자연언어의 한정사와 관련된 통사 및 의미 현상은 제2부에서 상세히 다루도록 하겠다.

이상에서 논의한 제 3장의 담화표상 구성 규칙에 의해 도입되는 담화표상조건들에 대한 입증조건은 (69)와 같이 정리된다.

(69) 담화표상조건의 입증조건

(K를 V와 R에 한정된 담화 표상, γ를 담화표상조건, f를 R에서 M으로 가는 내포함수라 하자.)

(i) f verifies the DRS K in M iff f verifies each of the conditions belonging to Con_K in M

(ii) f verifies the condition γ in M iff

(a) γ is of the form x=y and f(x)=f(y).

(b) γ is of the form π(x) and f(x) is the bearer of the name π.

(c) γ is of the form η(x) and f(x)∈F(η).

(d) γ is of the form xζ and f(x)∈F(ζ).

(e) γ is of the form xξy and <f(x), f(y)>∈F(ξ).

(f) γ is of the form ¬K and there is no embedding function g from R into M which extends f and verifies K in M.

(g) γ is of the form K1⇒K2 and, for every extension g of f such that $Dom(g)=Dom(f) \cup U_{K1}$ which verifies K1 in M there is an extension h of g such that $Dom(h)=Dom(g) \cup U_{K2}$ and h verifies K2 in M.

(i) γ is of the form K1<every> and, for every extension g of f such that $Dom(g)=Dom(f) \cup U_{K1}$ which verifies K1 in M there is an extension h of g such that $Dom(h)=Dom(g) \cup U_{K2}$ and h verifies K2 in M.

지금까지 담화지시체와 담화지시체에 대한 조건들로 구성된 담화표상의 입증조건들을 살펴보았다. 함수 f가 담화표상 K의 담화지시체를 모형 M의 개체에 사상하고 사상된 개체들이 담화표상조건에 명시된 조건들을 모형 M 안에서 참임을 입증할 때 이 함수(내포함수)가 담화표상 K를 M 안에서 참임을 입증한다. 그러나 (70)과 같이 담화표상 K의 담화표상조건 중에 K의 universe에 속하지 않는 담화지시체를 포함하고 있는 것이 있으면 이 담화표상의 진위를 결정할 수 없다. 담화표상 K의 universe에 속하지 않고 K의 담화표상조건에 포함되어 있는 (70)의 z와 같은 담화지시체를 자유 담화지시체(free discourse referent)라 한다.

(70)

x, y
John(x)
book(y)
x has z

이는 일차술어논리 언어에서 자유 변수(free variable)가 있는 표현의 의미값을 결정할 수 없는 것과 같다. 따라서, 담화표상에 대한 입증조건은 자유 담화지시체를 포함하지 않은 담화표상(proper discourse representation)에 한하여 주어질 수 있다.

어떤 담화표상 K를 주어진 모형 M 안에서 참으로 입증해 주는 내포함수 f가 최소한 하나가 존재할 때, 담화표상 K는 M 안에서 참이 된다. 또한 담화표상 K가 모든 모형에서 참이 된다면 K는 모든 모형에서 논리적으로 참이 된다(logically true in all models). 이 관계는 (71), (72)로 표현된다 (Reyle 1991, p.109).

(71) Let K be a proper DRS confined to V and R and M a model for V. We say that K is true in M iff there is an embedding f from R into M such that f verifies K in M.

(72) A DRS is logically true iff it is true in all models for V.

이제 담화의 진리조건을 알아보자. 여기서 담화는 문장들의 집합을 뜻한다. 따라서, 담화는 한 문장으로 구성될 수도 있다. 주어진 담화의 진리조건은 그 담화로부터 도출된 담화표상의 진리 여부에 따라 간접적으로 정의된다. 즉, 어떤 담화 D가 모형 M에 비추어 참인가를 알기 위해서는 그 담화로부터 도출된 담화표상이 모형 M의 모습을 참되게 표상하는가를 살펴보면 된다. 다시 말하여 담화 D는 이에 근거한 담화표상 K가 모형 M 에서 참이 될 때, 그 모형 내에서 참이 된다. 그러나 주어진 담화가 한가 지 이상의 의미로 해석되지 않은 경우라도, 즉 담화가 애매하지 않은 경 우에도 이로부터 무수히 많은 담화표상을 도출할 수 있다. 예를 들어 담 화 (73)으로부터 담화표상 (74)와 (75)를 도출할 수 있다.

(73) John loves Mary.

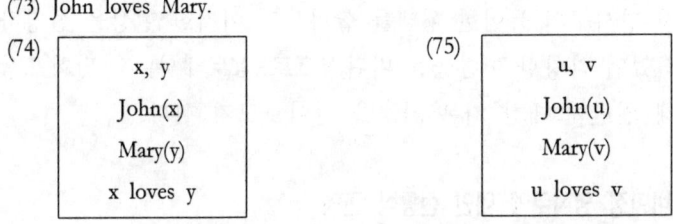

(74)
| x, y |
| John(x) |
| Mary(y) |
| x loves y |

(75)
| u, v |
| John(u) |
| Mary(v) |
| u loves v |

(74)와 (75)의 담화표상은 표상하는 의미가 동일하므로 이 둘을 표기적 변 이형(notational variants 또는 alphabetical variants)이라 한다. 그러면 애매하지 않은 담화란 그 담화로부터 도출 가능한 담화표상들이 표기적 변이형에 불과한 담화를 말한다고 정의할 수 있다. 따라서 담화 D로부터 도출할 수 있는 무수히 많은 담화표상이 표기적 변이형에 불과하다면 이 담화 D로 부터 도출 가능한 모든 담화표상이 모형 M에서 참이 되는 조건은 도출 가능한 담화표상 중의 하나가 모형 M에서 참이 되는 조건과 동일하다. 이 제 어떤 담화 D의 모형 M 안에서의 진리조건을 (76)과 같이 정리할 수 있 다.

(76) Let D be an unambiguous discourse confined to V and M for V. Then D is true in M iff any DRS derivable from D is true in M.

4.4. 담화표상 이론에서의 양화 문제

좁은 의미의 담화표상이론은 자연언어의 양화문제에 대한 새로운 접근 방법이다. 담화표상이론은 a student 등과 같은 비한정 명사구의 의미에 있어 Russell(1905) 등이 제시한 전통적 접근방법과 매우 다르다. 전통적 접근 방법과의 가장 큰 차이는 비한정 명사구를 양화표현으로 보지 않고 단순한 변수(variable)와 같은 역할을 하는 것으로 간주한다는 점이다. 이 부분에서는 비한정 명사구의 특이한 행태를 살펴보고 이러한 현상을 설명하기 위하여 제시되었던 다양한 이론들을 비판적으로 검토해 본 후 담화표상이론의 양화문제 일반에 대한 기본 가정을 알아보고자 한다.

4.4.1. 비한정 명사구에 대한 전통적 견해

자연언어의 양화문제에 대한 전통적 접근은 자연언어의 양화 현상은 통사 구조와 의미 구조의 관계가 명확하게 정의된 일차술어논리 언어(first-order predicate logical language)와 같은 인공언어를 통하여 설명되어질 수 있다는 태도로부터 기인한다. 일차술어논리 언어는 담화 영역(discourse domain)의 모든 개체(individual)가 어떤 기술(description)을 만족함을 나타내는 전칭 양화사($\forall$로 표기), 담화 영역 내에 어떤 기술을 만족시키는 개체가 존재함, 즉 그러한 개체가 최소한 하나는 있음을 나타내는 존재 양화사($\exists$로 표기), 그 값으로 개체를 취하는 변수(variable)를 포함한다. 이 양화사들은 문장의 앞에 붙어 다른 문장을 형성한다. 양화사가 부착되는 문장을 그 양화사의 양화 범위 또는 영향권(scope)이라 한다. 양화 범위는 표기 규약에 따라 [   ]로 표기하며 양화사의 범위가 명확할 경우에는 [   ]를 생략하기도 한다. 예를 들어 문장 (77)은 문장 (78)에 양화사 $\forall$가 부착되어 형성되며 문장 (78)은 이 양화사의 범위가 된다. 양화사 옆의 "x"는 변수로서 이 양화사가 이 변수에 제한되어 양화함을 보여 준다. M과 B를 어떤 일차술어논리 언어의 일항 술어(one-place predicate)라 하자.

(77) $\forall x[M(x) \rightarrow B(x)]$

(78) $M(x) \rightarrow B(x)$

양화사는 자신의 범위내의 지정된 변수만을 "구속할"(bind) 수 있다(또는 "묶을" 수 있다). 양화사 $\forall$은 문장 (79)에서 B(x)의 변수 x는 이 양화사의 범위 밖에 있으므로 묶을 수 없다. 또한 문장 (80)의 변수 y도 묶을 수 없는 데 이는 y가 이 양화사에게 지정된 변수가 아니기 때문이다.

(79) $\forall x[M(x)] \rightarrow B(x)$

(80) $\forall x[M(y) \rightarrow B(x)]$

양화사에 의하여 구속된 변수를 구속변수(bound variable)라 하고 구속되지 않은 변수를 자유변수(free variable)라 한다.

Russell은 영어의 every를 일차술어논리 언어의 전칭양화사 ($\forall$)에 그리고 a(n)을 존재양화사 ($\exists$)에 상응하는 기능을 가진다는 태도를 취한다. 이러한 견해는 Montague 등 형식의미론자들에게 그대로 받아들여졌다. 이러한 견해를 양화문제에 대한 전통적 접근방법이라 부르기로 하자. 전통적 접근방식을 따르면 (81)의 문장은 (82)의 일차술어논리 언어의 문장으로 번역되며 (83)은 (84)로 번역된다.

(81) Every student came in the room.

(82) $\forall x[\text{student}(x) \rightarrow \text{came-in-the room}(x)]$

(83) A student came in the room.

(84) $\exists x[\text{student}(x) \wedge \text{came-in-the-room}(x)]$

문장 (82)와 (84)는 문장 (81)과 (83)의 진리 조건적 의미를 충실하게 반영하고 있다. 즉, 일차술어논리 언어에서 정의한 문장 (82)와 (84)가 참이 될 수 있는 조건은 곧 문장 (81)과 (83)이 참이 될 수 있는 조건과 동일하다.

전통적 접근방법은 조응 대명사(anaphoric pronoun)를 공지시 대명사(co-referential pronoun)와 구속변수로서의 대명사(pronoun as a bound variable)로 이분한다. 공지시 대명사는 선행사가 지시 표현(referring expression)으로 대상 세계의 어떤 개체를 지칭할 때 이 개체(선행사의 지시체)를 그 자신의 의미값으로 취하는 대명사를 말하며 구속변수로서의 대명사는 선행사가 양화표현으로 자신의 지시체를 가지지 않을 경우 선행사의 의미값의 변화에 따라 그 의미값이 변화하는 대명사를 말한다. 문장 (85)에서 대명사 *his*는 공지시 대명사이며 문장 (86)의 대명사 *his*는 구속변수로서의 대명사이다.

(85) John$_i$ loves his$_i$ mother.
(86) [Every student]$_i$ loves his$_i$ mother.

공지시 대명사는 문장의 경계 밖에 있는 선행사와 연관될 수 있으나 구속변수로서의 대명사는 구속변수가 자신을 묶어 주는 양화사의 양화 범위 이내에 있어야 함과 같이 같은 문장 내에서 그 선행사를 찾아야 한다. 이러한 방식으로 두 종류의 조응 대명사의 성격을 규정함으로써 다음의 조응관계의 적형성을 설명할 수 있다. (87)에서 공지시 대명사 *He*는 문장 경계 밖의 명사구 *John*과 조응 관계를 형성하나 (88)에서 구속변수로서의 대명사 *He*는 양화 명사구 *Every student*를 선행사로 취할 수 없다.

(87) John came in. He sat on the floor.
(88) Every student came in. He sat on the floor.

그러나 문장 (83)에서와 같이 양화표현으로서의 의미를 지니는 *a student*와 같은 비한정 명사구는 조응관계에 있어 지시 표현(referring expression)과 같은 성격을 지닌다. 문장 (89)에서 *A student*는 문장 경계 밖의 대명사 *He*와 조응 관계를 이루고 있다. 다시 말하면 비한정 명사구는 지시 표현으로서의 속성과 양화 표현으로서의 속성을 동시에 지니고 있는 것처럼 보인다.

(89) A student came in. He sat on the floor.

비한정 명사구의 이상한 속성은 소위 말하는 당나귀 문장에서도 발견된다. 당나귀 문장은 비한정 명사구가 *if*절이나 관계절에 포함되어 있고 이를 선행사로 취하는 조응 대명사가 *if*절 밖이나 관계절 밖에 위치하는 형식을 갖는 문장을 일컫는다. 이러한 형태의 문장의 통사-의미적 속성은 그리스 시대 스토아 학파 철학자인 Chrysippos에 의해 연구되기 시작하였으므로 이를 Chrysippos 문장이라 부르기도 한다. 이 문제는 Geach(1962)에서 다시 논의되기 시작하였다. 문장 (90)과 (91)은 전형적인 당나귀 문장의 예이다. 문장 (90), (91)은 당나귀를 가지고 있는 농부는 자신이 가지고 있는 모든 당나귀를 때린다라는 의미를 갖는다.

(90) If a farmer owns a donkey, he beats it.
(91) Every farmer who owns a donkey beats it.

당나귀 문장에서의 비한정 명사구는 문장 경계 밖의 조응 대명사의 선행사가 될 수 있다는 점과 전칭 양화 의미를 지니는 점이 특이하다. 당나귀 문장 (91)은 (92)의 일차술어논리 언어 표현으로 번역된다.

(92) $\forall x \forall y[[\text{farmer}(x) \land \text{donkey}(y) \land x \text{ owns } y] \to x \text{ beats } y]$

위에서 살펴 본 비한정 명사구의 특이한 속성은 비한정 명사구를 존재
양화 표현으로, 조응 대명사를 공지시 대명사와 구속 변수로서의 대명사
로 이분하는 전통적 접근방법에 심각한 문제점을 야기한다. 다음에서 전
통적 접근방법의 테두리 안에서 비한정 명사구의 이러한 속성을 설명하려
고 했던 몇 가지 시도와 그 문제점을 살펴보고자 한다. (Heim 1982 참조)

4.4.2. Geach의 접근방법

Geach(1961)는 비한정 명사구는 양화 표현이며 이를 선행사로 취하는
문장 경계 밖의 대명사는 구속 변수라는 전통적 견해를 그대로 유지하면
서 비한정 명사구의 특이한 속성을 설명하고자 한다. 그에 의하면 a(n)은
존재 양화사의 기능을 가지나 every와 같은 양화사와는 다르게 그 양화 범
위가 문장이 아니라 담화(discourse) 전체라는 입장을 취한다. 즉, 두 문장
으로 구성된 (89)의 담화는 다음과 같이 일차술어논리 언어로 번역된다.

(93) $\exists x[\text{student}(x) \wedge x \text{ came in} \wedge x \text{ sat on the floor}]$

Geach와 같은 비한정 명사구의 처리는 담화 (89)의 진리조건을 잘 포착하
며 구속 변수로서의 조응 대명사의 역할도 잘 설명한다. 그러나 Geach의
설명은 몇 가지 문제점을 내포하고 있다. 첫째, 비한정 명사구의 양화 범
위가 담화 전체라고 한다면 두 명 이상의 화자가 포함되는 담화의 의미를
올바르게 기술할 수 없는 경우가 있다. 담화 (94)는 화자 A의 잘못된 지식
이나 믿음을 화자 B가 수정해 주는 상황하에서 그 진리값이 참이 된다.
그러나 비한정 명사구의 양화 범위가 담화 전체라면 담화 (94)는 (95)처럼
번역되어 항상 그 진리값이 0이 된다. 즉, 담화 (94)로 기술될 수 있는 상
황은 존재하지 않는다는 그릇된 결론에 도달하게 된다.

(94) A: A man fell over the edge.

B: He didn't fall; he jumped.

(95) ∃x[x is a man ∧ x fell over the edge ∧ ─x fell over the edge ∧ x jumped over the edge]

둘째, Geach의 설명 방법은 복수 비한정 명사구가 문장 경계 밖의 조응 대명사의 선행사가 되는 담화의 진리 조건을 올바르게 포착하지 못한다. (문장 경계밖에 있는 명사구를 선행사로 취하는 대명사를 Roberts(1987) 등을 따라 담화 대명사(discourse pronoun)라 부르기로 하자.) Evans(1980)가 제시한 (96)의 담화는 John이 두 마리 이상의 양을 가지고 있는데, 그는 자신이 가지고 있는 모든 양에게 예방 주사를 놓았다 라는 의미를 나타낸다.

(96) John owns some sheep. Harry vaccinated them.

Geach에 따르면 (96)의 담화는 (97)처럼 번역되어 John의 소유로서 John이 예방 주사를 놓은 양이 최소한 두 마리는 있다라는 의미를 나타낸다. |X| ≥2는 변수 X가 둘 이상의 개체로 이루어진 어떤 집단을 그 값으로 취한다는 것을 뜻한다.

(97) ∃X[sheep(X) ∧ |X| ≥2 ∧ John owns X ∧ John vaccinated X]

John이 다섯 마리의 양을 가지고 있으나 그 중에서 세 마리만 예방 주사를 놓았다면 담화 (96)은 거짓이나 (97)은 참이 된다. 즉, Geach의 방법은 (96)의 의미를 바르게 설명하지 못한다.

셋째, Geach의 방법은 양화사의 양화 범위에 관하여 비한정 명사구를 예외로 처리한다. (89), (98), (99)에서처럼 한정사 a(n)만이 문장 경계를 넘어서 그 양화력(quantificational force)을 행사하고 있다. 만약, 모든 양화사가 동일한 제약의 적용을 받도록 하면서 일견 예외적으로 보이는 비한정 명사구의 속성을 설명할 수 있다면 Geach의 접근방법보다 이 이론을 택하는 것이 보다 타당할 것이다.

(89) A student came in. He sat on the floor.

(98) Every student came in. He sat on the floor.

(99) No student came in. He sat on the floor.

넷째, Geach의 접근방법은 당나귀 문장의 양화 관계를 적절히 설명하지 못한다. 비한정 명사구가 양화 표현이며 그 양화 범위가 문장의 경계를 넘어 담화에 미친다는 가정은 (100)의 당나귀 문장에서 조응 대명사 it의 구속 변수로서의 속성을 설명할 수 있다. 그러나 비한정 명사구가 당나귀 문장에서 (101)과 같은 전칭 양화 의미를 부여받는 것은 설명하지 못한다.

(100) Every farmer who owns [a donkey]i beats iti.

(101) $\forall x \forall y[[farmer(x) \wedge donkey(y) \wedge own(x, y)] \rightarrow beat(x, y)]$

4.4.3. Kripke와 Lewis의 접근방법

Geach가 문장 (89)의 담화 대명사를 공지시 대명사가 아닌 구속 변수로서의 대명사로 취급하여 담화 (89)의 조응 관계를 설명하려 했다면, Kripke (1977)와 Lewis(1979)는 담화 대명사를 공지시 대명사로 보고 공지시 관계를 수정함으로서 이 문제를 해결하고자 한다. Kripke는 의미적 지시 (semantic reference)와 화자의 지시(speaker's reference)를 구별해야 한다고 주장한다. 어떤 표현의 의미적 지시체는 그 표현이 한 부분을 이루는 언어의 규칙에 의하여 결정된다. 반면에, 화자의 지시체는 어떤 표현을 발화할 때 화자가 마음속에 떠올리는 (또는 화자가 그것에 대하여 말하고 싶어하는) 특정 개체를 뜻한다. 어떤 명사구는 의미적 지시체와 화자의 지시체를 다 가지고 있으며, 어떤 표현은 화자의 지시체만을 가지기도 하고 어떤 표현은 둘 다 가지지 못하는 경우도 있다. 예를 들어, John과 같은 고유 명사는 의미적 지시체와 화자의 지시체를 가지며, a student와 같은 비한정 명사구는 양화 표현이므로 의미적 지시체는 없으나 그 표현을 발화할 때, 화자가 마음속에 떠올리는 어떤 특정한 개인이 있다면 이 개인이 화자의 지시체가 된다. 비한정 명사구의 화자의 지시체에 대하여 Kripke는 다음과 같이 표현한다.

When a speaker asserts an existential quantification, $(\exists x)(\phi x \ \& \ \Psi x)$, it may be clear which thing he has in mind as satisfying 'ϕx,' and he may wish to convey to his hearers that that thing satisfies 'Ψx.' In this case, the thing in question (which may or may not actually satisfy 'ϕx') is called the 'speaker's referent' when he makes the existential assertion. (Kripke, 1977, p.17)

Kripke는 공지시 대명사의 의미적 지시체는 그 선행사의 화자의 지시체와 동일하다고 대명사의 조응 관계를 정의한다. 따라서, 담화 (89)의 비한정 명사구 A student는 양화 표현으로 의미적 지시체는 없으나, 화자가 이 표현을 담화 (89)의 일부로서 특정 환경에서 발화할 때 이 표현으로 나타내기를 원하는 어떤 개인을 화자의 지시체로 가지게 되고 이 화자의 지시체가 공지시 대명사 He의 의미적 지시체가 된다. 이렇게 함으로써 Russell의 양화 문제에 대한 가정을 유지한 채로 (89)의 조응 관계를 설명할 수 있게 되었다. Kripke는 비한정 명사구와 담화 대명사간의 조응 관계를 다음과 같이 표현한다.

Often one hears it argued against Russell's existential analysis of indefinite descriptions that an indefinite description may be anaphorically referred to by a pronoun that seems to preserve the reference of the indefinite description. I am not sure that these phenomena do conflict with the existential analysis. In any event, many cases can be accounted for (given a Russellian theory) by the fact that: (i) existential statements can carry a speaker's reference; (ii) pronouns can refer to the speaker's referent.

Lewis(1979)는 '대명사는 발화 환경에서 가장 현저한(salient) 대상물을 그 지시체로 취할 수 있다'라는 입장을 취하여 Kripke의 견해를 확대한다. 어떤 대상물의 현저성은 그 대상물을 지시하는 표현의 사용에 의해 불러 일으켜진다. 예를 들어 비한정 명사구와 같은 양화 표현이 특정 환경에서 쓰일 때는 이 표현을 사용하도록 만든 어떤 개체를—비록 화자가 그 개체에 대한 특별한 정보가 없다 하더라도—현저하게 만든다. Heim(1982)이 제시한 다음의 경우를 살펴보자. 쓰레기통이 넘어져 있고 쓰레기 봉투가 찢겨져서 쓰레기가 여기 저기 널려 있는 광경을 목격하고 (102)를 말하였다고 하자. 화자가 어떤 특정한 개를 마음에 두고 있지 않는 상황에서도 (102)는 가능하다. 이 경우 화자의 지시체가 존재하지 않아 Kripke의 방식으로는 (102)의 조응 관계가 설명되지 않는다. 그러나 Lewis의 접근방법을 따르면 비록 어떤 특정한 개를 마음에 두고 있지 않더라도 어떤 개가 상황적 현저성을 부여받아 이 개가 비한정 명사구 A dog의 지시체가 되어 뒤에 오는 담화 대명사의 지시체로 작용하게 된다.

(102) A dog has been rummaging in the garbage can.
       It has torn open all the plastic bags.

어떤 개체가 상황적 현저성을 부여받는 것은 표현의 내용(또는 진리 조건)과 이 표현이 발화된 상황에 의해서만 야기되는 것 같지 않다. 다음의 두 문장에서 보는 것과 같이 명제적 내용이 어떠한 어휘들을 사용하여 표현되어졌는가 하는 것도 현저성을 불러일으키는데 있어 중요한 역할을 수행한다. (103)에서는 찾지 못한 10번째의 구슬이 명시적으로 표현되어 있

고 이 구슬이 후행하는 담화 대명사의 지시체로서 작용한다. 그러나 (104)
에서는 찾지 못한 10번째의 구슬이 명시적으로 표현되지 않았으며 이 구
슬은 후행하는 담화 대명사의 지시체로 여겨지지 못한다.

(103) I dropped ten marbles and found all of them, except for one. It is probably
under the sofa.

(104) ?I dropped ten marbles and found only nine of them. It is probably under the
sofa.

Postal(1969)이 "조응 섬(anaphoric islands)"이라 이름한 다음의 현상도 명시
적 표현이 가지는 현저성의 예가 된다.

(105) John owns a bicycle. He rides it daily.

(106) ?John is a bicycle-owner. He rides it daily.

(107) John has a spouse. She is nice.

(108) ?John is married. She is nice.

비한정 명사구를 양화 표현으로 보고 비한정 명사구가 담화 대명사의
선행사가 될 수 있는 현상을 비한정 명사구의 화자의 지시 또는 현저성이
라는 개념을 도입하여 설명하려는 Kripke나 Lewis의 방법을 취하면서 표현
이 가지는 조응관계에서의 중요성을 설명하려면 표현의 논리적 구조 (또
는 의미) 뿐 아니라 표현이 가지는 현저성을 불러일으킬 수 있는 잠재력
도 동시에 명시하여야 할 것이다. 다시 말하면 어떤 표현의 현저성은 그
표현의 내재적 의미이어야 한다. 즉, 비한정 명사구가 담화 대명사의 선행
사로 쓰일 수 있는 것은 비한정 명사구가 그 쓰이는 환경에서 화용적 해
석을 받아 지시표현으로서의 잠재력을 가지게 되기 때문이 아니라 비한정
명사구의 내재적 의미와 기능에 의하여 담화 대명사의 선행사가 되는 것
이다 라고 말할 수 있다.

Kripke나 Lewis의 접근 방법으로 당나귀 문장에서의 비한정 명사구의 의미를 설명하기가 매우 어렵다. 우선 당나귀 문장에서 비한정 명사구는 Kripke 등이 다루었던 예문과 다르게 지시적 의미를 지니고 있지 않으면서 문장 경계 밖의 담화 대명사의 선행사가 된다. 이 현상을 화용적으로 설명하기 위해서는 비한정 명사구와 담화 대명사간의 조응 관계를 새로운 각도에서 연구하여야 할 것이다. 또한 당나귀 문장에서 비한정 명사구가 왜 전칭 양화 의미를 지니게 되는가를 화용적 규칙을 활용하여 설명할 수 있어야 한다.

4.4.4. Evans의 접근방법

Evans(1979, 1980)는 비한정 명사구를 선행사로 하는 담화 대명사를 '가장한 한정 표현(disguised definite description)'으로 간주한다. 한정 명사구(또는 한정 표현)는 그 자체가 지시 표현(referring expression)이므로 조응 대명사를 구속 변수와 동일시하는 접근방법에서의 문제점이 발생하지 않는다. (109)의 예문에서 담화 대명사 it는 실제로 한정 표현 the dog that came in과 그 기능과 의미가 동일하다. 이와 같이 양화 표현을 그 선행사로 하나 양화 표현의 양화 범위밖에 있는(즉, 양화 표현에 의해 구속되지 않는) 대명사를 Evans는 E-type 대명사라 부른다. (109)의, it가 E-type 대명사의 한 예이다. E-type 대명사는 대명사를 가장한 한정 표현이므로 (109)는 (110)을 간단히 표기한 것에 불과하다.

(109) A dog came in. It lay down under the table.
(110) A dog came in. The dog that came in lay down under the table.

Evans는 한정사 the의 의미를 유일성(uniqueness)에 의존하여 정의하는 전통적 접근방법을 취한다. 즉 어떤 표현 the p q는 (i) p를 만족하는 어떤 개체 x가 존재하고 (ii) x는 q도 만족하며 (iii) 만약 p를 만족하는 개체가 있다면 그 개체는 반드시 x여야 한다 (p를 만족하는 개체는 하나밖에 없다)라는 태도를 받아들인다. 표현 the p q는 (111)로 번역된다.

(111) the p q = $\exists x[p(x) \wedge q(x) \wedge \forall y[p(y) \rightarrow y=x]]$

Evans에 의하면 (109)는 안으로 들어온 개가 오직 한 마리 있는데 그 개가 탁자 아래에 누었다 라는 것을 뜻한다. 그에 의하면 비한정 명사구는 원래 유일성을 함의하지 않는데 이것이 담화 대명사의 선행사로 사용되는 경우에는 유일성의 의미가 화용적으로 불러 일으켜 진다는 것이다. (109)의 첫 번째 문장은 안으로 들어온 개가 최소한 한 마리가 있다라는 것을 뜻하여 유일성의 의미를 띄지 않으나 첫 번째 문장의 비한정 명사구 a dog가 후속하는 문장의 대명사 it의 선행사로 쓰이는 순간 유일성의 의미를 부여받아 안으로 들어온 오직 한 마리의 개가 있는데 그 개가 탁자 아래 앉았다 라는 의미를 가지게 된다는 것이다. 그러나 Heim(1980) 등이 지적하는 바와 같이 비한정 명사구가 후속하는 담화 대명사의 선행사로 쓰일 때 유일성의 의미를 부여받는가 하는 것은 의문이다. Heim은 문장 (112)는 문장 (113)과 그 의미에서 차이가 나지 않으며 두 문장 모두 어제 밤에 깨어진 술잔이 최소한 하나는 있는데 이들 중 어떤 특정한 것이 매우 비싸다는 것을 뜻한다고 지적한다. 만약 Heim의 주장이 옳다면 Evans의 접근방법은 영어의 현상을 제대로 관찰하지 못한 셈이어서 관찰적 타당성을 지니고 있지 않다고 하여야 할 것이다.

(112) A wine glass broke last night. It had been very expensive.
(113) A wine glass which had been very expensive broke last night.

Evans의 접근방법은 당나귀 문장의 조응 관계를 잘 설명한다. 당나귀

문장의 조응 대명사는 E-type 대명사로 한정 명사구와 같은 기능을 가지
므로 선행사의 양화 범위밖에 있어도 무방하다. 즉 문장 (100)이 통사적으
로 적형한 것은 문장 (114)가 통사적으로 적형하기 때문이다.

(100) Every farmer who owns a donkey beats it.

(114) Every farmer who owns a donkey beats the donkey he owns.

Evans는 문장 (100)은 모든 농부는 각각 단 한 마리의 당나귀를 가지고 있
는데 그 당나귀를 때린다라는 의미를 가진다고 주장한다. 이러한 주장은
일반적으로 받아들여진 문장 (100)의 의미인 '모든 농부는 자신이 소유하
고 있는 모든 당나귀를 때린다'와 유일성의 측면에서 차이가 있다. 이 문
제는 과연 영어를 모국어로 사용하는 화자들의 직관이 무엇인가에 의해
결정될 경험적 문제이다. 연구자들에 따라 차이가 있기는 하지만 당나귀
문장이 유일성의 의미를 함의하지 않는다는 것이 일반적 견해이다.

　이상에서 비한정 명사구는 양화 표현으로 특정 개체를 지칭하지 않는다
는 Rusell의 주장을 받아들이면서 비한정 명사구의 조응 관계에 있어서의
특이성을 설명하려는 몇 가지의 시도를 살펴보았다. 이러한 태도는 비한정
명사구의 기본 의미를 존재 양화 의미로 인정하고 그 특이성을 화용론적
으로 부여된(pragmatically accommodated) 의미를 상정함으로서 설명하려는
시도라고 일반화 할 수 있을 것이다. 역동적 술어 논리(dynamic predicate
logic)나 일반 양화사 이론(generalized quantifier theory) 등 최근의 이론들도
근본적으로 비한정 명사구를 양화 표현으로 간주하고 있어 위에서 언급한
문제점들을 지니고 있다고 보아야 할 것이다.

4.4.5. 담화표상 이론에서의 양화 문제

　비한정 명사구는 위에서 살펴 본 것 같이 양화 표현과 지시 표현의 속

성을 다 가지고 있는 것처럼 보인다. Strawson(1952)이나 Chastain(1975) 등은 비한정 명사구를 양화 표현과 지시 표현으로서의 두 의미를 모두 기본 의미로 가지는 애매한 표현(ambiguous expression)으로 간주한다. 이것은 마치 bank라는 단어가 은행을 뜻하기도 하고 (강)둑을 뜻하기도 하는 것과 같다. bank라는 어휘는 우연히 발음이 동일한 두 개의 별개의 단어로 여겨지는 것과 같이 비한정 명사구도 별개의 의미를 지니는 발음이 동일한 두 개의 표현이라는 것이다. Chastain의 다음의 언급에서 이러한 태도가 잘 드러나고 있다.

Sentences containing indefinite descriptions are ambiguous. Sometimes 'A mosquito is in here' and its stylistic variant 'There is a mosquito in here' must be taken as asserting merely that the place is not wholly mosquito-less, but sometimes they involve an intended reference to one particular mosquito.

4.4.4.절은 비한정 명사구를 양화 표현으로 간주하고 지시 표현으로서의 의미를 화용적으로 추론하고자 하였다. 이와는 다르게 담화표상 이론에서는 비한정 명사구를 담화 상에서 마치 지시 표현인 것처럼 작용하고 그 담화의 의미값이 결정되는 모형 (또는 세계)에 비추어서는 변수처럼 작용하는 표현으로 본다. 즉, 담화 상에서 특정 개체 (담화 지시체)를 지시하고 이 담화 지시체는 내포함수에 의해 모형 내의 어떤 임의의 개체에 사상되는 것이다. 이제 고유 명사와 비한정 명사구의 행태를 비교하여 보자. 고유 명사 John은 담화상의 어떤 개체, 예를 들어 x를 지시한다고 하면 이 x는 모형 <A, F>의 F가 표현 John에 부여한 모형상의 개체, 예를 들어 a에 항상 연관된다. 그러나 비한정 명사구 a student가 담화 상에서 지시하는 어떤 담화 지시체 y는 주어진 모형 <A, F>에서 학생의 속성을 가지고 있는 개체 중의 하나에 연결된다. 즉, 담화를 모형에 내포하는 함수에 따라 그 값이 달라지게 된다. 다시 말하면 비한정 명사가 담화 상에서 지시하

는 개체는 모형에 준하여 보면 하나의 변수로서 작용한다. 또한 고유 명사가 지시하는 담화 지시체는 그 담화가 계속되는 동안 지시체로서의 기능을 수행하여 그 담화 내의 후속하는 대명사의 지시체가 될 수 있다. (이러한 담화 지시체를 Karttunen은 long-term discourse referent라 부른다.) 그러나 비한정 명사구에 의해 지시되는 지시체는 담화의 특정 구조 내에서만 지시체로서 작용한다. (Karttunen은 이를 short-term discourse referent라 부른다.) 이는 변수가 어떤 양화사(또는 연산자)의 범위 안에 있을 때만 그 양화사에 의해 묶일 수 있는 것과 같다. 이러한 방법으로 담화표상 이론은 비한정 명사구의 양화 표현과 지시 표현으로서의 속성을 설명한다. 요약하면 어떤 표현의 지시체는 담화 차원의 지시체와 모형 차원의 지시체로 나뉘어지며 담화 차원의 지시체는 다시 모형의 특정 개체와 일관되게 연결되는 것과 모형 내의 임의의 개체와 연결되는 것이 있다. 비한정 명사구가 담화 상에서 지시하는 담화지시체는 모형에 비추어 보면 구속 변수와 같다.

이제 양화 문제에만 한정하여 담화표상 이론이 비한정 명사구의 의미와 조응관계를 어떻게 다루는지를 살펴보자. 위에서 언급한대로 담화표상 이론은 비한정 명사구를 양화 표현이 아닌 단지 일차술어논리 언어의 변수와 같은 역할을 하는 표현으로 본다. 대명사도 단순히 구속 변수로서 작용한다. 선행사가 문장 안에 있던 문장밖에 있던 대명사는 구속 변수로 처리한다. 따라서 담화 (115)는 (116)으로 번역된다.

(115) A dog came in. It sat on the mat.
(116) dog(x) $\land$ x came in $\land$ x sat on the mat

그러나 (116)은 담화 (115)의 존재 양화 의미를 표현하지 못하며 변수 x를 구속할 양화사가 없다. 담화표상 이론은 존재 양화사가 어떤 표현에 의하여 도입되는 것이 아니라 어떤 구조적 원칙에 따라 주어지는 것으로 본다. 즉, (116)의 자유 양화사를 구속하기 위하여 문장이 아니라 담화 전체에 존재 양화사 ∃가 주어진다. 이를 존재 양화사에 의한 닫기(existential closure)라 한다. (116)이 존재 양화사에 의해 닫혀지면 (117)이 되어 담화 (115)의 존재 양화 의미를 포착할 수 있게 된다.

(117) ∃[dog(x) ∧ x came in ∧ x sat on the mat]

전통적 양화 이론과는 다르게 담화표상 이론은 양화사가 어떤 특정 변수만을 구속하는 것이 아니라 구조적 조건을 만족하는 모든 변수가 주어진 양화사에 의해 구속될 수 있다. 즉, 한 양화사는 서로 다른 두 개 이상의 변수를 동시에 구속할 수 있다. 이를 비선택적 구속(unselective binding)이라 하고 어떤 변수 x, y가 양화사 Q에 의해 구속될 때, 양화사 Q는 변수 x, y를 비선택적으로 구속한다라고 한다. 한 문장으로 구성된 담화 (118)은 (119)와 같은 의미관계를 표시한다.

(118) A dog chased a cat.
(119) ∃x∃y[dog(x) ∧ cat(y) ∧ x chased y]

담화 (118)의 두 개의 비한정 명사구 a dog와 a cat은 우선 변수로 처리되어 (120)으로 변환된다.

(120) dog(x) ∧ cat(y) ∧ x chased y

(120)의 담화는 존재 양화사로 닫혀져 담화 전체가 존재 양화사의 범위가 되며 이 양화사는 두 개의 변수를 비선택적으로 구속하게 된다. 즉 (121)은 (122)로 다시 쓸 수 있고 이는 (119)와 동일하다.

(121) ∃[dog(x) ∧ cat(y) ∧ x chased y]

(122) ∃x, y[dog(x) ∧ cat(y) ∧ x chased y]

비한정 명사구가 명백히 존재 양화 의미를 지니는 경우는 (123)과 같이 every 등과 같은 명백한 양화 표현의 핵범위 안에 있을 때이다. (123)은 (124)의 일차술어논리 언어 표현과 동일한 의미 관계를 나타낸다.

(123) Every farmer owns a donkey.

(124) ∀x[farmer(x) → ∃y[donkey(y) ∧ x owns y]]

Heim은 양화사 구문을 양화사, 양화사에 대한 한정부(restriction on the quantifier), 핵범위(nuclear scope)의 세 부분으로 구성된 구조(tripartite structure)로 분석한다. 문장 (123)은 (125)로 구조 분석된다. (125)의 구조에서 NP1은 양화사에 대한 한정부, S2는 양화사의 핵범위가 된다.

(125)

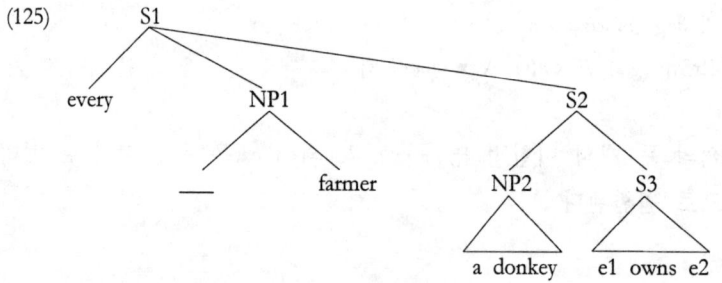

Heim은 (125)와 같은 양화 구문에서 양화사의 핵범위에 존재 양화사가 주어진다는 규칙을 설정한다. 따라서, 전체 담화와 양화사 구문의 핵범위는 존재 양화사에 의해 닫혀지게 된다. (125)의 핵범위에 존재 양화사가 부여되면 (125)는 (126)의 구조로 바뀐다.

(126)

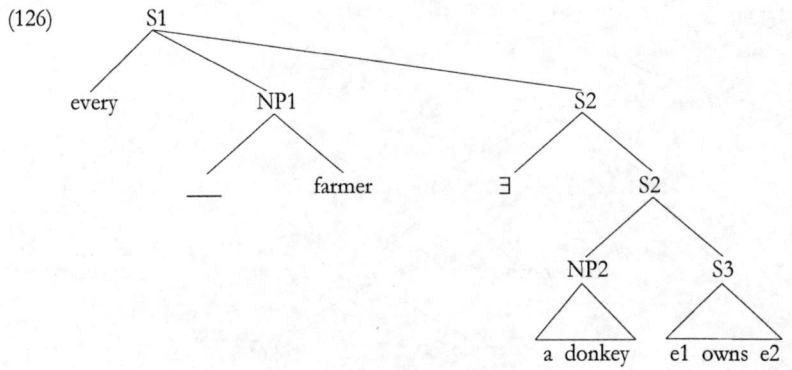

(126)은 (127)로 번역된다. (127)에서 변수 x는 전칭 양화사 ∀에 의해 구속되고 있으므로 존재 양화사 ∃는 변수 x와 y가 다 자신의 양화 범위 내에 있으나 y만 구속하게 된다. 따라서 (127)은 (124)와 동일하다.

(127) ∀[farmer(x) → ∃[donkey(y) ∧ x owns y]]

비한정 명사구가 전칭 양화 명사구에 내포되어 있는 당나귀 문장 (128)의 경우를 살펴보자. 문장 (128)은 (129)의 구조로 분석된다. 그런데 문장인 S3는 양화사를 포함하지 않고 또한 독립적인 담화를 형성하지도 못하므로 존재 양화사가 S3나 S3의 핵범위에 부여되지 못한다.

(128) Every farmer who owns a donkey beats it

(129)

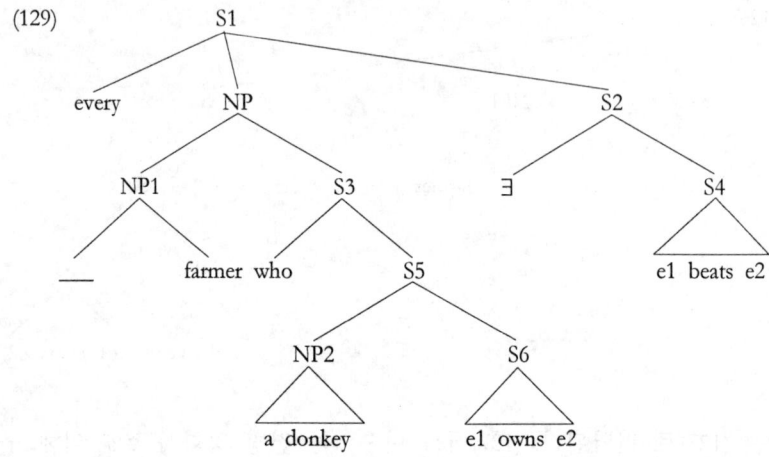

(129)의 구조는 (130)으로 바꾸어 쓸 수 있다. (130)에서 전칭 양화사 ∀은 두 개의 변수 x, y를 구속하고 존재 양화사 ∃은 자신이 구속할 변수가 없으므로 (130)은 (131)과 동일하며 (131)은 (132)로 다시 쓸 수 있다. (132)는 당나귀 문장 (128)의 의미에 대한 모국어 화자의 직관을 바르게 표상한다.

(130) ∀[[farmer(x) ∧ donkey(y) ∧ x owns y] → ∃[x beats y]]

(131) ∀x, y[[farmer(x) ∧ donkey(y) ∧ x owns y] → x beats y]

(132) ∀x∀y[[farmer(x) ∧ donkey(y) ∧ x owns y] → x eats y]

　이상에서 우리는 비한정 명사구의 특이성을 중심으로 담화표상 이론의 양화 문제에 대한 접근방법을 살펴보았다. 담화표상 이론의 양화 문제에 대한 태도는 다음과 같이 요약된다.

(133) 담화표상이론에서의 양화 문제
　(i) 대명사는 구속 변수(bound variable)이다.
　(ii) 비한정 명사구 "a (or some) + CN"는 양화 표현이 아니고 단순히 구속 변수로 작용한다.

(iii) 양화사는 자신의 양화 범위 안에 있는 하나 이상의 변수를 묶을 수 있다(unselective binding)

(iv) 존재 양화사(existential quantifier)는 어떤 구조(담화, 양화사의 핵범위 등)에 default로 주어진다(existential closure).

4.4.6. 담화표상의 일차술어논리 언어 표현으로의 번역

(133)에서 언급된 담화표상 이론의 양화 문제에 대한 가정이 네모 상자를 이용하여 담화를 표상하는 체계에서 어떻게 적용되고 있는가를 살펴보자. 한 문장으로 구성된 담화 (134)는 제 3장에서 설명한 비한정 명사구에 대한 담화표상 구성 규칙에 의해 (135)의 담화표상으로 처리된다.

(134) A farmer owns a donkey.

(135)
```
 x, y,
 farmer(x)
 donkey(y)
 x owns y
```

담화표상 (135)는 어떤 모형 M=<A, F>에 비추어서 담화지시체 x, y를 모형 M의 어떤 개체들 a, b에 사상하여 이 모형 M에서 a가 농부이고 b가 당나귀이며 a가 b를 소유하는 관계에 있게 하는 함수 f가 최소한 하나 이상 있을 때 이 담화표상은 주어진 모형에 비추어 참이며 문장 (135)도 이 모형에 비추어 참이 된다. 이러한 진리조건은 a가 농부이며 b가 당나귀이며 a가 b를 소유하는 관계에 있는 a와 b가 최소한 하나는 있어야 한다라는 조건과 동일하다. 즉, (135)의 진리조건은 (136)과 동일하다.

(136) $\exists x \exists y[farmer(x) \land donkey(y) \land x\ owns\ y]$

담화표상 (135)에서 담화지시체 x와 y는 일차술어논리 언어의 변수이며 담화표상 조건들은 변수에 대한 조건과 동일하므로 담화표상 (135)는 (137)의 표현과 대등하다.

(137) x, y[farmer(x) ∧ donkey(y) ∧ x owns y]

존재 양화사 닫기에 의해 존재 양화사가 부여되면 (138)이 도출되고 이것은 (136)과 동일하다.

(138) ∃x, y[farmer(x) ∧ donkey(y) ∧ x owns y]

이와 같이 담화지시체들의 집합 U와 담화지시체에 대한 조건들의 집합 Con의 순서쌍으로 정의된 어떤 담화표상 K를 일차술어논리 언어 표현으로 번역하려면 다음과 같은 절차를 거치게 된다.

(139) 담화표상의 일차술어논리 언어 표현에로의 번역 절차
  (i) 담화표상 조건들을 ∧로 연결하여 [   ] 안에 둔다.
  (ii) 담화 지시체들을 ,로 연결하여 [   ] 앞에 둔다.
  (iii) 담화 지시체들 앞에 존재 양화사 ∃를 붙인다.

담화표상은 형식적으로 담화 지시체들의 집합 U와 담화표상 조건들의 집합 Con의 순서쌍으로 정의된다. 그런데, 집합의 원소들 간에는 순서가 없으므로 이러한 원소들을 ∧나 ,로 연결하는 방식은 여러 가지가 가능하다. 그러나, 담화표상이 문장의 구조 분석으로부터 도출될 때는 구조의 위에서 아래로, 왼쪽에서 오른쪽으로 처리되므로 각 담화 지시체와 담화표상 조건이 도입되는 순서가 존재하여 특정 담화표상을 이룬다. 이제 이러한 점을 반영하여 담화 지시체들의 집합을 이루는 요소들이 네모 상자에 표상 되는 순서대로 왼쪽에서 오른쪽으로 순서 지워져 있고 담화표상 조

건들도 표상 되는 순서를 따라 순서 지워져 있다고 하자. 그리고 담화 지시체와 담화표상 조건들을 ∧나 ,로 연결할 때 이 순서대로 연결된다고 하면 주어진 담화표상은 특정한 일차술어논리 언어 표현으로 번역되게 된다.

담화표상조건은 문장의 통사분석에 담화표상 구성 규칙이 작용하여 도출된다. 담화표상 구성 규칙은 통사분석의 구조를 유지하며 명사구 등을 담화 지시체로 대체하거나 P(x) 또는 K1⇒K2와 같은 새로운 구조의 담화표상 조건을 도입하게 된다. 이렇게 도출된 담화표상 조건은 일차술어논리 언어 표현과 다른 구조나 표현 방식을 가질 수 있다. 예를 들어 A dog came in이라는 문장으로부터 x came in이라는 담화표상 조건이 도출되나 일차술어논리 언어 표현에서 이 문장은 통상 came-in(x)로 번역된다. 따라서 담화표상을 일차술어논리 언어로 번역하기 위해서는 담화표상 조건들을 이에 상응하는 일차술어논리 언어 표현으로 변환하여야 한다.

일차술어논리 언어는 그 이론적 가정들을 유지하면서 여러 가지 형태로 정의될 수 있다. 동일한 기본 어휘와 일차 양화사를 기저(base)로 하더라도 구성 규칙을 회기적 정의(recursion)에 기반을 두느냐 구구조규칙(phrase-structure rules)을 사용하느냐에 따라 다른 형태의 일차술어논리 언어가 정의되기 때문이다. 여기서는 Reyle(1991)을 따라 회귀적 구성 규칙을 사용하는 일차술어논리 언어 PL를 정의해 보고 이 특정한 언어로 담화표상을 번역하는 절차를 살펴보겠다.

PL은 논리적 어휘와 비논리적 어휘를 포함하는 기저부, 기저부의 어휘로부터 문장형(formula)을 만들어내는 구성 규칙(formation rules)으로 정의된다. 양화사 ∃, ∀는 한 개 이상의 변수를 동시에 구속할 수 있어 ∃x, y는 ∃x∃y와 동일하다.

(140) 일차술어논리 언어 PL

    (a) 논리적 어휘 항목 (logical vocabulary of PL)

(i) 변수: x, y, z, ..., x1, x2, x3, ...

(ii) 논리 상수(logical constants): ㄱ, ∧, ∃, ∀, →, =

(iii) 기타: (,), [,]

(b) 비논리적 어휘 항목(non-logical vocabulary of PL)

(i) 개체 상수(individual constants): John, Mary, Susan, Ulysses, ...

(ii) 일항 술어(one-place predicates): dog, donkey, book, sings, came-in, ...

(iii) 이항 술어(two-place predicates): loves, owns, beats, hates, is-in, ...

(c) 구성 규칙(formation rules)

(i) π가 일항 술어이고 τ가 변수이거나 개체 상수라면 π(τ)는 문장형이다.

(ii) π가 이항 술어이고 σ와 τ가 변수이거나 개체 상수라면 π(σ, τ)는 문장형이다.

(iii) σ와 τ가 변수이거나 개체 상수일 때 σ=τ는 문장형이다.

(iv) φ가 문장이면 ㄱφ는 문장형이다.

(v) φ1, ..., φn이 문장들이면 φ1 ∧ φ2, ..., ∧ φn은 문장형이다.

(vi) α1, ..., αn이 변수들이고, φ가 문장이면 ∃α1...αn[φ]는 문장형이다.

(vii) α1, ..., αn이 변수들이고, φ1과 φ2가 문장이면 ∀α1...αn[φ1 → φ2]는 문장형이다.

따라서, dog(x), owns(x, y), x=John, ㄱdog(x), dog(x) ∧ owns(x, y), ∃x, y[owns(x, y)], ∀x, y[dog(x) → owns(x, y)] 등은 PL의 문장형이다. 문장형 중에서 자유변수를 포함하지 않은 것을 특별히 문장 (sentence)이라 부른다.

　어떤 담화표상 K=<U, Con>이 담화 지시체들을 가지고 있지 않은 경우, 즉 U가 공집합인 경우에는 담화표상 조건들 각각을 PL의 문장형으로 바꾸어 각 조건들을 ∧로 연결하면 된다. K에 담화 지시체들이 있는 경우, 즉 U가 공집합이 아닌 경우에는 담화표상 조건들을 PL의 문장형으로 바꾸어 ∧로 연결한 후 이것을 [ ]에 넣고 [ ] 앞에 담화 지시체들의 연결체를 위치시킨 후 그 앞에 존재 양화사 ∃를 부착하면 된다. 담화표상 조건이나 담화 지시체를 연결할 때는 위에서 언급한 순서대로 한다. 이는 담화 지시체들의 집합 U와 담화표상 조건들의 집합 Con이 어떤 방식으로 순서 지워져 있다는 것을 명시하면 된다. 담화표상 조건들은 그 유형에 따라 적절한 문장형으로 번역된다. 예를 들어 x came in의 유형은 came-in(x)의 유형으로, x owns y의 유형은 owns(x, y)의 유형으로 번역된다. 담화표상 K로부터 PL로의 번역 과정이 (141)에 명시되어 있다. (Reyle 1991)

(141) 담화표상의 PL로의 번역

    (a) K가 담화표상 <U, Con>이라 하자.

      (i) U가 공집합 { }일 때, φ가 (φ_1 $\wedge$ φ_2 $\wedge$ ... φ_n)이고 i=1, ..., n 에 대하여 φ_i는 담화표상 조건 γ_i의 PL로의 번역이며 <γ_1, γ_2, ..., γ_n>은 순서 지워진 담화표상 조건들의 집합 Con이라면 φ는 담화표상 K의 PL로의 번역이다.

      (ii) U가 공집합이 아닐 때, φ가 $\exists\alpha_1...\alpha_n[\varphi_1$ $\wedge$ φ_2 $\wedge$ ... φ_n]이며 (φ_1 $\wedge$ φ_2 $\wedge$ ... φ_n)은 (i)과 같고 $\alpha_1...\alpha_n$은 순서 지워진 담화 지시체들의 집합 U라면 φ는 담화표상 K의 PL로의 번역이다.

    (b) γ가 담화표상 조건이라 하자.

      (i) γ가 $\upsilon(\alpha)$일 때 (υ는 고유 명사, α는 담화 지시체), γ의 PL로의 번역 φ는 $\alpha=\upsilon$,

      (ii) γ가 $\upsilon(\alpha)$일 때 (υ는 보통 명사, α는 담화 지시체), γ의 PL로의 번역 φ는 $\upsilon(\alpha)$,

      (iii) γ가 α υ일 때 (υ는 자동사, α는 담화 지시체), γ의 PL로의 번역 φ는 $\upsilon(\alpha)$,

      (iv) γ가 α υ β일 때 (υ는 고유 명사, α, β는 담화 지시체), γ의 PL로의 번역 φ는 $\upsilon(\alpha, \beta)$,

      (v) γ가 $\alpha=\beta$일 때 (α, β는 담화 지시체), γ의 PL로의 번역 φ는 $\alpha=\beta$,

      (vi) γ가 $\neg$K일 때 (K는 담화표상), γ의 PL로의 번역 φ는 $\neg\Psi$, (Ψ는 K의 PL로의 번역)

      (vii) γ가 K1$\Rightarrow$K2일 때 (K1, K2는 담화표상), γ의 PL로의 번역 φ는 $\forall\alpha_1...\alpha_n[[\Psi_1\wedge\Psi_2\wedge, ..., \Psi_n]\rightarrow\Psi]$, 단 $\alpha_1...\alpha_n$은 순서 지워진 K1의

담화 지시체들이며 Ψi는 K1의 담화표상 조건 γi의 PL로의 번역
이고 Ψ는 담화표상 K2의 번역.

(viii) γ가 K1<every>K2일 때 (K1, K2는 담화표상), γ의 PL로의 번역 φ
는 ∀α1...αn[[Ψ1∧Ψ2∧, ..., Ψn]→Ψ], 단 α1...αn은 순서 지워진
K1의 담화 지시체들이며 Ψi는 K1의 담화표상 조건 γi의 PL로의
번역이고 Ψ는 담화표상 K2의 번역.

복합 담화표상 조건들인 ¬K, K1⇒K2, K1<every>K2의 PL로의 번역 규
칙을 좀 더 자세히 살펴보자. 문장 John does not own a dog는 John이 소유
하고 있는 개가 한 마리도 없을 때 참이 된다. 이 문장은 일차술어논리 언
어 표현 (142)로 번역되며 (143)의 담화표상으로 표상된다.

(142) ∃x[x=John ∧ ¬∃y[dog(y) ∧ owns(x, y)]]

(143)

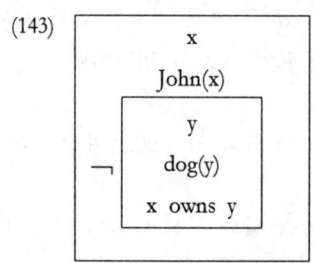

담화표상 (143)의 복합 담화표상 조건은 (141b)의 (vi)에 의해 내포된 담화
표상의 번역 ∃y[dog(y) ∧ owns(x, y)]에 부정 연산자 ¬가 첨가되어 ¬
∃y[dog(y) ∧ owns(x, y)]으로 되어 (143)은 결국 ∃x[x=John ∧ ¬∃y[dog(y) ∧
owns(x, y)]]로 번역된다. 이는 (142)와 같게 된다. 즉, 이 문장을 직접 PL로
번역한 것과 이 문장의 담화표상을 PL로 번역한 것이 같게 되어 담화표상
조건의 번역 규칙 (141b-vi)이 타당함을 알 수 있다.

조건문 (144)는 모국어 화자에 의해 (145)와 동일한 진리 조건을 가지고
있는 것으로 이해된다. 조건절에 있는 비한정 명사구는 전칭 양화 의미를

가지는 것으로 해석되는 반면 결과절의 비한정 명사구는 존재 양화 의미를 가지게 되는 현상을 분석해 보고자 한다.

(144) If a farmer is rich, he owns a donkey.
(145) $\forall x[[farmer(x) \wedge rich(x)] \rightarrow \exists y[donkey(y) \wedge owns(x, y)]]$

Heim은 Lewis(1975)의 양화의 부사 (adverbs of quantification)라는 개념을 받아들인다. 문장 (144)는 전칭 양화 부사 always를 가지고 있는 (146)과 그 의미관계가 동일하다. 따라서, Heim에 의하면 (144)는 명시적으로 표현되지 않은 전칭 양화 부사 always를 가지고 있는 것으로 이해되어야 한다.

(146) If a farmer is rich, he always owns a donkey.

(146)에서 양화 부사 always는 시점(points of time)에 대하여 양화하는 것이 아니라 사건/상태(events)에 대하여 양화한다. 문장 (146)은 어떤 한 농부가 부자인 모든 상태에서 그 농부는 당나귀를 최소한 한 마리 보유한다는 것을 나타낸다. 다시 말하면 모든 농부에 대하여 그 농부가 부자라면 그는 당나귀를 최소한 한 마리 가지고 있다는 것을 뜻하게 되어 결국 always는 개체들에 대하여 양화하는 기능을 하게 된다. 부사 always가 사건에 대하여 양화할 때, (146)은 개략적으로 (147)로 표현되며 이는 (148)과 논리적으로 동일하다. "e"는 사건/상태를 값으로 취하는 변수이다. 문장형 rich(x, e)는 x가 사건/상태 e에서 부자이다라는 것을 뜻한다.

(147) $\forall e[\exists x[[farmer(x) \wedge rich(x, e)] \rightarrow \exists y[donkey(y) \wedge owns(x, y, e)]]]$
(148) $\forall e \forall x[[farmer(x) \wedge rich(x, e)] \rightarrow \exists y[donkey(y) \wedge owns(x, y, e)]]$
(149) $\forall x[[farmer(x) \wedge rich(x)] \rightarrow \exists y[donkey(y) \wedge owns(x, y)]]$

양화 부사 always를 every와 같은 양화사처럼 개체에 대하여 양화한다면 문

장 (146)은 양화사 구문과 같은 3 부분 구조(tripartite structure)를 가지는 것
으로 통사 분석되어 조건절은 양화사의 한정부(restrictive clause), 결과절은
양화사의 핵범위(nuclear scope)가 된다. (150)은 문장 (146)의 통사분석이다.

(150)

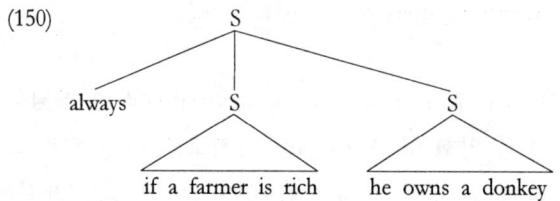

양화사의 핵범위에 존재 양화사가 부여되어(existential closure) (151)의 구조
를 이루며 비한정 명사구와 대명사가 변수로 번역되어 (152)가 되며 이는
(149)와 동일해진다.

(151)

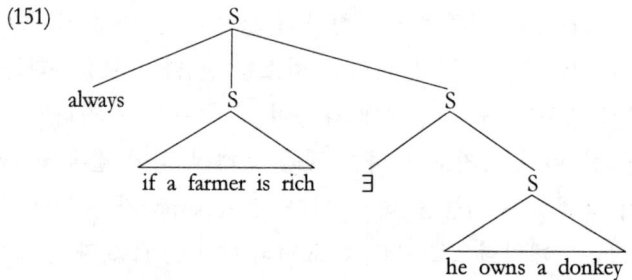

(152) always[[farmer(x) ∧ rich(x)]→∃y[donkey(y) ∧ owns(x, y)]]

이상에서 보인 바와 같이 (i)조건문은 양화 부사 always를 암시적으로 포
함하고 있으며, (ii)이 양화 부사로 인해 3부분 구조로 분석되고 양화 부사
의 핵범위에 존재 양화사가 default로 부여된다고 하는 담화표상 이론의
양화 문제에 대한 가정을 받아들임으로써 조건문의 의미를 바르게 기술할
수 있게 된다. 이러한 접근 방법이 Kamp식의 네모 상자로 표상되는 담화

표상이 일차술어논리 언어 PL로 번역되는 과정에 어떻게 작용하는지를
알아보겠다. 우선 문장 (144)는 (153)으로 담화표상된다.

(153)

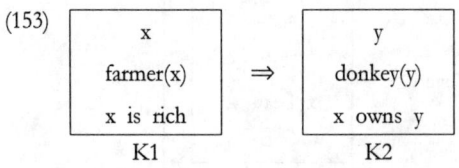

담화표상 K1은 문장 (144)의 3부분 구조 중 제한절로부터 도출되었고 담
화표상 K2는 (144)의 핵범위로부터 도출되었다. 담화표상 조건 (153)은 PL
로의 번역 규칙 (141 b)-(vii)에 의해 ∀x[[farmer(x)∧rich(x)]→K2']으로 번역된
다. K2'은 K2의 PL로의 번역이므로 ∃x[donkey(x)∧owns(x, y)]가 되어 (153)
의 번역은 ∀x[[farmer(x)∧rich(x)]→∃x[donkey(x)∧owns(x, y)]]이다. 이러한 과
정은 결국 조건문의 암시적 전칭 양화사가 조건문 전체를 그 범위로 가지
며, 조건문의 결과절은 default로 주어진 존재 양화사의 범위에 놓이게 된
다는 담화표상 이론의 양화 문제에 대한 접근방법을 충실히 반영하고 있
다. 즉, K1⇒K2의 PL로의 번역 과정은 ∀[K1→∃K2]에 상응하는 PL 표현을
부여하는 과정이라 하겠다.

　전칭 양화 구문으로부터 도출한 담화표상 조건 K1<every>K2는 K1⇒K2
와 동일하게 번역된다. 이 두 담화표상 조건은 전칭 양화사가 명시적으로
표현되었는가 암시적으로 이해되는가의 차이만 있을 뿐이다. 전칭 양화
구문의 양화 의미와 조응 관계는 양화사의 비선택적 구속, 변수로서의 비
한정 명사구와 조응 대명사, 핵범위에의 존재 양화사 부착 등의 기재를
통해 설명되며 K1⇒K2의 PL로의 번역 규칙 (141 b)-(viii)은 이러한 기재를
수용한 당연한 결과이다. 당나귀 문장 Every farmer who owns a donkey
beats it로부터 도출된 담화표상 조건 (154)는 PL 표현 (155)와 등가물인데
(155)는 이 당나귀 문장에 대한 원어민 화자의 직관을 정확히 표상하고 있

으므로 (154)는 주어진 당나귀 문장에 대한 타당한 표상이라고 볼 수 있다.

(154)

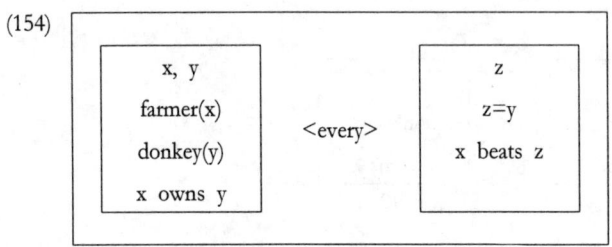

(155) $\forall x,\ y[[farmer(x) \wedge donkey(y) \wedge owns(x,\ y)] \rightarrow \exists z[z=y \wedge beats(x,\ z)]]$

PL 표현 (155)는 모형 M=<A, F>에서 x에 농부인 A의 어떤 개체를 사상하고 y에 당나귀인 어떤 개체를 사상하여 두 개체가 소유의 관계에 있게 하는 각 치할당 함수 f를 확장하는 함수 g가 최소한 하나 존재하여 g가 변수 z에 사상하는 개체가 함수 f가 y에 사상한 개체와 동일하고 함수 f가 x에 사상한 개체와 g가 z에 사상한 개체가 때리는 관계에 있을 때 표현 (155)는 참이 된다. 이러한 진리 조건은 4.3.1.2.에서 언급한 복합 담화표상 조건 K1<every>K2의 입증 조건과 동일하다.

4.5. 요약

이 장에서 담화의 통사 분석에 담화표상 구성 규칙이 작용하여 도출한 담화표상이 어떤 모형 M에 비추어 참이 되는 진리 조건을 살펴보았다. 어떤 담화표상 K는 K를 주어진 모형 M에 내포시키는 함수 f가 하나 이상 존재할 때, 이 모형 내에서 참이 된다. 어떤 함수 f가 K의 담화 지시체들을 M의 개체들에 사상하고 사상된 각 개체가 담화표상 조건들을 M 내에서 참임을 입증할 때 함수 f는 담화표상 K를 모형 M에 내포시킨다고 말

한다. 제 3장에서 언급한 담화표상 구성 규칙에 의하여 도입되는 각 담화
표상 조건에 대한 입증 조건을 살펴 본 후, 이러한 입증 조건들이 담화표
상 이론의 양화 문제에 대한 기본 가정들을 어떤 방식으로 구현하고 있는
가를 분석하였다.

담화표상이론의 확장

-담화표상이론에서의 배분성과 양화문제

Chapter 1. Introduction

1.1. Purpose and Scope

Kamp(1981) and Heim(1982) have introduced a new perspective on NP semantics by arguing that an indefinite NP is a variable but not a quantifying expression with existential quantificational force. Their semantic theory is generally called Discourse Representation Theory (DRT). As Heim(1990) points out, the term DRT refers to any semantic theories which take the assumptions[1] described in (1).

(1) (i)   Indefinites are bound variables.

     (ii) Anaphoric pronouns are plain bound variables.

     (iii) Quantificational determiners and the conditional operator are capable of binding multiple variables.

     (iv) Default existential generalization (existential closure in Heim (1982)) of free variables is needed.

These assumptions can be formalized in various ways, for example, by adopting Kamp (1981)'s system or Heim (1982)'s File-Changing semantics.

Kamp and Reyle (1990), who classify indefinite NPs into quantificational and non-quantificational, extend the DRT proposed in Kamp (1981) to cope with the NPs with various determiners such as *many, few, some, two*, etc.. They treat every quantificational NP as introducing a pair of DRSs. An individual discourse referent is introduced into the universe of the first DRS of the pair. For example, sentence (2) which contains a quantificational indefinite NP *every student* is reduced into DRS (3). The two DRSs are connected by the quantifier *every*.

(2)   Every student came in.

(3)

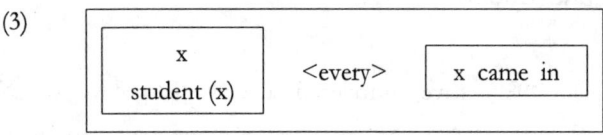

A non-quantificational indefinite NP introduces an individual discourse referent when it is singular (for example, *a student*) or a non-individual discourse referent when it is plural (for example, *two students*). The cardinality information which specifies how many atoms a group individual (or individual-sum, i-sum) has is represented as a DRS condition. Sentence (4) has two readings such that there were two students who individually lifted a piano (distributive reading) and a group of two students lifted a piano together (collective reading). DRS (5) represents the collective reading of sentence (4).

(4)   Two students lifted a piano.

(5)

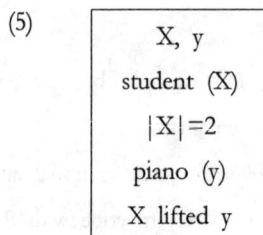

A non-quantificational NP can be followed by a distributive predicate as in (6). Sentence (6) reads that every member of a group of two students came in; that is, there are two individuals which are students and they both came in.

(6)   Two students came in.

Kamp and Reyle devise a DR construction rule which stipulates that when a non-individual discourse referent is followed by a distributive predicate, a pair of sub-DRSs be introduced. In the first sub-DRS (or the antecedent DRS) of the pair, a new discourse referent is introduced with conditions that the discourse referent is atomic and is an i-part of the non-individual discourse referent. Sentence (6) is first reduced into DRS (7) which is, in turn, further reduced into DRS (8) by the rule of Distributivity Expansion.[2] DRS(8) represents the reading that there is an i-sum consisting of 2 atomic individuals which are students and each of the i-parts of the i-sum came.

(7)   (8)

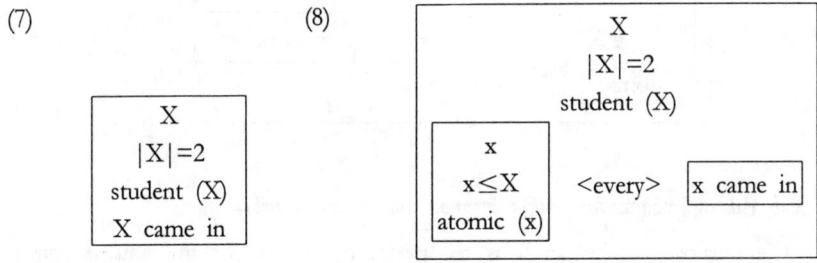

Note that the distributive reading of a sentence is captured either by the quantification as in DRS (3) or by Distributivity Expansion as in DRS (8). Roberts (1987), Root (1986), Kadmon (1987) and others also take this stand. I will call this approach *a non-unified approach toward the distributivity*.

In this study, I take the stance that the distributivity of sentence (2) is the same in nature as the distributivity of sentence (6). In both sentences, the distributivity is assigned when a distributive predicate takes an individual, atomic or i-sum, as its argument. In DRT terms, the distributivity is the result of Distributivity Expansion both in sentence (2) and in sentence (6). That is, the indefinite NP *every student* of sentence (2) introduces a non-individual discourse referent as *two students* of sentence (6) does. Then, sentence (2) should be reduced into DRS (9) rather than into DRS (8). The DRS condition $|X| = |student|$ represents the information that the discourse referent X must be mapped into an i-sum which has the same number of atomic individuals as the number of atomic individuals which are student.

(9)

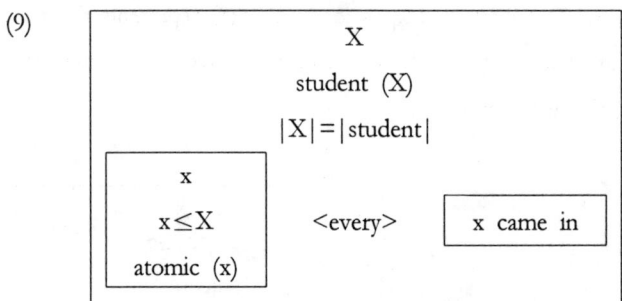

I call this approach *the unified approach toward the distributivity.*

The purpose of this study is to specify the system of the unified approach and to show that it should replace the non-unified approach by comparing the two approaches against some data of English and Korean. In short, I am going to argue for the hypothesis that every indefinite NP is translated into a variable. In Kamp's term, the hypothesis is that every indefinite NP introduces an individual or a non-individual discourse referent depending on the semantic number of the NP. (Later, I will address how the semantic number of an NP is determined.)

As a natural consequence of the hypothesis, quantificational forces cannot be provided by linguistic determiners since NPs with these determiners introduce just a variable of a quantifier-variable construction. Quantificational forces are provided either by default existential closure (existential closure in Heim (1982)'s sense) or by Distributivity Expansion (in this case, the universal quantifier is provided). I also assume that anaphoric pronouns are plain bound variables and that quantifiers can bind multiple variables (unselective binding), following Kamp (1981) and Heim (1982).

I will do two things in Chapter 2. The first is to examine the criteria for the classification of NPs into quantificational and non-quantificational (or quantificational and individual-denoting in Roberts' term). Since Roberts provides a set of such criteria, and Kamp and Reyle do not give explicit criteria for it, I will mainly examine and criticize the criteria provided by Roberts (1987). The second is to critically review how Roberts or Kamp and Reyle (I take theirs as typical non-unified approaches) deal with the following three sets of data.

(A)   Data about Number Agreement between a Pronoun and its Antecedent

Let's assume that a singular pronoun introduces an individual discourse referent which is to be linked to an accessible individual discourse referent, and that a plural pronoun introduces a non-individual discourse referent which is to be linked to an accessible non-individual discourse referent. Then, a non-unified approach, say Kamp and Reyle's approach, can explain the acceptability of sentences (10) and (11) since NPs *a student* and *every student* introduce a discourse referent. But sentences (12) and (13) are problematic since the NP *most students* introduces an individual discourse referent and *some students* introduces either a non-individual discourse referent or an individual discourse referent via Distributivity Expansion (in this case, *his teacher* must be judged acceptable in (13)).

(10)   [A student]$_i$ respects his$_i$/#their$_i$ teacher.

(11)   [Every student]$_i$ respects his$_i$/#their$_i$ teacher.[3]

(12)   [Most (Many, Few, All) students]$_i$ respect their$_i$/#his$_i$ teacher.

(13)   [Some (Several, Five) students]$_i$ respect their$_i$/#his$_i$ teacher.

The contrast between sentence (14) and sentence (15) shows another problem. The pronoun *they* is acceptable when it is not in the scope of *every student* (or is not c-commanded by *every student*) as in (15).

(14)   [A student]$_i$ came in. #They$_i$ gathered in the hall.

(15)   [Every student]$_i$ came in. They$_i$ gathered in the hall.

In sentence (15), the predicate *gathered in the hall* requires a non-individual discourse referent. Then, pronoun *they* must be reduced into a non-individual discourse referent which is to be linked to an accessible non-individual discourse referent. If *every student* introduces only an individual discourse referent, how can the pronoun be anaphorically related to its antecedent?

I will examine how Kamp and Reyle deal with the problems related to plural pronouns and criticize their approach.

(B)   Data about the Mode of Predication

As a line of departure, I will assume that there are three kinds of predicates (or VPs): distributive predicates which can take an atomic individual or an i-sum as its argument (for example, *is asleep*), collective predicates which require an i-sum as its argument (for example, *gathered in the hall*, *lifted a piano*, *together*) and ambiguous ones which are sometimes distributive and sometimes collective (for example, *built a cabin*, *lifted a piano*). This classification is also accepted in Frey and Kamp (1986), Root (1986) and Dowty (1986). Now, the acceptability or the unacceptability of sentences (16), (17) and (18) is explained by the non-unified approach. But sentence (19) is problematic since NP *most students* does not introduce a non-individual discourse referent in this approach.

(16)   #A student gathered in the hall.

(17)   #Every student gathered in the hall.

(18)   Some (Several, Five) students gathered in the hall.

(19)   Most (Many, Few, All, At least 5) students gathered in the hall.

(C)   Data about the Predication with Ambiguous Predicates

An ambiguous predicate like *built a cabin* can take an atomic individual as well as an individual-sum as its argument. When it takes an atomic individual, a distributive reading is necessarily assigned. When it takes an i-sum as its argument, a distributive or a collective reading is assigned as in (20) and (21).

(20)   John built a cabin.

(21)   John and Bill built a cabin.

   (i)   John built a cabin and Bill did, too.

   (ii)   John and Bill as a group built a cabin.

When some quantificational NPs such as *every farmer* and *most farmers* are followed by an ambiguous predicate, only a distributive reading is obtained. That is, sentences (22) and (23) have as their readings (22-i) and (23-i) but not (22-ii) and (23-ii). This result is predicted by the non-unified approach since a quantificational NP introduces only an individual discourse referent.

(22)   Every farmer built a cabin.

    (i)   For all individual farmers x, x built a cabin.

    (ii)   All the farmers as a group built a cabin.

(23)   Most farmers of the town built a cabin.

    (i)   For most farmers x, x built a cabin.

    (ii)   The majority of the farmers of the town as a group built a cabin.

However, when other quantificational NPs including *many farmers*, *few farmers*, *all farmers* and *at least five farmers* in Kamp and Reyle's system are followed by an ambiguous predicate, both readings are possible as in (24) and (25). If the NPs *many farmers* and *at least five farmers* are unambiguously quantificational as in Kamp and Reyle's system, these sentences are problematic to the non-unified approach (Kamp and Reyle treat *many* and *at least five* as quantificational).[4]

(24)   Many farmers lifted a huge rock.

    (i)   They individually lifted a huge rock.

    (ii)   They as a group lifted a huge rock.

(25)   At least five farmers lifted a huge rock.

    (i)   They individually lifted a huge rock.

    (ii)   They as a group lifted a huge rock.

In Chapter 3, I will first specify the system of the non-quantificational approach. I will classify NPs according to the kind of predicates which are able to follow them. Then, I will show how to represent them on a DRS. Secondly, I will show how the system explains the data provided above.

Chapters 4 and 5 are intended to provide further evidence for my approach specified in Chapter 3. In Chapter 4, I will deal with the set of data about the proportion problem in Kadmon (1987)'s term (Rooth (1986) calls it "asymmetric quantification").

D.   Data about Asymmetric Readings of Quantificational Determiners

Sentence (26) is false under the situation where 99 farmers own exactly one donkey each, and they do not beat the donkeys they own, and yet one farmer who has 200 donkeys beats all of the donkeys he owns.

(26)   Most farmers who own a donkey beat it.

If *most* is a quantificational determiner which can unselectively bind free variables in its scope, sentence (26) is reduced into DRS (27).

(27)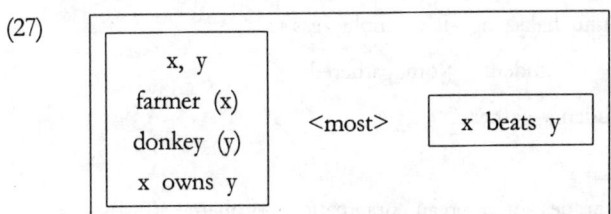

DRS (27) is true iff for most donkey-farmer pairs, the farmer beats the donkey. However, sentence (26) is true iff most donkey-owning farmers beat every donkey they own (cf. Heim 1990). This problem was noticed and diverse solutions were suggested by many linguists — Kadmon (1987, 1990), Partee (1990), Kratzer (1989), Reinhart (19), Chierchia (1993), and Kamp and Reyle (1990), to name a few. In this chapter I will take Kamp and Reyle's approach as a typical non-unified one, and I will compare their approach with mine (a unified account).

E.   Data about a Korean Determiner Kak (every) and a Pragmatic Morpheme -*Tul*

In Chapter 5, I will deal with the fact that Korean NP *kak haksayng* (every student) cannot be followed by a collective predicate such as *mohi-ess-ta* (gathered) but requires a distributive predicate as shown in (28).

(28)   a. #kak haksayng-i   mohi -ess -ta.
             every student Nom gather past IND
             'Every student gathered.'
        b. Modun haksayng -i   mohi-ess-ta.
             all   student Nom gathered
             'All students gathered.'
        c. Taybubunui haksayng -i   mohi -ess-ta.
             most   student Nom gathered
             'Most students gathered.'

As Lee, H. (1992) argues, a Korean pragmatic morpheme (PM)-*tul* can be attached to an adverbial when the triggering NP is semantically plural as in (29).

(29)   a. #John -i ppali   -tul o   -ess -ta.
             Nom quickly PM come past IND
          'John came quickly.'

       b. John -kwa Mary-ka   ppali -tul o   -ess -ta
               and   Nom quickly PM come past IND
          'John and Mary came quickly.'

However, NPs with *kak* can trigger the introduction of PM *-tul* as in (30).

(30)   Kak haksayng -i   ppali -tul o -ess-ta.
       every student Nom quickly PM came
       'Every student came quickly.'

If an NP with *kak* cannot be followed by a collective predicate because the NP does not introduce a non-individual discourse referent (this position would be taken by the non-unified approach if we try to extend its account of the unacceptability of "Every student gathered" to Korean), sentence (30) is problematic since PM -tul requires a semantically plural NP as its trigger.

Chapter 6 will be the conclusion of the theses.

1.2. Theoretical Framework—DRT

In this section, I will specify some notions and devices in DRT which the two approaches mentioned above have in common. One who is familiar with Kamp and Reyle (1990)'s work (or with Kamp (1981)) can safely ignore this part.

1.2.1. Discourse Referents

The term 'Discourse referent' originated in Karttunen (1976)[5]. It is distinct from an entity in a model (or in the real world). It refers to an entity in a DRS and is linked to an entity in a model by some function (embedding function; a discourse representation is regarded as a partial model). In this sense, a discourse referent is like a variable in predicate logic. Accordingly, a discourse referent can be linked to two or more entities in the model according to embedding functions (for example, for a discourse referent x, embedding function f1 links it to an entity a, and f2, to b, etc.) and two or more distinct discourse referents can be linked to the same entity.

Webber (1979)'s 'discourse entity' (she reserved the term referent to stand for a real world entity which a linguistic expression refers to) and Heim (1982)'s file-card express the same concept as 'discourse referent'. To make clearer the notion discourse referent, let's examine Heim's file-card metaphor. In a conversation, the task of a hearer is just like that of a secretary who updates her file consisting of some file cards in it. Suppose a hearer starts with an empty file which has no file-cards. Now, he hears an utterance (31).

(31)　　(a) A woman was bitten by a dog.

　　　　(b) She hit it.　　　　(Heim 1987, p.167)

The hearer puts into the file two file-cards which have an index and appropriate information when he hears sentence (a).

(32)

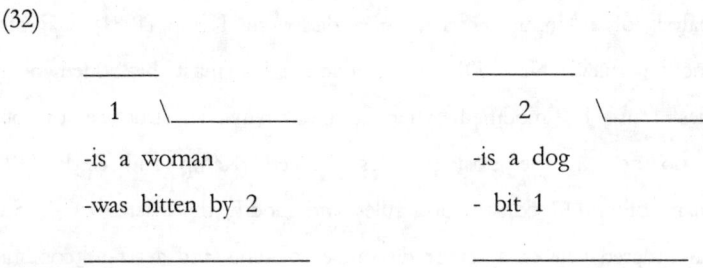

```
        ___                              ___
    1  _____              2    _____
    -is a woman                   -is a dog
    -was bitten by 2              - bit 1

    _____            _____
```

When he hears sentence (b), he updates them accordingly.

(33)

```
        ___                               ___
    1  _____               2    _____
    -is a woman                   -is a dog
    -was bitten by 2              -bit 1
    -hit 2                        -was hit by 1

    _____            _____
```

The file-cards represent some entities in a model which satisfy the conditions recorded on the cards. In the same vein, Webber (1983) uses the metaphor of a 'conceptual coathook' on which to "hang descriptions of the entity's real world or hypothetical world correspondent".

1.2.2. DR Construction Rules

DRT consists of 3 main parts: generative syntax, DR construction rules, and semantics defined in terms of an (proper) embedding (Kamp 1981). Among them, DR construction rules are a set of rules which derive a DRS from the syntactic analysis of an input sentence or a discourse. Kamp (1981) suggests 5 DR construction rules.[6] New DR construction rules must be added or the existing rules must be modified when a new syntactic structure or other expressions do not fit the existing rules. Indeed, Kamp and Reyle (1990) introduce many other DR construction rules and modify the existing rules. Since a DRS is an ordered pair of a set of discourse referents and a set of conditions on the discourse referents (<U, CON>), the DR construction rules are stated in relation to discourse referents and the conditions on them. For example, the DR Construction rule for a proper noun is informally stated as in (34). For other rules, see Kamp (1981).

(34)   DR Construction Rule for a Proper Noun

CR1. Suppose α is a proper name.

STEP 1.   Add a new discourse referent u to the universe of the main DRS.

STEP 2.   Add a condition u=α to the set of conditions (CON) of the main DRS.

STEP 3.   Add the condition ϕ' to the CON of the current DRS where ϕ' is the result of replacing α with u in ϕ, where ϕ is a syntactic analysis of a sentence.

DR construction rules reduce a syntactic analysis of a sentence to a complete DRS by recursively applying to it until there are no elements to be reduced further by DR construction rules (Reduction is a process to convert a sentence or a discourse into a DRS by applying DR construction rules). A syntactic analysis of a sentence is reduced in a top-down and left-to-right manner.

Kamp and Reyle (1990) defines a DR Construction rule by specifying (i) its triggering configuration or configurations and (ii) its modus operandi, manner of reducing the input configuration. For example, CR 1 of (34) is redefined as in (35). $\gamma \subseteq \bar{\gamma} \in$ ConK represents that "γ is the configuration that triggers the application of the rule and $\bar{\gamma}$ is the treated condition that contains it as a subtree (Kamp and Reyle 1990, p.116)."

(35)   CR. PN (proper noun)

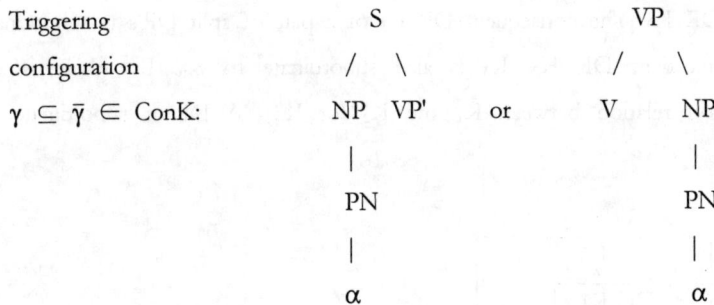

| Triggering configuration $\gamma \subseteq \bar{\gamma} \in$ ConK: | S / \ NP VP' \| PN \| α | or | VP / \ V NP \| PN \| α |

Introduce into the universe
of the main DRS: new discourse referent u

Introduce into the condition
set of the main DRS: new condition $\alpha(u)$

                                                              NP
                                                               |
Substitute in $\bar{\gamma}$:   u   for   PN
                                                               |
                                                              α

I will use this convention when there is a need to define a new DR Construction rule in the discussion.

1.2.3. Anaphora Resolution in DRT

Anaphoric resolution is a process in which a discourse referent introduced by an anaphoric expression is linked to an appropriate discourse referent among structurally accessible ones. A DR K is accessible to another DR K' iff K' is subordinate to K. In a schematic DRS (36), a nested DR K_1 is subordinate to the main DR K_0. The consequent DR K_3 of a pair of split DR's is subordinate to the antecedent DR K_2. K_3 is also subordinate to K_0. But there is no subordination relation between K_1 and K_2 (or K3). A DR is subordinate to itself.

(36)

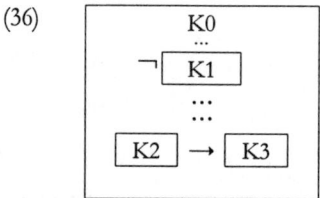

Then, K_0 is accessible only to itself, K_1 and K_2 are accessible to K_0 and themselves, and K_3 is accessible to K_2, K_0 and itself. That is, the accessibility relation is partially ordered (reflexive, transitive, anti-symmetric). A discourse referent of a DR K is accessible to a discourse referent of a DR which is accessible from DR K.

Selecting an appropriate discourse referent among accessible discourse referents is a complicated process. First, two discourse referents capable of being linked to each other (for example, x=y) must agree in their indexical values such as person, gender and number (more accurately, their values must be compatible). In this study I will include the number information for convenience's sake in the definition of accessibility such that a discourse referent is accessible to a discourse referent y iff they agree in number and they are "configurationally accessible" as defined above.

Semantic and pragmatic information is necessary to select an appropriate discourse referent which is linked to a discourse referent introduced by an anaphoric expression. I will not deal with this topic in this thesis.

1.2.4. Semantics

Kamp and Reyle (pp.226-227) give the semantics of DRT in terms of embedding functions from a DRS K into a model M which is an ordered set <D,F> where D is a set of individuals and F an interpretation function. I will follow their system in this study in general. Informally, a DRS K is true iff the DRS is compatible with a model with respect to which the DRS is evaluated. DRS K is compatible with model M iff it is a partial model of M. That is, when every individual of DRS K is in the universe of M and every condition on these individuals is satisfied in the model, DRS K is compatible with model M. However, DRS entities are discourse referents which act like bound variables. If a function f assigns an individual of the universe of the model to every discourse referent of DRS K, and those individuals satisfy in model M the conditions specified on DRS K, then, we say that the function f properly embeds DRS K into model M. Now, DRS K is true iff there is at least one embedding function f from DRS K onto model M.

Suppose a DRS which has a sub-DRS as its condition like (37).

(37)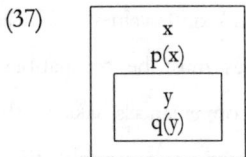

Let f be an embedding function for the main DRS, and g be an embedding function for the sub-DRS. Then, f and g must be related in some way. f maps x onto an individual **a** of a model M. But it is not specified onto which individual of M f maps y. g maps y onto **an individual b** of M. If g maps x onto an individual **c** of M instead of **a**, a crash occurs because f maps x onto **a** and g maps it onto **c** (a≠c). To be compatible with f, g must map x onto **a**. When two embedding functions f and g are compatible, and g is just the same as f except that it maps the discourse referents of the sub-DRS onto some individuals of M, we say that g extends f (or g is an extension of f). Let the domain of an embedding function f (represented as Dom(f)) be the set of all the discourse referents which f maps onto individuals of M. Now DRS (37) is true iff there is at least one embedding function f which (i) maps x onto **a**, a member of property p in M; (ii) there is at least one embedding function g which extends f in the way that the domain of g is the union of the domain of f (that is, {x}) and the set of discourse referents of the sub-DRS (that is, {y}), {x} ∪ {y} ={x,y}; (iii) g maps y onto **b**; (iv) **b** is a member of a property q in M; (v) and **a** likes **b** in M. In this case, we say that f verifies condition *p(x)*, and g verifies conditions *p(x)*, *q(y)*, and *x likes y*. When an embedding function f verifies all the conditions of a DRS K, we say f verifies DRS K. Then, in this case, g verifies DRS (31).

Verification conditions of a pair of split DRS's can be given similarly. Let K1 ⇒ K2 be a discourse condition where K1 and K2 are DRS's. Then K1 ⇒ K2 is verified iff for every embedding function f which verifies K1, there is at least one embedding function g which extends f, and g verifies K2. (Dom(f)=the universe of K1 (U_{k1}), Dom(g) = Dom(f) $\cup$ U_{k2})[7]

1.3. Plural Individuals

1.3.1. Plural Individuals

In Bennett (1974), a plural NP is treated as denoting a set of individuals. Following Montague (1974), Bennett assigns to a singular NP a denotation of type <<e,t>,t>, a set of sets of individuals.[8] Similarly, a plural NP denotes a set of sets of sets of individuals, an entity of <<<e,t>,t>,t> type. This treatment inevitably proliferates linguistic categories. For example, the category CN (common nouns) is divided into 2 types: singular CN (represented by CN) which is type <e,t> and plural CN (represented by $\overline{CN}$) which is of type <<e,t>,t>. Then, determiners must be categorized into singular determiners (DET) and plural determiners ($\overline{DET}$) to make singular NPs and plural NPs. With the same reason, we need plural VPs ($\overline{VP}$) as well as singular ones, plural prepositions as well as singular ones, and so forth. Besides the proliferation of types, his system should be relaxed to include the coordination between different types because it is natural to conjoin a singular NP with a plural one as in (38).

(38)   a. John and many students

b. John and the children

c. a teacher and five students

(for other criticisms on Bennett's treatment of plural, see Roberts (1987, pp.116-124).)

The idea that a conjoined NP denotes a new type of individual was first introduced in linguistic analyses by Massey (1976). He adopts the mereology of Leonard and Goodman (1940) who treat 'John and Bill' as denoting a third individual where John and Bill are parts of it but not a set of individuals {John, Bill}. The summing operation represented by + in Massey (1976) makes a new individual from other individuals. He does not distinguish the type of a plural NP from the type of singular one. That is, a conjoined NP (or, more generally, a plural NP) and a singular NP are the same in their types.

Link (1983) is basically in the same position as Massey (1776). He assumes that plural individuals (or individual sums, i-sum) are individuals of a new kind, not a set of individuals.[9] Landman (1987) takes the position that a plural NP denotes a set of individuals assuming that a singular term denotes a singleton set.[10] That is, 'John' refers to a singleton {j} instead of an individual j. However, if we set aside the ontological differences, the two approaches of Link and Landman explain the same range of data (cf. Kamp and Reyle, 1990).[11] I just take Link's position that a plural term denotes an individual-sum.

1.3.2. Nature of Plural Individuals

Here, I am going to make an assumption on the nature of a plural individual (or i-sum). Consider (39). In a theory which treats an NP *some men* as quantificational, (39) is true under the situation where there are at least two men who came in. That is, the cardinality of the intersection of the set of all the students and the set of all things which came in must be greater than or equal to 2 for (39) to be true. It does not require that more than two men came in at the same time, or as a group. In other words, the subject NP *some men* need not be any spatio-temporally regulated group of men.

(39)   Some men came in.

In a theory where the NP *some men* is treated as denoting an i-sum, sentence (39) is true iff at least one set of men whose cardinality is greater than or equal to 2 came in. If the truth conditions of (39) required that the set of men be a spatio-temporally regulated group of men, sentence (39) would be false if a man came in at 10 o'clock in the morning, and another man came in 3 o'clock in the afternoon, and no other men came in. But it is against the intuition of native speakers. So, I assume that a set (or a plural entity) need not be a spatio-temporally regulated entity. Then, sentence (40) can describe the two situations of (41) in a non-quantificational approach.

(40)   Three students met the principal.

(41)   a. Three students met the principal at the same time.
        b. Three students met the principal one by one.

1.3.3. Properties of Summing Operation

Link (1983, 1984, and 1987) develops lattice-theoretic semantics adopting summing operation and individual sum into his system. Following him, I will use the term *individual sum* to represent the denotation of a plural NP. The sign $\oplus$ is for the summing operation in the intensional language (its counterpart in semantics is V_i). Then, *John and Bill* is represented by j $\oplus$ b where j and b are translations of *John* and *Bill*, respectively. The properties of summing operation are as follows.[12]

(42)   Properties of Summing Operation

    Idempotency (a $\oplus$ a =a), as taking the sum of John and himself would not yield a new object.

    Commutativity (a $\oplus$ b = b $\oplus$ a), as *John and Mary met* is true just in case *Mary and John met* is true, and hence the two subject NP's should denote the same object

    Associativity (a $\oplus$ (b $\oplus$ c) = (a $\oplus$ b) $\oplus$ c), as *John, and Mary and Bill met* is true just in case *John and Mary, and Bill met* is true. Hence, the two subject NP's should denote the same object.

(Krifka, 1991, p.73)

An individual-sum has a part-whole relation to its members. Let a 2-place predicate Π be an i(ndividual)-part relation which expresses the "intrinsic ordering relation '$\leq_i$' on E" (Link 1983, p.307). The relation 'a is an i-part of b' is expressed as in (43).

(43)   a Π b $\leftrightarrow$ a $\oplus$ b = b

Since this relation is homomorphic to the relation 'is less than or equal to ($\leq$)' it has the following properties.

    Reflexive: a Π a

Antisymmetric: a Π b & b Π a $\leftrightarrow$ a = b

Transitive: a Π b & b Π c $\rightarrow$ a Π c

That is, the relation 'is an i-part of' is partially ordered. Among i-parts, atomic i-parts have special importance, which is defined as in (44).

(44)   Ata $\leftrightarrow$ $\forall$x(x Π a $\rightarrow$ x = a) where Ata represents that a is an atomic individual.

1.3.4. Model Structure Incorporating i-sums

As usual in modeltheoretic semantics, a model M is defined as an ordered pair of <A, F> where A is a set of individuals of a discourse (universe of the model) and F, interpretation functions. Now, the universe A is expanded so as to incorporate the complex individuals (i-sums) as well as atomic individuals. In other words, a model M is defined as in (45).[13, 14, 15, 16, 17]

(45)   M = <<A, V_i, $\leq_i$, AT>, F>

          where A is a complete free atomic join semi lattice closed
          under V_i, $\leq_i$, and AT. (AT: set of atomic individuals)

                              (cf. Link 1983, Link 1987)

V_i is a join operator which forms a summed individual (i-sum) from 2 or more individuals (atomic or non-atomic). In this study, I will use the symbol + instead of Vi. Then, a+b is a complex individual generated from individuals a and b. The symbol $\leq_i$ is the partial order understood as the part-whole relation between 2 individuals.

The universe of a model is a complete atomic free semi join lattice generated from the set of atomic individuals. It means that (i) the universe is finite because it is complete,[18] (ii) any two individuals, each of which contains at least one distinct atomic individuals as its parts are different from each other (since it is free), (iii) there is no such element (or individual) which is a part of every individual since it is a semi join lattice, and (iv) as a consequence of (iii), a singular individual such as j for 'John' is atomic, and the whole lattice is generated by a set of atomic individuals. For example, if AT is a set of three atomic individuals, a, b, and c, then the universe of the model is a set of all the individuals which consists of a, b, c and all the i-sums illustrated in (46).

(46)   AT = {a,b,c}

complete atomic free semi join lattice generated by AT

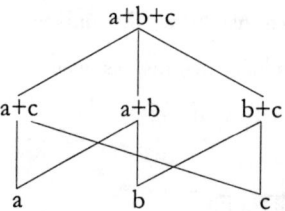

A = {a, b, c, a+b, a+c, b+c, a+b+c}

The interpretation function F assigns an atomic individual to a singular term, and an i-sum (non-atomic individual) to a plural term. To a 1-place predicate, it assigns a set of atomic individuals, a set of i-sums, or a set of atomic individuals and i-sums, according to its kind. To a n-place predicate, it assigns n-tuples of appropriate kinds of individuals.

1.3.5. Uncommutative/Unassociative NP Conjunctions

Following Link (1983), I defined the universe of a model incorporating i-sums as a complete free join semi-lattice generated from atomic individuals of the universe. If the summing operation is not associative or not commutative, the individuals generated by the summing operation does not form such a lattice. For example, if a+b is differentiated from b+a, we might have to assume four individuals (a, b, a+b, b+a) which do not constitute even a semi lattice since in a semi lattice, any two individuals must have one and only one supremum. And if the summing operation is not associative, an i-sum (a+b)+c must be differentiated from an i-sum a+(b+c). If these i-sums are elements of a lattice, the lattice is not atomic since an i-sum (a+b)+c consists of an i-sum and an atom.

In natural languages, some NP conjunctions do not observe the commutativity. The truth conditions of sentence (47) are different from those of sentence (48).

(47)   Tom and Bill love Mary and Susan, respectively.

(48)   Bill and Tom love Mary and Susan, respectively.

In some NP conjunctions, the associativity is violated as in (50) and (51).

(50)   Napoleon and [Wellington and Blücher] fought against each other on Waterloo Plain.

(51)   [Napoleon and Wellington] and Blücher fought against each other on Waterloo Plain.

In this study I want to maintain the assumption that the universe of a model is a complete atomic free semi join lattice generated by summing operation from the set of atomic individuals of the model. In this respect, I will generally follow Krifka (1991) who argues that the universe of a model is a complete free join semi lattice while the summing operation in a DRS is uncommutative. That is, in a DRS, a non-individual discourse referent x $\oplus$ y is distinguished from a non-individual discourse referent y $\oplus$ x. Then, an embedding function f assigns the same individual, say, **a+b**, to them.

Link(1984) introduces new plural entities called 'group individuals' in addition to sum individuals(i-sums). A group individual (or a group) is regarded as an atomic individual. It differs from an i-sum in some aspects. The main motivation of introducing the notion is the existence of collective nouns such as *committee, family, parliament*, etc.. These entities are different from i-sum individuals obtained through the sum operation.[19]

The problem of the unassociativity of conjunction is solved by admitting the group (formation) operation while retaining the property of associativity of the sum operation. In sentence (50), the group operation applies to the i-sum of w+b (Wellington and Blücher), yielding a group $\uparrow$ (w+b). Then, the conjunct Napoleon and Wellington and Blücher denotes an i-sum of n+ $\uparrow$ (w+b) which is distinct from $\uparrow$ (n+w)+b. Since a group is an atomic individual, the problem of unassociativity disappears.[20]

The universe of a model must be enlarged to include the group individuals. Link (1984) assumes two disjoint sets of atoms, the set of pure atoms (AT_p) and the set of impure atoms (AT_i). An impure atom, a group individual, is formed from an i-sum by the group formation operator. The atoms, pure and impure, generate a free complete semi join lattice. This lattice is the universe of the model.

He does not allow the iterative group formation. But Landman (1989) argues that it is needed to describe the semantics of a natural language. In (52) the group of the committees of the State Department is controlling the group of the committees of the CIA, and vice versa. That is, the subject NP denotes a sum of two groups.

(52)   The committees of the State Department and the committees of the CIA control each other. (Landman 1989, p.579)

Since a committee is a group, a group of groups must be in the universe of a model. That is, the iterative group formation must be allowed. According to Landman, the universe of a model must be large enough to allow an indefinite iteration of the group formation. Then the whole structure of the universe is no longer a complete join semi lattice because the whole lattice itself does not have a supremum.

The iterative group formation proposed in Landman (1989) is mainly motivated by the existence of collective nouns such as *committee, family*, some terms about organizational institutes, etc.. Landman gives examples of iterative groups by citing some terms in *Das Kapital: The Farmers* and *the City-proletarians* are type-1 groups; *The Working Classes* consisting of the farmers and the city proletarians is type-2 groups; The State consisting of the working classes and the exploiting classes is a type-3 group, and *The States of Central Europe* and *the States of Western Europe* who distrust each other is a type-4 group.

However, Krifka (1991) argues that the relationship between a group individual denoted by a collective NP (collective objects in Krifka's term) and its members is not systematic: assume that j and m are pure atomic individuals of a model. Then, j and m may join to form different couples, committees, societies, etc. (Krifka 1991, p.83). That is, an i-sum can be mapped into infinitely many collective objects. If the group formation operation ↑ is an injection, a one-to-one function as specified in Landman (1989), the operation cannot be regarded as an operation from an i-sum to a collective object because the mapping of an i-sum into a collective object is not a function. When this operation applies to an i-sum **a+b**, it must uniquely generate a group ↑**(a+b)**. Thus, it is reasonable to assume that the group formation operation applies to an i-sum and generates the unique group from it. Consequently, it means that a collective object denoted by a collective NP is not obtained from an i-sum by the operation.

I, following Krifka (1991), assume that a collective NP denotes a collective object and that the membership relation among members of a collective object is defined appropriately. Then, the group formation operation applies only to an i-sum, yielding a group. The i-sum is obtained by NP conjunction or by the plural quantification. Now, the plural entities are of 3 kinds − i-sums, collective objects and groups. Collective objects and groups participate in the lattice formation as atoms.

Notes to Chapter 1

1. Heim (1990) states that indefinites and anaphoric pronouns are (un)bound variables. DRT differentiates indefinite NPs from quantificational NPs as stated in (1). At the outset of DRT, this classification did not cause any problems because only two extreme cases of the two categories – *a(n) CN* and *every CN* – were treated. However, as Heim(1982, p.267) points out, a quantifying NP is also an indefinite NP. Then, the assumption (1-i) must be further restricted to the extend that indefinite NPs whose determiners are not quantifying are bound variables. In this study, I just follow the tradition that indefinite NPs refer to some "noble" entities which are not familiar to the speaker and (or) the hearer.

2. I will deal with distributivity and some related problems in Chapter 3.

3. Here, I do not consider the non-sexist usage of pronoun *they*. It is reported that *they* is used instead of *he* to prevent a sexist's implication. I will deal with this matter, later.

4. As professor Zucchi pointed out to me, the data are not problematic if these NPs are treated as having a cardinal reading. That is, if these NPs introduce either a non-individual discourse referent or an individual one, the data are explained. However, I stick to the proposition that NPs are not ambiguous in their reading following Kamp and Reyle and Roberts (1987).

5. Karttunen (1976) classifies discourse referents introduced by indefinites into two categories – permanent referents and short-term referents. Permanent discourse referents are introduced by (1) indefinites with the widest scope and

(2) non-specific (not having the widest scope) indefinites in an affirmative sentence "Just in case the proposition represented by the sentence is asserted, implied, or presupposed by the speaker". Short-term referents whose "life span is limited in a certain domain" are introduced when an indefinite is in the scope of other quantifiers or when it is in the scope of modals or propositional attitude verbs.

6. DR Construction rules for proper names, singular indefinite NPs, universal NPs, anaphoric pronouns and conditional constructions.

7. For more verification conditions, see Kamp and Reyle (1990). Verification conditions for other DRS's will be given in the discussion whenever required.

8. In this study, I will not deal with the intensionality. Bennett (1974) actually assigns intensional types to those expressions.

9. In this respect, he follows the nominalist tradition which maintains that there are no entities except individuals.

10. It is known as Quine's innovation. Cf. Quine (1960).

11. Link's arguments for a new kind of individuals are summarized in Landman (1989, p.565).

> 1. Sets are abstract objects, while plural individuals can be regarded as concrete entities.

2. If John, Paul and Mary is a set then the following sentence should be true, but it seems strange.

John, Paul and Mary has three elements.

3. The denotation of a singular and plural terms should be treated on a par: the following question can be answered with a plural as easily as with a singular:

Who made a mess of the living room?   David/My kids

It implies that a singular term must be of the same type as a plural term (cf. Bennett, 1974).

4. There are undeniable analogies between plural terms and mass terms. It is impossible to treat mass terms in a set theoretic framework.

5. "In general (...) the introduction of a collective term (...) is indicative of connotations being added enough for it to refer to a different individual; for instance, a committee is not just a collection of its members, etc.. ... There might be two different committees which necessarily consist of the same members (Link 1983, p304)."

Landman (1989) also points out some problems in Link's arguments for introducing i-sums into the semantics of plurals.

12. In some situations, commutativity and associativity are not observed in natural language coordination. Sentence (i) and sentence (ii) have different truth conditions. Here, the associativity of the summing operation is violated.

(i) Napoleon and [Wellington and Blücher] fought against each other on Waterloo Plain.

(ii) [Napoleon and Wellington] and Blücher fought against each other on Waterloo Plain.

Several solutions have been proposed to this phenomenon. Link (1984) and Landman (1989) maintain that the summing operation is still associative in this case and propose the group formation operation which converts an i-sum into a group. Then, in (i), the summing operation takes two arguments, n denoted by Napoleon and a group formed from w+b. Thus, sentence (i) does not pose a problem concerning the associativity. Hoeksema (1983) and Lasersohn (1988, 1990) take the position that the natural language coordination is unassociative. They enlarge the universe of a model so as to cope with the unassociative summing operation. Krifka (1991) solves the problem by admitting two kinds of summing operations − the unassociative summing operating on discourse referents and the associative summing operating on individuals of a model. Schwarzschild (1991) argues that the summing is associative and the unassociativity is due to pragmatic factors.

The commutativity is also violated as in sentences (iii) and (iv) which have different truth conditions.

(iii) Tom and Bill like Mary and Susan, respectively.

(iv) Bill and Tom like Mary and Susan, respectively.

For more discussion on this matter, see Schwarzschild (1991), Krifka (1991), Link (1984) and others cited there.

13. A poset (partially ordered set) is a lattice if a supremum of set {a,b} and an infimum of {a,b} exist for all a,b which are members of a set A. A supremum of {a,b} is called a join of a and b, and an infimum of {a,b}, a meet of a and b.

14. A join semi lattice is a poset any two of whose elements have a supremum (join) but need not have an infimum (meet).

15. A complete lattice is a poset in which every subset has a supremum and an infimum.

16. Lattice A is atomic iff for all b ∈ A: there is an a ∈ AT (the set of atomic individuals) such that a ≤ b.

17. A lattice is free when it is the richest in its structure among all the lattices generated by the same atoms (Landman 1989, pp.569-570)

18. If a generator set is infinite, it cannot be complete since not every subset of A does not has a supremum (the entire set in this case cannot have a supremum).

19. Landman (1989) gives three arguments for groups in terms of upward closure, involvement, and the distributivity in conjunction construction.

20. Another operator is needed to specify the members of a group (member specification, $\downarrow$, in Landman's term. For example, sentence (i) is true iff members of Committee A gathered in Room 705. Let the members of the committee be **a, b,** and c. Then, Committee A is $\uparrow$(**a+b+c**). And what gathered is the i-sum of **a+b+c** obtained from the group by the member specification.

(i)   Committee A gathered in Room 705.

Chapter 2. Non-Unified Approaches Toward the Distributivity

2.0. Introduction

This chapter aims to specify the system and problems of the non-unified approaches proposed in Roberts(1987) and Kamp and Reyle(1990). Their approaches are based on the following set of assumptions which have become traditional in literatures assuming DRT as their framework (Heim, 1990).

(1) (i)   Indefinites are bound variables.

  (ii)   Anaphoric pronouns are plain bound variables.

  (iii)   Quantificational determiners and the conditional operator are capable of binding multiple variables.

  (iv)   Default existential generalization (existential closure in Heim (1982)) of free variables is needed.

The approaches of Roberts(1987) and Kamp and Reyle(1990) can be understood as an attempt to incorporate the semantics of various natural language quantifiers into the theory proposed by Kamp(1981). To be in accordance with the assumptions of (1), they classify indefinite NPs into quantificational NPs and non-quantificational (or individual-denoting) ones.

In section 2.1, I will specify Roberts(1987)' and Kamp and Reyle (1990)'s systems focusing on (i) how they classify noun phrases, (ii) how they treat those NPs in terms of reduction into a DRS, and (iii) how they treat anaphoric relations where pronouns and their antecedents are not in the same sentence. In section 2.2, I will point out some problems in their approaches.

2.1. Systems of Non-unified approaches

2.1.1. NP Classification

Roberts (1987) classifies NPs into quantificational and individual-denoting NPs. Individual-denoting NPs, according to Roberts, include proper names, pronouns and those NPs with determiners listed under "individual denoting" in (2) which are interpreted as variables.[1] Quantificational NPs, "whose determiner sets up a relationship between the denotation of the CN and that of the predicate of which the NP is subject (Roberts 1987, p.191)," are NPs with quantificational determiners listed in (2).[2]

(2)   Classification of Determiners (Roberts 1987, p192)
        individual denoting   quantificational

                a   each
                $some_{sg/pl}$ every
                1,2,3, ... $no_{sg/pl}$
                $the_{sg/pl}$ most
                this, that   few
                these, those   many
                                            both
                                            neither

Roberts' system is distinguished from that of Scha(1981)'s described in (3) in that Roberts' system does not allow any ambiguous determiners (Roberts 1987, p.192). According to Roberts, whether or not an NP can be followed by a collective predicate is not an essential criterion to classify determiners.

(3)   Classification of Determiners (Scha 1981)

Distributive	Collective
each	
every	
a	
both	
0	0
all	all
$some_{sg/pl}$	$some_{pl}$
$no_{sg/pl}$	no_{pl}
2,3,4, ...	2,3,4, ...
the_{sg}	the_{pl}

2.1.2. DR Construction Rules for NPs

Roberts (1987) suggests that the scope of an argument be represented in the syntactic analysis by giving S-node the indices of arguments. These are arranged so as that the one with the wider scope comes to the left of the one with the narrower scope. For example, in representation (4), the NP with index j has the wider scope than the NP with i.

(4)   S: j/i

Now, Roberts gives the following DR construction rules.[3]

(5)   Mapping Algorithm for DRs

To map a constituent with root node C onto a DR,

(a) if C is indexed :i ..., map the first (moving from top to bottom, left to right) constituent NP_i dominated by C into the DR. Then remove the index i from C.

(b) if C has no indices, map in turn its daughter constituents, left to right.

(6)   Mapping Individual-denoting NPs onto a DR,

To map a constituent of the form $[...[DET\ CN]_i...]_s$ onto a DR, where NP_i is individual-denoting, enter a discourse referent x_i into the DR, along with the condition $CN(x_i)$. Then, enter the nuclear scope of the NP into the DR, where the nuclear scope is S with the variable x_i in place of NP_i.

(7)   Mapping Quantificational NPs onto a DR:

To map a constituent of the form $[...[DET\ CN]_i]_s$ onto a DR, where NP_i is quantificational, form two subordinate boxes, the left accessible to the right; enter a discourse referent x_i into the left-hand box of the DR. DET serves to characterize the relation between the two boxes in the embedding into a model.

According to her rule system, sentence (8) and (10), which include an individual-denoting NP and a quantificational NP, respectively, are reduced into (9) and (11).

(8)   [The man]ᵢ lifted a piano.

(9)

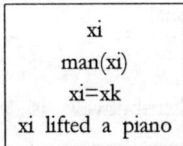

(Roberts 1987, p311)

(10)   Few men lifted a piano.

(11)

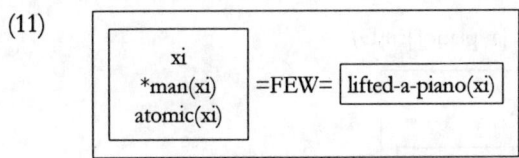

(Roberts 1987, p313)

The distributivity of a predicate is marked on the index of its argument on S-node, representing that the NP with the index is an argument of a distributive predicate as in (12).

(12)   S: i(D)

Then, Roberts proposes a rule for the distributivity of a sentence which does not have any quantificational NPs.

(13)   Algorithm for the Treatment of Nuclear Scope with D:
        To map a structure of the form [... eᵢ ...]s: (D)... onto a DR, where
        the structure is the nuclear scope of NPᵢ, introduce a conditional
        structure, with a new discourse referent xₖ, in the lefthand box, along

with the conditions i-part(x_k,x_i) and atomic(x_k). Remove (D) from the index on S, replace e_i, throughout with e_k, and introduce this remainder in the right box of the conditional.

In Roberts' system, sentence (14) which reads distributively is syntactically represented as in (15). An S-structure (15) is reduced into DRS (16) by rule (13) and other appropriate rules.

(14) Some men lifted a piano.

(15) [[Some men]$_i$ lifted [a piano]$_j$]s:i(D)

(16)

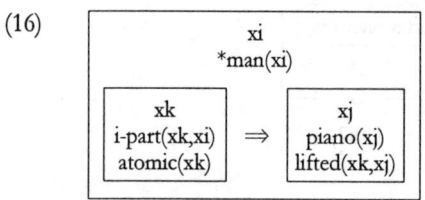

(Roberts 1987, p321)

Kamp and Reyle (1990)'s treatment of quantificational and non-quantificational NPs is equivalent to Roberts' in nature. Quantificational NPs introduce a pair of sub-DRSs connected by a quantificational determiner. Non-quantificational plural NPs introduce a plural (or non-individual) discourse referent into the current DRS.[5] The two DR construction rules are formulated in (17) and in (18).

(17) CR.NP [Quant=+] (Kamp and Reyle 1990, p.316)

Triggering configurations

(i) [$_S$ [$_{NP}$ [$_{DET}$ δ] [$_N$ β]] [$_{VP}$ η]]

(ii) [$_{VP}$ [$_V$ η] [$_{NP}$ [$_{DET}$ δ] [$_N$ β]]]

$\gamma \subseteq \bar{\gamma} \in \mathrm{Con_k}$: with δ a quantifying determiner.

Operations: Choose a new discourse referent x.

Replace $\bar{\gamma}$ by the duplex condition

$$\boxed{\begin{array}{c} x \\ [N](x) \end{array}} \quad \left\langle \begin{array}{c} \delta \\ x \end{array} \right\rangle \quad \boxed{\gamma'}$$

where γ' resulted from $\bar{\gamma}$ by substituting x for [NP $\alpha\beta$].

(18) CR.NP [Quant = ind/ Num = plur] (Kamp and Reyle 1990, p.322)

Triggering (i) $[_S [_{NP} [_{DET} \delta] [_N \beta]] [_{VP} \eta]]$

configurations (ii) $[_{VP} [_V \eta] [_{NP} [_{DET} \delta] [_N \beta]]]$

$\gamma \subseteq \bar{\gamma} \in \mathrm{Con_k}$:

Operations: (a) Introduce a new plural discourse referent X into the universe of the DRS K

(b) Add $\beta(X)$ to $\mathrm{Con_K}$

(c) Substitute in $\bar{\gamma}$: u for $[_{NP} \delta\beta]$.

When a non-quantificational NP is the subject of a mixed predicate, the resulting sentence is ambiguous in terms of distributivity. Sentence (19) "can mean either that a group consisting of three lawyers jointly hired a single secretary or that each lawyer in the group hired a new secretary on his own (Kamp and Reyle 1990, p.334)."

(19)   Three lawyers hired a new secretary.

To capture this ambiguity, they consider two alternatives: (i) treating the NP *three lawyers* as being ambiguous – sometimes quantificational and sometimes non-quantificational, and (ii) treating it as being non-quantificational in any case and capturing the distributive reading by the rule of distributive expansion. According to the first alternative, when the NP *three lawyers* of sentence (19) is treated as being quantificational, sentence (19) is reduced into DRS (20) without introducing a plural discourse referent.

(20)
$$\boxed{\begin{array}{c} x \\ \text{lawyer(x)} \end{array}} \quad \left\langle \begin{array}{c} \text{three} \\ x \end{array} \right\rangle \quad \boxed{\text{x hired a new secretary}}$$

According to the second alternative, sentence (19) is temporarily reduced into DRS (21).

(21)
$$\boxed{\begin{array}{c} X \\ \text{lawyer* (X)} \\ |X|=3 \\ \text{X hired a new secretary} \end{array}}$$

DRS (21) has a group reading such that a group of three lawyers hired a new secretary. To represent the distributive reading, condition X *hired a new secretary* must be further reduced. Kamp and Reyle introduce a DR construction rule of "Optional Distribution" as in (22).

(22)   Optional Distribution

Triggering   (i) $[_S X [_{VP} ...]]$
configurations   (ii) $[_{VP} V X]$
$\gamma \subseteq \bar{\gamma} \in Con_k$:

Operations: Then, $\bar{\gamma}$ may be replaced by the duplex
                               condition

$$
\boxed{\begin{array}{c} x \\ x \in X \end{array}} \; \left\langle \begin{array}{c} every \\ x \end{array} \right\rangle \; \boxed{\begin{array}{c} \gamma' \end{array}}
$$

where x is a new individual discourse
referent and γ' is obtained from $\bar{\gamma}$
through replacing X with x.

By Optional Distribution, DRS (21) is further reduced into DRS (23) which
represents the distributive reading of sentence (19).

(23)

$$
\boxed{\begin{array}{c} X \\ lawyer^*(X) \\ |X|=3 \\[6pt] \boxed{\begin{array}{c} x \\ x \in X \end{array}} \; \left\langle \begin{array}{c} every \\ x \end{array} \right\rangle \; \boxed{\begin{array}{c} y \\ secretary(y) \\ x \; hired \; y \end{array}} \end{array}}
$$

Kamp and Reyle take the second alternative supplemented with a DR construction
rule for distributive expansion.[6]

In summary, the distributivity of a sentence which does not have any quantificational NPs is captured by the rule specified in (14) in Roberts' approach while in Kamp and Reyle's by the rule of Optional Distributivity defined in (22). The two approaches share the same spirit except that in Roberts' approach the application of the rule is triggered by the presence of a distributive predicate but in Kamp and Reyle's this condition is not specified.

2.1.3. Pronouns in Non-Unified Approaches

2.1.3.1. Unbound Pronouns

In this section, I will define the term unbound pronouns and specify the problems concerning the anaphoric potential of these pronouns. It was Russell (1905) who acknowledged that there are two kinds of pronouns: referential pronouns and pronouns as bound variables. In (24), the pronoun *he* refers back to the individual which the expression *John* also refers to. In this sense, the pronoun *he* is (co)referential.

(24)   John$_i$ went to the store. He$_i$ bought a computer.

The pronoun *his in* (25) is an example of pronouns as bound variables. Compared with *he* in (24), *his* in (25) cannot refer back to the individual referred to by its antecedent *every man* since the NP *every man* does not refer at all. It is like a bound variable in the sense that the referent of *his* is determined by what value the antecedent is assigned by an assignment function f. Sentence (25) is translated into a formula of the first-order predicate language as in (26). The pronoun *his* gets **a** as its referent if f assigns **a** to variable x. It gets **b** as its referent if f assigns **b** to x.

(25)   [Every man]$_i$ loves his$_i$ mother.

(26) $\forall x[man(x) \rightarrow x$ loves x's mother]

Pronouns as bound variables can get their values if and only if they are in the scopes of quantifiers which do not span over sentence boundaries. This property distinguishes referential pronouns from pronouns as bound variables. In (27), *he* cannot be translated into a bound variable since it is out of the scope of the quantifier *every* while *he* can be coreferential with *John* in (28).

(27)   Every man attended the party. He was drunk.

(28)   John attended the party. He was drunk.

However, *They* in sentence (29) exemplifies the third kind of pronoun according to the non-unified approach. It is not referential since *every man* is not a referential expression. It is not bound since it is out of the scope of *every*. But it can be translated into a variable which acts as if it were bound by the quantifier of its antecedent as in (29)b. Pronouns of this kind are called *pronouns as unbound variables*, or just *unbound pronouns*.[7]

(29)   a. [Every man]$_i$ attended the party. They$_i$ were drunk.

        b. $\forall x[man(x) \rightarrow$ (attended-the-party (x) & was-drunk $(x))]$

A singular indefinite NP can serve as an antecedent of an unbound pronoun. Here, the pronoun agrees with its antecedent in number. It seems that the pronoun can be translated just into a bound variable as in (30)b.[8]

(30)   a. [A student]$_i$ attended the party. He$_i$ was drunk.

b. $\forall$x [student (x) & attended-the-party (x) & x was drunk]

A plural indefinite NP (or plural individual denoting NP in Roberts' terms) can also serve as an antecedent of an unbound pronoun as in (31).

(31)   [Some students]$_i$ attended the party. They$_i$ were drunk.

However, sentence (31) cannot be translated into (32) where *some x [P(x)]* is true iff for there are at least 2 assignment functions f such that each of them assigns a distinct value to x and f(x) is a member of f(P). (32) represents the reading that the number of the students who attended the party and were drunk is at least 2.

(32)   Some x[student(x) & attended-the-party(x) & were-drunk(x)]

Then, sentence (32) must be true in the situation where 5 students attended the party and 2 of them were drunk. Nevertheless, sentence (31) asserts that at least 2 students attended the party and all the students who attended the party were drunk. That is, the reading of (31) is correctly represented by (33).

(33)   Some x [student(x) & attended-the-party(x)] &
        $\forall$x[(student(x) & attended-the-party(x)) $\rightarrow$ were-drunk(x)]

It means that they in (31) cannot be translated into a variable which is to be bound by the quantifier of its antecedent.

A quantificational NP (or intrinsically distributive NP) can serve as an antecedent of an unbound pronoun. In this case, the pronoun must be plural.[9]

(34)   a. [Every student]ᵢ attended the party. *Heᵢ was drunk.

b. [Every student]ᵢ attended the party. Theyᵢ were drunk.

Unbound pronouns can be followed by a collective VP as in (35). To translate the second sentence in a logical form, a set type variable whose value is dependent on the set of all the values the antecedent can have must be introduced.

(35)   Every studentᵢ (Some studentsᵢ, many studentsᵢ, most studentsᵢ or few studentsᵢ) attended the party. Theyᵢ gathered in a hall after the party.

There are another kind of pronouns which are in the scope of a quantifier but are not translated as a bound variable. In (36), the antecedent of *their*, *every student*, introduces an individual type variable but not a set type variable. But *their* cannot be translated into an individual type variable as in (37). In (36), *their* is construed as a set of all the students in the room.

(36)   [Every student]ᵢ in the room is proud of theirᵢ joint project.
(37) $\forall x$[student-in-the-room(x) $\rightarrow$ $\exists y$[x's project(y) & x is-proud-of y]]

I will include this kind of pronouns into unbound pronouns, too. Then for a pronoun to be an unbound pronoun, (i) the pronoun must be out of the scope of the quantifier or (ii) the type of variable introduced by the pronoun must be different from the type of variable introduced by its antecedent.

2.1.3.2. C-command Bound Pronouns and Discourse Bound Pronouns
I am concerned with the anaphoric use of pronouns. In this study, I will

ignore other uses of pronouns, for example, deictic use of pronouns.[10]

Following Kamp and Reyle, I will call the discourse referent introduced by an antecedent expression "an antecedent discourse referent". Accordingly, an anaphoric relation is regulated by the configuration of a Discourse Representation System (DRS), a set of Discourse Representations (DRs), and by other conditions applied to those discourse referents introduced by an anaphoric expression and its antecedent. In short, the anaphoric relationship between two linguistic expressions is reduced to a relationship between two configurationally accessible discourse referents.[11,12]

Roberts (1987) differentiates the c-command binding from the discourse binding, and defines the two bindings in the following way:

"... there are two kinds of structures which permit binding between an NP and a pronoun. One is established solely intrasententially, making reference in a configurational language like English to the relation of c-command. I will call binding licensed by these structural relations *c-command binding*. The other kind of structure is the hierarchical discourse structure we considered in Chapter 1, where the possibility of anaphoric relations is dependent upon the relation of accessibility. Such structures license discourse binding (Roberts 1987, p68)."

Then, she maintains that only the pronoun which is c-command bound by its antecedent gets the same index as that of the antecedent. When a pronoun and its antecedent in a sentence have the same index and the sentence is marked with (D), the sentence is reduced by the set of DR construction rules specified in section 2.1.2. Let's consider how this condition works in sentence (38) which has a reading that "each of the two individuals **John** and **Mary** invited his or her parents to the place where they lived together (Roberts 1987, p337)."

(38)   John and Mary invited their$_{dist}$ parents to their$_{coll}$ place.[13]

If coreferential terms share the same index, sentence (38) would be represented as in (39) since *their* in *their* parents and *their* in *their place* refer back to the same individual **j+m**.

(39)   [[John and Mary]$_i$ invited [their$_i$ parents]$_k$ to [their$_i$ place]$_m$]$_s$:i(D)

Since NP *John* and *Mary* is individual denoting, by rules (5) and (6) in section 2.1.2, the indexed structure (39) is reduced into an incomplete DRS (40).

(40)
$$\begin{array}{|l|}
\hline
\quad x_i, \ x_1, \ x_n \\
\quad x_i = x_1 \oplus x_n \\
\quad \text{John}(x_1) \\
\quad \text{Mary}(x_n) \\
[x_i \ \text{invited} \ x_i\text{'s parents to} \ x_i\text{'s place}]\text{:(D)} \\
\hline
\end{array}$$

By rule (13) repeated as (41), (40) is further reduced into (42):

(41)   Algorithm for the Treatment of Nuclear Scope with D:
        To map a structure of the form [... e$_i$ ...]s: (D)... onto a DR, where
        the structure is the nuclear scope of NP$_i$, introduce a conditional
        structure, with a new discourse referent x$_k$, in the left-hand box, along
        with the conditions i-part(x$_k$,x$_i$) and atomic(x$_k$). Remove (D) from the
        index on S, replace e$_i$, throughout with e$_k$, and introduce this
        remainder in the right box of the conditional.

(42)

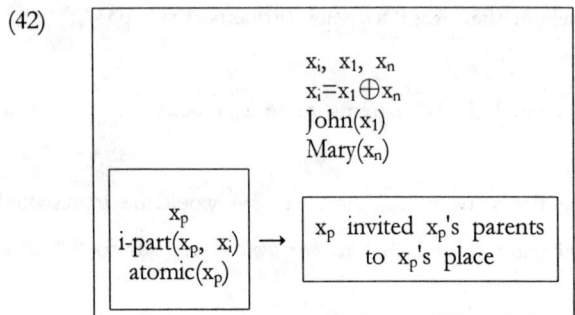

DRS (42) represents the reading that John invited his parents to his place and Mary invited her parents to her place, which is not intended by sentence (38).

Roberts solves this problem by stipulating that the first *their* is bound via c-command binding and the other *their* is bound via discourse binding. Then, sentence (38) is indexed as in (43) since only the pronoun which is c-command bound gets the same index as that of the antecedent.

(43)　　[[John and Mary]$_i$ invited [their$_i$ parents]$_k$ to [their$_j$ place]$_m$]s:i(D)

Again by rules of (5), (6) and (13), the indexed structure (43) is reduced into DRS (44) which represents the intended reading. Notice that the discourse referent x_j can be linked to discourse referent x_i since x_i is accessible to x_j (discourse binding).

(44)

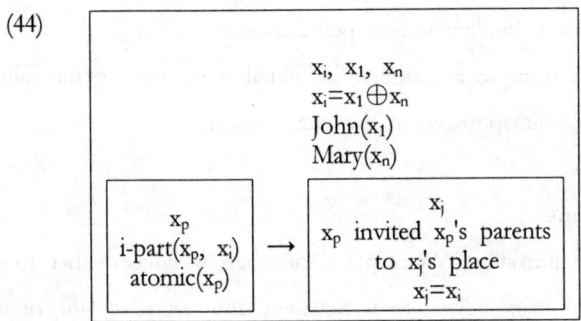

$$x_i, x_1, x_n$$
$$x_i = x_1 \oplus x_n$$
$$John(x_1)$$
$$Mary(x_n)$$

$$\begin{array}{c} x_p \\ i\text{-part}(x_p, x_i) \\ atomic(x_p) \end{array} \longrightarrow \begin{array}{c} x_j \\ x_p \text{ invited } x_p\text{'s parents} \\ \text{to } x_j\text{'s place} \\ x_j = x_i \end{array}$$

A problem of her approach is how to determine that the first *their* is c-command bound while the second one is not. Moreover, sentence (38) can have four readings as illustrated in (45).

(45)   John and Mary invited their parents to their place.

a.	dist	dist
b.	dist	coll
c.	coll	dist
d.	coll	coll

What I am going to propose is to treat c-command bound pronouns as a subset of discourse bound pronouns. Then, c-command pronouns should observe the conditions on the anaphora resolution (in short, choose an appropriate discourse referent among accessible ones) as discourse bound pronouns. They should also observe some syntactic conditions such as being c-commanded by its antecedent. It is a refinement of Roberts' position about the relation between the two bindings. She specifies the relation between the two bindings in that "discourse binding may take place in structures where c-command binding is also permissible." My position is stronger than hers in that discourse binding must take place where c-command binding is also permissible.

Since Kamp and Reyle propose a treatment of plural pronouns in the same direction, I will examine their approach in the next section.

2.1.3.3. Plural Pronouns

The discourse referent introduced by a plural pronoun is linked either to a singular discourse referent as in (48) which is obtained from sentence (46), or to a plural discourse referent as in (49) which is a representation of sentence (47). DRS (48) represents the reading that John drove his own car and Bill drove his own car (distributive reading) and DRS (49) represents that John and Bill drove their jointly owned car.

(46) John and Bill drove their cars to school.

(47) John and Bill drove their car to school.

(48)
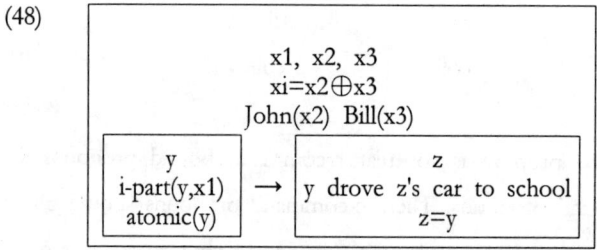

(49)
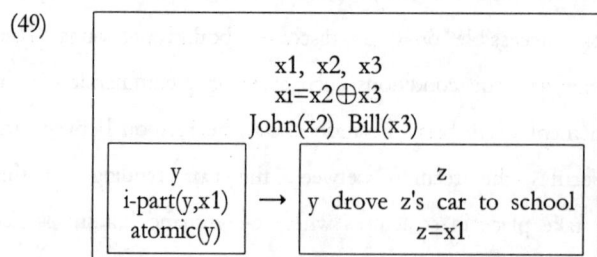

The discourse referent introduced by *their* can be linked to a singular discourse referent introduced by a syntactically plural quantifying NP but not to a singular discourse referent introduced by a syntactically singular quantifying NP as in (50).

(50) a. [Most students]$_i$ love their$_i$ mothers.

  b. *[Every student]$_i$ loves their$_i$ mother.

Kamp and Reyle(1990, p375) stipulate that a plural pronoun introduces a discourse referent which is neutral with respect to the number. A neutral discourse referent can be linked either to an individual or an i-sum (or non-individual) discourse referent which is accessible from it. However, a neutral discourse referent cannot be linked to an individual discourse referent introduced by a syntactically singular NP as in (50). Sentences in (51) provide further evidence.

(51) a. [John and Bill]$_i$ admire their$_{dist,i}$ parents.

  b. *John$_i$ admires their$_i$ parents.

To cope with this fact, Kamp and Reyle further stipulate that a plural quantifying NP introduces a singular discourse referent superscripted with *pl*. When a plural discourse referent is an argument of a distributive predicate, it introduces a pair of DRSs such that the first DRS of the pair contains a singular discourse referent superscripted with *pl*. Then, they propose the DR construction rule for plural pronouns as in (52).

(52)   CR. PRO [NUM = plur] (Kamp and Reyle 1990, p377)

	S			VP	
Triggering	/	\		/	\
configurations:	(i) NP	VP		(ii) V	NP
$\gamma \subseteq \bar{\gamma} \in Con_k$:	|	|		|	|
	β	η		η	β

Operations: (a)   Introduce a neutral discourse referent ξ into U_k, the universe of the current DRS.

(b)   Add to Con_k a condition of the form $\xi = \alpha$ where either (i) α is an available non-individual discourse referent accessible from the position of the pronoun; or (ii) α is an individual discourse referent marked *pl*, which, again, is accessible from the position of the pronoun.

(c)   Replace $\bar{\gamma}$ by r′ where r′ is obtained through substitution of ξ for the processed NP.

Then, the example (53) which gives trouble to Roberts′ DR construction algorithms can be explained by (52).

(53)   [John and Mary]$_i$ invited their$_{i,dis}$ parents to their$_i$, $_{coll}$ place.

DR construction rule (52) with other appropriate DR construction rules can represent the intended readings of (53) with treating c-command bound pronouns as a subset of discourse bound pronouns as in (54).[14]

(54)

$$
\boxed{
\begin{array}{c}
X,u,v \\
X=u \oplus v \\
John(u) \\
Mary(v) \\[4pt]
\boxed{\begin{array}{c} x^{pl} \\ i\text{-part}(z,X) \\ atomic(z) \end{array}}
\;\rightarrow\;
\boxed{\begin{array}{c} w,y,\xi,\zeta \\ \xi\text{'s parent}(w) \quad \zeta\text{'s place}(y) \\ \xi=z \quad \zeta=x \\ z \text{ invited } w \text{ to } y \end{array}}
\end{array}
}
$$

2.1.3.4. Unbound Pronouns in Non-Unified Approaches

Heim (1982) argues that the semantics of a singular unbound pronoun, for example *it* in (55), cannot be properly explained by treating a singular indefinite determiner as a quantifier.

(55)   Every farmer who owns [a donkey]$_i$ beats it$_i$.

Instead, she proposes that an indefinite NP is translated into an expression containing a free variable which may be bound by a quantifier which does not belong to the translation of the indefinite. A pronoun with an indefinite as an antecedent is also translated into a bound variable. This proposal is one of the crucial tenets of DRT presented in Kamp(1981).

However, DRT of Kamp (1981) cannot explain the semantics of a plural unbound pronoun whose antecedent is a universally quantified NP as in (56). In DRS (57) which is obtained by reducing sentence (56), a non-individual discourse referent X introduced by *they* cannot be linked to x introduced by *every student* since x is neither accessible from X nor is the same type as X.[15]

(56)   [Every student]ᵢ came in. Theyᵢ sat on the floor.

(57)

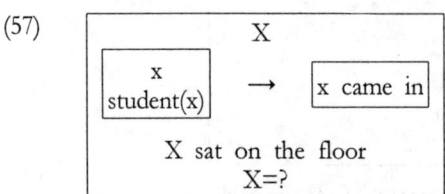

Van Eijk(1983) tries to solve this problem by stipulating that *they* in (56) is not anaphoric to a full NP but is anaphoric to a common noun(CN: *student* in (56)). Every common noun introduces a discourse referent of set-type since a CN denotes a set of individuals. That is, the discourse referent is of the same type as a discourse referent introduced by *Tom and Bill* since it denotes a set of individuals: **{Tom, Bill}**, according to his ontology. Now, the anaphoric linking of *they* in (56) is explained: the discourse referent X of (57) is to be linked to a non-individual discourse referent introduced by CN *student*.

(58)

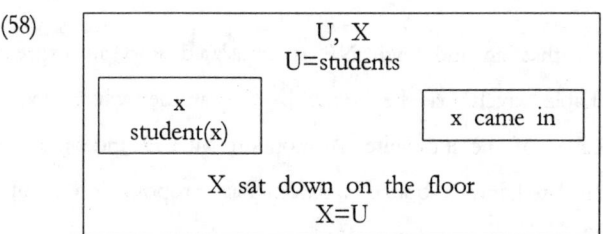

An embedding function f verifies the condition U=students iff f(U) exists and equals to F(student) where F is the interpretation function of a model M.

Even if a CN introduces a non-individual discourse referent, van Eijk's system fails to account for the anaphoric linking between *they* and *most students* in (59). The second sentence does not mean that every student sat down on the floor.

Rather, it means that every student who came in sat down on the floor. That is, the discourse referent introduced by *they* cannot be linked to the discourse referent introduced by CN *student*. Similarly, since *most CN* is, according to him, undefined like *every* CN in terms of the semantic number, it cannot introduce a non-individual discourse referent.

(59)   [Most students]$_i$ came in. They$_i$ sat down on the floor.

A similar problem is pointed out by Root(1986, p35). The unbound pronoun *they* refers back to the set of proposals all the students submitted. If *they* is a CN-anaphor, then it must refer back to all the proposals in model M. It is, however, not compatible with the intended meaning of (60).[16]

(60)   Every student submitted a proposal but they were returned unopened. (Root 1986, p34).

The above counter-arguments against van Eijk's approach do not prove that a CN should not introduce a non-individual discourse referent if the denotation of the CN contains more than one individuals. Rather, they ensure that there must be another mechanism which takes care of (59), (60) and the likes.

2.1.3.4.1. Unbound Pronouns in Kamp and Reyle

In Kamp and Reyle, a pronoun, when its antecedent is not a quantifying NP, introduces a discourse referent linkable to the discourse referent introduced by its antecedent as in (61). This kind of unbound pronoun does not pose any problem in the anaphoric resolution.

(61)   [Some students]ᵢ came in. Theyᵢ gathered in a hall.

However, when an unbound pronoun has a quantificational NP as its antecedent, the anaphoric linking cannot be represented properly. The neutral discourse referent η introduced by *they* cannot be linked to an discourse referent introduced by its antecedent *every* student. Discourse referent x is not accessible from η as in (63). But the discourse of (62) is perfectly acceptable.

(62)   [Every student]ᵢ came in. Theyᵢ gathered in a hall.

(63)

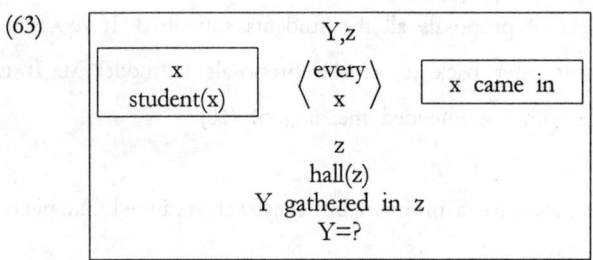

A non-individual discourse referent to which Y is to be linked must be provided. That is, an appropriate discourse referent to be linked to a discourse referent Y must be accommodated pragmatically. Intuitively, *they* in (63) refers to the set of all the students in the model (or an i-sum which is the supremum of property **student**) or equivalently to the set of the students who came in. In discourse (64), *they* refers to the set of students who came in.

(64)   [Few students]ᵢ came in, Theyᵢ gathered in a hall.

In cases of (62) and (64), *they* refers to the set of the students who came in. That is, in the main DRS, a discourse referent must be introduced which is to be mapped into the set of the students who came in (or an i-sum which is the supremum of the intersection of property **student** and property **came in**).

For this purpose, Kamp and Reyle introduce an operation which forms a non-individual discourse referent, taking a DRS as its argument. They call this operation *Abstraction*. They define the operation as in (65).

(65)   Abstraction (Kamp and Reyle, p330)

Triggering configurations

$\gamma \subseteq \bar{\gamma} \in Con_K$:

$$\boxed{\quad K1 \quad} \left\langle \begin{matrix} every \\ x \end{matrix} \right\rangle \boxed{\quad K2 \quad}$$

Operations: Form the union K0 = K1 $\cup$ K2 of the two component DRSs of this condition.[17] Choose a discourse referent w from U_{K0}. Introduce into U_K a new discourse referent Y and add to Con_K the condition

$$Y = \Sigma w: K0$$

In DRS (63), by the abstraction, a new discourse referent X is introduced in the universe of the main DRS. The DRS condition (66) is introduced as a condition of the main DRS.

(66)

$$X = \Sigma x: \boxed{\begin{matrix} x \\ student(x) \\ x \ came \ in \end{matrix}}$$

Now, discourse (62) is reduced into (67) where Y is linked to the discourse referent X which is introduced by the abstraction.

(67)

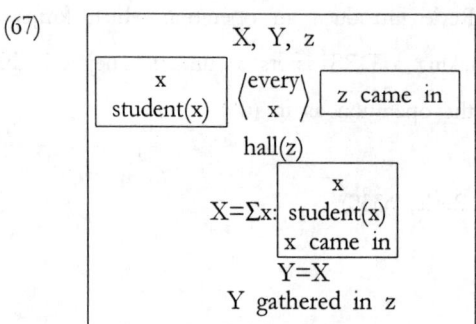

An embedding function f verifies the condition specified in (66) iff f maps X into the set of all the individuals which are students and which came in (or the i-sum generated from all the individuals which are students and came in).[18]

Root(1986) proposes a very similar approach toward the problem. She introduces "the sub-embeddings of a DRS K with respect to a proper embedding f" which she informally defines as "the extensions of f which map the reference markers of K and all its sub-DRSs to objects in the model M (Root 1986, p48)." Let a proper embedding f be a sub-embedding. Then, the sub-embeddings of f are actually f itself and all the extensions of f. As an example, let's examine discourse (67) (=(2.4) of hers). The first 2 sentences are reduced into (68).

(67)   An agent entered.
        Every farmer asked *him a question.*
        They were hostile.

(68)

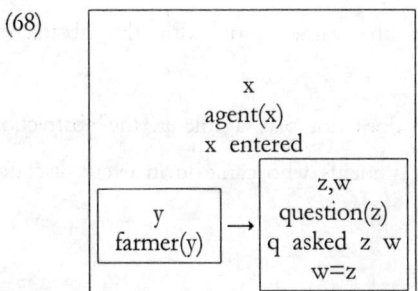

For *they* to be properly linked to a discourse referent which is related in some way to *a question*, she introduces a set type discourse referent X with the condition X={z}. Now, DRS (68) is further reduced into (69).

(69)

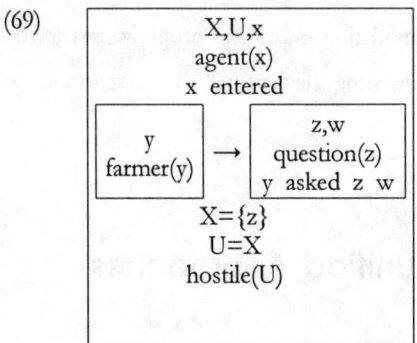

The embedding conditions for X={z} is given as in (70) by Root.

(70)   Assume that f is a proper embedding of some DRS K. f verifies the condition "X={z}" iff $f(X)=\{\alpha \in U_M|$ there is some function g, a sub-embedding of K, and $g(z)=\alpha\}$.

The embedding condition (70) shares the same spirit with the abstraction function of Kamp and Reyle(1990).

Notice that the quantifier of an NP does not play a role in the abstraction. Pronoun *they* refers to the set of all the students who came in in every discourse of (71).

    (71)   a. [Most students]$_i$ came in. They$_i$ gathered in a hall.

              b. [Many students]$_i$ came in. They$_i$ gathered in a hall.

              c. [Few students]$_i$ came in. They$_i$ gathered in a hall.

              d. [At least 3 students]$_i$ came in. They$_i$ gathered in a hall.

Abstraction is a pragmatic function in nature. As Roberts (1987), Kadmon (1987) and Asher(1992) argue, accommodation must be properly restricted. If not, it is too powerful to be an interesting device for the description of a natural language.

2.2. Problems of Non-Unified Approaches

2.2.1. Classification of NPs

I will examine the criteria for the classification of NPs into quantificational and non-quantificational (or quantificational and individual-denoting in Roberts' term). Since Roberts provides a set of such criteria, and Kamp and Reyle do not give explicit criteria for it, I will mainly examine and criticize the criteria provided by Roberts (1987). Recall that Roberts (1987) classifies NPs into quantificational and individual-denoting categories as in (72).

(72)   Classification of Determiners   (Roberts 1987, p192)

Individual denoting	quantificational
a	each
some$_{sg/pl}$	every
1,2,3, ...	no$_{sg/pl}$
the$_{sg/pl}$	most
this, that	few
these, those	many
	both
	neither

Roberts' criterion for the classification of plural NPs is whether or not they have a group reading. She provides a set of tests for whether or not an NP has a group reading. After illustrating her Criteria, I will evaluate them in order to examine if they are rigid enough as classificatory criteria.

The first test provided in Roberts(1987) to classify determiners into individual-denoting or quantificational is that quantificational NPs cannot be antecedents of discourse anaphora as in (73).

(73)   a. [Every student]$_i$ came in. *He$_i$ sat down on a couch.

b. [Some students]$_i$ came in. They$_i$ sat down on a couch.

But this test is misleading because a quantificational NP can be an antecedent of a discourse pronoun *they* as in (74). Note that pronoun *they* but not *he* can be used in this situation.[19]

(74) a. Every man came in. They gathered in the hall.

b. [Most students]$_i$ came in. They$_i$ sat down on a couch.

c. [Many students]$_i$ came in. They$_i$ sat down on a couch.

d. [Few students]$_i$ came in. They$_i$ sat down on a couch.

The second test is that only an individual-denoting NP contributes a sloppy reading as well as a nonsloppy one (strict reading) in "sloppy identity construction". Sentence (75) has at least two readings as indicated. However, (76) is not ambiguous--it has only a sloppy reading.

(75) Mary, Susan and Kathy love their mother, and Bob does too.

(i) love-(**m+s+k**)' mother (**m+s+k**) & love-(**m+s+k**)'s mother(**b**)

(nonsloppy reading)

(ii) love-(**m+s+k**)'s mother (**m+s+k**) & love-**b**'s mother (**b**)

(sloppy reading)

(76) Every student loves his mother and Bill does, too.

(i) Every x [student(x) → love-x's mother (x)] & love-**b**'s mother (**b**)

This test is also dubious as a criterion to distinguish a quantificational NP from individual-denoting one. Roberts admits that even in sentences where individual-denoting indefinites are subjects of the first sentence of a sloppy-construction, the non-sloppy reading is hard to get. According to her, when the determiner *some* is stressed, the non-sloppy reading is hard to get from (77)a. It is harder to get the non-sloppy reading in (77)b than in (77)a. Note that *some* and *four* are individual-denoting.

(77)   a. Some girls like their teacher, and Bernie does too.

        b. Four girls like their teacher, and Bernie does too.

Then, the best we can generalize about this phenomenon is as follows: when a non-sloppy reading is hard to get in a sloppy-construction, the subject of the first sentence tends to be quantificational. Now, the basically pragmatic notions such as tendency, preference, context, etc. play a role in the tests provided by Roberts.

The third test is that only individual-denoting NP can occur "felicitously" as the subject of a predicate with a floated quantifier, and NP's with *most, many* or *few* cannot felicitously occur at those positions.

(78)   a. The students all left.

        b. #Few students all left.

However, this test is simply inappropriate as a criterion that the NP is either individual-denoting or quantificational. This criterion is rather for whether or not an NP is definite according to Dowty (1986, p110). He puts the asterisk * to sentence (79) and attributes the ill-formedness of (79) to the fact that the NP *some students* is not definite. If floated *all* can be compatible with an individual-denoting NP, (79) must be judged acceptable since *some CN* is individual-denoting according to Roberts' classification.

(79)   *Some students all left.

The fourth criterion is that when one of the conjuncts is a quantificational NP, the whole conjoined NP contributes only a distributive reading. Sentence

(80)a has only a distributive reading while (80)b can have a distributive as well as a collective reading (Roberts 1987, p199).

(80)   a. Both apartments and most of the mobile homes have a fire extinguisher in the kitchen.

    b. Two movers and some neighbors carried the piano into the house.

Here again, pragmatic information plays a role in determining the acceptability of a sentence. For example, in sentences (81)a and b, a conjoined NP which has an NP with *most*, *many* or *few* as its conjunct contributes a collective reading to a sentence. Then, according to this criterion, NPs *many students* and *most of his roommates* must be classified into individual-denoting NPs.

(81)   a. John and many students lifted a piano (together).

    b. John and most of his roommates played football (together).

The fifth test for whether or not an NP denotes a group is that the prepositions *among* and *between* take (only) a group denoting complement (Roberts 1987, p199).

(82)   a. Ellen found a thistle among some roses.

    b. #Ellen found a thistle among few roses.

    c. Jonathan found a poem stuck between (the) pages of logical formulae.

    d. #Jonathan found a poem between both pages of logical formulae.

However, Root(1986) reports that NPs with stressed *some* or numerals are not accepted as a complement of *among*. Since SOME and *five* are classified as individual-denoting, the NPs with *SOME* or *five* must be judged acceptable according to Roberts' criterion.

(83)   *among many (every, most, SOME, five) ducks

Lastly, according to Roberts, the test whether or not an NP can take a collective predicate like *gather* is not relevant to determine whether or not an NP denotes a group. Determiners *many* and *few* are "restricted plural quantifiers". I will deal with the notion "restricted plural quantification" later, and will point out some problems of this approach there.

To recapitulate the discussion above, Roberts' criteria for classifying NPs into quantificational or individual-denoting are not reliable. Without reliable criteria, it is impossible to assign an NP into one of the two categories.

2.2.2. Number Agreement between a Pronoun and its Antecedent

The (un)acceptability of sentences (86) and (87) is problematic to the non-unified account if we assume that a singular pronoun introduces an individual discourse referent and a plural pronoun introduces a non-individual discourse referent.

(84)   [A student]$_i$ respects his$_i$/#their$_i$ teacher.

(85)   [Every student]$_i$ respect his$_i$/#their$_i$ teacher.[20]

(86)   [Most (Many, Few, All) students]$_i$ respect their$_i$/#his$_i$ teacher.

(87)   [Some (Several, Five) students]$_i$ respect their$_i$/#his$_i$ teacher.

Van Eijk (1983) generalizes that a pronoun which is translated into a bound variable of an intensional language agrees with the syntactic number of its antecedent and that a pronoun translatable into an unbound variable agrees with the semantic number of its antecedent. Since the pronouns in above sentences are translated into a bound variable, they must agree with the syntactic numbers of their antecedents. This generalization correctly captures number agreement in these sentences. However, without designing some devices which can express the notions bound and unbound variables in DRT terms, van Eijk's generalization cannot be implemented on DRT since DRT does not differentiate a bound variable from an unbound variable (a discourse referent is always regarded as a bound variable).

To solve this problem, Kamp and Reyle suggests rule (88) by introducing some stipulations of (89). Note that this approach can also explain the number agreement in sentence (87) when it reads distributively.

(88)   A singular pronoun introduces an individual discourse referent and a plural pronoun introduces a neutral discourse referent. A discourse referent introduced by a plural pronoun must be linked to an accessible non-individual discourse referent or an accessible individual discourse referent with superscripted pl.

(89)   A (syntactically) plural quantificational NP introduces an individual discourse referent superscripted with pl. When a non-individual discourse referent is further processed by Distributivity Expansion, an individual discourse referent with superscripted pl is introduced in the antecedent DRS of a duplex condition.

The rule (88) incorporates the syntactic number agreement into anaphora resolution by introducing diacritic *pl* on the discourse representation level. Let's examine how the acceptability of sentence (86) is explained with rules (88) and (89). Sentence (86) is reduced into DRS (90). Since *most students* is syntactically plural, it introduces a discourse referent superscripted with *pl*.

(90)

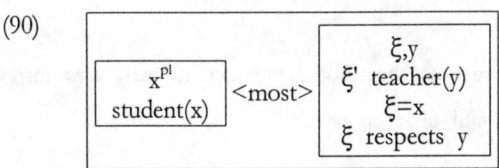

In a similar way, the acceptabilities of the above sentences are explained.

However, their account cannot account for the anaphoric relations in sentences (91) and (92). According to my informants, sentence (91) is acceptable when it means that all the students in the room are engaging in their joint project and each of them is proud of the project. Sentence (92) is acceptable when it means that all the sons of John intended to buy a ring for a woman, Susan for example, who is their mother.

(91)   [Every student in the room]ᵢ is proud of theirᵢ joint project.

(92)   [Every son of John]ᵢ contributed money to buy a diamond ring for
        theirᵢ mother.

According to Kamp and Reyle, pronoun *their* introduces a neutral discourse referent which must be linked to an accessible discourse referent with superscripted *pl*. But its indicated antecedent *every student in the room* or *every son of John* does not introduce a discourse referent with the diacritic. Even abstraction operation cannot provide an appropriate discourse referent to which the neutral discourse referent is to be linked to.

Another problem is about "non-sexist's use of pronoun they." Roberts (1987) reports that sentence (93) is widely accepted to prevent the sexist's prejudice.

(93)   [Every student]$_i$ keeps their$_i$ ID handy.

But as Choi (1987) argues, there must be another reason in using *their* instead of *his* because sentence (94) is still unacceptable.

(94)   *[A student]$_i$ keeps their$_i$ ID handy.

It means that *their* in (93) is not a mere substitute for *his* or *her* (let's call it THEIR) but still a plural pronoun. Then, rule (88) and (89) cannot explain the acceptability of (93). Note that NP *every student* in (93) is followed by a singular VP. If we admit sentence (93) and sentence (95) to be grammatical, and therefore weakening the syntactic agreement rule between a pronoun and its antecedent, we need to modify Kamp and Reyle's device.

(95)   [Every student]$_i$ keeps his$_i$ ID handy.

We can find almost the same phenomenon in Korean. I will deal with this matter in Chapter 5.

2.2.3. Problems about the Mode of Predication

The acceptability of sentences (96), (97) and (98) is explained by the non-unified approach. But sentence (99) is problematic since NP *most students* does not introduce a non-individual discourse referent according to non-unified approaches.

(96)   #A student gathered in the hall.

(97)   #Every student gathered in the hall.

(98)   Some (Several, Five) students gathered in the hall.

(99)   Most (Many, Few, All, At least 5) students gathered in the hall.

2.2.3.1. Root's Approach

I will examine two attempts suggested to solve the problem mentioned above assuming an non-unified approach – those of Root (1986) and of Roberts (1987). Root(1986) who cites Frey and Kamp[1986]'s unpublished work pays attention to the special property of collective predicates like *gather* such that "they are similar to pure distributives in that the contribution of the individual members of a member set is roughly the same (Root 1986, p107)." To capture this property of predicate *gather*, she adopts Frey and Kamp's idea that an operator which "takes a collective predicate and yields the associated individual predicate" must be introduced. DRS (100) shows the operation of this operator.

(100)

$$
\boxed{\;\boxed{\begin{array}{c} x \\ man(x) \end{array}} \quad \left\langle \begin{array}{c} many \\ \Rightarrow \end{array} \right\rangle \quad \boxed{x\; Ind_y\; [Y_{col}\; gathered]}\;}
$$

(Root 1986, p108)

Root(1986, p108) explains the intended reading of DRS (100) as follows:

The exact embedding conditions of the statement "x IndY [Y_{col} gathered]" are not specified, but the idea is roughly that x performed the individual contribution to some collective gathering. As things are presented here, there is nothing which represents the fact that the sentence entails that the mentioned men were part of the same event of gathering. In the Frey and Kamp account, the collective marker introduced by the subject noun phrase serves this purpose.

The quotation assures that Root tried to solve other problems concerning the special property of the predicate *gather* but she does not do anything for the problem of how a non-individual discourse referent (Y in DRS (100)) is introduced by a quantificational NP. Frey and Kamp's position that the non-individual discourse referent Y of (100) is introduced by NP *many men* is only against the non-unified approaches. In the end, the problem is left unsolved in her approach.

2.2.3.2. Roberts' Approach

If *most, many* and *few* are quantifiers which range over atomic individuals denoted by a common noun, the acceptability of sentences in (101) cannot be appropriately explained since predicates like *gather* and *agree on this issue* require plural individuals as their arguments. Sentences (101)b and c are examples of Roberts (1987, p190).

(101)   a. Most students of the class gathered in the hall.

b. Many people agree (with each other) on this issue.

c. Few people agree (with each other) on this issue.

Roberts argues that these quantifiers quantify over i-sums generated by the property denoted by their head noun or quantify over atomic individuals, the members of the property denoted by the head noun. Then, a collective predicate *gathered in the hall* takes one of those i-sums as its argument.

In the following sub-sections, I will examine the notion "plural quantification" which was first introduced by Link (1987). Then, I will examine how Roberts modifies the notion to deal with sentences in (101). Finally, I will point out some problems of her approach to show that sentences in (101) cannot be explained by the quantificational approach enforced with the (modified) plural quantification.

2.2.3.2.1. Plural Quantification

Link (1987) claims that there is a phenomenon where the quantification ranges over i-sums rather than atomic individuals in the denotation of a common noun. In sentence (102), the determiner *all* quantifies over groups (or i-sums) of companies which are competing with each other but not over individual companies. Sentence (102) is true iff every i-sum which consists of at least two companies which are competing with each other has common interests. (103) is the logical form of (102).

(102)   All competing companies have common interests.

(103) $\forall x$ [company* (x) & $|x| \geq 2$ & competing (x) $\rightarrow$ x has common

interests]

Logical form (103) is equivalent to DRS (104) in its truth conditions.

(104)

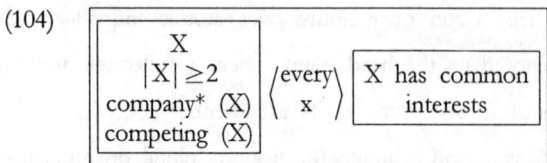

Sometimes, the cardinality of i-sums which a quantifier quantifies over is explicitly expressed as in (105). *Any* in (105) quantifies over i-sums whose cardinality is 11.

(105)　　Any 11 students can make a soccer team.

Sometimes, the cardinality of such i-sums is contextually determined. Sentence (106) means that "between many pairs of adjacent houses, there was a fence (Roberts 1987, p190)." That is, the determiner *many* quantifies over pairs of houses.

(106)　　Between many houses, there stood a picket fence.

2.2.3.2.2. *Most, Many* and *Few* as Plural Quantifiers

If we admit that quantifiers such as *most, many* and *few* ranges over i-sums, the fact that an NP with one of these quantifiers can be followed by a collective VP seems to be no longer a problem to the quantificational approach of Roberts (1987) and Kamp and Reyle (1990). Sentence (101)b repeated as (107) is acceptable since a collective predicate takes an i-sum individual (or a non-individual discourse referent) which is one of the i-sums which the quantifier *few* quantifies over.

(107)   Few people agree (with each other) on this issue.

Sentence (107) would be reduced into DRS (108) if *few* is a quantificational determiner which quantifies over i-sum individuals. The condition X *agrees on this issue* is well-formed since X is a non-individual discourse referent.

(108)

$$\boxed{\quad \boxed{\begin{array}{c} X \\ person^* \ (X) \\ |X| \geq 2 \end{array}} \quad \left\langle \begin{array}{c} few \\ x \end{array} \right\rangle \quad \boxed{\begin{array}{c} X \ agrees \ on \\ this \ issue \end{array}} \quad}$$

However, DRS (108) does not represent the reading of (107) since DRS (108) is true iff the number of the i-sums of persons who agree on this issue are "few"[21]. But sentence (107) is about the cardinality of an i-sum of people who agree on the issue. The quantificational approach equipped with the plural quantification is still inappropriate to solve the problem concerning sentence (107).

2.2.3.2.3. Restricted Plural Quantification

Roberts, realizing the problems of the plural quantificational approach to sentence (107), argues that "what seems to be at issue is the cardinality of the maximal collection of people who agree on the issue." To support this intuition, she introduces a new notion of "restricted plural quantification." Consider the following quotation from Roberts (1987).

..., consider a situation in which there are twenty people and some burning political issue. Suppose that two of them agree on one potential solution to the problem, while three others agree on a different solution, and none of the others agrees with anyone on any solution. I think the relevant question is 'what's the largest number of people who agree?' .... One way to represent this intuition might be via a logical form such as (128):

(128)   FEW (σx[$\exists$y (*person (y) & agree (y) & x = |y|)
      & $\forall$z (*person (z) & agree (z) $\longrightarrow$ x $\geq$ |z|)])

where |y| means 'the number of atomic i-parts of y,' and *agree (y) means* that all i-parts of y agree in the same way. (128) means that the cardinality of the largest i-sum of people who agree in the same way is FEW. Though (128) does involve plural quantification, it is over a restricted type of i-sum, those which are a group of people who agree in the same way, and not all i-sums which are in the lattice *person.   (Roberts 1987, pp182-183)

Here, 'FEW' is a characteristic function from a certain number, n, to truth values, 1 or 0, such that if n is regarded as 'few', FEW (n) is 1 and if not, FEW (n) is 0. Then, logical form (128) can be converted into DRS (109).

(109)

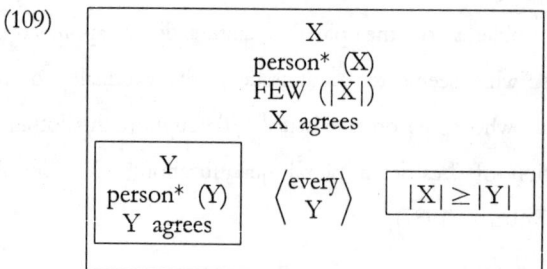

The determiner *many* is treated similarly. In summary, she solves the problem by defining *many* and *few* as plural quantifiers as in (110).

(110) Few: $\lambda CN \ \lambda VP \ FEW \ (\sigma x[\exists y \ (CN(y) \ \& \ VP(y) \ \& \ x=|y|)$

$\& \ \forall z \ (CN(z) \ \& \ VP(z) \ \rightarrow \ x \ \geq \ |z|)])$

Many: $\lambda CN \ \lambda VP \ MANY \ (\sigma x[y \ (CN(y) \ \& \ VP(y) \ \& \ x=|y|)$

$\& \ \forall z \ (CN(z) \ \& \ VP(z) \ \rightarrow \ x \ \geq \ |z|)])$

(Roberts 1987, pp183-184)

2.4.2.4. Problems of Roberts' Approach

Although DRS (109) captures the reading of sentence (107) correctly, Roberts' approach has some problems. First, she does not specify how the existential quantifier in the denotations of *few* and *many* is introduced. The quantifier is just stipulated. In the logical form of (128) and its corresponding DRS (109), there is no quantifier corresponding to the determiner *few*. The role of *few* here is to specify the cardinality of the largest i-sum which agrees on the issue, but it is not that of a quantifier. Second, if they are restricted plural quantifiers as argued by Roberts, *few* in sentence (107) must be translated into a quantifier which ranges over all the i-sums of persons which agree on the issue but not over all the i-sums generated by the property denoted by CN *people*. Sentence (107) might be represented as in (111) which captures the spirit of the restricted plural quantification, more or less.

(111) $\forall x \ (*person \ (x) \ \& \ agree \ (x) \ \rightarrow \ FEW \ (x))$

(Roberts 1987, p184)[22]

However, there is no quantifier corresponding to the determiner *few*. And it is still necessary to explain how the universal quantifier is introduced. Furthermore, (113) is not an appropriate logical form of sentence (112) as she herself points out. According to her, sentence (112) is true iff the cardinality of the largest i-sum among the i-sums which agree on the issue is MANY. But for (113) to be true, the cardinalities of every i-sum which agrees must be MANY.

(112) Many people agree on this issue.

(113) $\forall$x (*person (x) & agree (x) $\rightarrow$ MANY (x))

Third, if we admit that *few* and *many* with denotations given in (110) are plural quantifiers, we have to treat *few* and *many* as plural quantifiers differently from *few* and *many* which quantify over atomic individuals. For example, a schema *Few P Q* is reduced into DRS (114) when *few* is regarded as a restricted plural quantifier, into DRS (115) when it is a quantifier over atomic individuals and into DRS (116) when it is a usual plural quantifier. Sentences (117) and (118) fit schematic DRSs (115) and (116), respectively.

(114)

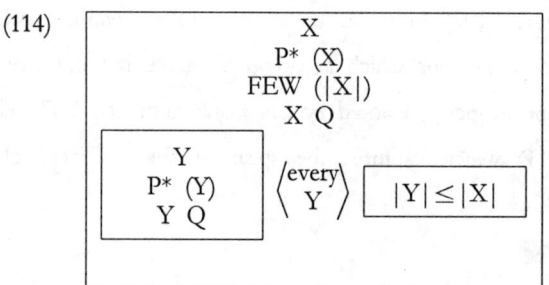

(115)   (116)

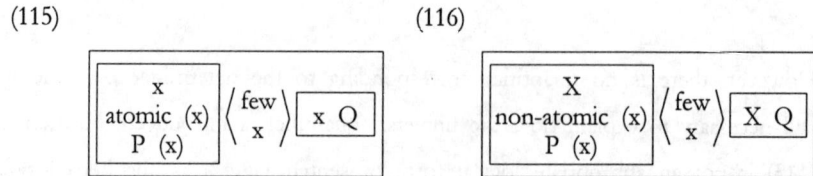

(117)   Few students wore blue jeans.

(118)   Few competing companies have common interests.

Fourth, it is not always required to consider every i-sum to determine the truth value of a sentence which has a quantificational NP as its subject and a collective VP. For example, sentence (119) is true if there is at least one i-sum of persons who agrees on the issue in the same way and the cardinality of the i-sum is a member of one-place predicate MANY. The i-sum need not be the largest among the i-sums of persons which agree on the issue. That is, sentence (119) should be reduced into DRS (120) rather than DRS (121).

(119)   Many people agree on this issue.

(120)
$$\boxed{\begin{array}{c} X \\ \text{person* } (X) \\ \text{MANY } (|X|) \\ X \text{ agrees on this issue} \end{array}}$$

(121)

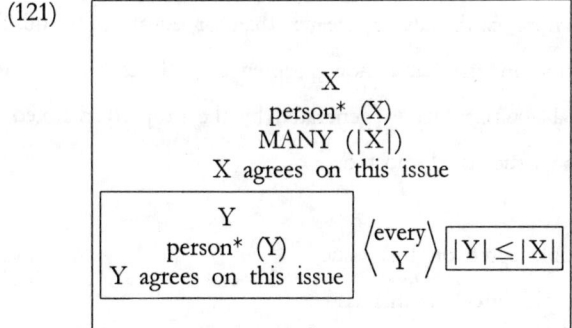

Then, the NP *many people* introduces a non-individual discourse referent just like a group-denoting NP such as *some people*. Sentence (122) is true iff there is an i-sum which agrees on the issue and the cardinality of the i-sum is a member of SOME.

(122) Some people agree on this issue.

Then, why is it necessary to consider every i-sum of people which agrees on the issue to determine the truth value of sentence (107)?

(107) Few people agree on this issue.

I believe that the monotonicity of a quantifier plays a role here[23]. When an NP with a quantifier which is not monotone-increasing is followed by a collective VP, the cardinality of the maximal i-sum must be considered. This generalization is further evidenced by the contrast between the truth conditions of sentence (113) with a monotone increasing quantifier, *at least 5*, and sentence (114) with a non-monotonic quantifier, *at most 5*. Sentence (123) is true iff there is at least one i-sum of persons whose cardinality is greater than or equal to 5 and the i-sum agrees on the issue in the same way. Sentence (124) is true iff the cardinality of the maximal i-sum, which is generated by the property denoted by person and agrees on the issue, is at most 5.

(123) At least 5 people agree on this issue.
(124) At most 5 people agree on this issue.

Based on this observation, I will treat the maximality condition which is represented as a duplex condition on a DRS as being accommodated by the non-monotonicity of a quantifier. Now, denotations of *few* and *many* given in

(100) are modified as in (125).

(125)   Few: λCN λVP FEW (σx[$\exists$y (CN(y) & VP(y) & x=|y|)])

   Many: λCN λVP MANY (σx[$\exists$y (CN(y) & VP(y) & x=|y|)])

Denotations in (125) are equivalent to those in (126).

(126)   Few: λCN λVP [$\exists$y (CN(y) & VP(y) & FEW (|y|)]

   Many: λCN λVP [$\exists$y (CN(y) & VP(y) & MANY (|y|)]

These denotations are similar to denotations of group-denoting determiners such as *some* and *five*.

(127)   Some: λCN λVP [$\exists$y (CN(y) & VP(y) & SOME (|y|)]

   Five: λCN λVP [$\exists$y (CN(y) & VP(y) & FIVE (|y|)]

In DRT terms, NPs *few CN* and *many CN* introduce a non-individual discourse referent by specifying the cardinality of the discourse referent just like group denoting NPs.

In the end, Roberts' approach toward a sentence which has a quantificational NP as its subject and is followed by a collective VP is not a quantificational approach but a typical non-quantificational one like mine.[24]

2.2.4. Predication with Ambiguous Predicates

An ambiguous predicate like *built a cabin* can take an atomic individual as well as an individual-sum as its argument. When it takes an atomic individual, a distributive reading is necessarily obtained. When it takes an i-sum as its argument, a distributive reading is optional as in (128) and (129).

(128) John built a cabin.

(129) John and Bill built a cabin.

(i)   John built a cabin and Bill did, too.

(ii) John and Bill as a group built a cabin.

When some quantificational NPs such as *every farmer* and *most farmers* are followed by an ambiguous predicate, only a distributive reading is obtained as in (130) and (131). This result is predicted by the quantificational approach.

(130) Every farmer built a cabin.

(i)   For all individual farmers x, x built a cabin.

(ii) $\neq$ All the farmers as a group built a cabin.

(131) Most farmers of the town built a cabin.

(i)   For most farmers x, x built a cabin.

(ii) $\neq$ The majority of the farmers of the town as a group built a cabin.

When quantificational NPs *many farmers*, *few farmers*, *all farmers* and *at least five farmers* are followed by an ambiguous predicate, both readings are possible as in (132) and (133). These data are problematic to the quantificational approach. Until now, I have not seen any attempts to solve this problem in the quantificational approach.

(132)   Many farmers lifted a huge rock.

   (i)   They individually lifted a huge rock.

   (ii)   They as a group lifted a huge rock.

(133)   At least five farmers lifted a huge rock.

   (i)   They individually lifted a huge rock.

   (ii)   They as a group lifted a huge rock.

2.2.5. Problems about Abstraction

When a pronoun is not in the scope of its antecedent (or is not c-commanded by its antecedent) as in (134) and (135), the syntactic number agreement between them is not observed.

(134)   [Every student]$_i$ came in. They$_i$ gathered in the hall.

(135)   Every student submitted [a proposal]$_j$, but they$_j$ were returned unopened. (Root 1986)

Sentence (134) poses another problem: the predicate *gathered in the hall* requires a non-individual discourse referent. Then, the pronoun *they* must be reduced into a non-individual discourse referent which is to be linked to an accessible non-individual discourse referent. If *every student* introduces only an individual discourse referent, how can the pronoun be anaphorically related to its antecedent?

Kamp and Reyle (1990) introduce an operation which accommodates a non-individual discourse referent from a duplex condition. Consider the first sentence of (135) which is reduced into DRS (136). DRS (136) does not contain any non-individual discourse referent which can be picked up as an antecedent of the discourse referent introduced by *they* of the second sentence. Kamp and Reyle, like Roberts (1987) and Root (1986), take the position that a non-individual discourse referent is accommodated to be mapped into an i-sum. Each atomic i-part of the i-sum is a proposal submitted by a student. Similarly, another non-discourse referent is accommodated to be mapped into an i-sum whose i-parts are students who submitted a proposal.

(136)

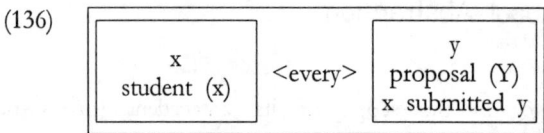

Kamp and Reyle call the operation Abstraction. Abstraction has two parts: one is to make a union of the two DRSs of a duplex condition. For example, from the duplex condition of (136), DRS (137), the union of the two DRSs, is obtained.

(137)

> x,y
> student (x)
> proposal (y)
> x submitted y

The second part of Abstraction abstracts a non-individual discourse referent from the union of the two DRSs with respect to a chosen discourse referent of the union. In (137), when x is chosen as a base of the operation, a non-individual discourse referent is obtained which is to be mapped into an i-sum whose i-parts satisfy the conditions in (137). Now, the anaphoric relations in (135) and (136) are explained as usual.

This approach has some problems. First, it cannot explain the anaphoric relations in sentences (138) and (139). For example, sentence (139) is reduced into DRS (140). Notice that the discourse referent introduced by the pronoun *their* is in the second DRS of the duplex condition. It is impossible to accommodate a non-individual discourse referent which is to be linked to x.

(138)   Every student in the room is proud of their joint project.

(139)   Every son of John contributed money to buy a diamond ring for their mother[25].

(140)

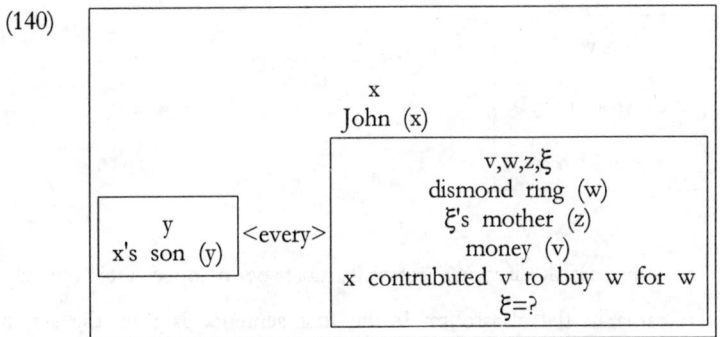

Second, the abstraction operation cannot accommodate a non-individual discourse referent to which the discourse referent introduced by *they* in the second sentence of (141) is linked. The first sentence of (141) is reduced into DRS (142).

(141)   No student came into the classroom. They gathered on the lawn to protest Dean's decision.

(142)

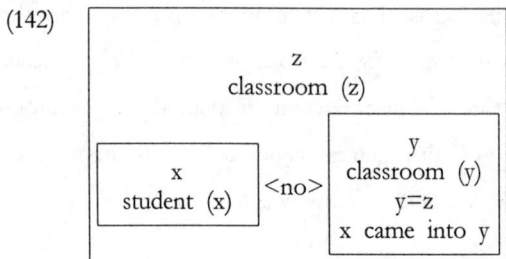

The union of the two DRS of the duplex condition of DRS (142) is DRS (143).

(143)

```
x,y
student (x)
classroom (y)
y=z
x came in y
```

Then, the accommodated discourse referent must be mapped into the set of students who came in the classroom. If the first sentence is true, the set must be empty since there was no student who came in the classroom. Of course, this non-individual discourse referent cannot be an antecedent of the discourse referent introduced by the pronoun they of the second sentence of (141).

2.3. Conclusion

I have specified the system of ununified approaches by examining (i) how an NP is classified into one of the two categories--quantificational and non-quantificational, (ii) how an NP is reduced by DR Construction Rules and

(iii) how unbound pronouns are treated. I have also pointed out some problems of ununified approaches in such areas as NP classification, number agreement, predication mode, ambiguity in predication, and the abstraction operation.

Notes to Chapter 2

1. Individual denoting NPs denote atomic individuals or i-sum individuals.

2. Kamp and Reyle(1990, p311) classify quantifiers into three categories: quantificational indefinite, non-quantificational indefinite and definite as in Heim(1982). The following is their classification. It differs from Roberts' in that it includes *all* and modified numerals (for example, *at least two*) in quantificational determiners.

Classification of Determiners

	Num=plur	Num=sing
Quant=+	most, many, few no, all, at least two, at most two, exactly two, ...	every
Quant=-	some, several, two, ∅, ...	a,
Definite	the, ...	the, ...

3. For more information, see Roberts (1987, pp309-328).

4. Heim (1982) assumes the tri-partite structure of quantification. Sentence (i) has (ii) as its LF structure.

(i)   Every student came in.

(ii)

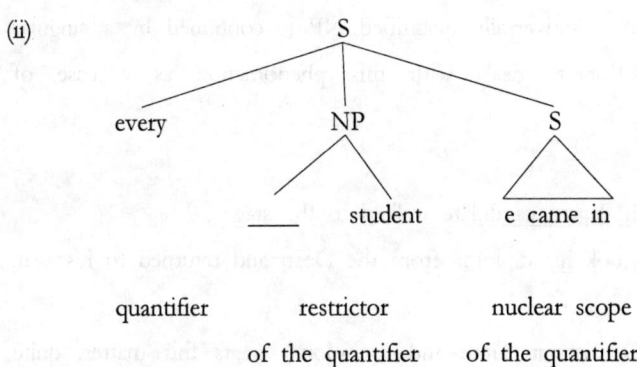

quantifier   restrictor   nuclear scope
              of the quantifier   of the quantifier

5. A non-individual discourse referent X is the conventionalized representation of the information that the discourse has a condition of *non-individual* (x).

6. Notice their DR construction rule of the distributive expansion differs from Roberts' treatment of the distributive expansion in that rule (23) does not require a distributive predicate. The distributive expansion is optional, according to them. Then, as professor Zucchi pointed out to me, there must be some restrictions on the rule which prevents the rule from applying to sentence (i) which does not have a distributive reading. But they don't deal with this matter.

(i)   Three men lifted a piano together.

7. Evans (1978, 1980) calls them E-type pronouns.

8. Geach (1967) takes this position. For more criticism against his approach, see Heim (1982), Chapter 1.

9. Roberts (1987, p38) reports a case which Partee names "the telescoping phenomenon." In (i), a universally quantified NP is continued by a singular pronoun (he, his). Roberts deals with this phenomenon as a case of "subordination"

(i)   a. Each degree candidate walked to the stage.

        b. He took his diploma from the Dean and returned to his seat.

10. Kamp(1983) (SID without Time and Questions) treats this matter, quite massively. Heim(1982) just assume that the deictic use of pronouns is a case of the anaphoric use of them. For example, when a hearer hears that a speaker uses a deictic pronoun with some indicating motion or gesture, the hearer accommodates some relevant information on the entity indicated by the motion. The hearer now links the entity introduced by the deictic pronoun to the accommodated entity. However, pragmatic information such as hearer's (or speaker's) intention plays an important role in determining which entity is accommodated by the indication motion. Morgan (1978) gave an example.

"... imagine a jar of sugar with a glass lid, on which the word *sugar* is painted in blue; and imagine that someone puts her fingertip just under the letter *u* of the word *sugar* and says, "What's that?" "Our answer might be, among other things, *the letter* **u**, *the word* **sugar**, *paint, blue paint, blue, English, a lid, glass, a glass lid, a jar, sugar, a jar of sugar,* and so on, depending on our interpretation of the person's interest — is she learning English, the use of seasoning, physics, or what? (p264)"

11. Chierchia and Rooth (1984) attempted to get rid of the configurationality

from a DRS by filtering out the anaphoric linking which does not meet the configurational requirements by manipulating the mapping from a DRS into a model. However, Kamp and Reyle (1990) and Roberts (1987) maintain that the configurationality plays a role in determining an acceptable anaphoric linking between two discourse referents. I also assume the configurationality in this study.

12. Here, the distinction between bound pronouns and unbound ones disappears since both of them introduce a discourse referent which must be linked to an accessible discourse referent. In Heim(1982)'s term, all the anaphoric pronouns are bound variables which are to be bound by a quantifier (explicit or provided by the existential closure).

13. This sentence was first discussed in Link (1987).

14. However, some stipulations are needed to get DRS (54): (i) each of the two pronouns introduces a distinct discourse referent even though the two pronouns bear the same indices, (ii) when a pronoun and an NP is coindexed, the discourse referent introduced by the pronoun must be linked either to the discourse referent introduced by the NP, or to the discourse referent which is an i-part of the discourse referent introduced by the NP. With these stipulations, sentence (53) is easily processed into (54).

15. Even though we admit that a plural pronoun introduce a neutral discourse referent η, it cannot be linked to x since it is not accessible to x and x is not carrying the diacritic pl (*every student* is not syntactically plural).

16. For other problems, see Root(1986, pp 30-35).

17. Let DRS K1 = < U_{K1}, CON_{K1}> where U_{K1} is the set of discourse referents of DRS K1 and CON_{K1} is the set of conditions of DRS K1. Similarly, let DRS K2 = <U_{K2}, CON_{K2}>. Then the union of DRSK1 and DRSK2 is <$U_{K1}U_{K2}$, $CON_{K1} \cup CON_{K2}$> by definition.

18. More formally, an embedding function f verifies condition (66) iff f(X)={a: $\exists$g[g $\supseteq$K1 f & g(x)=a & g verifies K1 in M} where K1 is the DRS of condition (66).

19. She argues that in (74) quantificational NPs are not antecedents of discourse pronoun *they*. The antecedents are accommodated. However, she does not say how and why the antecedents are accommodated.

20. Here I ignore the non-sexist use of *they*.

21. Kratzer (p.c. with Roberts reported in Roberts 1987) also recognizes a similar problem of this approach. Let a schema *few* P Q be true when the number of individuals which satisfy P and Q is smaller than the number of individuals which satisfy P but not Q. Kratzer's argumentation is summarized as follows: Consider a situation where there are four individuals, a,b,c and d such that a,b and c agree on the issue while d does not agree with any of them. Among 11 i-sums generated by the set {a,b,c,d}, 4 individuals, a+b, a+c, b+c, and a+b+c agree on the issue while 7 i-sums, a+d, b+d, c+d, a+b+d, a+c+d, b+c+d, a+b+c+d do not. If *few* is a plural quantificational quantifier, sentence (107) must be predicted to be true in this situation. But empirically, sentence (107) is

judged false in this situation. In general, if among m atomic individuals, n atomic individuals agree on the issue, the number of i-sums which agree on the issue is always smaller than the number of i-sums which do not unless n is equal to m. For more detailed discussion on this matter, see Roberts (1987, pp180-182).

22. If FEW is a characteristic function which takes a number and yields 1 or 0, (111) must be rewritten as in (i) where $|x|$ is the cardinality of x.

(i) $\forall x$ (*person (x) & agree (x) $\rightarrow$ FEW ($|x|$))

23. The monotonicity of a determiner is about "how information expressed in natural language in inferential pattern is preserved or lost by manipulating models (Partee et al. 1990, p380)." The monotonicity of determiners "is based on increasing or decreasing the number of entities in the relevant set A (CN-interpretation) and B (VP-interpretation)." Determiners are classified as follows:

left monotone increasing: (DAB & A $\subseteq$ A' $\rightarrow$ DA'B

right monotone increasing: (DAB & B $\subseteq$ B' $\rightarrow$ DAB'

left monotone decreasing: (DAB & A' $\subseteq$ A) $\rightarrow$ DA'B

right monotone decreasing: (DAB & B' $\subseteq$ B) $\rightarrow$ DAB'

I will take up the monotonicity related to determiners in Chapter 3, again.

24. Professor Zucchi pointed out to me that frequently determiners *many* and *few* are treated as cardinal determiners which contribute a non-quantificational reading to a sentence. If then, these determiners must be classified into

non-quantificational (or individual-denoting) determiners in Roberts' system. (They might be treated as being ambiguous between quantificational and individual-denoting. However, Roberts does not admit ambiguous determiners in her classification of determiners.) In addition, an NP with *most* can also be followed by a collective predicate like *gathered on the play ground* as in (i).

(i)   Most students (of the class) gathered on the play ground.

25. The preferred reading of sentence (139) is that all the sons of John wanted to buy a diamond ring for a certain woman, Susan, for example, who is the mother of all the sons of John. Compare sentence (139) with sentence (i) which has only one reading that every son of John has his own mother for whom he wanted to buy a diamond ring.

(i)   Every son of John contributed money to buy a diamond ring for his
        mother.

Chapter 3. A Unified Approach toward the Distributivity

3.0. Introduction

The purpose of this chapter is to specify my alternative, a unified approach toward distributivity. As I mentioned in Chapter 1, I take the following set of assumptions:[1]

(i)   Indefinites whether or not they are quantificational are bound variables.

(ii) Anaphoric pronouns are plain bound variables.

(iii) Default existential generalization (existential closure in Heim(1982)) of free variable is needed.

(iv) Quantifiers are capable of binding multiple variables (unselective binding).

Note that quantificational NPs in Kamp and Reyle's system are treated as variables in my approach since they are also indefinites. In this chapter, I will specify what kind of variables (or discourse referents) a quantificational NP introduces and what conditions the discourse referent must be assigned. The second question to be addressed is how a quantificational force is introduced if a quantificational NP of Kamp and Reyle's system introduces a discourse referent in the main DRS like a non-quantificational NP such as *two students*. For example, the NP *every student* in sentence (1) introduces a non-individual discourse referent into the main DRS. DRS (2) which is obtained from sentence (1) represents the reading that all the student (of a model) lifted a piano as a group contrary to the meaning of sentence (1). The universal quantifier over individual students must be provided in some way.

(1)   Every student lifted a piano.

(2)

$$\begin{array}{|c|}\hline X, y \\ \text{student } (X) \\ |X| = |\text{student}| \\ \text{piano } (y) \\ X \text{ lifted } y \\ \hline \end{array}$$

The third question is how to explain the three sets of data in (2), (3) and (4). The first set of data is about the anaphoric relation between a singular (or a plural) pronoun and its antecedent which is quantificational. The second set is about the case where a quantificational NP is followed by a collective predicate. The third one is about the predication with ambiguous predicates.

(2)   a.   [Every boy]$_i$ loves his$_i$ mother.

          b.   [Every son of John]$_i$ contributed money to jointly buy a diamond ring for their$_i$ mother.

(3)   a.   *Every student gathered.

          b.   Most (Many, Few) students gathered.

(4)   a.   "Many students lifted a piano" reads as

   (i) The students lifted a piano, individually, or

   (ii) The students as a group lifted a piano.

b.   "Every student lifted a piano" reads as

        (i) The students lifted a piano, individually, but not as

        (ii) The students as a group lifted a piano

As shown in Chapter 2, (2)b, (3)b and (4)a are problematic to the non-unified approach. I will show how the unified approach toward distributivity copes with these data. In the other hand, (2)a, (3)a and (4)b are problematic to the unified approach: in (2)a, if *every student* introduces a non-individual discourse referent into the main DRS and the singular pronoun *his* introduces an individual discourse referent, the two discourse referents cannot be linked to each other; in (3)a, if the NP *every student* introduces a non-individual discourse referent, it must be able to combine with a collective predicate; in (4)b, if the NP *every student* is the same as the NP *many* students in that they introduces a non-individual discourse referent, sentence (4)b must be ambiguous as (4)a is.

   In section 3.1, I will deal with how to represent the distributivity in the unified approach. In section 3.2, I will classify the NPs of English based on the kinds of predicates they can combine with. In section 3.3, I will define denotations of English quantifiers. In section 4, I will deal with the data given in (2) through (4).

3.1. Distributivity in the Unified Approach

This section is to specify how the unified approach deals with distributivity.

As shown in chapter 1, the approach assumes that the VP of a sentence is responsible for the distributive or collective reading of the sentence. In this section, I will give some evidence to the claim that VP is the source of distributivity. Then, I will specify the DR construction rule for distributivity.

3.1.1. Ambiguity with respect to Distributivity and Collectivity

A sentence containing a conjoined NP as the subject can be ambiguous in some cases. Sentence (5) is paraphrasable as (6)a or (6)b according to its distributive and collective readings, respectively. In the reading of (6)a, there were two piano-carrying events, while in (6)b, there was only one such event.

(5)   John and Mary carried the piano upstairs.

(6)   a.   John carried the piano upstairs, and Mary did too.

        b.   John and Mary carried the piano upstairs together.

Now, let's examine the source of ambiguity of (5). Two alternatives are possible.[2] One is that the ambiguity is due to the ambiguity in the denotation of the subject conjoined NP (here, *John and Mary*).[3] In other words, the subject denotes $(\lambda P P(j)$ & $\lambda P P(m))$ V $(\lambda P P(j \oplus m))$. In this case, the denotation of the predicate is determined. That is, the predicate denotes a set of all the individuals and groups (or i-sums) who carried the piano upstairs. Then, (5) is true either when John and Mary carried the piano upstairs, individually or when they did it in group. The readings of (6)a and b are represented as in (7).

(7)   a. $(\lambda P P(j)$ & $\lambda P P(m))$ (carried-the-piano-upstairs')

=carried-the-piano-upstairs'(j) & carried-the-piano-upstairs' (m)

b. $\lambda PP(j \oplus m)$(carried-the-piano-upstairs')

=carried-the-piano-upstairs'(j $\oplus$ m)

The second approach states that the source of the ambiguity is the ambiguity of the verb phrase. The subject conjoined NP has a uniquely determined denotation. The VP is either distributive or collective. On the collective reading, the VP contains in its denotation the set of all the i-sums and atomic individuals that carried the piano upstairs. On the distributive reading, the VP denotes all the atomic individuals that carried the piano upstairs and all the i-sums of these atomic individuals. This approach needs an operator which ensures that when an i-sum is predicated of by a predicate, its every i-part is also predicated of by the same predicate (that is, an operator which makes a predicate distributive). Following Link(1983) and others, I introduce the operator *, "working on 1-place predicates P, which generates all the individual sums of members of the extensions of P" (Link 1983,p306). Then, *P is actually the complete free join semi lattice generated by $\parallel P \parallel$. Following him (1983, 1985), I am going to use the raised 'D' as the distributive operator. By definition, $^{D}*P(x) \leftrightarrow \forall y[y\Pi x$ & AT(y) $\rightarrow$ P(y)]. Now, the two readings of (5) are obtained as in (8).

(8)   a.   distributive reading

$^{D}*$carried-the-piano-upstairs (j $\oplus$ m) =

carried-the-piano-upstairs(j) & carried-the-piano-upstairs(m)

b.   collective reading

*carried-the-piano-upstairs (j $\oplus$ m)

I take the second approach in this chapter with the following evidence:

1. There are "intrinsic distributive (or collective) predicates" such as *be-asleep*. These predicates are always distributive since there are no cases in which, for example, John is not asleep and Mary is not asleep but the i-sum of *John and Mary is asleep*. Then, according to the first approach, the sentence *John and Mary are asleep* must be ambiguous as in (9) since the subject *John and Mary* are not specified in terms of distributivity. But it is against the intuition of a native speaker.

(9)   a. $(\lambda PP(j)$ & $\lambda PP(m))$ (are-asleep) = is-asleep(j) & is-asleep(m)
        b. $\lambda PP(j \oplus m)$ (are-asleep) = are-asleep$(j \oplus m)$

2. The conjoined subject NP of a distributive (or collective) sentence can be the antecedent of plural pronoun *they* which is the subject of a sentence with a collective (or a distributive) reading as in (10).

(10)   a. [Tom and Bill]$_i$ were asleep soundly. They$_i$ lifted a piano, together during the day.
        b. [Tom and Bill]$_i$ lifted a piano, together. They$_i$ were asleep soundly at night.

In (10)a, *Tom and Bill* is the subject of an unambiguous distributive sentence, and *They* is the subject of an unambiguous collective sentence (and vice versa in (10)b). If the first approach is correct, *Tom and Bill* must be translated into $\lambda PP(t)$ & $\lambda PP(b)$ or $\lambda PP(t \oplus b)$ where t, b and t$\oplus$b are translations of 'Tom', 'Bill' and 'Tom and Bill' respectively. In (10)a, Tom and Bill must be $\lambda PP(t)$ &

λPP(b) since the sentence is distributive. But as the antecedent of they, *Tom and Bill* must be λPP(t⊕b). This fact cannot be properly explained by the first approach. In the second approach, *Tom and Bill* is always translated into an i-sum t⊕b, and is the antecedent of *they*.

3. As first pointed out by Dowty (1986), the coordination of an intrinsic distributive VP and an intrinsic collective VP provides another fact against the first approach. Sentence (11) is adopted from Lasersohn (1989: his example sentence (6)). In (11), VP *met in the bar* is unambiguously collective and VP had a beer is distributive.

(11)   John and Mary met in the bar and had a beer.

To explain (11), the first approach must regard *John and Mary* as being distributive as well as collective such that when it is predicated of by *met in the bar*, it is collective and when it is predicated of by *had a beer*, it is distributive. Actually, this position is taken in Gillon (1990). According to him, *John and Mary* denotes two different 'covers' each of which is predicated of by one of the two VP's. But, it is still dubious that an NP can simultaneously have the two denotations incompatible to each other. I will deal with Gillon's position in section 3.4. In the second approach, this phenomenon can be explained in a compositional way. A coordinated VP denotes the intersection of the denotations of conjunct VP's. By the closure condition described above, a distributive VP *had a beer* denotes a set {j,m, t, b, j+m, t+b, ...}. A collective VP *met at the bar* denotes a set {j+m, t+b, ...}. Then, the VP *met at the bar and had a beer* denotes {j+m, t+b, ...}. Proposition denoted by (8) is true because j+m is a member of the denotation of the coordinated VP.

3.1.2. DR Construction Rule for Distributivity

Following Roberts(1987), I will represent as NP(D) the NP which is translated into an argument of a distributive predicate.[5] I just mark (D) on an NP node directly as in (12).

(12)

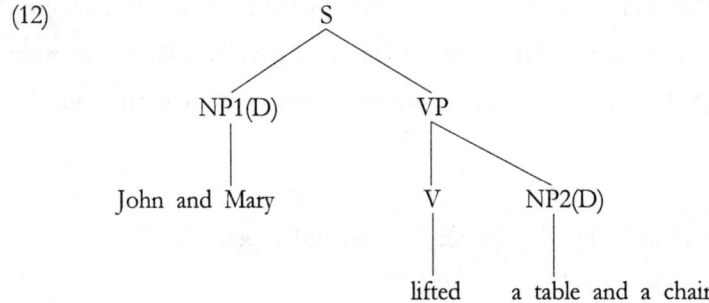

One thing must be assumed to maintain this alternative. When an NP is marked with (D), the rest of the sentence must be understood as being interpreted as a distributive predicate which takes the NP as its argument. Then, *John and Mary* is interpreted as an argument of a predicate which is, in turn, an interpretation of *lifted a table and a chair* (λx[x lifted a table and a chair]). For NP2(D), the predicate is λx[John and Mary lifted x]. I will take this option to represent distributivity on a syntactic analysis tree.

The basic tenet of a unified approach about distributivity is that a distributive reading is rendered when a distributive predicate takes an i-sum as its argument. (Recall that in Kamp and Reyle's system, this position is taken to explain the distributivity in a sentence where a non-quantificational NP is the subject of a distributive predicate, but is not taken to explain the sentence where a quantificational NP is the subject of a distributive predicate.) Then, DR

Construction rules for distributivity must be specified in terms of the relation between a predicate and every (atomic) i-part of a non-individual discourse referent which is to be mapped into an i-sum individual. Assume that an NP is already reduced, introducing a non-individual discourse referent according to some DR construction rules. Now, an NP(D) is replaced by X(D) according to the rules.

In the unified approach, DR Construction rule for distributivity need not be sensitive to the kinds of NPs (for example, individual denoting NPs or quantificational NPs, etc.). Therefore, the construction rule is given simply as in (13).

(13)   CR.X(D)   (DR Construction Rule for the Distributivity)
        Triggering
        Configurations   [S ..., X(D), ...]
        $\gamma \subseteq \bar{\gamma} \in$ Conk:

        Operations: Replace $\bar{\gamma}$ by the duplex condition[6]

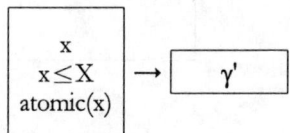

                        where x is a new discourse referent and γ' is
                        obtained from $\bar{\gamma}$ through replacing X by x.

The syntactic analysis tree of (12) is reduced by CR.X(D) into DRS (14)b via DRS (14)a. DRS (14)b represents the reading that each of John and Mary lifted each of a table and a chair.

(14)　　a.

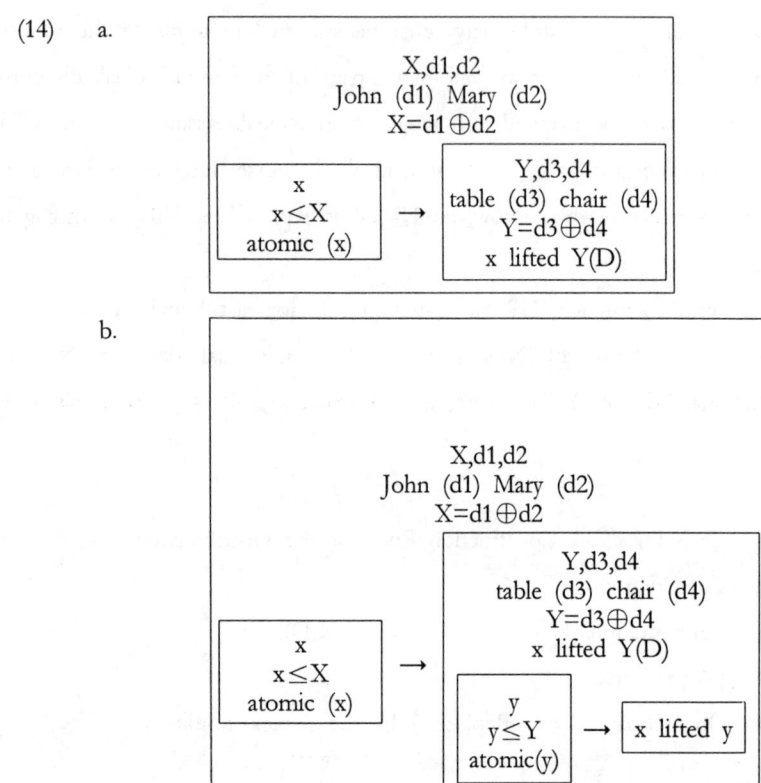

　　　b.

3.2. System of the Unified Approach

Van Eijk (1983) classifies NPs with respect to their syntactic and semantic numbers. He defines the notion of semantic number of an NP based on the denotation of the NP given in the generalized quantifier theoretical terms. He defines the semantic number of an NP as follows:

(15)   NP denotation [| a |] is proper iff [| a |] is defined and [| a |] $\neq$ 0 and [| a |] $\neq$ Þ(U) (Þ(U) ; the power set of the universe of a model)

(i)   s.n. (a) = 1   iff in every M (=<U, [| |]>) where [| a |] is proper, 0 is not a member of [| a |] and [| a |] contains at least one singleton set.

(ii)   s.n. (a) = 2+ iff in every M where [| a |] is proper, [| a |] has only sets as its elements that contain at least two members.

(iii)   s.n. (a) is undefined in all other cases.

(s.n. : semantic number of, 1: singular, 2+: plural)

NP *a man* is defined iff |man'| $\neq$ 0. Whenever it is defined, it is proper since [| a man |] is a set of sets of individuals which contain at least one man (it cannot be 0 since it must contain at least one individual which is a man, and it cannot be the power set of U since sets which do not contain any man cannot be member of [| a man |]. Moreover, the empty set which is a member of the power set is not a member of [| a man |]). It must contain at least one singleton set whose member is a student by the definition of [| a man |]. Therefore, its semantic number is 1. NP *three men* is defined iff |man| is greater than or equal to 3. Similarly, whenever it is defined, it is proper and every set of individual which is a member of [| three men |] must contain at least 2 members which are men (in this case, at least 3 members). Therefore, it is semantically plural. NP *every man* is always defined. But when $|man| = \phi$, $[|$ every man $|] = Þ(U)$ since every set contains the empty set as its subset. It does not satisfy the conditions of (i) since when $|man|=1$, it contains at least one singleton set, but when $|man| \geq 2$, it cannot contain any singleton set. It does not satisfy the conditions of (ii) with the same reason. Therefore, the semantic number of *every man* is undefined. Now, NPs are classified as follows:

(16)	syntactic number	semantic number
John	singular	singular
John and Bill	plural	plural
a man	singular	singular
five men	plural	plural
some men	plural	plural
few men	plural	plural
many men	plural	plural
many a man	singular	plural
most men	plural	undefined
every man	singular	undefined
all men	plural	undefined
no men	plural	undefined

I will group semantically plural NPs and semantically undefined NPs into semantically non-singular NPs.[7]

The basic ideas of the unified approach are now summarized as follows:[8]

(17)   Tenets of the Unified Approach

A.   A semantically singular NP is an individual variable. In DRT terms, it
         introduces an individual discourse referent.

B.   A semantically non-singular NP is a non-individual variable. In DRT
         terms, it introduces a non-individual discourse referent.

C.   A singular pronoun introduces an individual discourse referent; a plural
         pronoun introduces a neutral discourse referent whose number
         information is not specified (same as in Kamp and Reyle)

D.   The existential quantifier ($\exists$) is provided by Default Existential
         Generalization (Existential Closure); the universal quantifier ($\forall$) is
         provided by Distributivity Expansion but not by determiners such as
         every, all, and each.

E.   The role of a determiner is to specify the size of the i-sum (i.e. how
         many atomic individuals the i-sum has) denoted by an NP with the
         determiner. A linguistic determiner does not have quantificational
         forces.

With this set of assumptions, sentences (18) and (19) are reduced into DRSs (20)
and (21). DRS (20) is true iff there is a group of 5 students and each of the
students respects his teacher. DRS (21) is true iff there is a group consisting of
all the students and each of the students respects his teacher.

(18) [Five students]ᵢ respect theirᵢ teachers.

(19) [Every student]ᵢ respects hisᵢ teacher.

(20)   (21)

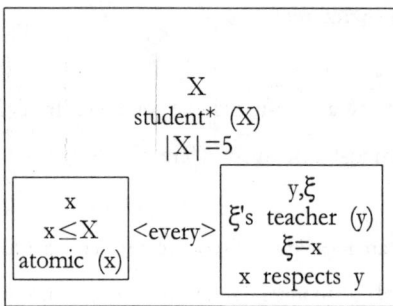 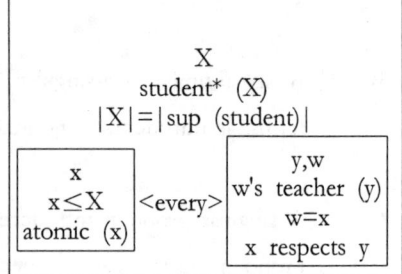

Let CN student denote a set {a,b,c}. Then *student** is a complete atomic free semi join lattice generated from {a,b,c}, that is, {a,b,c,a+b,a+c,b+c,a+b+c}. Then, condition *student** *(x)* is verified by an embedding function f iff f assigns to x some individual which is a member of the lattice generated from the property denoted by *student* (‖ student ‖). The function *sup* takes a property (or a set of individuals) and yields an i-sum which is the supremum of the property. In this case, *sup* *(student)* is an i-sum, a+b+c. Then, DRS (21) represents the reading that there is an i-sum which is the supremum of the property **student**, and for every i-part of the i-sum, x, x respects x's teacher.

3.3. Classification of Determiners

Scha (1981) classifies a determiner as distributive or collective based on whether or not an NP with that determiner can be followed by a collective VP. If the NP can be followed by only a distributive VP, the determiner of the NP is classified as a distributive one. If an NP can be followed by a collective VP, the determiner of the NP is a collective one. Then, determiners such as *most*, *many* and *few* must be classified as collective determiners since NPs with these determiners can be followed by a collective VP as in (22)-(24).

(22)   a. Most farmers (of the town) gathered in Town Hall.

    b. Most farmers (of the town) work, together.

    c. Most students fought one another.

    d. Most farmers have a common interest.

(23)   a. Many farmers (of this town) assembled in Town Hall.

    b. Many farmers (of the town) worked together.

    c. Many students fought one another.

    d. Many students have a common interest.

(24)   a. Few farmers (of this town) gathered in Town Hall.

    b. Few farmers (of the town) worked together.

    c. Few students fought one another.

    d. Few farmers have a common interest.

Here, how to categorize predicates becomes essential. Actually, Kamp and Frey cited in Root(1986) treat *gathered* as a mixed predicate which is ambiguous with respect to the distributivity/collectivity.[9] However, Dowty(1986) provides convincing arguments against their classification (cf. Dowty 1986, pp108-111). According to him, mixed predicates of Kamp and Frey are collective predicates with "distributive sub-entailments". He informally presents what the term "sub-entailment" means as follows:

Although collective predicates like gather obviously do not distribute down to the members of the groups of which they are predicated in a literal way (i.e. *The students gathered* doesn't entail **Every student individually gathered*), this doesn't really mean that such predicates completely lack entailments about the individual members of their group subjects. Consider what is required of individual students for the sentence *The students gathered in the hall* to be true. Clearly, every student in the group referred to by the students (or "most every student") must come into the hall and remain long enough that they are all there at a common time. Thus, gather distributively entails some property of members of its group subject (each undergoing a change of location), but *gathering* itself can only be true of the group *qua* group.

Dowty also introduce the notion "collective sub-entailments" whose definition is alluded in the following quotation. Even though he does not give an explicit definition of it, we can infer that collective sub-entailments are group actions entailed by a predicate. I will use the term in this sense.

.... It has frequently been observed that ordinary singular effected-object sentences such as (28a) have causative entailments, that is, that (28a) entails that some action that John performed, presumably a complex one, brought about the existence of the cabin. I think (28b) should be no different, except that the entailment is that some "group action" by a subset of the group of students in question brings about the existence of the cabin.

(28) a. John built that cabin.
b. The students built that cabin.

Now I don't have a fully-developed theory of group actions, but fortunately I only need to make some very weak assumptions about what a group action is: namely an action by a group takes place whenever every member of the group does something. (Dowty 1986, pp 104-105)

Then, when a collective predicate P which takes an i-sum X as its argument distributively sub-entails a property Q, every atomic i-part of X has the sub-entailed property Q. When a collective predicate P which takes an i-sum X as its argument collectively sub-entails a property Q, a non-atomic i-part Y of the i-sum (possibly, the i-sum, itself) has the property Q.

He classifies predicates as in (25) (Dowty 1986, p112).

(25)   Classification of Predicates

    I. Purely distributive predicates: fall asleep, be pregnant

    II. Collective predicates with distributive sub-entailments:
        A. Collectives whose only entailments may be distributive sub-entailments("disguised distributives): gather, ...

        B. Collectives with both collective and distributive entailments: be a happy couple, surround the fort

    III. Purely collective predicates:
        be numerous, be few in number, be a large group

    IV. Predicates ambiguous between Collective (II-B) and Distributive: build a cabin, carry the piano upstairs

    V. Predicates ambiguous between Collective (II-B) and indexically-collective distributive[10]: count, enumerate

I follow Dowty(1986) in classifying predicates.

Now, I will classify NPs according to what predicates they can take. To do this, I will examine whether or not there are restrictions on the combination of an NP with a predicate. Clearly, a semantically singular NP of van Eijk's classification cannot combine with any collective VP as in (26).

(26)   a. John fell asleep.

       b. *John gathered.

       c. *John surrounded the fort.

       d. *John is numerous.

Semantically non-singular NPs can combine with distributive VPs as in (27).

(27)   a. John and Bill fell asleep.

       b. Every student fell asleep.

       c. Most students fell asleep.

       d. Many students fell asleep.

       e. Some students fell asleep.

       f. 5 students fell asleep.

       g. The students fell asleep.

However, *every-CN*, *each-CN* and *both-CN*[11] cannot combine with any collective VP as in (28).

(28)   a. *Every student gathered in the hall.

       b. *Each student surrounded the fort.

       d. *Both students are a happy couple.

Most-CN, many-CN and *few-CN* can be followed by a collective VP with distributive sub-entailments, but not by a purely collective one as in (29).

(29)   a. Most (Many or Few) students gathered in the hall.

        b. *Most (Many or Few) students are a big (or small) group.

Among them, when a *most CN* is followed by a VP with collective as well as distributive sub-entailments, the sentence is unacceptable or very odd, as in (30).

(30)   a. #Most musicians performed a symphony.

        b. #Most soldiers surrounded the fort.

Intuitions about determiner *few* is quite shaky. Sentences in (26) are judged unacceptable or questionable.[12] However, sentences in (27) which have an NP with a *few* instead of few are judged acceptable.

(26)   a. #(?)Few musicians performed a symphony.

        b. #(?)Few soldiers surrounded the fort.

(27)   a. A few musicians performed a symphony.

        b. A few soldiers surrounded the fort.

This indeterminacy is also found when an NP with *few* is followed by an ambiguous predicate. Some informants judge that sentences in (28) have only a distributive reading, but others judge that they are ambiguous between a distributive reading and a collective reading. However, sentences in (29) can have both readings.

(28) a. Few students made a cabin.

b. Few students lifted a huge rock.

(29) a. A few students made a cabin.

b. A few students lifted a huge rock.

Taking a risk of the over-generalization, I will classify *most* and *few* into the same category with respect to the mode of predication.

Determiners, *many, some, several, all,* etc are similar to a *few* in that NPs with these determiners can combine with a distributive predicate, a collective with distributive sub-entailments and a collective with collective sub-entailments as in (30). But they cannot combine with purely collective predicates.

(30) a. Many (some, several or all) students fell asleep.

b. Many (some, several or all) students gathered in the hall.

c. Many (some, several or all) musicians performed a symphony.

d. *Many (some, several or all) students are numerous/a small group.

NPs with numerals and definite articles can be followed by a distributive VP, a collective VP with distributive sub-entailments and a purely collective one.

(31) a. The students (or 100 students) fell asleep.

b. The students (or 100 students) gathered in the hall.

c. The students (or 100 students) met for lunch.

d. The students (or 100 students) is a big group.

Table (32) summarizes the combinatorial characteristics of NPs with predicates.

(32)

	Type I	Type II	Type III	Type IV
	every	most	many	the
	each	few	a few	the two
	both,...		all, some	two
distributive predicates	O.K.	O.K.	O.K.	O.K.
collectives with distributive sub-entailments	No	O.K.	O.K.	O.K.
collectives with dis. sub-entailments and collective sub-entailments	No	No	O.K.	O.K.
purely collective predicates	No	No	No	O.K.

Then, purely collective predicates require as an argument a Type IV NP. Collective predicates with distributive sub-entailments require a Type IV, a Type III or a Type II NP. Distributive predicates require as an argument an NP of any type.

Table (32) indicates that NPs are ordered with respect to their possibility to combine with a certain predicate. That is, if an NP can combine with a purely collective predicate, it also can combine with any other kinds of predicates. But the fact that an NP can combine with a distributive predicate does not guarantee that the NP can combine with a purely collective NP. From Table (32), the ordering of (33) is inferred.[13]

(33)   Type I NPs < Type II NPs < Type III NPs < Type IV NPs

I will define "minimal requirement" as in (34).

(34)   A predicate P minimally requires as an argument an NP of Type α iff when the predicate takes an NP of Type β such that $\beta < \alpha$, the resulting sentence is ill-formed.

Then, a purely collective predicate minimally requires an NP of Type IV, a collective predicate with distributive as well as collective sub-entailments requires an NP of Type III, a collective predicate with distributive sub-entailments minimally requires an NP of Type II, and a distributive predicate minimally requires a Type I NP.

Ambiguous predicates are ambiguous in that they minimally require an NP of Type I or an NP of Type III. That is, if they follow an NP of Type I or II, they are interpreted distributively but not collectively. If they follow an NP of Type III or IV, they are interpreted distributively or collectively.

Based on the above discussion, I classify NPs as in (35). First, I classify them into semantically singular and semantically non-singular. Semantically non-singular NPs are further classified into Type I through Type IV NPs.

(35) Classification of NPs

        Semantically singular: John, NPs with *a(n)*

        Semantically non-singular

                Type I: NPs with *every, each, both, no,* ...

                Type II: NPs with *most, few,* ...

                Type III: NPs with *many, a few, some, several, all,* ...

                Type IV: John and Mary, NPs with *the, the two, two,* ...

3.4. Denotations of Quantified NPs in the Unified Approach

In this section, I will specify what denotation an NP, specially a quantified NP, is assigned in the unified approach toward distributivity. The basic principle of the approach is to treat every NP equally as something like a referring expression. That is, *some students* refers to an i-sum with the cardinality of greater than or equal to two which is a member of the pluralized property of **student** represented by ***student**.[14] Strictly speaking, *some students* is translated as a variable which is to be bound by a contextually provided existential quantifier (existential closure in Heim(1982)'s sense).

3.4.1. DR Construction Rules for Indefinite NPs

I will follow Heim(1982) who treats definiteness as familiarity. I will concentrate on how to represent various kinds of indefinite NPs on DRSs. My DR construction rules for indefinite NPs are quite similar to van Eijk (1983)'s in that a semantically singular NP introduces an individual discourse referent into a current DRS and a semantically plural NP introduces a non-individual discourse referent into a current DRS. For the DR Construction rule for a semantically singular NP, I will adopt that of Kamp and Reyle's. For the DR construction rule for a semantically non-singular NP, I will slightly modify the DR construction rule for indefinite non-quantificational plural NPs of Kamp and Reyle specified in (36) (Kamp and Reyle 1990, p322). CR.NP[semantically plural] is defined as in (37). CR (37) is in effect the same as CR (36) except that rule (37) can apply to a quantificational NP of Kamp and Reyle's system as well as to an indefinite plural NP.

(36)   CR.NP[Quant=ind/Num=plur]

Triggering	(i)	$[_S [_{NP} [_{DET} \delta] [_N \beta]] [_{VP} \eta]]$
configurations	(ii)	$[_{VP} [_V \eta] [_{NP} [_{DET} \delta] [_N \beta]]]$[15]

$\gamma \subseteq \bar{\gamma} \in Con_K$:

Operations:	(a)	Introduce a new plural discourse referent X into the universe of the DRS K.
	(b)	Add $\beta^*(X)$ to Con_K.
	(c)	Substitute in $\bar{\gamma}$: X for $[_{NP} \delta\beta]$.

(37)   CR.NP[indefinite/semantically plural]

Triggering	
configurations:	same as (36)

Operations: a-c. same as (36)

                          d. Add $|X| = \delta'$

                                 where $|X|$ is the cardinality of X, and δ'

                                 is the number information expressed by

                                 δ.[16]

In the following section, I will specify how δ' is obtained from δ.

3.4.2. Type II and Type IV NPs in Non-quantificational Approach

I am going to stick to the assumptions of DRT (or File-Changing Semantics) one of which is that a singular indefinite denotes neither a (generalized) quantifier nor an individual, but it is represented as a variable with an associated descriptive condition. In the same vein, I take the position that a quantified NP is also represented as a variable (or it introduces a discourse referent).

Then, it is straightforward that an NP like *two students* or *some men* is translated into a variable. Let the cardinality of a variable X be $|X|$. A formula $|X| = n$ is true iff an assignment function assigns an i-sum individual **a** to X, and **a** has n atomic i-parts. The function of quantifiers such as *two* or *some* is to specify the value of n. Now, sentence (38) is translated into (39) in a predicate logical language.

(38)   a. Two students gathered in a hall.

            b. Some students gathered in a hall.

(39)   a. *student'(X) & $|X|=2$ & gathered-in-a-hall' (X)

            b. *student'(X) & $|X| \geq 2$ & gathered-in-a-hall' (X)

By existential closure, formulas in (39) are provided the existential quantifier, resulting in (40).

(40) a. $\exists X$ [*student'(X) & $|X|=2$ & gathered-in-a-hall'(X)]

   b. $\exists X$ [*student'(X) & $|X| \geq 2$ & gathered-in-a-hall'(X)]

DRSs (41)a and b are equivalent to (40)a and b in their truth conditions, respectively.

(41) a.

| X,y |
| *student(X) |
| $|X|=2$ |
| hall(y) |
| X gathered in y |

b.

| X,y |
| *student(X) |
| $|X| \geq 2$ |
| hall(y) |
| X gathered in y |

Kamp and Reyle (1990), Asher (1991), and Roberts(1987) also treat these quantifiers similarly. That is, a plural individual denoting NP introduces a non-individual type discourse referent and a condition of cardinality specification (i.e. $|X|=2$).

   DRS (41)a is true iff there is at least one embedding function f which maps X into an i-sum individual **a** with just two atomic i-parts of the universe of a model which is a member of a property ***student**, and it maps y into an atomic individual **b** which is a member of a property **hall** and **a** gathered in **b**. According to these truth conditions for DRS (41)a, it is true when the model contains one or more i-sums with two atomic i-parts which are members of ***student** and gathered in **b**.

3.4.3. Non-Monotonic Quantifiers

Now, let's examine quantifiers *at least two*, *exactly two*, and *at most two*. Sentence (42) is intuitively true when 3 students lifted a piano, together. Suppose a model where only one i-sum **c** with 3 atomic i-part which is a member of ***student** and lifted a piano **b**, and no other individuals lifted **b**. In this situation, DRS (43)a is false while (43)b is true. Therefore, (43)b with the condition $|X| \geq 2$ is the proper DRS for sentence (42).

(42)   At least two students lifted a piano, together.

(43)   a.

X,y
*student(X)
$|X| = 2$
piano(y)
X lifted y, together

b.

X,y
*student(X)
$|X| \geq 2$
piano(y)
X lifted y, together

Here, the function of *at least two* is to specify the cardinality of a non-individual type discourse referent, too. What about quantifier *exactly two* or *at most two*? Let's examine quantifier *exactly two*, first. Sentence (44)a and b contain a collective VP and a distributive one, respectively. Sentence (44)a is true if and only if there is at least one group of exactly two students who lifted the piano, together. Suppose the situation where students John and Bill lifted the piano, together, and Mary and Beth lifted the piano, together, and no group of students did. In that situation, the sentence is true. However, sentence (44)b is false if there is more than one group of exactly 2 students who attended the party. For (44)b to be true, all the students who attended the party must be exactly 2.

(44)   a. Exactly two students lifted the piano, together.

        b. Exactly two students attended the party.

Let's represent a distributive VP as ^{D}VP following Roberts (1987). Assume a syntactic tree of [s X ^{D}VP] to be further reduced by a DR Construction rule which was discussed in section 3.1.3.3. into a pair of split DRSs as in (45).[17]

(45)

$$\boxed{\begin{array}{c} x \\ x \leq X \\ atomic(x) \end{array}} \longrightarrow \boxed{x\ VP}$$

Now, (44)b is reduced into (46) by a series of DR Construction rules.

(46)

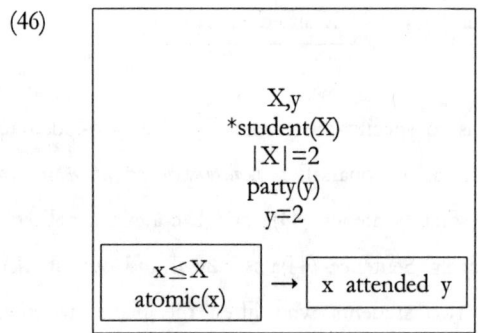

However, DRS (46) does not represent the reading of sentence (44)b correctly since (46) is true when there are two embedding functions f and g such that f and g map X into different i-sum individuals of a model and they embed all the conditions of (46) properly into the model, too.

This phenomenon is not restricted to quantifier *exactly n*. The phenomenon is witnessed when an NP with a quantifier which is not (right) monotone increasing is followed by a distributive VP (cf. van der Does 1992, p48). Monotonicity is defined as in (47) (Partee et al. 1990, p381).

(47)   (Right) Monotonicity

(i)   right monotone increasing
            If D CN VP1, then D CN VP2 (where VP1 $\subseteq$ VP2)
            ((DAB & B $\subseteq$ B') $\rightarrow$ DAB')

(ii)   right monotone decreasing
            If D CN VP1, then D CN VP2 (where VP2 $\subseteq$ VP1)
            ((DAB & B' $\subseteq$ B) $\rightarrow$ DAB')

Exactly n is not (right) monotonic since exactly 2 students came by 10 a.m. does not imply that exactly 2 students came by 11 a.m. (therefore, it is not right monotone increasing) and exactly 2 students came by 11 a.m. does not imply that exactly 2 students came by 10 a.m. (therefore, it is not right monotone decreasing). *At most n* is right monotone decreasing since at most 2 students came by 11 a.m. implies that at most 2 students came by 10 a.m.. Similarly, *few* and *no* are right monotone decreasing.

When sentence (48) is reduced into DRS (49), the DRS does not represent the reading of (48) properly since if there are 2 or more i-sums with at most 2 atomic i-parts which slept until 5 in the morning, sentence (48) is false.

(48)　　At most two students slept until 5 in the morning.

(49)

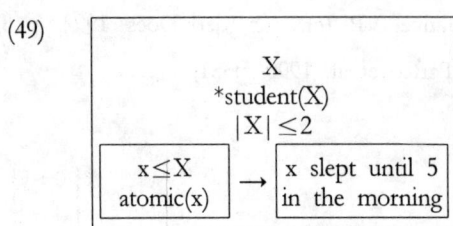

If *at most two students* is regarded as a quantificational NP, this kind of problem might disappear since the distributivity is directly captured as a result of the quantification. For example, (48) is processed into (50) which is true iff there are at most 2 embedding functions which map x into an individual of the model which is a student and it slept until 5 in the morning.

(50)

$$\boxed{\begin{array}{|c|}\hline x \\ student(x) \\ \hline\end{array} \;\; <\text{at most 2}> \;\; \begin{array}{|c|}\hline \text{x slept until 5} \\ \text{in the morning} \\ \hline\end{array}}$$

But this approach has some problems. First, it is impossible to capture a collective reading of a sentence which has as the subject an NP with a non-monotonic or monotone decreasing quantifier, without stipulating some rules. For example, to process (44)a repeated as (51), A DR construction rule is needed in which an NP with a non-monotonic quantifier introduces a non-individual discourse referent.

(51)　　Exactly two students lifted a piano, together.

This problem occurs whenever a quantified NP can be followed by a collective as well as a distributive predicate.[18] Second, in this approach, it is hard to explain the anaphoric relation between an anaphoric expression and its antecedent. For example, (48) can be continued as in (52).

(52)   [Exactly two students]$_i$ slept until 5 this morning. They$_i$ were late for class.

If the NP *exactly two students* does not introduce a non-individual discourse referent, the discourse referent introduced by *they* cannot be linked to an appropriate discourse referent.[19]

My solution in favor of the unified approach is as follows: Let D[non-mon] be a non-monotone increasing quantifier. A schema D[non-mon] P Q where P is a CN and Q is a distributive VP is processed so as to guarantee that the discourse referent introduced by an NP D[non-mon] P is the only one discourse referent which satisfies the subsequent conditions. For example, sentence (48) is processed into DRS (53).

(53)

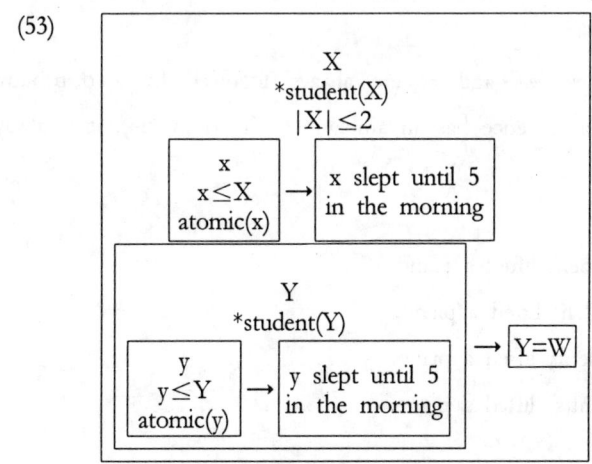

DRS (53) is true iff there is at least one embedding function f which embeds X into an i-sum **a** of the model with at most two atomic i-parts which is a member of *student. For each atomic i-part of **a**, it slept until 5 in the morning. And for all the individuals in the model whose atomic i-parts slept until 5 in the morning, they must be **a**. Since Y can be an individual discourse referent (in this case, an individual **b**, which Y is mapped into by an embedding function g, is an atomic i-part of itself), DRS (53) represents the readings of (48) correctly.[20]

This approach can deal with the problems stated above without positing other stipulations: it can deal with the collective reading contributed by a non-monotone increasing NP since the NP introduces a non-individual type discourse referent. Consequently, anaphoric problems shown in discourse (52) does not occur since there appears an accessible non-individual type discourse referent (X in (53)) to which a discourse referent introduced by *they* is to be linked.

3.4.4. Quantifiers Which Require Distributive Predicates

Quantifiers *each*, *every*, *both* and *no* are always followed by a distributive predicate. Even when a sentence has an ambiguous VP as in (54), it is always distributively read.

(54)   a. Every student lifted a piano.

         b. Each student lifted a piano.

         c. Both students lifted a piano.

         d. No student(s) lifted a piano.

An NP with *each*, *every* or *both* cannot be followed by a collective VP as in (55). This differentiates them from quantifiers such as *many*, *most* and *few* which can take a collective VPs as in (56).

(55) a. *Each student of the class gathered in a hall.

b. *Every student of the class gathered in a hall.

c. *Both students gathered in a hall.

(56) a. Most students of the class gathered in a hall.

b. Many students of the class gathered in a hall.

c. Few students of the class gathered in a hall.

However, an NP with *no* can be followed by a collective VP as in (57).

(57) No students of the class gathered in a hall.

It seems that quantifier *no* must be classified into Type II like *many* or *most*. But notice that sentence (57) is true iff it is not the case that a group of students of the class did not gather in a hall. (58) represents the reading of (57).

(58) $\forall X[(*\text{student-of-the-class}'(X)$ & $\text{non-atomic}(X)) \rightarrow \neg(\text{gathered-in-a-hall}'(X))]$

In other words, *no* is distributive over non-atomic entities in (58). In this respect, *no* is different from *many*, *few* and *most*.

3.4.4.1. *Each* and *Every*

I will recapitulate the semantics of an NP of the form "all CN" in the unified approach. An NP *all CN* denotes the i-sum individual generated by individuals which are the members of the property $[|CN|]$. That is, $[|all\ CN|]$ is the supremum of the lattice generated by $[|CN|]$. For example, let $[|student|] = \{a,b,c\}$. Then, $[|all\ students|] = a+b+c$. In DRT terms, *all CN*, as an indefinite NP, introduces a new discourse referent, X, into the universe of the current DRS and a new condition of $X=\sigma(CN')$.[21] Further, an embedding function f maps $\sigma(CN')$ into the supremum of $f(CN')$. When such an NP is followed by a distributive predicate, the sentence has a distributive reading. When it is followed by a collective predicate, a collective reading is resulted. In other words, the quantifier *all* denotes $\lambda P\lambda Q\exists X[X=\sigma(P)\ \&\ Q(X)]$. If Q is distributive, *all* actually denotes $\lambda P\lambda Q\exists X[X=\sigma(P)\ \&\ \forall x[x\leq X \rightarrow Q(x)]]$. Accordingly, sentences in (59) are interpreted as in (60). Sentence (59)a has a distributive VP and (59)b has a collective VP.

(59)　　a. All students wore blue jeans.

　　　　b. All students gathered in a hall.

(60)　　a. $\exists X[X=\sigma(student)\ \&\ \forall x[x\leq X\ \&atomic(x) \rightarrow wore\text{-}blue\text{-}jeans'(x)]]$

　　　　b. $\exists X[X=\sigma(student)\ \&\ gathered\text{-}in\text{-}a\text{-}hall'(X)]$

Every and *each* has been treated as a universal quantifier over atomic individuals.[22] Sentence (61) is translated as in (62).

(61)　　Every student wore blue jeans.

(62)　　$\forall x[student'(x) \rightarrow wore\text{-}blue\text{-}jeans'(x)]$

The truth conditions of (60)a and (62) are equivalent if the cardinality of the property **student** is equal to or greater than one. If the cardinality is zero, (62) is true since student'(x) is always false. (60)a is true since x≤X is always false (x is a variable over atomic individuals of the universe of a model and f(X) is a zero element. Thus, any individual cannot be an i-part of f(X).). Therefore, (60)a and (62) have the same truth conditions. It means that *every* and *each* denote $\lambda P \lambda Q^D \exists X[X=\sigma(P)$ & $^D Q(X)]$ (it is equal to $\lambda P \lambda Q \exists X[X=\sigma(P)$ & $Q(X)$ & distributive(Q)]).

Then, *every CN* denotes a zero element when the cardinality of the CN is zero, an atomic individual when the cardinality is one, and an i-sum individual when the cardinality is greater than one just like *all CN*. It is distinguished from *all CN* in that it is required to be followed by a distributive predicate. In other words, an *every CN* is minimally required by a distributive predicate (i.e. it is of Type I). In other words, it cannot be followed by other kinds of predicates. In DRT terms, a schematic sentence 'every P Q.' is represented as in (63).

(63)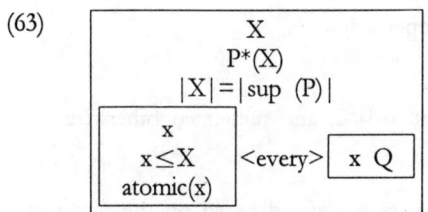

Condition $|X|$ = $|\sup (P)|$ is verified iff there is at least one embedding function of the main DRS, f, such that the cardinality of f(X) is the same as the cardinality of the supremum of property P (= σP). Actually, Two conditions P*(X) and $|X|$ = $|\sup (P)|$ is merged into one condition of X = sup (P). That is, DRS (63) is equivalent to DRS (64). In the following discussions, I will use

DRS (63) and DRS (64), interchangeablely.

(64)

$$
\boxed{
\begin{array}{c}
X \\
X = \sup (P) \\
\boxed{
\begin{array}{c}
x \\
x \leq X \\
\text{atomic}(x)
\end{array}
} \quad \langle \text{every} \rangle \quad \boxed{x \; Q}
\end{array}
}
$$

3.4.4.2. Both

Barwise and Cooper(1981) treats *both* as a definite determiner equivalent to *the two* which is, in turn, defined as in (65).

(65)   the *two* (s) = *every* (s) if $|s| = 2$, and undefined otherwise

Since *every* (s) is defined as a set of sets of individuals (or a set of properties) each of which contains the property s as its subset (or subproperty), *both* is defined as in (66) in Barwise and Cooper's system.

(66)   *both* (s) = $\{X \subseteq E| \; s \subseteq X\}$ if $|s| = 2$, and undefined otherwise

In the unified approach, the definiteness is defined based on the familiarity as stated above. Then, *both CN* denotes a non-individual variable which is to be assigned by an assignment function an i-sum individual which has two atomic i-parts. The i-sum individual must be familiar to the interlocutors at the stage where the NP is uttered. Moreover, it requires a distributive VP to follow it. In DRT terms, *both CN* introduces a non-individual discourse referent, X, in the universe of the current DRS, and conditions of $|X| = 2$ and $X = Y$ where Y is a discourse referent already introduced in the DRS. Now, *both* is translated as in (67). A formula *both CN VP* is reduced into (68).[23]

(67) $[|both|] = \lambda P \lambda Q \exists X[*P(X) \ \& \ |X|=2 \ \& \ Q(X) \ \& \ distributive(Q)]$

(68)

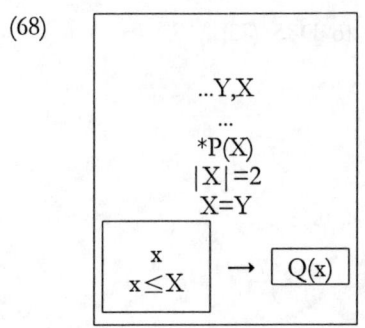

3.4.4.3. *No*

Sentence (69) is true iff it is not the case that for an individual, x, x is a student and x came in. That is, sentence (69) is correctly translated into (70).

(69)   No student came in.

(70) $\neg \exists x[student'(x) \ \& \ came\text{-}in'(x)])$

Formula (70) is equivalent to (71) which is true iff for every x which is a student, it is not the case that x came in.

(71) $\forall x[student'(x) \rightarrow \neg(came\text{-}in(x)]$

In the unified approach toward the distributivity, formula (71) is rewritten as in (72) where the distributivity is resulted when a distributive predicate applies to an i-sum individual.

(72) $\exists X[X=\sigma(\text{student})$ & $\forall x[x \leq X$ & $\text{atomic}(x) \to \neg(\text{came-in}(x))]]$

Formula (72) is truth-conditionally equivalent to DRS (73).

(73)

That DRS (73) is the representation of sentence (69) is evidenced by discourse (74) where a discourse anaphoric relation is established across the sentence boundary. A discourse referent introduced by *they* can be linked to X of DRS (73).

(74) [No student]$_i$ came in. They$_i$ gathered on the ground.

Quantifier *no* is translated as in (75).

(75) $\lambda P \lambda Q \exists X[X=\sigma(P)$ & $\neg^D Q(X)]$

        where $\neg^D Q(X) =_{df} \forall x[x \leq X$ &atomic(x) $\to \neg Q(x)]$

No can be followed by a plural CN as well as a singular one as in (76). When the VP is distributive, the reading of the sentence is the same as the one where *no* is followed by a singular CN. That is, sentence (76) has the same reading as sentence (69).

(76)   No students came in.

As in the translation of (75), the NP *no CN* requires a distributive VP. However, it can combine with a collective VP as in (77). In this case, the predicate distributes over non-individual i-sums as I have discussed above. Thus, the requirement that a VP be distributive need not be modified.

(77)   a. No students (of the class) gathered on the ground.

        b. No students (of the class) lifted a piano, together.

        c. No two students (of the class) lifted a piano, together.

(77)a (or b) is roughly paraphrased as any (non-singleton) sets of students did not gather on the ground (or lift a piano, together). (92)c is paraphrased as any sets of two students did not lifted a piano, together.[24] Then, (77)a and c are translated as in (78)a and b.

(78)   a. $\exists X[X=\sigma(\text{student})$ & $\forall x[x \leq X$ & $|x| \geq 2 \rightarrow \neg\text{gathered-on-the-ground}'(x)]]$

        b. $\exists X[X=\sigma(\text{student})$ & $\forall x[x \leq X$ & $|x|=2 \rightarrow \neg\text{lifted-a piano-together}'(x)]]$

To cope with sentences in (77), I modify the condition of (75) so as to guarantee that if Q is a distributive VP, it distributes over atomic i-parts of the i-sum, and if Q is a collective VP, it distributes over non-atomic i-parts.

(79) $\lambda P\lambda Q \exists X[X=\sigma(P)$ & $\neg^{D}Q(X)]$ where

$\neg DQ(X)=\forall x[x \leq X$ &atomic(x) $\rightarrow \neg Q(x)]$ if Q is distributive,

$\neg DQ(X)=\forall x[x \leq X$ &non-atomic(x) $\rightarrow \neg Q(x)]$ if Q is collective

Note, however, that the translation of (79) does not mean that the determiner *no* is ambiguous. Rather I maintain the position that there are two kinds of distributivity – distributivity over atomic individuals and distributivity over i-sum individuals, following Link (1987).[25]

Since *no* is a monotone decreasing quantifier, *no CN* is required to denote a unique i-sum individual with respect to a model. The denotation of *no* of (79), however, need not specify the uniqueness condition unlike such quantifiers as at *most n*, *exactly n*, and *few* because X in (79) is unique in itself in a model (if P is unique in a model, $\sigma(P)$ is also unique in the model).

3.4.5. *Most*, *Many* and *Few*

The denotations of these quantifiers are context-dependent. It is hard to determine how many is *many* without considering context in sentence (80). Sentence (80) can be understood that the number of 'straight-A' students are greater than a certain proportion of the students of a model. The proportion is to be determined by the context. When 10 % of the students got straight-A's this year, but usually 5 % of the students got them, sentence (80) might truthfully represent the situation (cf.Partee et al. 1990, p390).

(80)   Many students got straight A's this year.

Partee et al. 1990 (p395) distinguishes 4 denotations of *many* as in (81). Here, quantifiers are defined as a relation between two properties denoted by the CN of the subject and the VP of a sentence. In (81)a, *many* is defined with respect to the size of the universe of a model. In (81)b, it is defined with respect to the number of the atomic individuals contained in the property denoted by CN and contextually determined parameter (representing "constant or normal frequency"). In (81)c, the contextual parameter is explicitly defined in terms of the number of the atomic individuals of the universe and the number of the atomic individuals of the property denoted by VP. In (81)d, *many* is interpreted in terms of the number of the atomic individuals in the property denoted by VP and contextually determined parameter.

(81)   a. $\text{many}^1 E \ AB = \text{many}^1 E \ A(A \cap B)$ where $|(A \cap B)| > f(E)$

       b. $\text{many}^2 E \ AB = \text{many}^2 \ A(A \cap B)$ where $|(A \cap B)| > c.|A|$

       c. $\text{many}^3 E \ AB = \text{many}^3 \ A(A \cap B)$ where $|(A \cap B)| > |B|.|A|/|E|$

       d. $\text{many}^4 E \ AB = \text{many}^4 \ A \ (A \cap B)$ where $|(A \cap B)| > c.|B|$

In the unified approach stated above, *many* CN denotes a variable which is to be mapped into an i-sum by an embedding function. The cardinality of the variable is determined as in (81). Then, *many* is translated as in (82).

(82)   a. many1 : $\lambda P \lambda Q \exists X[*P(X) \ \& \ |X| > f(E) \ \& \ Q(X)]$

       b. many2 : $\lambda P \lambda Q \exists X[*P(X) \ \& \ |X| > c.|P| \ \& \ Q(X)]$

       c. many3 : $\lambda P \lambda Q \exists X[*P(X) \ \& \ |X| > |Q|.|P|/|E| \ \& \ Q(X)]$

       d. many4 : $\lambda P \lambda Q \exists X[*P(X) \ \& \ |X| > c.|Q| \ \& \ Q(X)]$

When I am not concerned with the exact number of atomic individuals of an i-sum into which X is to be mapped, I will just represent the number information as $|X|$=many. In this situation, many is defined as $\lambda P \lambda Q \exists$ $X[*P(X)$ & $|X|$=many & $Q(X)]$. *Few* and *most* is defined similarly except the number information.[26]

The second characteristic of *most CN*, *many CN* and *few CN* is that they require a predicate with distributive sub-entailments as in (83).[27]

(83) a. Most (Many or Few) students wore blue jeans, yesterday.

b. Most (Many or Few) students fell asleep during the class.

c. Most (Many or Few) students gathered on the ground.

d. *Most (Many or Few) students are numerous.

e. *Most (Many or Few) trees are denser in the middle of the forest.

According to Dowty(1986), all the distributive predicates and some collective ones have a distributive sub-entailment (or just sub-entailment) discussed in section 3.2. But the degree of the distributive sub-entailment is varied one by one. In (74)a, predicate "*vote to accept X* has the sub-entailment of *an individual vote to accept X* " (Dowty 1986, p101). However, "this predicate itself only entails that a certain percentage of members of the group must have the sub-entailed property in order for the group-property to obtain-at least 51 % of them." However, predicate *gather* "seems to require that the distributive sub-entailment apply to almost all members of the group."

(84) a. The students voted to accept the proposal.

b. The students gathered in a hall.

When *all* comes before *the* as in (85), both sentences have the readings where the sub-entailments apply to all members of the group.

(85) a. All the students voted to accept the proposal.

  b. All the students gathered in a hall.

A distributive predicate has itself as the sub-entailment, according to Dowty. That is, a distributive predicate is a special case of predicates with sub-entailments. The degree variation is also found among distributive predicates. Sentence (86)a properly describes the situation where only a small number of the reporters asked a question. But when *all* is placed, every reporter was required to ask a question for (86)b to be true.

(86) a. At the end of the press conference, the reporters asked the president questions. (Dowty 1986, p103)

  b. At the end of the press conference, all the reporters asked the president questions.

Dowty calls the effect of *all* "maximizing effect of *all* " which is summarized as in (87) (=his 19).[28]

(87) Hypothesis: the effect of *all* on a collective predicate is to fully distribute the predicate's sub-entailments to every member of the group argument: Instead of merely holding of some (proper) subset of these members, as required by the predicate by itself, *all* requires that these sub-entailments hold of every member of the group.

The same thing can be said to *most, many* and *few* as in (88).

(88)   Determiners *most, many* and *few* have the same maximizing effect as *all* described in (87).

Sentences (83)d and e are bad because the VPs are *numerous* and *are denser in the middle of the forest minimally* require Type IV NPs and the NP *most (many, few) students (or trees)* belongs to Type II (or Type III) NPs. (83)a and b are acceptable, and have a distributive reading because predicates have sub-entailments (the predicates themselves) which must apply to all the atomic members (or all the atomic i-parts) of [|most (many or few) students|] owing to the maximizing effect of *most (many or few)*.

Now, the schematized sentence (89) is processed into DRS (90). Let R be a distributive sub-entailment of predicate Q.

(89)   Most (Many or Few) P Q.

(90)

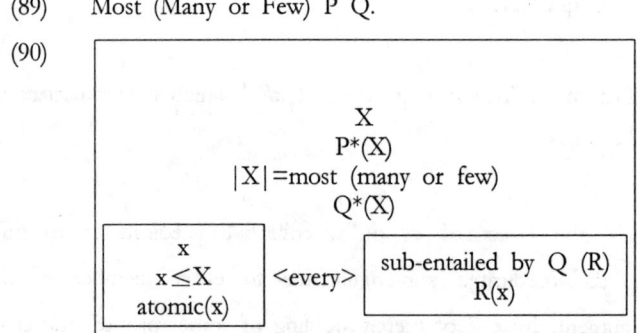

When Q is distributive a main DRS condition $Q^*(X)$ is vacuous since $Q^*(X) = \forall x[x \leq X \rightarrow Q(x)]$ and R=Q (that is, the duplex condition of (90) is obtained from DRS condition $Q^*(X)$).

3.5. Number Agreement

In my approach, semantically non-singular NP's such as *every student, most students, some students, John and Mary,* etc. introduce non-individual discourse referents. When a non-individual discourse referent is an argument of a distributive predicate, by the rule of Distributivity Expansion, a duplex condition is introduced. The universe of the antecedent DRS of the duplex condition contains an individual discourse referent and some relevant conditions on it. In this section, I will show how my approach explains the number agreement between a pronoun and its antecedent.

First, I will examine how Kamp and Reyle (1990) explain the number agreement in sentences (91)-(94).

(91)   John$_i$ respects his$_i$/*their$_i$ teacher.
(92)   [Every student]$_i$ respects his$_i$/*their$_i$ teacher.
(93)   [Some students]$_i$ respect their$_i$/*his$_i$ teachers.
(94)   [Many students]$_i$ respect their$_i$/*his$_i$ teachers.

They propose a number agreement rule of (95) to take account of the number agreement between a syntactically plural pronoun and its antecedent with the convention of (96).

(95)   A singular pronoun introduces an individual discourse referent and a plural pronoun introduces a neutral discourse referent. A discourse referent introduced by a plural pronoun must be linked to an accessible non-individual discourse referent or an accessible individual discourse referent with superscripted *pl.*

(96)   A (syntactically) plural quantificational NP introduces an individual
         discourse referent superscripted with *pl*. When a non-individual
         discourse referent is further processed by Distributivity Expansion, an
         individual discourse referent with superscripted *pl* is introduced in the
         antecedent DRS of a duplex condition.

Now, in sentence (91), the pronoun is not acceptable since it introduces a
neutral discourse referent which should be linked either to a non-individual
discourse referent or to an individual discourse referent marked with *pl*.
However, the indicated antecedent *John* introduces neither a non-individual nor
an individual discourse referent marked with *pl*. The same explanation can be
given to sentence (92). In (93), the plural pronoun is acceptable since *some
students* introduces a non-individual discourse referent and since the discourse
referent is an argument of a distributive predicate, an individual discourse
referent marked with *pl* is introduced which is accessible from the neutral
discourse referent introduced by the pronoun of (93). In (94), the plural pronoun
is acceptable since *many students*, a quantificational NP, introduces a split DRSs
with an individual discourse referent with *pl* in the antecedent DRS and the
pronoun introduces a neutral discourse referent in the consequent DRS.

By adopting abstraction accommodation into their system, Kamp and Reyle
can explain the number agreement in sentences (97)-(99). In (97), the pronoun
they is not acceptable since *John* introduces an individual discourse referent
without *pl*. In (98), the pronoun *they* is acceptable since the neutral discourse
referent introduced by the pronoun is linked to a non-individual discourse
referent accommodated from the split DRSs reduced from the first sentence of
(98). The acceptability of *they* in (99) can be explained straightforwardly.

(97)   John$_i$ came in. He$_i$/*They$_i$ wore blue jeans.

(98)   [Every student]$_i$ came in. They$_i$/*He$_i$ wore blue jeans.

(99)   [Some students]$_i$ came in. They$_i$/*He$_i$ wore blue jeans.

However, their approach has a problem in explaining the number agreement in sentence (100) since abstraction operation does not provide an appropriate discourse referent to which the neutral discourse referent introduced by the pronoun *they* is to be linked (see Chapter 2).

(100)   [Every son of John]$_i$ contributed money to buy a diamond ring to their$_i$ mother.

I will develop a way which can overcome the shortcomings of Kamp and Reyle's approach in number agreement. Here, I adopt Kamp and Reyle's idea that a plural pronoun introduces a neutral discourse referent. As the point of departure, I propose hypothesis (101).

(101)   A neutral discourse referent must be linked either to a non- individual discourse referent or an individual discourse referent which is introduced as an atomic i-part of a non-individual discourse referent.

With hypothesis (101), number agreement in sentences (91), (93), (94), (97)-(100) is explained since the NPs *every student, some students* and *many students* introduce a non-individual discourse referent. For example, sentence (94) is first reduced into DRS (102) where a non-individual discourse referent X is introduced. DRS (102) is further reduced into DRS (103) since the predicate *respect their teacher* is distributive.

(102)

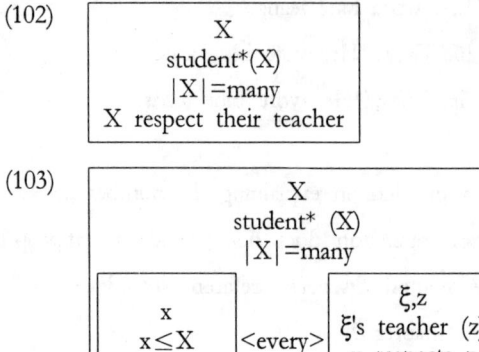

(103)

However, the unacceptable anaphoric relation in (104) is problematic to generalization (101).[29] Since a plural pronoun *their* introduces a neutral discourse referent which can be linked to an individual discourse referent which is an i-part of non-individual discourse referent, the anaphoric relation in (104) must be predicted as acceptable.

(104)   #[Every student]ᵢ respects theirᵢ teacher.

Sentence (104) is supposed to be reduced into a well-formed DRS (105). Let ξ be a neutral discourse referent.

(105)

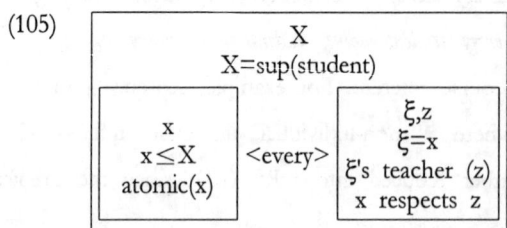

Recall that van Eijk (1983) proposes that a pronoun which is to be translated into a bound variable of an intensional language agrees with the syntactic number of its antecedent while a pronoun which is to be translated into an unbound variable agrees with the semantic number of its antecedent. His generalization can also capture the acceptability of the anaphoric relation in (100) which is problematic to Kamp and Reyle's account. By the definition given in section 3.2.2, pronoun *their* in (100) is an unbound pronoun. (It is translated into a variable which ranges over sets of individuals (or i-sums) rather than over atomic individuals.)

(100)   [Every son of John]$_i$ contributed money to buy a diamond ring for their$_i$ mother.

However, since every pronoun is treated as a bound variable in DRT (that is, there is no distinction between a bound variable and an unbound variable), his generalization faces a fundamental difficulty. Kamp and Reyle's account has a merit over van Eijk's in that their account does not depend on the distinction of pronouns into the two categories.

Adopting van Eijk's idea on the number agreement between a pronoun and its antecedent, I am going to reformulate his proposal without differentiating the two kinds of pronouns. His approach can be rewritten in my approach in a way that a bound pronoun in his approach introduces a discourse referent to be linked to an individual discourse referent which is introduced as an i-part of a non-individual discourse referent. Similarly, an unbound pronoun in his approach introduces a discourse referent to be linked to a discourse referent which is not an i-part of another discourse referent. Then, van Eijk's generalization on the number agreement between a pronoun and its antecedent can be rewritten as in (106).

(106) (i) When a pronoun introduces a discourse referent which is to be linked to a discourse referent which is an i-part of a non-individual discourse referent, the pronoun must agree with the syntactic number of the NP.

(ii) When a pronoun introduces a discourse referent which is to be linked to a discourse referent which is not an i-part of another discourse referent, the pronoun must agree with the semantic number of its antecedent.

The generalization (106) represents the fact that the information on the syntactic number of an NP plays a role in antecedent-anaphora relation. To implement this idea on DRT, I am going to adopt Kamp and Reyle's idea of the diacritic *pl.*

Kamp and Reyle stipulate that a discourse referent introduced by a syntactically plural quantificational NP (for example *most students*) carry the diacritic. According to them, a syntactically plural non-quantificational NP such as *some students* need not introduce a discourse referent with the diacritic *pl* since such an NP always introduces a non-individual discourse referent. Now, a neutral discourse referent introduced by a plural pronoun can pick up as its antecedent an individual discourse referent with the diacritic (as in sentence 107), an individual discourse referent which is introduced as an atomic i-part of a non-individual discourse referent (as in sentence 108), or a non-individual discourse referent (as in sentence 109).

(107)   [Most students]ᵢ respect theirᵢ teachers.
(108)   [Some students]ᵢ raised theirᵢ hands.

(109)   [Some students]ᵢ already finished theirᵢ joint project.

I am, however, going to change the diacritic introducing mechanism in the following way since in my approach a syntactically singular quantificational NP of Kamp and Reyle's classification also introduces a non-individual discourse referent. First, I will assume that a non-individual discourse referent introduced by a syntactically plural NP is assigned the diacritic. Second, when an individual discourse referent is introduced by Distributivity Expansion as an i-part of a non-individual discourse referent which is introduced by a syntactically plural NP, the individual discourse referent is also assigned the diacritic *pl*. According to these conventions, an NP *most students* introduces a non-individual discourse referent with the diacritic *pl*, and, an individual discourse referent which is an i-part of the non-individual discourse referent, in turn carries the diacritic. An NP *every student* introduces a non-individual discourse referent which does not carry the diacritic, and thus, an i-part of it cannot carry the diacritic. Now, a rule for the anaphoric linking can be stated as in (110).

(110)   (i) An individual discourse referent introduced by a singular pronoun must be linked to an accessible individual discourse referent which does not carry the diacritic *pl*.

(ii) A neutral discourse referent introduced by a plural pronoun must be linked either to an accessible non-individual discourse referent or to an accessible individual discourse referent with the diacritic *pl*.

Now, we have a device to explain the acceptability of the anaphoric relations in (111) and (112) with retaining the assumption that an NP of the form *every*

CN is reduced into a non-individual discourse referent.

(111) [Every student]$_i$ respects his$_i$ teacher.

(112) [Most students]$_i$ respect their$_i$ teacher.

Sentence (111) is reduced into a DRS (113) where an individual discourse referent x does not carry the diacritic pl since the non-individual discourse referent X does not carry the diacritic. The discourse referent y introduced by the pronoun his can be linked to x.

(113)

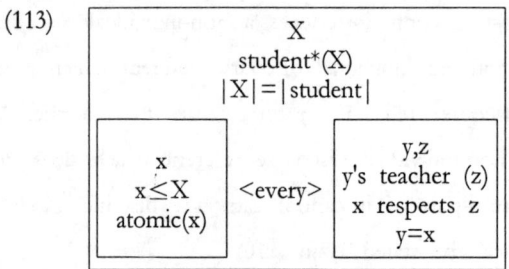

When sentence (112) is reduced into a DRS, the NP *most students* introduces a non-individual discourse referent superscripted with pl (X^{pl}). Since this discourse referent is an argument of a distributive predicate, an individual discourse referent carrying the diacritic (x^{pl}) is introduced, which is, in turn, a possible antecedent of the neutral discourse referent introduced by the pronoun *their*.

(114)

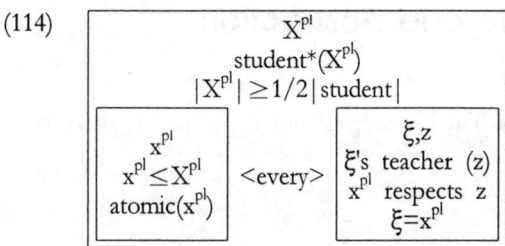

The anaphoric relation in sentence (115) is not acceptable when the sentence means that for every student x, x respects x's teacher. (Here, I ignore the non-sexist's usage of a plural pronoun *they*.) This unacceptability is predicted since an individual discourse referent, which is an i-part of a non-individual discourse referent introduced by the NP *every student*, does not carry the diacritic pl, and since the neutral discourse referent introduced by a plural pronoun must be linked either to a non-individual discourse referent or to an individual discourse referent with pl.

(115)   #[Every student]$_i$ respects their$_i$ teacher.

In addition, according to the mechanism described above, it is also predicted that a plural pronoun can have an NP of the form *every CN* as its antecedent when the pronoun refers back to the supremum of the property denoted by the CN since a neutral discourse referent introduced by a plural pronoun can be linked to a non-individual discourse referent. This prediction is evidenced by sentences such as (116).[30,31]

(116)   [Every son of John]$_i$ contributed money to buy a ring for their$_i$ mother.

3.6. Determiner *No* and Abstraction

I treat schema 'No P Q' as if it is 'Every P not Q'. That is, determiner *no* has the following translation.

(117) $[|no|] = \lambda P \lambda Q \exists X \; [*P \; (X) \; \& \; |X| \; = \; |sup \; (P)| \; \&$
$\forall x \; [x \; \leq \; X \; \& \; atomic \; (x) \; \rightarrow \; \neg Q(x)]]$

That is, 'No P Q' is reduced into DRS (118).

(118)

$$
\begin{array}{|c|}
\hline
X \\
P*(X) \\
|X| = |sup \; (P)| \\
\hline
\begin{array}{|c|} \hline x \\ x \leq X \\ atomic \; (x) \\ \hline \end{array} \; <every> \; \begin{array}{|c|} \hline x \; \neg Q \\ \hline \end{array} \\
\hline
\end{array}
$$

Now, the anaphoric relation in discourse (119) is no longer problematic since the discourse referent introduced by *They* is to be linked to the non-individual discourse referent introduced by *No student*.

(119) No student came in. They gathered on the lawn, instead.

Recall that in the non-unified approach, the first sentence of (119) is reduced into a duplex DRSs connected by the quantifier *no*. Thus, the accommodated discourse referent by abstraction operation must be mapped into the set of individuals (or the corresponding i-sum) who were students and came in, which is necessarily an empty set. Accordingly, in this approach, the anaphoric linking in (119) is problematic. Abstraction operation can accommodate a desirable discourse referent only when the scheme of *no P Q* is treated as *every p not Q*.

3.7. Problems with respect to the Mode of Predication

In my approach, the fact that some quantificational NPs in Kamp and Reyle's term can be followed by collective predicates such as *gathered in the hall* and *agree on this issue* is naturally explained since these NPs introduce a non- individual discourse referent which can be an argument of a collective predicate.

(120)   Most (Many, Few, All) students gathered in the hall.

The fact that sentence (121) has only (i) as its reading is no problem to the non-unified approach since quantifier *most* is a quantificational determiner in this approach. Since NP *most students* is a quantificational NP like *every student*, it does not introduce a non-individual discourse referent. Therefore, the sentence cannot get a collective reading. This phenomenon is observed whenever an NP with *most* or *few* is followed by an ambiguous predicate.

(121)   Most students lifted a piano.

    (i)   Students lifted a piano, individually.

    (ii)   Students as a group lifted a piano.

In my approach, NPs with these quantifiers are treated as Type II NPs which can be followed by distributive predicates or collective predicates with distributive sub-entailments. Ambiguous predicates are ambiguous, according to Dowty (1986), in that they are distributive predicates or collective predicates with collective sub-entailments. A sentence with a Type II NP can have a distributive reading or a collective reading with distributive sub-entailments but it cannot have a collective reading with collective sub-entailments or a collective reading which devoids any sub-entailments. However, Type III NPs can trigger a distributive reading, a collective reading with distributive sub-entailments and a collective reading with collective sub-entailments.

Then, when an ambiguous predicate is actually a distributive one, it can take an NP of any type as its argument. When it is a collective predicate with collective sub-entailments, it requires an NP of Type III or of Type IV as its argument (Type I NPs and Type II NPs cannot be followed by a collective predicate with collective sub-entailments). These characteristics of Type II NPs and ambiguous predicates provide reasons why when a Type II NP is followed by an ambiguous predicate, the sentence renders only a distributive reading.

3.8. Is a Sentence Multiply Ambiguous?

In the unified approach, the ambiguity is treated as being rendered owing to the ambiguity of the predicate. If we maintain the unified approach specified above, and if a sentence is ambiguous in many ways, VP must be multiply ambiguous. As discussed by other linguists (Roberts 1986, Link 1983, and others), the ambiguity of a VP is disambiguated by positing some VP operators such as the distributivity operator. However, it is unimaginable to assume as many VP operators as the number of the different readings of a sentence if a sentence is multiply ambiguous. In this sense, the problem of the multiple ambiguity of a sentence might provide a counter example against the unified approach. In the following sections, I will argue that a sentence is not multiply ambiguous by giving counter-arguments against Scha (1981) and Gillon (1987) who have maintained that a sentence can be ambiguous in many ways.

3.8.1. Scha (1981)

Scha (1981), taking for granted that NP is the source of the ambiguity in terms of distributivity/collectivity, proposes that an NP can contributes three readings to a sentence − a distributive reading, a collective reading and a cumulative reading. For example, sentence (122) has three readings − (1) each of the 600 Dutch firms has 5,000 American computers, (2) 600 Dutch firms as a group have the total of 5,000 American computers. In this reading, there can be Dutch firms which do not have any American computers, and (3) the number of the Dutch companies which own one or more American computers is 600 and the number of the American computers owned by those firms is 5,000.[32]

(122)   600 Dutch firms have 5,000 American computers.

However, as Link(1984, pp21-22) argues, the distinction of the collective reading from the cumulative reading is dubious. According to Link, the cumulative reading is a subcase of the collective reading, and this difference need not be specified in semantics. Moreover, sentence (123) reads that the total of the people who participated in any demonstrations throughout the country is 5,000. Certainly, it does not mean that the number of the people gathered in one demonstration is 5,000. It is impossible to a subset of the set of 5,000 people gathered throughout the country. The subset can gathered only in a specific space.[33]

(123)   5,000 demonstrators gathered throughout the country.

3.8.2. Gillon

According to Gillon (1987), sentence (124) (his example sentence (1)) is truly affirmed when "the men" denotes Mozart, Handel, Gilbert, and Sullivan.

(124)   The men wrote operas.

But it is not true on the collective reading since the four men never wrote an opera together. It is not true even on the distributive reading since neither Gilbert nor Sullivan ever wrote an opera on his own. Assuming an NP can be multiply ambiguous, he adopts Higginbotham(1981)'s truth schema for sentences which have plural noun phrases for subjects as given in (125).

(125) $[_S NP_{+PL}$ VP] is true iff there is a partition of the set denoted by NP such that VP is true of each element in it.

'Partition' is defined as in (126) where P(B) and $\cup A$ represents the power set of B and the union of all the elements of A, respectively.

(126)   A partitions B iff $A \subseteq P(B) \land \phi \in A \land \cup A = B \land$
$$\forall x,y \in A(x \cap y \neq \phi \rightarrow x=y)$$

Let Mozart, Handel, Gilbert, and Sullivan denote individuals m, h, g and s, respectively. Then, $\{\{m\},\{h\},\{g\},\{s\}\}$, $\{\{m\},\{h\},\{s,g\}\}$, $\{\{m,h\},\{s,g\}\}$ are partitions of $\{m,h,g,s\}$. But $\{\{m,h\},\{m,s,g\}\}$ is not a partition of it. By (126), sentence (124) is true since there is a partition $(\{\{m\},\{h\},\{g,s\}\})$ each of which is truly predicated of by the VP *wrote operas*.

But (126) is too strong because it wrongly predicts that sentence (127) is false under the situation that 'the men' denotes Rogers, Hammerstein and Hart (a set $\{r, hm, hr\}$), and Rogers and Hammerstein collaborated to write musicals and Rogers and Hart do, too.

(127)   The men wrote musicals.

To cope with this case, Gillon modifies (125) into (128) using the term *minimal cover* which is defined as in (129).

(128)   [s NP$_{+PL}$ VP] is true iff there is a minimal cover of the set denoted by NP such that VP is true of each element in it.

(129)   a. A covers B iff $A \subseteq P(B) \wedge \cup A = B \wedge \phi \in A$.
        b. A minimally covers B iff A covers $B \wedge \forall X(X$ covers $B \wedge X \subseteq A$
           $\rightarrow X = A)$

Then, the set $\{\{r,hm\},\{r,hr\}\}$, $\{\{r,hm\},\{hm,hr\}\}$ are some minimal covers of $\{r,hm,hr\}$. Now, (127) is true under the given situation since there is a cover $(\{\{r,hm\},\{r,hr\}\})$ each of whose elements is truly predicated of by *wrote musicals*.

According to him, a distributive reading is obtained when there is a minimal cover whose elements are all singleton sets such that every element is truly predicated of by the predicate denoted by the given VP. Similarly, a collective reading of a sentence is obtained when there is a minimal cover which has only one element − a set consisting of all the (atomic) individuals in the denotation of a conjoined NP. Actually, a distributive and a collective readings are only two instances of a multiply ambiguous plural NP in this approach. Needless to say, the source of ambiguity between the distributive and collective readings is the subject NP, not the VP.[34]

But this approach has some problems. For example, in (130) pronoun *they* and its antecedent *Tom and Bill* must have different minimal covers since the first sentence reads distributively while the second one reads collectively.

(130)   [Tom and Bill]$_i$ came into the room. They$_i$ lifted a piano, together.

Tom and Bill of the first sentence must denote $\{\{t\}, \{b\}\}$ which is a minimal cover of the set $\{t,b\}$ where t and b are individuals denoted by *Tom* and *Bill*, respectively. Pronoun *They* of the second sentence must have a minimal cover $\{\{t,b\}\}$ as its referent to contribute a collective reading to the sentence, according to Gillon. Only when it is assumed that a pronoun replaces a linguistic expression and the denotation of the pronoun is independent from the denotation of its antecedent, this approach can explain the data. (Because there can be many minimal covers for a plural NP, it is a mere accident that the antecedent is a minimal cover whose elements are all singleton sets and the pronoun denotes a minimal cover which has only one element.) But this kind of anaphor-antecedent relation does not seem plausible.

In addition, Lasersohn (1989,1990) points out some problems in Gillon's approach. First, his approach assigns very large number of readings to certain sentences. For example, when the subject NP is the *real numbers*, its minimal covers are infinitely many. That is, sentences with the NP as the subject can have infinitely many readings. "It seems unlikely that natural language grammars actually assign this many readings to a sentence (Lasersohn 1990, vi)." Second, the number of readings assigned to a sentence depends on facts about extralinguistic reality, not on the basis of the lexicon and grammar of the language. For example, the number of readings of *the men wrote operas* depends on the number of men in the model. "The usual notion of ambiguity requires the readings of a sentence to be differentiated solely on the basis of the grammar and lexicon of the language involved."

Third, Gillon's approach assigns incorrect truth conditions in "a number of cases". For example, if John, Mary and Bill are the TA's in a department, and were paid exactly 7,000 dollars last year, his analysis wrongly predicts that sentence (131) (from Lasersohn 1989, and 1990) is true since each element of the minimal cover {{John, Mary}, {Mary, Bill}} was paid exactly $14,000.

(131)   The TA's were paid exactly $14,000 last year.

But it is hard to judge this sentence is correct in the given situation. The fourth problem is the problem of the conjunction of a collective VP to a distributive one as in (132). In this case, the subject NP must be assigned two different covers, simultaneously.

(132)   Five students lifted a piano together and drank beer.

Then, how do we explain the fact that sentence *the men wrote operas* is truly affirmed in the circumstance described above? Lasersohn(1989) solves it simply by introducing a lexical meaning postulate stipulated in (144) where ‖ write ‖ is the relation denoted by *write*, and w, x, y, and z are i-sums or individuals. x ∪

y is a set union of x and y (or a new i-sum, x+y)

(144) $||\text{write}||(w,y)$ & $||\text{write}||(x,z)$ → $||\text{write}||(w \cup x, y \cup z)$

This meaning postulate ensures, for instance, that if the group of Rogers and Hammerstein wrote *Oklahoma!* and the group of Rogers and Hart wrote *Babes in Arms*, then the group of Rogers, Hammerstein and Hart wrote the group of *Oklahoma!* and *Babes in Arms*. I adopt his position.

3.9. Conclusion

In this chapter, I specified my approach toward distributivity and quantification by showing that the following assertions are empirically evidenced.

I.   A semantically singular NP introduces an individual discourse referent.

II.   A semantically non-singular NP introduces a non-individual discourse referent. A quantificational NP as well as a group-denoting NP in Roberts (1987)'s term introduces a non-individual discourse referent.

III.   The existential quantifier ($\exists$) is provided by default existential generalization (existential closure); the universal quantifier ($\forall$) is provided by distributive expansion but not by determiner quantifiers such as every or each.

IV.   The role of a determiner quantifier is to specify the number of atomic individuals of an i-sum denoted by an NP with the determiner. Accordingly, determiners need not be classified into quantificational and individual-denoting.

V.   NPs are classified into four types with respect to the combinatorial possibility with predicates which are classified into distributive predicates, collective predicates with distributive sub-entailments, collective predicates with collective sub-entailments, purely collective predicates and ambiguous predicates.

VI.   Distributivity is a property of predicates; when a sentence is ambiguous with respect to distributivity/collectivity, the source of the ambiguity is the predicate of the sentence but not the subject NP of it.

I have also classified NPs with respect to the kind of predicates they are required to take. Then, I have examined the characteristics of NPs of each category. I have showed how my approach can solve the problems to the non-unified approach pointed out in Chapter 2.

Notes to Chapter 3

1. The term "indefinite" has the technical sense such that an indefinite NPs introduces a novel discourse referent in a DRS (see Heim 1982). That is, the definiteness is defined based on the notion novelty (or familiarity).

2. Theoretically, it is possible that the subject NP and the VP of the sentence are both ambiguous. However, as Lasersohn(1990) argues, this alternative can be reduced to the first or the second approach if it shares with them that the denotation of a distributive VP is closed under summing operation or at least a distributive VP can contain i-sums in its denotation. Dowty(1986) argues for the closure condition of distributive predication assuming that the denotation of a conjoined VP is the intersection of the denotations of conjunct VPs. If the denotation of a distributive VP does not contain any i-sums, the intersection of the denotations of a distributive VP and of a collective one must be empty. Therefore, sentence (i) is necessarily a false proposition because the *VP are a happy couple* is intrinsically collective, and *are (each) well-adjusted individuals* is distributive. But (i) can be a true proposition according to an appropriate model.

(i)   John and Mary are a happy couple and are (each) well-adjusted individuals, too. (Dowty 1986,p)

If his assumption is correct, a distributive VP must contain i-sums in its denotation. In other words, the denotation must be closed under the summing operation. Many other persons argue for the closure condition (Roberts 1987, Scha 1981, Hoeksema 1983) or assume it (Link 1983, 1984, 1986, 1987,

Landman 1989, Krifka 1991, and others). Following them, I assume the closure condition on the denotation of a distributive predicate. Now, I eliminate the third alternative in favor of the first or the second alternative.

3. Scha (1981) and Gillon (1987) take this position.

4. Roberts(1987) adopts a similar notation. In her system, every NP carries its index. The information that an NP with index i is interpreted as an argument of a distributive predicate is represented on S(entence)-node as i(D).

5. The duplex condition is a notational variant of (i). The two notations are interchangeable.

(i)   John and Bill lifted a piano.

(ii)

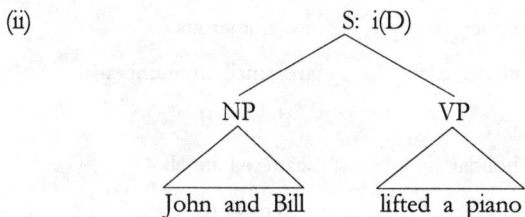

6. The duplex condition is a notational variant of (i). The two notations are interchangeable.

(i)

$$\boxed{\begin{array}{c} x \\ x \leq X \\ \text{atomic}(x) \end{array}} \quad \text{<every>} \quad \boxed{\gamma'}$$

7. I will specify the reasons why I integrate semantically plural NPs and semantically undefined NPs into semantically non-singular NPs when I deal with the number agreement between a pronoun and its antecedent.

8. I am adopting the assumptions of Heim (1982), Kamp (1981) and Kamp and Reyle (1990) except that I assume every indefinite is a bound variable. The other changes are naturally derived from this assumption.

9. Their classification of predicates are illustrated in (i).

(i)

Distributive Predicates	Mixed Predicates	Collective Predicates
were asleep	gathered in the room	can be counted on the
ate apples	surrounded the fort	fingers of one hand
own a car	met for dinner	are numerous
	often wrote to each	are small in number
	other	dispersed
	went on holiday	scattered in all
	together	directions

10. I do not deal with predicates of this kind in this study.

11. I am using *every-CN* as an abbreviation of an NP with *every* as its determiner and any common noun as its head noun.

12. Here, I do not mean that the intuitive judgment of an informant is shaky between unacceptable and questionable. Around 7 out of 10 judged these

sentences are not acceptable.

13. The ordering relation $\alpha < \beta$ means that the combinatorial power of β with a predicate is stronger than that of α. That is, β can combine with more predicates than α does.

14. The operator * takes a property to yield a complete atomic join semi lattice generated by the property. For example, if **student** is a set of atomic individuals $\{a,b,c\}$, then *student is a set of atomic and non-atomic individuals which consists of a complete join semi lattice, that is, $\{a,b,c,a+b,a+c,b+c,a+b+c\}$. Then, some students refers to either a+b, b+c, a+c, or a+b+c.

15. $[_{NP} \dots]$ here must be understood as $[_{NP[Quant=ind/Num=plur]} \dots]$.

16. Actually, this condition is also admitted in Kamp and Reyle. For example, sentence (i) is represented as in (ii) where a condition on the cardinality of an i-sum into which discourse referent X must be mapped is expressed. Then, CR.NP[semantically plural] of (37) is just the same as CR.NP[Quant=ind/Num=plur] of (36).

(i)   Two men met.

(ii)

X
$\|X\|=2$
man*(X)
X met

17. The condition $x \leq X$ represents that an individual into which x is mapped is an i-part of an i-sum into which X is mapped, and atomic(x) represents that

x is expected to be mapped into an atomic individual.

18. If an NP is ambiguous in many ways, the problem might be solved. However, this assumption has to face some difficulties which will be discussed shortly.

19. The Abstraction Operation discussed in Chapter 3 can provide a non-individual discourse referent to which a discourse referent introduced by the pronoun is linked. However, as I pointed out in Chapter 3, this approach has some problems.

20. Kadmon (1987, 1990) discusses uniqueness conditions extensively. She argues that the uniqueness condition is accommodated when an indefinite is anaphorically related to a pronoun. But in my treatment of non-monotonic NPs, the accommodation of the uniqueness condition occurs even though the NP is not anaphorically related to a pronoun.

21. $X = \sigma(CN')$ is a complex condition such that CN' (X) & $|X| = |\sigma(CN')|$ (or just $|X| = |CN'|$).

22. I ignore the difference in the uses of the two quantifiers. Rather, I will treat them as universal distributive quantifiers, equally. See Aldridge (1976) for further reference.

23. In (82), the familiarity condition is not incorporated into the translation.

24. This definition of *no* predicts that when a group of three students lifted a

piano, together and no one else did, sentence (92)c should be true. My informants affirm this prediction.

25. In the discussion of the meaning of *many* and *few*, Partee (1988) maintains the position that these expressions are ambiguous in that they can have either a cardinal reading or a proportional one. According to her, when they have a cardinal reading, they behave like intersective adjectives and when they have a proportional one, they behave like a quantifiers such as *every* and *most*. Here, I do not pursue this position, though.

26. Recall that since *few* is a monotone decreasing quantifier, when *few CN* is followed by a distributive VP, the uniqueness condition is specified according to the DRS construction rule for non monotone decreasing quantifiers.

27. These distributional constraints are (almost) the same as those of *all*. Sentences (i)c and d are from Dowty (1986).

(i)   a. All the students wore blue jeans, yesterday.

         b. All the students gathered on the ground.

         c. *All the students are numerous.

         d. ?All the trees are denser in the middle of the forest.

28. He explains the anomaly of (i)c and d of foot note 31 based on (102): since pure cardinality collective predicates such as be numerous and be dense are "completely devoid of distributive sub-entailments, then according to Hypothesis (102) *all* should have nothing to operate upon here, so the anomaly of just this class of collectives is to be expected (Dowty 1986, p102)."

29. Here, I don't consider the non-sexist use of *they*.

30. It has been reported that the pronoun *their* is widely used in the place of *his* as in (i) and (ii) to avoid sexist's prejudice (cf. Roberts 1987, Choe 1987).

(i)   [Every student]$_i$ keeps his$_i$ ID handy.

(ii)   [Every student]$_i$ keeps their$_i$ ID handy.

If we consider this kind of plural pronouns to be a 'disguised singular pronoun', the number agreement mechanism developed so far can be maintained in tact with the stipulation that a plural pronoun used to avoid sexist? prejudice introduces an individual discourse referent which is to be linked to an individual discourse referent which does not carry the diacritic pl. If we consider these pronouns to be reduced into a neutral discourse referent like ordinary plural pronouns, we should modify the number agreement mechanism to the extent that a neutral discourse referent can be linked either to a non-individual discourse referent or to an individual discourse referent without regarding whether or not the discourse referent carries the diacritic pl. However, this modification is too weak because, as Choe points out, the non-sexist's pronoun cannot be used when its antecedent is semantically singular as in (iii).

(iii)   *[A student]$_i$ keeps their$_i$ ID handy.

Then, the number agreement mechanism must be stated to the effect that a neutral discourse referent must be linked either to a non-individual discourse referent or to an individual discourse referent introduced as an i-part of a non-individual discourse referent whether or not it carries the diacritic pl.

31. The rule of anaphoric linking must be further relaxed to cope with Korean data. In Korean, a discourse referent introduced by a singular pronominal expression can be linked to an individual discourse referent which is an i-part of a non-individual discourse referent as well as to a discourse referent introduced by a semantically singular NP. A neutral discourse referent introduced by a plural pronominal expression must be linked to either a non-individual discourse referent or to an individual discourse referent introduced as an i-part of a non-individual discourse referent. For example, sentence (i) can be put either into (ii) a or (ii)b in Korean. In (ii)a, a singular reflexive *caki* is used while in (ii)b, a plural reflexive *caki-tul* is used.

(i)   Every student loves his mother.

(ii)   a.   kak haksaeng -i   caki -ui   emeni-lul cohahanta.

                  every student Nom self poss mother Acc love

          b.   kak haksaeng-i   caki-tul-ui   emeni -lul   cohahanta.

                  every student Nom self pl poss mother Acc love

To cope with these data, the rule of anaphoric linking must be relaxed as in (iii). Note that the diacritic is no longer used in (iii). I will take rule (iii) as the rule of anaphoric linking of Korean.

(iii) Rule of Anaphoric Linking of Korean

        (i) An individual discourse referent introduced by a singular pronoun must be linked to an individual discourse referent.

        (ii) A neutral discourse referent introduced by a plural pronoun must be linked either to a non-individual discourse referent or an individual discourse referent which is introduced as an atomic i-part of a non-individual discourse referent.

I just conjecture that Korean and English share a universal anaphoric linking rule with language specific parameters. I will pursue this issue in a separate study.

32. Van der Does (1992, p30) gives the denotations to a numeral determiner adopting Scha's position.

(i)   a. distributive: $\lambda X \lambda Y.\ |\{d \in X:\ \mathbf{Y}([d])\}| = n$

           b. collective: $\lambda X \lambda Y.\ \exists Y \subseteq X\ [|Y| = n\ \&\ \mathbf{Y}(Y)]$

           c. cumulative: $\lambda X \lambda Y.\ |\cup \{Y \subseteq X:\ \mathbf{Y}(Y)\}| = n$

where d is an atomic individual

33. That is, the denotation of (i)c of foot note 32 which is responsible for the cumulative reading is not relevant, here, as shown in (ii).

(i)   5,000 demonstrators gathered throughout the country.

(ii) $|\cup \{\mathbf{Y} \subseteq [|{*}\text{demonstrator}|]\ \wedge\ \text{gathered-throughout-the-country}'(Y)\}|$
           $= 5,000$

34. This approach can provide an answer why a conjoined NP expresses the unity even when the sentence with it has a distributive reading if we regard a set as representing something concrete just like an individual-sum (cf. Landman 1989, p567) since a cover is a set.

Chapter 4. Asymmetric Quantification
– the Proportion Problem

4.0. Introduction

The purpose of this and the following chapters is to provide more empirical evidence for my approach specified in Chapter 3.

Chapter 4 will be about the proportion problem reported in Heim (1982), Partee (1984), Kadmon (1987, 1990) and Chierchia (1988). Suppose among the farmers of model M, five farmers own at least one donkey. One farmer owns 10 donkeys and he beats all the donkeys he owns. The other 4 farmers have exactly one donkey and they do not beat them. In this situation, sentence (1) is false. Actually, this section will deal with the validity of the duplex condition proposed in Kamp and Reyle. Recall that in sentence (2), they can have *most farmers who own a donkey* as its antecedent.

(1)   Most farmers who own a donkey beat it.

(2)   They are rich.

I will also be concerned with how the two approaches deal with the fact that in discourse (3), *they* cannot have a *farmer* as its antecedent while in (4), *they* can. What is the difference between the *every-construction* and the *if-then* construction? What is the similarity between them?

(3)   If [a farmer]$_i$ owns a donkey, he beats it. *They$_i$ are unhappy.

(4)   [Every farmer]$_i$ who owns a donkey beats it. They$_i$ are unhappy.

4.1. The Proportion Problem

The proportion problem has been discussed widely among linguists in various theoretical frame-works (Partee 1984, 1990, and 1991, Buerle and Egli 1985, Root 1986, Kadmon 1987, Heim 1990, Gronendijk and Stokhof 1990, Chierchia 1988, 1990, Pelleitier and Schubert 1988, and Kratzer 1989, Kamp and Reyle 1990, to name a few).[1] Here, I will be concerned mainly with those works which assume DRT. The purpose of this section is to show that my approach can provide a simple way to explain this complex problem.

One of the basic assumptions of DRT is that a quantifier can bind two or more distinct variables whenever the configurational relation between the quantifier and the variable satisfies certain conditions. This assumption is known as "unselective binding." Another assumption is that an indefinite NP behaves like a variable. Consequently, the donkey sentence (5) is logically represented as in (6). The indefinite NP a donkey is translated into a variable but does not introduce the existential quantifier.

(5)   Every farmer who owns a donkey beats it.

(6) $\forall x,y[\text{farmer}(x) \ \& \ \text{donkey}(y) \ \& \ x \text{ owns } y \longrightarrow x \text{ beats } y]$

With this assumption, the parallelism can be explained between the quantification induced by determiner quantifiers (D-quantification in Partee (1990)) and the adverbial quantification studied in Lewis (1975) (A-quantification in Partee (1990)). Lewis argues that adverbs like *always, usually* and *most of the time* are not just quantifiers over *times* or events. Rather, sometimes, they behave just like determiner quantifiers. For examples, sentence (7) means that most quadratic equations have two different solutions. It does not mean that there is a quadratic equation that usually has two different solutions.

(7)   A quadratic equation usually has two different solutions.

Heim (1982) proposes that when the adverbial quantifier is implicit in an *if-then* construction, it is equated to *always*. That is, sentence (8) can be rewritten as (9).

(8)   If a farmer owns a donkey, he beats it.
(9)   Always, if a farmer owns a donkey, he beats it.

Then, (8) is represented as in (10) which is equivalent to (11) under the unselective binding assumption.

(10) $\forall$ <x,y> [farmer(x) & donkey(y) & x owns y $\longrightarrow$ x beats y]
(11) $\forall$x $\forall$y[farmer(x) & donkey(y) & x owns y $\longrightarrow$ x beats y]

The parallelism between the adverb *always* and the determiner *every* is explained since sentence (8) is shown to have the same meaning as sentence (5). That is, under the unselective binding assumption, quantification applies to the set of donkey-farmer pairs but not to the set of farmers or the set of donkeys. Sentences (5) and (8) are true iff for every farmer-donkey pair, the farmer of a pair owns the donkey of the pair and he beats it.

However, the unselective binding assumption seems to be untenable when the determiner of the subject NP followed by a relative clause is not fully universal.[2] Let's consider sentence (12). Suppose there is one woman who owns fifty dogs and talks to them all, while there are ten other women with one dog each, who don't talk to their dog.

(12)   Most women who own a dog talk to it (Kadmon 1987).

Under the unselective binding, sentence (12) is translated into (13). Let the denotation of *most* be a relation between two properties.[3]

(13)   Most x,y [(woman (x) & dog (y) & x owns y), (x talks to y)]

Roughly, logical form (13) is true iff for most woman-dog pairs, the woman of a pair owns the dog of the pair and she talks to it. Assume fifty out of sixty satisfies the proportion expressed by the determiner *most*. Then, under the situation described above, sentence (12) must be predicted as being true according to the unselective binding. But it is judged false. Again suppose there is a woman who owns fifty dogs and does not talk to any of them and there are ten other women with one dog each who talk to their dog. Under this situation, (12) is true even though it must be false according to the unselective binding hypothesis.

The proportional problem seems to be a counter-example against the unselective binding. But there are some phenomena which evidence the unselective binding hypthesis. First of all, donkey sentences (5) and (8) are good examples for the hypothesis. Second, as Partee(1990) argues, when the quantificational force is expressed by an adverb, and the antecedent clause of an if-then construction contains a stage level predicate,[4] the symmetric quantification (or unselective binding) is strongly favored as in (14).

(14)   Almost always, if a woman sees a dog, she talks to it.

Sentence (14) is true under the situation where a woman sees fifty dogs and she talks to each of them and the other two women who each see a dog do not talk to it. That is, in (14), quantification applies over woman-dog pairs. The quantification which observes the unselective binding is called "symmetric quantification," while the quantification which does not observe it is called "asymmetric quantification." The question here is whether or not the unselective binding must be maintained. If yes, an answer should be given to the question how asymmetric quantification is explained. If no, an alternative way must be sought which keeps the assumption that indefinites are mere variables.

What quantificational force does the indefinite of sentence (15) have? According to Heim (1990), the indefinite has a universal reading. She paraphrases sentence (15) into (16).[5]

(15)   Most people that owned a slave also owned his offspring.

(16)   for *most* people that owned a slave: for *every* slave they owned: they also owned his offspring.

Heim (1990) reports that this point has been acknowledged by many authors including Bäuerle and Egli (1985), Root (1986), Rooth (1987), and Reinhart (1987). Kamp and Reyle (1990) also judge that the indefinite NP in sentence (15) has a universal reading.[6] Interestingly, in a determiner donkey sentence, an indefinite NP which occurs in the relative clause is interpreted universally regardless of the determiner of the subject NP of the sentence. Consider sentences in (16) and their logical representations in (17). (17)d and e represent the distributive readings of sentences (16)c and d. Let's assume that the logical connector @ is appropriately defined.[7]

(15)　　a. Many man who own a donkey beat it.

　　　　b. Few men who own a donkey beat it.

　　　　c. No man who owns a donkey beats it.

　　　　d. Some men who own a donkey beat it.

　　　　e. Three men who own a donkey beat it.

(16)　　a. many$_x$ every$_y$[(man(x) & donkey(y) & x owns y) @ (x beats y)]

　　　　b. few$_x$ every$_y$[(man(x) & donkey(y) & x owns y) @ (x beats y)]

　　　　c. every$_x$ every$_y$[(man(x) & donkey(y) & x owns y) @ $\neg$(x beats y)]

　　　　d. some$_x$ every$_y$[(man(x) & donkey(y) & x owns y) @ (x beats y)]

　　　　e. three$_x$ every$_y$[(man(x) & donkey(y) & x owns y) @ (x beats y)]

Then, the question why the implicit operator must be *every* should be answered.

In summary, I have discussed three points about the proportion problems: (i) there are cases where quantification applies over certain individuals (asymmetric quantification) rather than over certain tuples of individuals (symmetric quantification). When the quantificational force is provided by a non-universal determiner and the predicate is an individual level one, the asymmetric quantification occurs. (ii) In the asymmetric quantification, the unselective binding hypothesis seems to be violated. However, the hypothesis is still needed to describe the symmetric quantification which is common among adverbial quantifications. (iii) In an asymmetric donkey sentence, an indefinite NP which occurs in the relative clause of the sentence is interpreted as being universally quantified. Any approach toward the proportion problem should predict these facts.

4.2. DRT Approaches toward the Proportion Problem

As I have mentioned above, many solutions are proposed to the proportion problem. In this section, I will select two approaches which assume DRT as their framework—Kadmon (1988, 1990) and Kamp and Reyle (1990), and critically review them.

4.2.1. Kadmon (1988, 1990)

Kadmon's judgment on an asymmetric quantificational sentence is different from the judgment on this sentence described in section 4.1. She interprets sentence (17) to have the reading of (18). That is, sentence (17) has the reading that most farmers who own exactly one donkey beat the unique donkey they own.

(17)   Most farmers who own a donkey beat it.

(18) Most_x [farmer (x) & $\exists y$ [donkey (y) & x owns y] @ $\exists y$ [x beats y] & $\forall z$[[donkey (z) & x owns z] $\rightarrow$ z=y]]

In her system, uniqueness effect (i.e., $\forall z[[donkey\ (z)\ \&\ x\ owns\ z]\ \rightarrow\ z=y]$ of (18)) is pragmatically accommodated. Here, I will not address the matter of uniqueness effect.[8] Rather, I will be concerned with that (i) how the second existential quantifier of (18) is introduced and (ii) whether the unselective binding is observed or not in her system.

Kadmon argues that "the asymmetric examples differ from the symmetric ones in the internal structure of the restriction, in that the dependent is bound, within the restriction, by existential quantification (Kadmon 1990, p305)." In case of symmetric examples, she follows the usual Lewis/Kamp/Heim's treatment which assumes the unselective binding. For example, sentence (19) is reduced into DRS (20).

(19)   Mostly, if a semanticist hears of a good job, she applies for it.

(20)

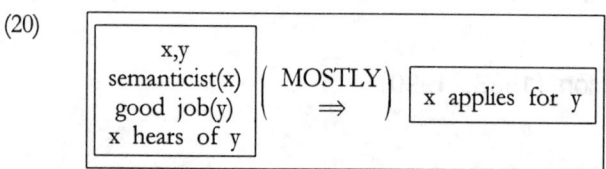

An asymmetric example of (21) is reduced into DRS (22). The indefinite *a dog* is bound by the existential quantification introducing a subordinate DRS.

(21)   Most women who own a dog are happy.

(22)

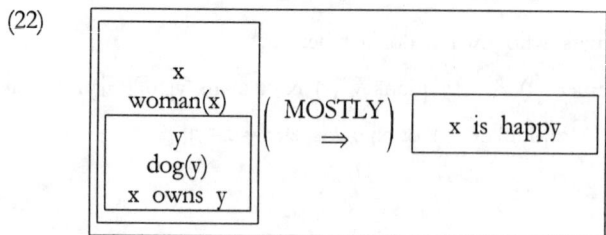

DRS (22) can be represented as in (23) where an indefinite *a dog* is treated as being existentially quantified.

(23)   Most$_x$ [woman(x) & $\exists$y[dog(y) & x owns y], x is happy]

However, if the indefinite NP *a dog* in sentence (24) introduces a discourse referent in a box subordinate to the current DRS, the discourse referent is not accessible to the discourse referent introduced by the pronoun *it*. That is, if *a dog* is an existentially quantified expression, the pronoun *it* cannot be a bound variable since it is not in the scope of the indefinite.

(24)   Most women who own <u>a dog</u> talk to <u>it</u>.

(25)

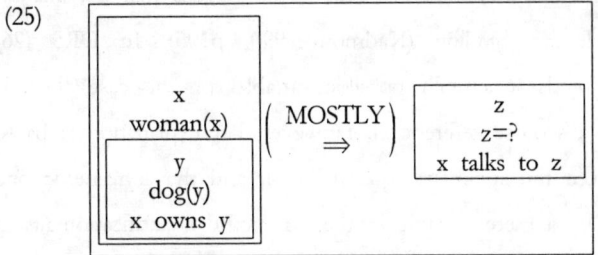

(26)   Most$_x$ [woman(x) & $\exists$y[dog(y) & x owns y] @ x talks to it]

To remedy this problem, she proposes the accommodation of the conditions of the inner-most DRS of the left hand side to the DRS of the right hand side. Then, (25) is changed into (26). Now, discourse referent z can be linked to discourse referent y.

(26)

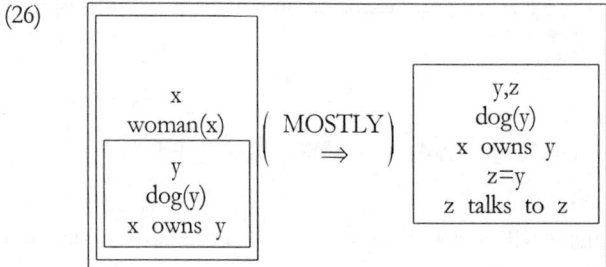

Kadmon asserts that the accommodation has no effect on the truth conditions since DRS (26) means that "mostly, if a woman x is such that **there is a dog that she owns**, then there is a dog that she owns, and she talks to that dog.

Now, the asymmetric reading of sentence (24) is explained by letting an indefinite NP introduce a subordinate DRS. She further argues that her analysis keeps intact the unselective binding (Kadmon 1990, p305). In DRS (26) MOSTLY unselectively binds structurally possible variables (in this case, there is only one such variable, discourse referent x). However, her explanation is based on the difference between the symmetric quantification and the asymmetric one such that an indefinite be a mere variable in the symmetric quantification (as in (20)) and that it be existentially quantified in the asymmetric quantification (as in (26)). That is, indefinites are sometimes mere variables and sometimes quantificational expressions. It means that she discards one of the basic assumptions by which the unselective binding is motivated -- an indefinite is not an existentially quantified expression, but it is translated just into a variable. If an indefinite is existentially quantified, the unselective binding is at best vacuous.

4.2.2. Kamp and Reyle (1990)

Kamp and Reyle propose a solution to the proportion problem by stipulating embedding conditions of a duplex condition in a way to make sure that the quantifier of the duplex condition binds the designated variable and the implicit universal quantifier binds the other variables of the duplex condition. The designated variable (the principal discourse referent in Kamp and Reyle's terminology) is a variable which ranges over the set of individuals denoted by the head noun of an NP modified by a relative clause.[8] Kamp and Reyle represent the principal discourse referent under the quantifier of a duplex condition. For example, sentence (27) is reduced into the duplex condition (28). Discourse referent 'x' is the principal discourse referent.

(27)   Most farmers who own a donkey beats it.

(28)
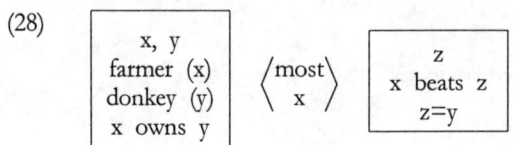

In this respect, their approach is not different from Büerle and Egli (1985);s, Rooth's (1987) and Reinhart (1987)'s approach which treats donkey-sentences with relative clauses as if they contain not one but two quantifying operators. For example, the determiner *most* of sentence (29) is actually treated as being a complex quantifier, *most-every*, in Kamp and Reyle's account. According to them, sentence (29) would be translated into (30).

(29)   Most people that owned a slave also owned his offspring.

(30)   most$_x$ every$_y$ [(people (x) & slave (y) & x owned y) @ (x also owned
                                                            y's offspring)][9]

(Heim 1990, pp162-163)

Adopting the view that a determiner denotes a relation between two properties denoted by the head noun of the subject and the VP of a sentence, Kamp and Reyle stipulates verification conditions for a duplex condition as in (31).

(31) $M \models_f$ [x] $\left\langle \begin{array}{c} Q_0 \\ x \end{array} \right\rangle$ [ ]

                K1   K2

iff $<A,B> \in R_0$, where Q_0 denotes R_0 and

$A = \{b: b \in U_M \ \& \ (\exists g) \ (f \cup \{<x,b>\} \subseteq U_{K1-\{x\}} g \ \& \ M \models_g K1)\}$

and

$B = \{b: b \in U_M \ \& \ (\exists g) \ (f \cup \{<x,b>\} \subseteq U_{K1-\{x\}} g \ \& \ M \models_g K1 \ \&$

$\forall g(f \cup \{<x,b>\} \subseteq U_{K1-\{x\}} g \rightarrow (\exists h)(g \subseteq U_{K2} h \ \& \ M \models_h K2)))\}$

The verification (31) is rephrased as in (32).

(32): The duplex condition is verified with respect to a model M and an embedding function f iff the two sets A and B which are defined below satisfy the relation denoted by the quantifier of the duplex condition.

A is the set of individuals each of which is assigned to discourse referent x and for such an individual b, there is at least one embedding function g which assigns b to x and some individuals to all the discourse referents in K1 except x such that those individuals satisfy all the conditions of K1.

B is the set of individuals each of which is assigned to x and for such an individual b, (i) there is at least one embedding function g which assigns b to x and some individuals to other discourse referents of K1 such that those individuals satisfy all the conditions of K1, and (ii) for every such function g, there is at least one embedding function h, an extension of g, which properly embeds DRS K2 into M. Then, B is a sub-set of A.

To get the idea, let's consider the duplex condition (33). Assume a model specified in (34).

(33)

$$\boxed{\begin{array}{|c|}\hline \text{x,y} \\ \text{woman(x)} \\ \text{dog(y)} \\ \text{x owns y} \\\hline\end{array}\left\langle\begin{array}{c}\text{almost every}\\ \text{x}\end{array}\right\rangle\boxed{\text{x talks to y}}}$$

(34)   M=<U,F>
U= {m1,m2,m3,m4, d1,d2,d3,d4,d5,d6}
F(woman)={m1,m2,m3,m4}
F(dog)={d1,d2,d3,d4,d5,d6}
F(own)={<m1,d1>,<m1,d2>,<m2,d3>,<m2,d4>,<m3,d5>,<m4,d6>}
F(talk-to)={<m1,d1>,<m3,d5>,<m4,d6>}

Let the antecedent DRS of the duplex condition K1 and the consequent DRS, K2. Then, according to (31), m1 is a member of set A since there is an embedding function g which assigns m1 to x and d1 to y (for m1, there is another embedding g' which assigns m1 to x and d2 to y). Individuals m2, m3 and m4 are also members of set A with the same reason. That is, A = {m1,m2,m3,m4}. m1 cannot be a member of set B since for g' which assigns m1 and d2 to x and y, respectively, there is no extension h of g' (here, g' itself) which properly embeds DRS K2. (That is, the requirement that every extension g of f ∪ {<x, m1>} must have an extension h which embeds DRS K2 is violated here.)   Similarly, m2 is not a member of set B (no extension h of g, at all). But m3 and m4 are members of B. That is, B = {m3,m4}. If 2 out of 4 is not regarded as being in the denotation of almost every, according to (31), the duplex condition (33) is not verified with respect to f and M.

Their approach solves the proportion problem without pragmatic accommodation. It also captures the fact that the indefinite NP of a donkey sentence which occurs in the relative clause has the universal quantificational force regardless of the quantifier of the subject NP. However, the fact that the indefinite NP is universally quantified is just stipulated in the verification conditions rather than being explained. Heim (1990) points out two problems in this kind of approach:

There are two big questions about this kind of approach: One is whether there is any principled way of predicting the force of the implicit secondary quantifier. .... The second question is how to implement the analysis without ad hoc maneuvers in either the syntax or the semantics. .... The authors that have pursued this type of analysis have generally opted for the horn of the dilemma: keep the LFs close to the surface and put the fancy footwork into the semantic interpretation rules. (Heim 1990, p163)

Secondly, the unselective binding hypothesis is relativized in their system. Let's consider a schematic duplex condition (35) where more than two discourse referents are in the antecedent DRS of the duplex condition.

(35)

$$\boxed{\begin{array}{l} x,y,z \\ P\ (x) \\ R\ (y) \\ S\ (x,y,z) \end{array}} \quad \left\langle \begin{array}{c} most \\ x \end{array} \right\rangle \quad \boxed{T\ (x,y,z)}$$

K1　　　　　　　　　　　　　K2

With verification condition (31), the duplex condition (32) is translated into (36). Note that only the principal discourse referent, x, of (35) is bound by the quantifier of the condition, *most*, and the other discourse referents are bound by an implicit universal quantifier which is stipulated in (31). It can be rewritten as in (37).

(36) $most_x$ $every_{y,z}$ [(P(x) & R(y) & S(x,y,z)) @ (T(x,y,z))]

(37) $most_x$ $every_y$ $every_z$ [(P(x) & R(y) & S(x,y,z)) @ (T(x,y,z))]

Then, we can say that the quantifier of a duplex condition unselectively binds the principal discourse referents if there are at least two principal discourse referents and an implicit quantifier *every* unselectively binds other discourse referents.

Now, let's examine a donkey sentence which involves the determiner *every* as in (38) which gave the original motivation to the unselective binding hypothesis.

(38)   Every farmer who owns a donkey beats it.

Sentence (38) is translated as in (39) where there is only one quantifier $\forall$ which unselectively binds the variables x and y.

(39) $\forall$x,y [(farmer (x) & donkey (y) & x owns y) $\rightarrow$ x beats y]

However, it is now hard to argue that sentence (38) is an example of the unselective binding since variable y introduced by a donkey can be bound by an implicit universal quantifier as in (40).

(40) $\forall x \forall y$ [(farmer (x) & donkey (y) & x owns y) $\rightarrow$ x beats y]

Kamp and Reyle take this position when they represent sentence (38) as DRS (41).

(41)

$$
\boxed{\quad\boxed{\begin{array}{c} x,y \\ \text{farmer } (x) \\ \text{donkey } (y) \\ x \text{ owns } y \end{array}} \quad \left\langle \begin{array}{c} \text{every} \\ x \end{array} \right\rangle \quad \boxed{\begin{array}{c} w \\ w=y \\ x \text{ beat } w \end{array}} \quad}
$$

Then, even though the unselective binding hypothesis is also maintained in Kamp and Reyle's account, the motivation for the unselective binding is weakened considerably. If implicit quantifiers can be provided freely,[10] there is no need to introduce the unselective binding mechanism.

4.3. The Unified Approach toward the Proportion Problem

4.3.1. Numeral Based Donkey Sentences

A D(eterminer)-donkey sentence has a following syntactic structure. In a nutshell, the VP of a sentence contains a pronoun which is anaphorically related to an indefinite NP of a relative clause which modifies the head noun of the subject NP of the sentence.

(42)

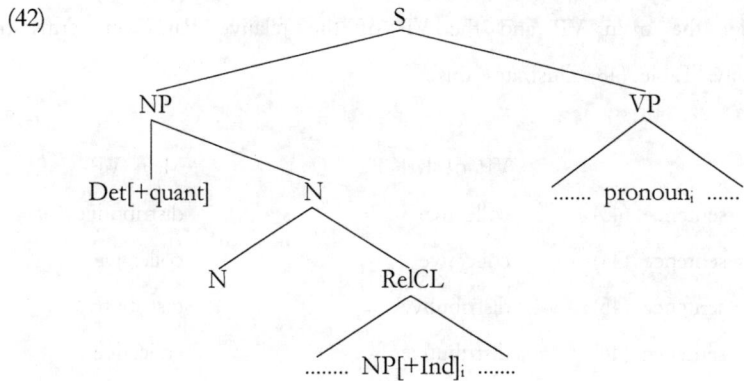

Even in a sentence where the determiner of the subject is not quantificational (in Kamp and Reyle's system), this kind of anaphoric relation is also found. In this case, the anaphoric relation is more complicated than in a donkey sentence with a quantificational determiner. In sentences (43), (44) and (45), the pronoun *it* in the main VP can be anaphorically related to an indefinite NP in the relative clause of the subject NP. In (46), such anaphoric linking is impossible. Sentence (43) has the reading that a group of seven students bought a car together and each of them love to drive that car. Sentence (44) has the reading that a group of seven students bought a car together and they gathered around the car. Sentence (45) has the reading that seven Ford-owning students hate the car they individually own. Sentence (47) reads that a group of seven Ford-owning students gathered in the garage.

(43)   Seven students who bought [a car]$_i$ together love to drive it$_i$.

(44)   Seven students who bought [a car]$_i$ together gathered around it$_i$.

(45)   Seven students who (individually) own [a Ford]$_i$ hate it$_i$.

(46)   *Seven students who (individually) own [a Ford]$_i$ gathered around it$_i$.

(47)   Seven students who (individually) own a Ford gathered in the garage.

Consider the main VP and the VP of the relative clause in terms of distributivity. Table (48) illustrates this.

(48)

	VP of RelCL	Main VP
sentence (43)	collective	distributive
sentence (44)	collective	collective
sentence (45)	distributive	distributive
sentence (46)	distributive	collective
sentence (47)	distributive	collective

In this section, I will deal with (i) how to build a DRS for each of these sentences and (ii) how to explain the anaphoric linkings in sentences (43) through (47).

Roberts (1987) also deals with sentence (49) which is originated from Rooth (1986)[11] who calls this kind of sentences "numeral based donkey sentences." This sentence can be rewritten as in (50). An example of a donkey sentence which has a distributive predicate and its relative clause also has a distributive predicate like sentence (45). Notice that in (49), the indefinite NP *two children* cannot be an antecedent of the discourse pronoun *they* as in a donkey sentence which has a quantificational NP as its subject. But the whole subject NP *seven fathers with two children* can be an antecedent of such pronoun.

(49)   [Seven fathers with [two children]$_j$]$_i$ send them$_j$ (both) to Montessori school.

    a.   #They$_j$ love it.

    b.   They$_i$ think it's a good investment.

(Roberts 1987, p226)

(50)   [Seven fathers who have [two children]ⱼ]ᵢ send themⱼ (both) to
Montessori school.

4.3.2. DR Construction Rule for Relative Clauses in Kamp and Reyle

The DR construction from a syntactic analysis is processed in a "top-down
and left-to-right" manner in Kamp and Reyle as well as in Kamp (1981).[12]
Sentence (51) is syntactically analyzed as in (52).

(51)   A farmer owns a donkey.

(52)

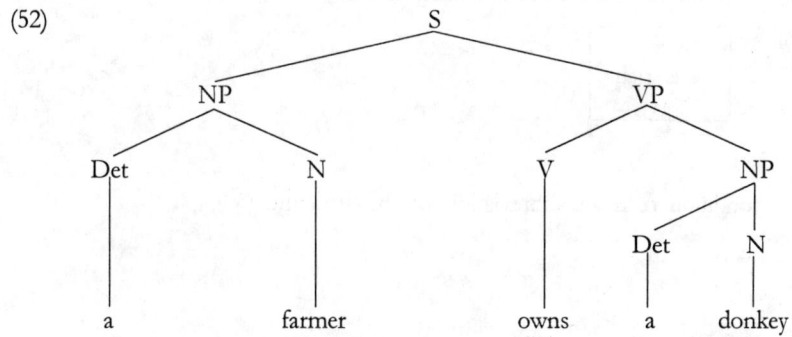

From the top node (S), the subject NP is the first NP. Since it is an indefinite
NP, by the DR Construction rule for indefinite NPs, (52) is first reduced into
an incomplete DRS of (53).

(53)

$$
\begin{array}{|c|}
\hline
x \\
\text{farmer}(x) \\
[_S\ x\ [_{VP}[_V\ \text{owns}\ ]\ [_{NP}\ [_{Det}\ a]\ [_N\ \text{donkey}]]]] \\
\hline
\end{array}
$$

The condition [$_S$ x [$_{VP}$[$_V$ owns [$_{NP}$[$_{Det}$ a] [$_N$ donkey]]]] still has an indefinite NP which is to be reduced further. The final DRS for sentence (52) is (54).

(54)

> x,y
> farmer (x)
> donkey (y)
> [$_S$ x [$_{VP}$[$_V$ owns] y]]

Sentence (55) with a relative clause is first reduced into (56) by the construction rule for indefinites.

(55)   A farmer who owns a donkey is rich.

(56)

> x
> x is rich
> α

The condition α is an abbreviation of the structure (57).

(57)

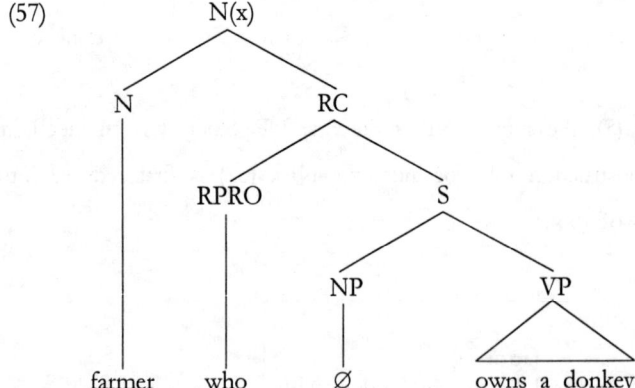

For a noun modified by a relative clause, Kamp and Reyle (p.119) propose a DR Construction rule as in (58).

(58)   CR.NRC

Triggering
configuration
$g \in Con_K$:

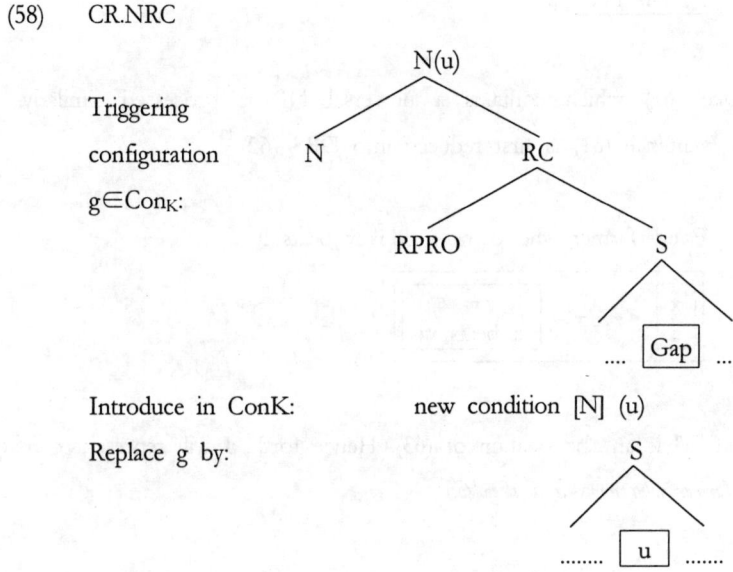

Introduce in ConK: new condition [N] (u)
Replace g by:

Now, by CR.NRC, condition (57) is further processed into (59).

(59)   farmer (x)
       x owns a donkey

After CR.ID (DR construction rule for indefinite NPs) applies again to reduce NP *a donkey*, sentence (55) is finally reduced into DRS (60).

(60)

```
┌─────────────┐
│ x,y         │
│ farmer (x)  │
│ donkey (y)  │
│ x onws y    │
│ x is rich   │
└─────────────┘
```

Sentence (61) which contains a universal NP is processed similarly. By CR.every, sentence (61) is first reduced into DRS (62).[13]

(61)   Every farmer who owns a donkey beats it.

(62)

```
┌──────────────────────────┐
│ ┌───┐          ┌────────┐ │
│ │ x │ <every>  │   w    │ │
│ │ a │          │x beats w│ │
│ └───┘          └────────┘ │
└──────────────────────────┘
```

Condition "a" is an abbreviation of (63). Hence forth, I will represent condition (63) as *farmer who owns a donkey (x)*.

(63)

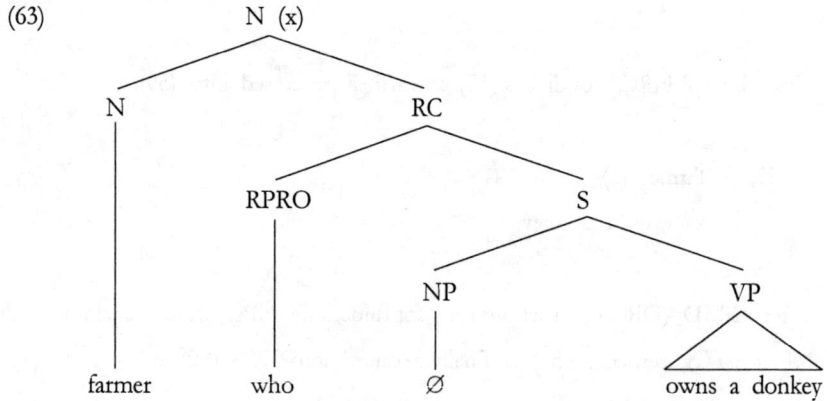

Condition (63) is further reduced into the two conditions specified in (64).

(64)   farmer (x)

x owns a donkey

Finally, sentence (63) is reduced into DRS (65).

(65)

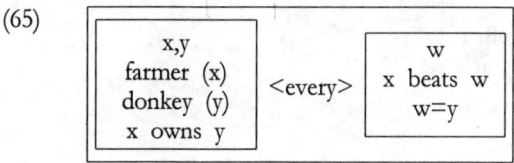

4.3.3. Problems of CR.NRC

Now, I am going to examine how CR.NRC formulated in (58) reduces numeral based donkey sentences (43)-(47).

(43)   Seven students who bought [a car]$_i$ together love to drive it$_i$.

(44)   Seven students who bought [a car]$_i$ together gathered around it$_i$.

(45)   Seven students who (individually) own [a Ford]$_i$ hate it$_i$.

(46)   *Seven students who (individually) own [a Ford]$_i$ gathered around it$_i$.

(47)   Seven students who (individually) own a Ford gathered in the garage.

Sentence (43) is reduced into DRS (66) by CR.NRC and other construction rules.

(66)

$$\boxed{\begin{array}{c} X \\ \text{student* (X)} \\ |X|=7 \\ X \text{ bought a car together} \\ X \text{ love to drive it} \end{array}}$$

Condition *X bought a car together* is further reduced so as to reduce the indefinite *a car* as in (67).

(67)

```
┌─────────────────────────────┐
│           X,y               │
│        student*(X)          │
│          |X|=7              │
│    X bought y, together     │
│     X love to drive it      │
└─────────────────────────────┘
```

Since the predicate *love to drive it* is distributive, condition *X love to drive it* is reduced by Distributivity Expansion as in (68). The anaphoric relation is also resolved on this stage.

(68)

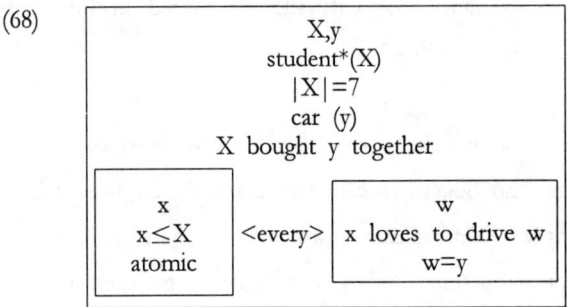

The unacceptability of the anaphoric relation in (46) is also captured by CR.NRC, Distributivity Expansion and other rules. Sentence (46) is first reduced into DRS (69).

(46)   *Seven students who (individually) own [a Ford]ᵢ gathered around itᵢ.

(69)

```
┌─────────────────────────┐
│           X             │
│      student* (X)        │
│        |X|=7            │
│      X  own  a  Ford     │
│   X  gathered  around  it │
└─────────────────────────┘
```

Since *(individually) own a Ford* is a distributive predicate, condition *X own a Ford* is further reduced as in (70). Note discourse referent y which is introduced by *a Ford* is not accessible from the discourse referent w which is introduced by *it*.

(70)

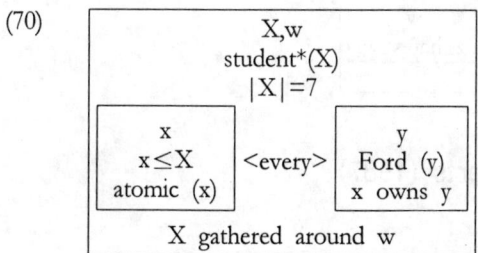

Sentences (44) and (47) are processed similarly. The anaphoric relations are also captured naturally.

However, sentence (45) is problematic. Note that the main VP and the VP of the relative clause are distributive. Sentence (45) would be reduced first into DRS (71).

(45)   Seven students who (individually) own [a Ford]ᵢ hate itᵢ.

(71)

```
┌─────────────────────┐
│          X          │
│     student* (X)     │
│       |X|=7         │
│    X  own  a  Ford   │
│      X  hate  it     │
└─────────────────────┘
```

DRS (71) is further reduced by Distributive Expansion into (72). But in (72), discourse referent w introduced by *it* is not accessible to discourse referent y which is introduced by *a Ford*.

(72)

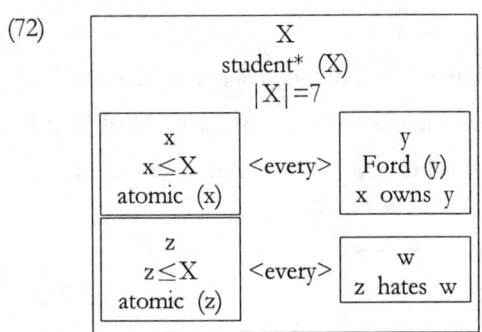

4.3.4. Solutions in Roberts (1987)

Roberts (1987), using the plural operator * of Link (1983), represents sentence (73) as in (74).[14]

(73)   The fathers with two children send them (both) to Montessori school.

(74)   [The *[fathers with [two *children]ᵢ]]ⱼ send themᵢ (both) to Montessori school.

Syntactic analysis (74) is reduced into DRS (75).

(75)

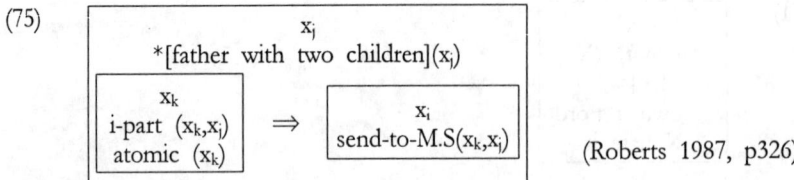

(Roberts 1987, p326)

However, in DRS (75), the discourse referent x_i introduced by the pronoun *them* is not linked to a discourse referent which should be introduced by *two children*. To solve this problem, she argues that the information that "all atomic i-parts of the lattice *CN are elements in the singular denotation" may be accommodated into the nuclear scope of the subject NP. That is, the entailed information that x_k is a member of the property [father with two children] may be accommodated into the left-hand DRS of the duplex condition of (75) as in (76).[15] (Since *children also carries *, it must be further reduced as in (76).) In DRS (76), the discourse referent introduced by *them* is linked to the discourse referent introduced by *two children*. The accommodation of the information that every atomic i-part of * [CN] is a member of the denotation of the singular CN resolves the anaphoric relation in sentence (73).

(76)

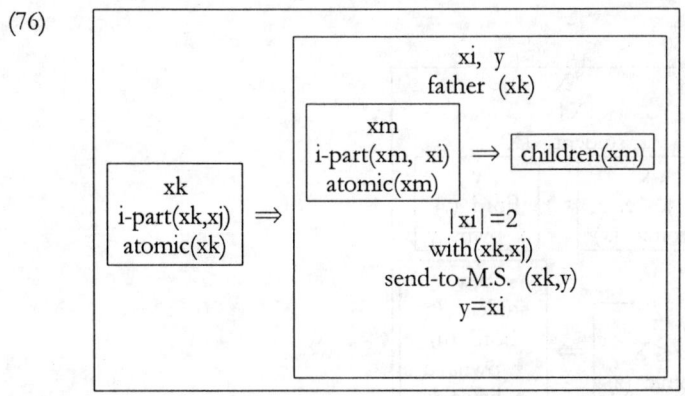

(cf. Roberts 1987: 329)

According to her approach, sentence (77) will be reduced into DRS (78).

(77)　　Seven students who own [a Ford]$_i$ hate it$_i$.

(78)

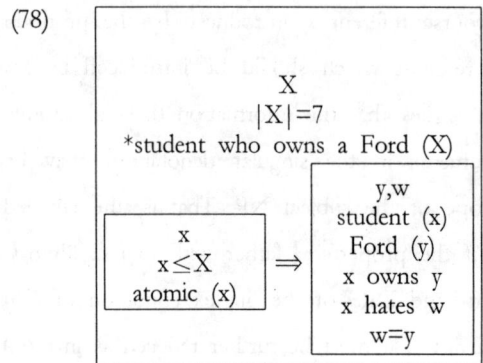

The condition *student who owns a Ford (X)* can be verified iff an embedding function f assigns to X an i-sum which is a member of the join of the two properties, ⟦ student ⟧ and ⟦ owns a Ford ⟧ (⟦ student ⟧ ∧ ⟦ owns a Ford ⟧). Or the condition may be further reduced by the CR.NRC as in (79).

(79)

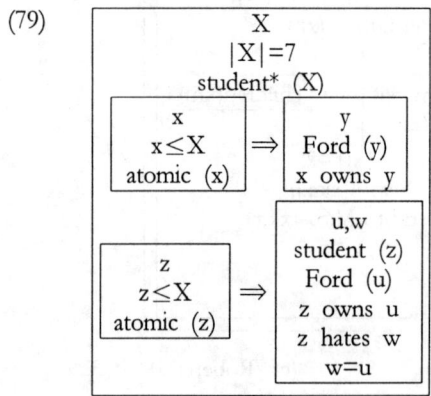

The information conveyed by the first duplex condition of DRS (79) is redundant. But it is not harmful. DRS (79) correctly represents the reading of sentence (77) and captures the anaphoric relation in the sentence.

However, it is unclear why only the specific entailment is accommodated. Others might be entailed by the *CN. Moreover, the accommodation of this kind of entailments is meaningful only when a sentence whose VP is distributive contains a relative clause (or a PP) which reads distributively. For example, this kind of accommodation is not necessary to process sentences in (80)-(82) if CR.NRC is adopted.[16]

(80)   Seven students own a car, individually.

(81)   Seven students who own a car together love to drive it.

(82)   Seven students who own a car individually gathered.

4.3.5. An Alternative

In this section, I will propose an alternative approach toward the NPs modified by a relative clause while preserving the spirit of Kamp and Reyle's CR.NRC specified in (58).

In Kamp and Reyle's system, a syntactic analysis tree is reduced in a top-down, left-to-right manner.[17] That is, a sentence schema (83) containing a relative clause is first reduced into (84) as usual. Let q be a determiner quantifier, and q' be the cardinality information expressed by q.

(83)   q CN RC VP

(84)
$$\begin{array}{|c|}\hline x \\ |x|=q' \\ CN\ RC\ (x) \\ x\ VP \\ \hline \end{array}$$

A DRS condition of DRS (84) *CN RC (x)* must be reduced earlier than a DRS condition x *VP* since an NP *q CN RC* comes left to the VP of (83) and is a sister of the VP, so the NP must be fully reduced before the reduction process moves to the VP. Now, DRS (84) is further processed by CR.NRC into DRS (85). Let x-W be obtained by getting rid of the relative pronoun of the RC and by replacing the gap of the RC with the discourse referent x.

(85)

$$\boxed{\begin{array}{l} x \\ |x| = q' \\ CN \ (x) \\ x\text{-}W \\ x \ VP \end{array}}$$

Now, for the sake of simplicity, let x of x-W be in the subject position and W be a VP. When W is a distributive VP, the condition x-W is further reduced into a DRS-condition (86) by the rule of Distributivity Expansion.

(86)

$$\boxed{\begin{array}{l} y \\ y \leq x \\ atomic \ (z) \end{array}} \ <every> \ \boxed{y\text{-}W}$$

Now, DRS (85) is reduced into DRS (87).

(87)

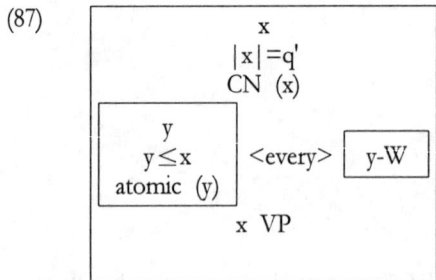

When the VP of x *VP* is distributive, the rule of Distributivity Expansion is applied, yielding DRS (88) from DRS (87).

(88)

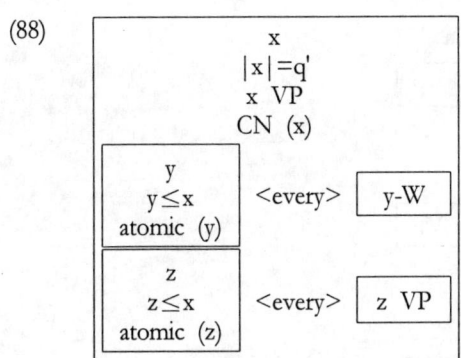

However, I have shown that DRS (88) is inappropriate to treat the anaphoric relation in a sentence *Seven students who individually own a car love to drive it.* To remedy this, I am going to propose an assimilation. Suppose a DRS already has (89) as its DRS condition.

(89) $\boxed{K1}$ <every> $\boxed{K2}$

When a DRS-Construction rule introduces another DRS condition of (90) where DRS K3 is a notational variant of DRS K1, it seems that a cognitive rule assimilates K3 to K1. That is, a cognitive process applies in a way that DRS condition (90) is a condition on discourse referents appearing in DRS K1.

(90) $\boxed{K3}$ <every> $\boxed{K4}$

For example, in DRS (88), the second duplex condition repeated in (91) becomes the DRS condition of (92).

(91)

$$
\boxed{\begin{array}{c} z \\ z \leq x \\ \text{atomic } (z) \end{array}} \ \text{<every>} \ \boxed{z \ \text{VP}}
$$

(92)

$$
\boxed{\begin{array}{c} y \\ y \leq x \\ \text{atomic } (y) \end{array}} \ \text{<every>} \ \boxed{y \ \text{VP}}
$$

DRS-Construction rule specified in (93) captures this point.

(93)   CR. Assimilation

        Triggering Configurations g:

$$
\boxed{K1} \ \text{<every>} \ \boxed{K2}
$$

$$
\boxed{K3} \ \text{<every>} \ \boxed{K4}
$$

        where DRS K3 is a notational variant of DRS K1

        replace γ with

$$
\boxed{K1} \ \text{<every>} \ \boxed{K2}
$$

$$
\boxed{K1} \ \text{<every>} \ \boxed{K4'}
$$

        where DRS K4' is obtained from DRS K4 by replacing every discourse referent introduced in DRS K3 with its corresponding discourse referent introduced in DRS K1[18]

Still we need another operation. In DRT, conditions on a discourse referent are regarded as being cumulative. To introduce a new DRS condition on a discourse referent is to add up that condition to previously introduced conditions on that discourse referent. Suppose that DRS condition (94) is previously introduced. When DRS (95) is introduced, it actually represents the conditions on the discourse referent 'x' which is a part of 'x' and owns 'x' which is to be mapped into an individual which is a donkey.

(94)

| x |
| x≤X |
| atomic (x) |
<every>
| y |
| donkey (y) |
| x owns y |

(95)

| x |
| x≤X |
| atomic (x) |
<every>
| x is rich |

That is, DRS (95) cumulatively represents the information of DRS (96).

(96)

| x,y |
| x≤X |
| atomic (x) |
| donkey (y) |
| x owns y |
<every>
| x is rich |

The following rule of merge is formulated to ensure this cumulative nature of DRS conditions.

(97)   Merge of Consequent DRS
       Triggering Configuration

       | K1 | <every> | K2 |

       | K1 | <every> | K2 |

Operations: merge DRS K2 into DRS K1 of the second duplex condition, making the DRS K1 into DRS K4 as in

$$\boxed{K1} <\text{every}> \boxed{K2}$$

$$\boxed{K4} <\text{every}> \boxed{K3}$$

where K4 is the union of DRS K1 and DRS K2 which is an ordered pair of $<\text{drf}_{K1} \cup \text{drf}_{K2}, \text{con}_{K1} \cup \text{con}_{K2}>$, where drf_K is the set of discourse referents introduced in DRS K and con_K is the set of DRS conditions of K

This accommodation captures the fact that when a sentence with a relative clause has a distributive reading and the relative clause also has a distributive reading, the relative clause is a restriction on an atomic individual which the main sentence describes.

With these devices, the anaphoric relation in sentence (77) is no more problematic. Sentence (77) is first reduced into DRS (98).

(77)   Seven students who (individually) own [a Ford]i hate iti.

(98)
```
┌─────────────────┐
│        X        │
│  student* (X)   │
│     |X|=7       │
│  X own a Ford   │
│   X hate it     │
└─────────────────┘
```

Since predicates *own a Ford* and *hate it* are distributive, by the rule of distributive expansion, DRS (98) is further reduced into DRS (99).

(99)

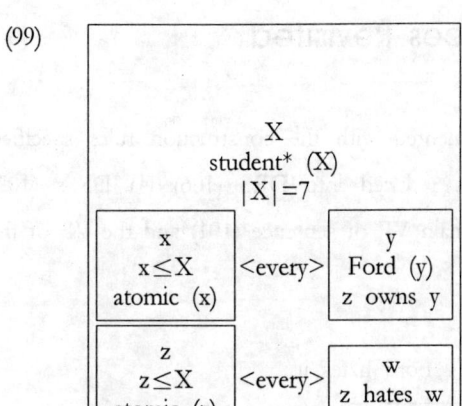

By the rule of assimilation and the rule of merge of consequent DRS specified above, DRS (99) is finally reduced into DRS (100) where the anaphoric relation of sentence (77) is resolved.

(100)

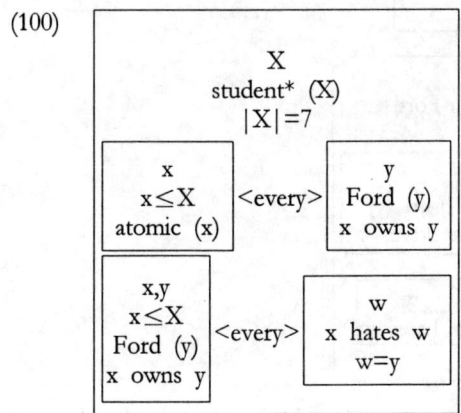

4.4. Donkey-Sentences Revisited

According to my approach augmented with the construction rules specified above, a donkey sentence (101) is reduced into DRS (106) via DRSs (102) through (105). Note that both the main VP of sentence (101) and the VP of the relative clause are distributive.

(101) Every farmer who drives a Ford hates it.

(102)

X
farmer who drivers a Ford* (X)
$|X| = |$ farmer $\wedge$ drive-a-Ford!
X hates it

(103)

X
$|X| = |$ farmer $\wedge$ drive-a-Ford!
Farmer* (X)
X drivers a Ford
X hates it

(104)

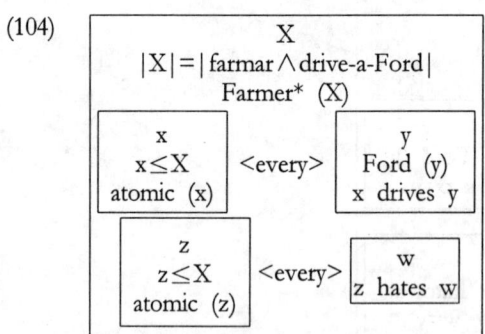

(by the rule of distributivity expansion; both *drives-a-Ford* and *hates it* are distributive predicates)

(105)

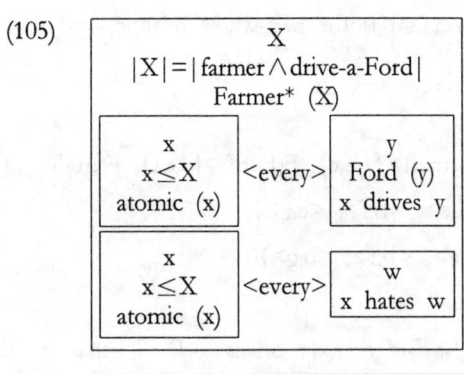

(by the rule of assimilation)

(106)

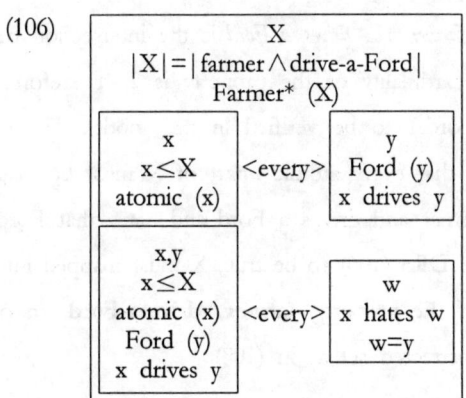

(by the rule of merge of the consequent DRS)

The DRS-condition $|X| = |\text{farmer} \wedge \text{drive-a-Ford}|$ is verified iff the number of atomic individuals of an i-sum into which a non-individual discourse referent X is mapped is the same as the number of atomic individuals contained in a composite property **farmer ∧ drive-a-Ford** which is the intersection of a property **farmer** and a property **drive-a-Ford**. Suppose the following model.

(107) $M = \langle\langle U, A, +, \leq_i \rangle, F\rangle$ where U is the complete free atomic join semi lattice generated from the set A of atomic individuals and the

intrinsic ordering relation $\leq i$ is the part-whole relation, and F is the interpretation function.

$A = \{a,b,c,d,e,f,g\}$, $F(farmer)=\{a,b,c\}$, $F(Ford)=\{d,e,f\}$, $F(Audi)=\{g\}$,
$F(drive) = \{<a,d>, <a,e>, <b,f>, <c,g>\}$,
$F(hate) = \{<a,d>, <a,e>, <b,f>, <b,g>\}$

The property denoted by *drive(s)-a-Ford* is $\lambda x[x$ drives a Ford], that is, $\{a,b\}$. Then, the property denoted by *farmer who drives a Ford* is the intersection of $\{a, b, c\} \cap \{a,b\} = \{a,b\}$ and the cardinality of the property is 2. Therefore, the cardinality of X must be 2 in order to be verified in this model. The other conditions in DRS (106) require that every atomic i-part of X must be mapped into an individual which is a farmer and drives a Ford and hates that Ford he drives. That is, in this model, for DRS (106) to be true, X must mapped into an i-sum of **a+b**, the supremum of the property, **farmer∧drive-a-Ford.** In other words, X is equivalent to the abstracted set as in (108).

(108)

$$\Sigma_x \quad \boxed{\begin{array}{l} x,y \\ farmer\ (x) \\ Ford\ (y) \\ x\ drives\ y \end{array}}$$

4.5. Proportion Problems

A donkey sentence with a non-universal quantifier like (109) is reduced into DRS (111) through DRS (110) in my approach. Here, I treat the determiner *most* as *more than or equal to the half of* for the sake of simplicity.

(109)   Most farmers who own a donkey beat it.

(110)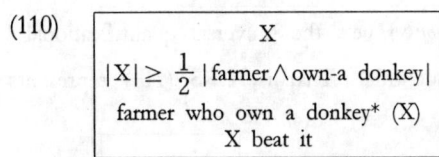

(111)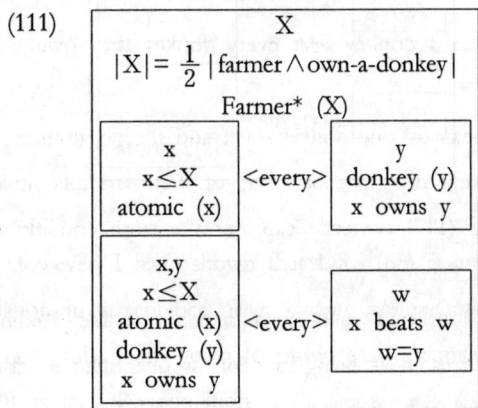

DRS (111) is true iff: (i) there is an embedding function f such that f(X) is a member of F(***farmer**) and the cardinality of f(X) is greater than or equal to the half of the cardinality of **farmer & own-a-donkey**, (ii) for every extension g of f such that g(x) is an atomic i-part of g(X) (=f(X)), there is at least one extension h of g such that h(y) is a member of F(dog), and <h(x) (or g(x)), h(y)> is a member of F(own), and (iii) for every h, an extension of g, such that h(x) is an atomic i-part of h(X), h(y) is a member of F(donkey), <h(x), h(y)> is a member of F(own), there is at least one extension j of h such that <j(x), j(w)> is a member of F(beat) and j(w)=j(y). Here, F is an interpretation function of a model.

In my approach, the proportion problem related to sentence (109) is no longer a problem. The unselective binding is intact while the quantification is actually over the set of farmers who own a donkey but not over the set of farmer-donkey pairs. Indefinite *a donkey* gets the universal quantificational force by being bound by a universal quantifier. That is, DRS (111) represents the reading of (112).

(112)　Most farmers who own a donkey beat every donkey they own.

Suppose that two farmers own exactly one donkey each and they beat them, and one farmer who owns 10 donkeys does not beat any of them. In this situation sentence (109) is true and DRS (112) correctly captures the truth conditions of sentence (109).

An indefinite NP is always treated just as a variable unlike Kadmon's approach where an indefinite is treated as being existentially quantified in case of the asymmetric quantification and as a simple variable in case of the symmetric quantification. For example, sentence (113) is reduced into (114) as usual. Here, an indefinite is also treated as a variable but not as being existentially quantified.

(113)　If a farmer owns a donkey, he beats it.

(114)

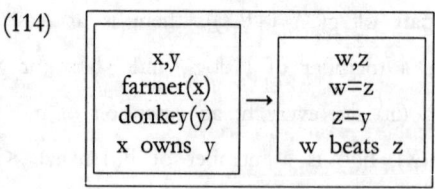

My approach does not need the principal discourse referent unlike Kamp and Reyle's approach. Moreover, a duplex condition is not needed to express the quantification induced by a determiner. At the outset of the discourse representation theory, for example, in Kamp(1981) and Heim(1982), sentence (113) and sentence (115) are treated as being equivalent in their meaning. It is one of the important motivations for the unselective binding. Both sentences are reduced into (114).

(115)   Every farmer who owns a donkey beats it.

With the introduction of a duplex condition with a principal discourse referent and its verification conditions specified above, the parallelism cannot be maintained any more. The difference between the two sentences is further evidenced by the fact that sentence (115) is felicitously continued by (116) where the pronoun *they* is mapped into the set of all the farmers who own a donkey and beat it. But sentence (113) cannot.

(116)   They are unhappy. (they=the set of all the farmers who own a donkey
and beat it)

That is, the abstraction operation cannot take the DRS obtained from sentence (113). It seems that for this and other reasons, they maintain a DR construction rule which processes a conditional sentence into a complex condition of K1 $\Rightarrow$ K2. The verification conditions for K1 $\Rightarrow$ K2 is given as in (117).

(117)   M $|=_f$ K1   K2 iff for every extension g of f to U_{K1} such that
M $|=_g$ K1 there is an extension h of g to U_{K2} such that M $|=_h$ K2.

Note that the verification conditions in (117) are in effect equal to the verification conditions of a duplex condition when the quantifier of the duplex condition is *every*, and has an arbitrary principal discourse referent chosen in the universe of K1. That is, the complex condition K1 $\Rightarrow$ K2 can be represented as a duplex condition of (118).

(118) $\Box$ $\left\langle \begin{array}{c} \text{every} \\ \text{x} \end{array} \right\rangle$ $\Box$

    K1   K2

Nevertheless, when a conditional sentence has an adverb of quantification which is not universal (i.e. usually, mostly, frequently, etc.), it cannot be represented as a duplex condition with a principal discourse referent since the quantification in this case is symmetric even in Kamp and Reyle's system. Consider sentence (119). Since the quantification is symmetric, neither the discourse referent introduced by a *farmer* nor the discourse referent introduced by *a dog* can be selected as a principal discourse referent.

(119) Almost always, if a woman sees a dog, she talks to it.

Sentence (119) can be represented as in (120) with the verification conditions specified in (121).

(120)

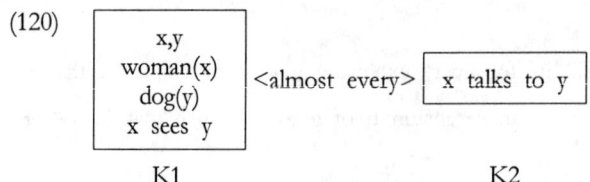

        K1   K2

(121)   A duplex condition (120) is verified iff for almost every extension g
of f to U_{K1} such that $M \mid =_g K1$ there is an extension h of g to U_{K2}
such that $M \mid =_h K2$.

In my approach, D(eterminer)-quantification and A(dverbial)-quantification are
represented as a duplex condition without a principal discourse referent. Recall
that D-quantification is a case of the distributivity expansion which occurs when
a non-individual discourse referent is an argument of a distributive predicate in
my approach. Accordingly, the difference between the two types of quantification
is that in case of D-quantification, a non-individual discourse referent is
introduced by a (non-singular) NP. I replace $\rightarrow$ which connects the two DRSs
of a complex condition by <every> which connects the two DRSs of a duplex
condition. Now, sentences (122)-(124) are processed into DRSs (125)-(127).

(122)   Every farmer who owns a donkey beats it.

(123)   If a farmer owns a donkey, he beats it.

(124)   Mostly, if a farmer owns a donkey, he beats it.

(125)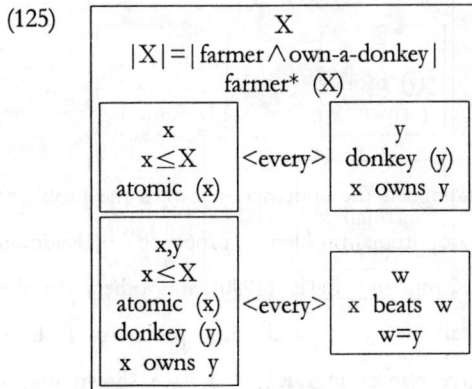

(126)

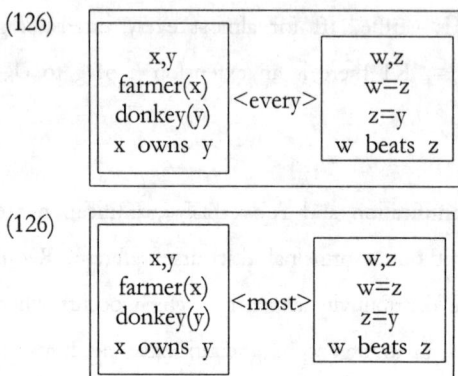

(126)

The verification condition for a duplex condition $K1< Q > K2$ where $K1$ and $K2$ are DRSs and Q is a quantifier is given in (128). Let **Q-many** be the quantity expressed by Q.[19]

(128)   A duplex condition $K1< Q > K2$ is verified iff for **Q-many** extensions g of f to U_{K1} such that $M \models_g K1$ there is an extension h of g to U_{K2} such that $M \models_h K2$.

4.6. Conclusion

In this chapter, I have critically examined the approaches toward the problems of asymmetric quantification (or proportion problems) proposed in Kadmon (1987, 1990), Roberts (1987) and Kamp and Reyle (1990) and others. In the course of developing my own alternative toward this problem, I have re-examined how to deal with relative clauses in DRT, and have shown that a donkey sentence which has a quantificational NP as its subject is nothing but a sentence whose subject NP contains a relative clause. The VPs of the main clause and the relative clause are distributive in these constructions. I have extended Kamp and Reyle's DR construction rule for relative clauses by introducing new DR construction rules which are needed to properly reduce sentence (129) into a DRS. Note that the main VP and the VP of the relative clause are distributive.

(129)   Seven farmers who drive a Ford hate it.

These rules capture the fact that when the VPs of the main clause and the relative clause are distributive, the relative clause is interpreted as a restriction on the atomic individuals of the property denoted by the head noun of the complex NP.

I have shown that problems associated with asymmetric quantification are explained by keeping intact the assumptions that a indefinite NP is a bound variable and a quantifier can bind two or more variables (unselective binding) in the unified approach augmented with the rule of assimilation and the rule of merge of consequent DRS.

Notes to Chapter 4

1. Partee (1990) presents an extensive summary of the approaches toward the problems related to donkey-sentences.

2. For example, determiners such as *most, many, almost all,* etc., and adverbials such as *almost always, mostly,* etc.

3. The Generalized Quantifier Theory treats every determiner as denoting a relation between two properties (properties denoted by the head CN of the determiner and by the VP of the sentence). Kamp and Reyle (1990) also treat all quantificational determiners this way. In this sense, I will treat formula (i) and formula (ii) equivalently. Let Q be a quantifier and a logical connective @ defined appropriately.

(i)   Qx,y [P(x,y), R(x,y)]

(ii)   Qx,y [P(x,y) @ R(x,y)]

4. Following Carlson (1977), I will use the term *individual level predicate* as a predicate which denotes (relatively) a property of an individual, meaning an individual object or a kind of thing. A stage level predicate is a predicate which denotes a property of a stage of an individual or a "spatio-temporal slice of an individual"(Partee 1990, p25). For example, according to her, *own* is an individual level predicate and *see* is a stage level predicate.

6. However, Heim (1982, p62) confesses that her intuitions vacillate between the two paraphrases of (i).

(i)　　Most men who own a donkey beat it.

(ii)　　a. Most men who own a donkey beat every donkey they own.

　　　　b. Most men who own a donkey beat one of the donkeys they own.

(iii)　　for *most* people that owned a slave: for *every* case (minimal situation) **s**
　　　　where they owned a slave: they also owned the offspring of the slave
　　　　that they owned in **s**.

5. Most informants of mine told me that the indefinite NP of a donkey sentence
can have a universal reading even though the determiner of the subject NP of
that sentence is not *every*.

6. Heim (1990) admits that the indefinite NP of a donkey sentence sometimes
has an existential reading:

　　Suppose we view donkey sentences with relatives as involving not one but
　　two quantifying operators. One is the QDet (determiner-quantifier), and the
　　other is an implicit quantifier of sometimes universal, some times existential
　　force, and this binds the indefinite and pronouns anaphoric to it (Heim 1990,
　　p162).

However, an implicit quantifier of existential quantificational force is provided
only when QDet is negative such as *no* and *neither* as in (a). (a) (i) is the
paraphrase given by Heim (1990).

(a) No parent with a teenage son lends him the car.

　　(i) for no parent with a teenage son: for any teenage son he or she has: he or she lends him the car.

(ii) no_x $some_y$ [(parent (x) & teenage son (y) & with (x, y)) &

(x lends y the car)]

Note that the logical representation in (a) (ii) is logically equivalent to (b).

(b)　　$every_x$ $every_y$ [(parent (x) & teenage son (y) & with (x, y)) $\longrightarrow$

(x does not lend y the car)]

If we view the schema *no P Q* as *every P not Q* as in Chapter 3, we can generalize that the implicit operator must be *every* in all cases.

7. Kadmon follows Evans (1977, p535) in this respect. According to Evans, sentence (i) means that most men who own at most one car, wash the unique car on Sundays.

(i)　　Most men who own a car wash it on Sundays.

Kadmon (1990) argues that the uniqueness effect is accommodated into a discourse when an indefinite is an antecedent of a pronoun, following Evans (1980) who argues that an E-type pronoun refers to a maximal collection determined by the clause containing the antecedent NP (Kadmon 1990, p274). One who are interested in this matter, see section 1.4 of Heim (1982) and Kadmon (1988, 1990).

8. Kamp and Reyle (1990) do not define the term "principal discourse referent."

However, I believe that the definition given here does not contradict their intention about this term. A duplex condition can have more than one variable when the head noun is a relational one such as *friend or relative*. Kamp and Reyle write:

The phrase *three friends*, for instance, as we find it in the sentence

4.75)   Three friends bought a sailboat.

is typically understood as denoting not a set each member of which is 'a friend' (in the sense of being someone or other's friend), but rather a set each member of which is a friend of the set's other two members. Thus the extension of the plural noun *friends* is defined in terms of the relation **x is a friend of y**, and is not computable from the set of those people who are a (i.e. somebody's) friend in the way that the extension of book is computable from the set of things that are **books**. Even in the case of relational nouns it is possible to characterize the denoted set in terms of its members, but here the characterization is relational. Thus the DRS condition friends (X) could be extended to

(4.76)

$$\boxed{\begin{array}{c} x,y \\ x \in X \\ x =/=y \\ y \in X \end{array}} \quad \left\langle \begin{array}{c} \text{every} \\ x,y \end{array} \right\rangle \quad \boxed{x \text{ is a friend of } y}$$

(Kamp and Reyle 1990, p347)

9. Heim (1990) provides the denotation of a complex determiner *most-every* as in (i). Equipped with this denotation, the logical form of (30) has desired truth

conditions.

(i) $[\![[\text{most}_x \ \forall_y]\varphi]\!]^g$ **is true iff**

$|\{a: \{b: [\![\zeta]\!]^{g_{x=a,y/b}}=\text{true}\} \subseteq \{b: [\![\varphi]\!]^{g_{x=a,y/b}}=\text{true}\}\}| > \dfrac{1}{2} |\{a: \exists_y:$

$[\![\zeta]\!]^{g_{x=a,y/b}}=\text{true}\}|$

10. If one implicit quantifier is provided, another implicit quantifier must be able to be provided with the modification of the semantics. For example, in a case where an implicit quantifier is assumed to bind two or more variables unselectively, two or more implicit quantifiers can be introduced without assuming the unselective binding.

11. Roberts (1987) summarizes Rooth (1986)'s account of numeral based donkey sentences which adopts Barwise (1985)'s notions of 'dynamic interpretation' and 'parametrized sets.' For details, see Roberts (1987, pp226-232).

12. This procedure is typical in studies assuming DRT. Notable exceptions are Klein (1986) and Asher (1992) who build a DRS in a bottom-up fashion which enables compositional semantics.

13. I did not specify the principal discourse referent in DRS (64) for the sake of simplicity.

14. Recall that the plural operator * takes a property denoted by a singular common noun as an argument and yields a complete atomic free semi join lattice. For example, if $[\![\text{father}]\!] = \{a, b, c\}$, $[\![\text{fathers}]\!] = *[\![\text{father}]\!] = \{a, b, c, a+b, a+c, b+c, a+b+c\}$.

15. Only a proposition entails another proposition. But Roberts (1987) seems to claim that a property entails a proposition when she says that "perhaps this fact (=that all the atomic i-parts of the lattice *CN are elements in the singular denotation) should be taken to be an entailment of *(father with two children)." (Roberts 1987, p328). The term 'entailment' used here should be understood in this sense.

16. If Roberts' approach does not need CR.NRC, sentence (i) cannot be reduced into a proper DRS. Note that the CN *students who own a car together* does not denote a semi lattice *(student who own a car together). Then the information that all the atomic i-parts of the lattice are elements in the singular denotation cannot be entailed, and thus, cannot be accommodated.

(i) Seven students who own a car together love to drive it.

Sentence (i) will be processed into DRS (ii) according to her.

(ii)

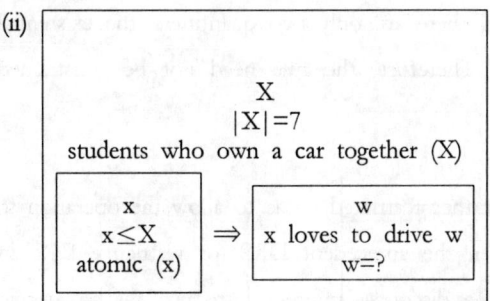

The discourse referent introduced by the pronoun *it* cannot find an appropriate discourse referent in (ii).

17. Kamp (1981) also takes this approach. Roberts (1987), Root (1986), Kadmon (1987, 1990), and van Eijk (1983) also take this methods. However, Klein (1987) and Asher (1992) take the bottom-up, left-to-right approach.

18. Notice that in this rule, the quantifier (*every*) plays a role. If the quantifier is not universal, this rule cannot be applied. For example, if sentences (i) and (ii) are true, then if an individual which is a student came, it also wore blue jeans.

(i) Every student came.
(ii) Every student wore blue jeans.

But, even though sentences (iii) and (iv) are true, it is not guaranteed that if an individual which is a student came, he or she also wore blue jeans.

(iii) Many students came.
(iv) Many students wore blue jeans.

However, note that in my system, there are only two quantifiers, the existential quantifier and the universal one. Therefore, the rule need not be constrained with regard to the quantifier

19. The abstraction operation is further restricted so as to allow the operation to take a duplex condition only when the antecedent DRS (or restrictive DRS in Kamp and Reyle's term) contains a discourse referent introduced as an atomic i-part of a non-individual discourse referent.

Chapter 5. Proper Distributivity
-- Evidence from Korean

5.0. Introduction

A rule of thumb to determine whether or not an NP introduces a
non-individual discourse referent on a DRS is whether or not the NP can be
followed by a collective predicate.[1] If an NP can be followed by a collective
one, it introduces a non-individual discourse referent. If an NP is followed by
only a distributive predicate, it does not introduce a non-individual one. In this
section, I will examine some Korean data which can be properly explained when
the rule of thumb is discarded. If so, and if the findings in this section are
applicable to English data, intrinsically distributive NPs (or quantificational NPs
in Kamp and Reyle's term) must be treated as being able to introduce
non-individual discourse referents. I will examine two Korean phenomena which
require a plural NP in some place of the construction; NP-*ssik* construction
which contributes a distributive reading to a sentence and the phenomena
studied under the rubric of plural marker copying. For example, sentence (1)a is
unacceptable but (1)b is O.K. Similarly, sentence (2)a is bad but (2)b is
acceptable.

(1)   a. #Suncay-ka   12-si 30-pwun -ey ku kakey-eyse pwungsen
                 NOM hour   minute at the store at   balloon

    hana-ssik -ul   sa   -ess -ta.

    one each ACC buy   past IND

    'Suncay bought a balloon each at the store at 12:30.'

b. Suncay-wa Chunwu-ka 12-si 30-pun   -ey   ku kakey-eyse

         and   NOM   hour minute at   the store at

    pwungsen hana-ssik -ul   sa   -ess -ta.

    balloon one   each ACC buy past IND

    'Suncay and Chwunwu bought a balloon each at the store at

    12:30.'

(2)   a. #cey-ka   hakkyo-ey-<u>tul</u> kasseyo.

        I NOM school to pl   went

        'I went to school.'

    b. haksayng-tul-i   hakkyo -ey-<u>tul</u> kasseyo.

        student pl NOM school to pl   went

        'Students went to school.'

                                                (H.K. Lee, 1992, p47)

Before discussing those phenomena, I will deal with the Korean quantifier system briefly.

5.1. Korean Quantifier System

Listed in (3) are Korean quantifiers and their English correspondents. I include numerals into this category. Most quantifiers have a post-nominal as well as a pre-nominal form. Post-nominal forms are in (   ).

(3)   Korean   English

         kak (kakkak)   each, every

         modun (modwu)   all

         taybwubwun-ui (taybwubwun)   most

         manun   many

         yere (yeret)   many, several

         myech (myech)   some, a few

         --   few

         --   no

         --   both

         --   neither

         --   not every, not many,

                                             not a, ...

         han (hana)   one

         twu (twul)   two

         sey (seyt)   three

         ney (neyt)   four

A quantifier can follow its head noun if it has the post-nominal form. For example, an NP *all (the) students* corresponds to *modun haksayng* or to *haksayng modwu*. Table (4) shows this relation.

(4)   modun haksayng   haksayng modwu

         taybwubwun-ui haksayng   haksayng taybwubwun

         manun haksayng   - - -

         han haksayng   haksayng hana

Korean quantifiers except *kak* (each), *modun* (all), *taybwubwun* (most) and *manun* (many) usually combine with classifiers determined by head nouns. For example, when the head noun is human, classifier *myeng* (person) is used. When quantifier+classifier comes at a pre-nominal position, it must be followed by the possessive particle -ui .

(5)　　a. yere myeng-ui haksayng　　'many students'
　　　　b.*yere myeng haksayng
　　　　c. haksayng yere myeng　　　'many students'

All the NPs with the quantifiers except *kak* can be followed by a distributive as well as a collective predicate. I will use *mohi-ta* (gather) and *hamkke x-lul tuleoli-ta* (lift x together) as examples of collective predicates. As shown in (6), *kak CN* can be followed by only a distributive predicate.[2]

(6)　　a.　modun haksayng-(tul) -i　mohi　-ess　-ta.
　　　　　all　　　student　pl　NOM gather past IND
　　　　　'All the student gathered.'
　　　　b.　taybwubwun-ui haksayng-(tul)-i mohi　-ess-ta.
　　　　　'Most students gathered.'
　　　　c.　manun haksayng -(tul) -i　piano-lul　hamkke　tuleoli-ess-ta.
　　　　　many　student　　pl NOM piano ACC together lift past IND
　　　　　'Many students lifted a piano, together.'
　　　　d.　#kak haksayng-i mohi-ess-ta.
　　　　　'Every student gathered.'
　　　　f.　#kak haksayng -i piano-lul hamkke tuleoli-ess-ta.
　　　　　'Every student lifted a piano, together.'

g.   modun haksayng-i noray -lul pwulwu-ess-ta.

        song   sing

'Every student sang a song.'

h.   kak haksayng-i noray -lul pwulwu -ess-ta.

'Every student sang a song.'

Some bound morphemes called delimiters by I.Yang(1973) show the same distribution as quantifier *kak*. A delimiter -*mata* which attaches to a noun has a similar function as *kak*. When delimiter -*(i)na* attaches to an NP with a wh-word which acts as an indefinite article, the whole NP shows the same distributional restriction as *kak CN*.

(7) a. haksayng-mata noray -lul pwulwu -ess -ta

    student del   song ACC sing   past IND

   'Every student sang a song.'

  b. #haksayng-mata mohi -ess -ta.

    student   del   gather past IND

   'Every student gathered.'

  c. enu   haksayng -ina noray -lul   pwulwu -ess-ta.

    which(or a) student   del song   ACC   sing   past IND

   'Every student sang a song.'

  d. #enu haksayng -ina piano-lul hamkke tuleoli-ess-ta.

        piano   together lift

   'Every student lifted a piano, together.'

Although the Korean quantifier system has many other interesting characteristics, I do not deal with them here simply because the characteristics mentioned above can, I believe, provide sufficient background information to the discussion which will be presented in the following subsections.[3]

5.2. Distributivity Triggered by Particle —ssik

Particle -ssik as a bound morpheme attaches to an NP. It usually combines with the subject NP, the direct object NP or the indirect NP as in (8) (Choe, 1987).[4] It must attach to the post-nominal form of a quantifier (except kak (every), modun (all), taybwubwun (most), and manun (many)) or a quantifier phrase (quantifier + classifier).

(8)   a.   [hyengsa-twu-myeng-ssik] -i   yonguica-tul-ul ccocho-ko-iss-ta
             detective two CL   NOM suspect pl ACC chase prog IND
             'Two detectives are chasing each suspect.'

        b.   ai   -tul -i   pwungsen hana-ssik-ul sa -ess -ta.
             child pl NOM balloon   one   ACC buy past IND
             'The children bought a balloon each.'

        c.   emma-tul-i   (chaykimciko)
             mommy pl NOM with a sense of responsibility
             ai   yel-myeng-ssik-eykey ku   sosik -ul cenhayssta.
             child ten CL   DAT the news ACC told
             'Mothers told ten children each the news.'

The contrast in (9) shows the function of -ssik as a distributivity trigger. Sentence (9)a has a collective or a distributive reading while sentence (9)b has only a distributive reading.

(9)   a.   John-kwa Mary-ka   pwungsen   hana -lul   sa   -ess -ta.

                and   NOM balloon   one   ACC buy past IND

        (i) John and Mary bought a balloon, together.

        (ii) John and Mary bought a balloon each.

    b.   John-kwa Mary-ka   pwungsen   hana-ssik-ul sa -ess -ta.

        'John and Mary bought a balloon, each.'

Next, I will discuss the semantic function of *-ssik*. I will regards *-ssik* as a distributivity operator which takes a predicate and make it distributive following Link (1987) and Roberts (1987) who treat the shifted *each* in (10) as a distributivity operator on a predicate.[5]

(10)   The children bought a balloon each.

Recall that a predicate need not be a syntactic constituent such as VP. As Roberts (1987) argues, a set of individuals obtained by λ-abstraction is also a predicate. To clarify the function of *-ssik*, let's compare the function of shifted *each* with that of *every*. According to ununified approaches, an NP with *every* introduces a discourse referent in the antecedent DRS of a duplex condition even when it is not the subject of a sentence since it is quantificational. In my term, *every CN* requires a distributive predicate and thus, it always participates in the predication as the argument of the distributive predicate. For example, sentence (11) is processed as if the predicate is *John bought __* , that is, λx(John bought x).

(11)   John bought every balloon.

    a. $\forall x$ [**balloon**(x) $\rightarrow$ **John bought** x]

b. $\exists Y$ [Y=sup(**balloon**) & $^D\lambda x$(**John bought** x) (Y)]

$= \exists Y$ [Y=sup(**balloon**) & $\forall y$[y is an atomic i-part of Y $\rightarrow$

John bought y]

In other words, *every* is a marker which indicates that an NP with it is the argument of a distributive predicate (Sorting Key in Choe's term). Korean *kak*, *-mata*, and *enu ... na* are such markers.

Similarly, shifted *each* makes a predicate distributive. But contrary to *every*, it marks that the NP it combines with cannot be an argument of a distributive predicate but it must be a part of it (in Choe's term, it marks an NP as a distributive share). Because of the dual function of shifted *each*, in some cases, the lambda abstraction must occur to get a new predicate which the NP with shifted *each* is a part of. This is why the lambda abstraction must occur in (12). Accordingly, (12) is translated as in (13). I treat a definite NP as being anaphoric.

(12)   One interpreter each was assigned to the visitors.

(Choe 1987, p147)

(13) $^D\lambda x$(one interpreter each was assigned to x) (the visitors)

$= \exists X,Y$ [visitor*(X) & Y=X & $^D\lambda x$(one interpreter was assigned to x) (Y)]

$= \exists X,Y$ [visitor*(X) & Y=X & $\forall y$[y is an atomic i-part of Y $\rightarrow$

$\exists z$[interpreter(z) & x is assigned to y]]

Korean *-ssik*, just like shifted *each*, morphologically marks that an NP with *-ssik* must have two functions--as a distributivity operator on a predicate and as an indicator which indicates that an NP with it must be a part of a distributive predicate. Then, the sentences in (8) are translated as in (14) which fit the intuitive readings given in English in (8).

(8)   a.   [hyengsa-twu-myeng-ssik] -i   yonguica-tul-ul ccocho-ko-iss-ta

         detective two CL   NOM suspect pl ACC chase prog IND

         'Two detectives are chasing each suspect.'

      b.   ai   -tul -i   pwungsen hana- ssik-ul sa -ess -ta.

         child pl NOM balloon   one   ACC buy past IND

         'The children bought a balloon each.'

      c.   emma-tul-i   (chaykimciko)

         mommy pl NOM with a sense of responsibility

         ai   yel-myeng-ssik-eykey   ku   sosik -ul   cenhayssta.

         child ten CL   DAT   the news ACC told

         'Mothers told ten children each the news.'

(14) a. $^D\lambda x$(two detectives are chasing x) (some suspects)

      = $\exists Y$ [suspect*(Y) & $^D\lambda x$(two detectives are chasing x) (Y)]

      = $\exists Y$ [suspect*(Y) & $\forall y$[y is an atomic i-part of Y $\rightarrow$

              λx(two detectives are chasing x) (y)]]

      = $\exists Y$ [suspect*(Y) & $\forall y$[y is an atomic i-part of Y $\rightarrow$

                 $\exists z$ [detective*(z) & $|z|$=2 & z is chasing y]]]

      b. $^D\lambda x$(x bought a balloon) (the children)

      = $\exists X,Y$ [child*(X) & Y=X & $^D\lambda x$(x bought a balloon) (Y)]

      = $\exists X,Y$ [child*(X) & Y=X & $\forall y$[y is an atomic i-part of Y $\rightarrow$

                 $\exists z$ [balloon(z) & atomic(z) & y bought z]]]

      c. $^D\lambda x$(x told ten students the news) (some mothers)

      = $\exists Y$ [mother*(Y) & $^D\lambda x$(x told ten students the news) (Y)]

$$= \exists Y \; [\text{mother}^*(Y) \; \& \; \forall y \; [y \text{ is an atomic i-part of } Y \rightarrow$$
$$\exists w,u,v \; [\text{student}^*(w) \; \& \, |w| = 10 \; \& \; \text{news}(u) \; \& \; v=u \; \&$$
$$x \text{ told } w \; v]]]$$

A predicate which is assigned the distributivity by particle *-ssik* (I will call it a *ssik-predicate*) is different from an ordinary (or lexical) distributive predicate in that the former requires as an argument an NP which is to be processed into a non-individual discourse referent while the latter can have a (semantically) singular NP as an argument. Choe puts this fact as a Sorting Key must be semantically plural (Choe 1987, p32). Sentences in (15) show that a *ssik*-predicate requires as an argument a plural NP which introduces a non-individual discourse referent. Sentences in (16) show that a lexically distributive predicate such as *ca-ta* 'sleep' can have a singular NP as its argument.

(15) a. #haksayng han myeng-i   ejey   12-si 30-pwun-ey ku
         student   one CL NOM yesterday hour   min.   at the
         kakey-eyso pwungsen hana-ssik-ul   sa-ess-ta.
         store at   balloon   one   ACC buy past IND
         'A student bought a balloon each at the store at 12:30, yesterday.'

     b. haksayng twu myeng -i ejey 12-si 30-pwun-e ku kakey-
        eyse pwungsen hana-ssik-ul sa-ess-ta.
        'Two students bought a balloon each at the store at 12:30, yesterday.'

(16) a. haksayng han myeng-i   ca -ko-iss-ta.
        student one CL   NOM sleep be-ing
        'A student is sleeping.'

b.   haksayng twu myeng-i ca-ko-iss-ta.

'Two students are sleeping.'

I will call a distributive predicate which requires a plural argument "a proper
distributive predicate." That is, a proper distributive predicate requires a
non-individual discourse referent as its argument in a DRS.

It is possible for an NP which cannot be followed by a collective VP to be
an argument NP of a *ssik*-predicate. Intrinsically distributive NPs of Korean such
as *kak CN*, *NP-mata*, and *enu CN-na* are perfectly acceptable as an argument of
ssik-predicate as in (17).

(17)   a.   kak   haksayng-i   pwungsen hana-ssik sa-ess-ta.

         every student NOM balloon   one   buy past IND

         'Every student bought a balloon each.'

       b.   haksayng-mata   pwungsen hana -ssik sa-ess-ta.

         student del.(every) balloon one   bought

         'Every student bought a balloon each.'

       c.   enu haksayng-ina   pwungsen hana -ssik sa-ess-ta.

         which student del balloon one   bought

         'Every student bought a balloon each.'

According to Kamp and Reyle, sentence (17)a will be reduced into DRS (18). But
the condition *x-ka y hana-ssik sa-ess-ta* (x bought a balloon each) is an ill-formed
condition because predicate *y hana-ssik sa-ess-ta* requires a non-individual discourse
referent.

(18)

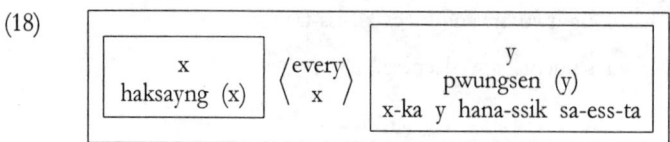

One possible objection to my treatment of *ssik*-construction might be that a predicate containing *ssik*-NP syntactically agrees with its controller, that is, the controller must be syntactically plural but need not introduce a non-individual discourse referent. But this objection is problematic. An NP which cannot be followed by a collective predicate cannot be pluralized by plural morpheme *-tul* as in (19) when the NP is about (atomic) individuals but not groups of individuals.

(19) a. kak   haksayng -i   noray hana-ssik pwulwu-ess-ta.
          every student NOM song one   sing   past IND
          'Every student sang a song.'

      b. kak   haksayng-tul-i   noray hana-ssik pwulwu-ess-ta.
          every student pl NOM song one   sing   past IND
          'Every group of students sang a song.'

      c. *kak haksayng-tul-i noray hana-ssik pwulwu-ess-ta.
          'Every student sang a song.'

Another possible approach toward the behavior of *-ssik* is to treat *-ssik* as an operator which makes a predicate properly distributive and when a proper distributive predicate predicates of a quantificational NP, it becomes an ordinary distributive one. This approach can describe the distributivity induced by *-ssik* correctly. However, if there are no sufficient reasons why it should be when it predicates of a quantificational NP, this kind of approach is too ad-hoc to be accepted.

According to my approach, a unified one, an NP which is followed only by a distributive predicate also introduces a non-individual discourse referent. Thus, the discourse referent introduced by such NP can be an argument of a proper distributive predicate. In my approach sentence (17)a is reduced into DRS (20). I will represent a proper distributive predicate P as PD(P). Since PD(P) is also a distributive predicate, the rule of distributivity expansion applies to the condition X PD(pwungsen hana-lul sa-ess-ta), further reducing DRS (20) into DRS (21).

(20)

(21)

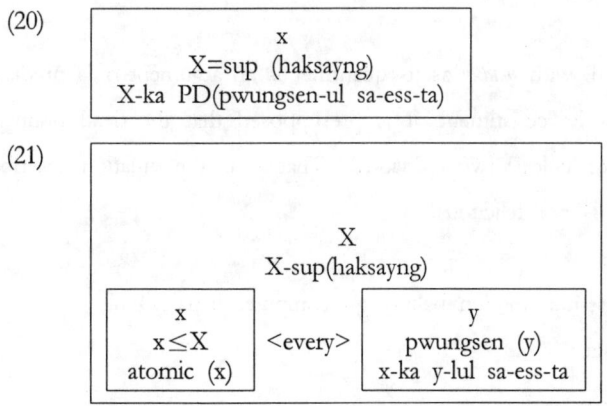

Korean quantifier *kak* is felicitously used only when the head noun denotes a set of at least two individuals. If a speaker knows that there is only a student in this room, he does not say sentence (22) to express the fact that the student owns a computer even in a hyperbolic manner. Rather, he uses (23) where *modun* (all, every) replaces *kak* of (22) in that situation. Quantifier *modun*, just like English *every*, can be felicitously used when the head noun denotes a singleton set or an empty set.

(22) i -pang -ey iss-nun   kak haksayng-i computer-lul

   this room in be rel.-marker every student NOM   ACC

   kaci-ko-iss-ta.

    own

   'Every student in this room owns a computer.'

(23) i-pang-ey iss-nun modun haksayng-i computer-lul kaciko-iss-ta

   'Every student in this room owns a computer.'

However, when an NP with *modun* as its quantifier is an argument of a predicate containing *ssik-NP* as its constituent, it is presupposed that the head noun of *modun* denotes a set of at least two individuals. That is, in the situation described above, sentence (24) is not felicitous.

(24) i-pang-ey iss-nun modun haksayng-i computer hana-ssik-ul

   kaci-ko-iss-ta.

The treatment of *-ssik* in the unified approach captures this intuition correctly.

The same thing can be said about shifted *each* of English. If Roberts (1987) is correct who treats shifted *each* as a distributive operator on a predicate (VP or λ-abstracted predicate), quantificational NPs must be able to introduce a non-individual discourse referent since those NPs can be a controller of shifted *each* as in (25). Note that it cannot have a semantically singular NP as its controller in (26).

(25) a. ?Every student bought two balloons each.

   b. Most students bought two balloons each.

      c. Many students bought two balloons each.

      d. Few students bought two balloons each.

(26)   a. John and Bill bought two balloons each.

        b. *John bought two balloons each.

        c. Two students bought two balloons each.

        d. *A student bought two balloons each.

If quantificational NPs do not denote i-sums, the acceptability in (25) cannot be properly explained with retaining the function of shifted each as described above.

The existence of properly distributive predicates both in English and Korean evidences the hypothesis that an NP which is required to be followed by a distributive VP does not have to denote an atomic individual. The fact also gives an evidence on the position that a quantificational NP of Kamp and Reyle's system denotes an i-sum just as a plural non-quantificational NP does.

5.3. −*tul*, a Pragmatic Morpheme (PM−tul) of Korean

5.3.1. -*tul* as a Sub-Entailment Trigger

H. Lee (1992) distinguishes two uses of Korean bound morpheme -*tul* : -*tul* as a nominal plural marker like -*(e)s* of English (PL-tul, in his term) and -*tul* as a pragmatic morpheme (PM-*tul*) which, according to him, "doesn't affect the literal meaning of the phrase (H. Lee 1992, p44)." He lists syntactic and morphological differences between the two uses of *-tul*. For example, morphologically, PL-*tul* combines only with a lexical noun while PM-*tul* attaches to any major categories other than adjectives as in (27)

(27) a. haksayng-tul (PL-tul)

   b. ppalli -tul (PM-tul)   (Adv-PM-tul)
       quickly PM   'quickly'

   c. Seoul-eyse-tul   (P-PM)
           in PM 'in Seoul'

   d. ai -tul -i   cip -ey kasseyo-tul   (V-PM)
       child PL NOM home to went   PM
       'The children went home.'

For other differences, see H. Lee (1992, pp 44-46).

The pragmatic function of PM-*tul* is to mark that every atomic i-part of an i-sum denoted by a controller of PM-*tul* is an argument of an inferable one-place predicate from the proposition denoted by the sentence. For example, PM-*tul* in (28) contributes an additional reading that every child is healthy to sentence (29) which is just the same as (29) except PM-*tul*.

(28) Yonghi-ka   ai-tul-ul   kenkanghake -tul kiwuessta.
         NOM child PL ACC healthily PM raised
      'Yonghi has raised her children healthily.'

                                              (H. Lee 1992, p55)

(29) Yonghi-ka ai-tul-ul kenkanghake kiwuessta.
      'Yonghi has raised her children healthily.'

The treatment of PM-*tul* by H. Lee is similar to the treatment of floated *all* of English by Dowty (1986) even though he (H. Lee) provides a pragmatic account of the fact that in some cases, PM-*tul* contributes a distributive reading to the sentence. According to Dowty (1986), verbs including some collective ones have some "distributive sub-entailments."[6] For example, a collective predicate *be alike* has an sub-entailment of "having an individual property that other group members share." H. Lee's remarks that "a proposition that is inferable from a sentence containing X (the controller of PM-*tul*)" is comparable to the notion of "sub-entailments."

H. Lee argues that PM-*tul* tends to contribute a distributive reading to the sentence where it occurs but the reading is cancelable without rendering contradiction because the reading is "figured out from its sense by the hearer." Sentence (30) usually has a distributive reading such that every student bought balloons (or a balloon). But when it is continued as in (31), the distributive reading is cancelled, meaning that the students as a group bought balloons (H. Lee 1992, P67).

(30)   haksayng-tul-i   pwungsen -ul   sasseyo-tul.
       student   PL NOM balloon ACC   bought PM
       'Every student bought balloons.'

(31)   haksayng-tul-i   pwungsen-ul sasseyo-tul. kulende,
        student PL NOM balloon ACC buy PM By the way
       tanchero   sasseyo.
       in a group bought
       'The students bought balloons. By the way, they bought them as a
       group."

In my account of PM-*tul*, the collective and the distributive readings are due to the fact that predicate *pwungsen-ul sasseyo* is a mixed predicate (that is, it can be distributive or collective). When it is a distributive one, the sub-entailment triggered by the predicate is the same as the predicate itself. Accordingly, the sentence has a distributive reading. When it is a collective one, a different sub-entailment such as 'having participated in buying balloons in some way' is triggered by PM-*tul*. Then, PM-*tul* contributes an additional reading that every member of the group participated in buying balloons in some way to the reading that the boys as a group bought balloons. Under the situation where there were 5 students and 4 of them contributed money to buy balloons and one student went to the store and bought the balloons with the money, sentence (31) is true. But when one of the five student did not involve in buying the balloons in any way, the sentence is false. Consider sentence (32) which lacks PM-*tul*. Sentence (32) is true in both situations described above if the five students are regarded as members of a group.

(32)   haksayng-tul-i tanchero   pwungsen-ul   sasseyo.
       student   PL NOM in a group balloon ACC   bought
       'The students bought balloons as a group.'

The cancelation of the distributive reading of the first sentence of (31) might be explained like this: when a predicate is a mixed one, a hearer interprets it as a distributive one in default. After hearing the word *kuronde* (by the way) which forces him to discard the default interpretation, if possible, he interprets the predicate as collective and invokes an appropriate sub-entailment.

In short, H. Lee's treatment of PM-tul can be restated in terms of sub-entailments as follows:

(i)   PM-*tul* requires that a certain sub-entailment of a predicate (VP or λ-abstracted) be realized,

(ii)   a sub-entailment of a predicate is a distributive predicate (by definition of sub-entailment), and

(iii)   the expression to which PM-*tul* is attached is assigned some pragmatic function.[7]

5.3.2. DR Construction Rule for PM-*tul*

H. Lee and other writers (Kuh, 1986, Hong, 1990) who deal with PM-*tul* have shown that PM-*tul* requires a plural controller. The contrast in grammaticality of sentences in (33) and (34) supports this generalization.

(33)   a. <u>haksayng-tul-i</u>   hakkyo-ey-<u>tul</u> kasseyo.
            student PL NOM school to PM went
            'The students went to school.'
        b. nay-ka   <u>ai-tul-eykey</u> ton   -ul -<u>tul</u> cuesseyo.
            I NOM child PL to   money ACC PM gave
            'I gave money to the children.'
        c. nay-ka   <u>ai -tul-ul</u>   kyosil -lo-<u>tul</u> ponayssta.
            I   NOM child PL ACC classroom to PM sent
            'I sent the students to a classroom.'

                                                (H. Lee, 1992, chapter 3)

(34) a. *<u>haksayng han-myeng</u> -i   hakkyo -ey -<u>tul</u> kasseyo.

         student one CL NOM school   to PM went

         'A student went to school.'

    b. *nay-ka   <u>ai   han myeng-eykey</u> ton -ul   -tul cuesseyo.

         I NOM child one CL   to   money ACC PM gave

         'I gave money to a student.'

    c. *nay-ka   ai   han myeng-ul kyosil   -lo-tul ponayssta.

         I NOM child one CL ACC classroom to PM sent

         'I sent a child to a classroom.'

Now, I will deal with how to reduce into a DRS a sentence with a collective predicate which has sub-entailments. Let NP[+pl] P[coll, +α-tul] be a schema for those sentences and Q be a predicate sub-entailed by P. First, as usual, the plural subject NP introduces a non-individual discourse referent X into a current DRS. Accordingly, the sentence is reduced into DRS (35).

(35)
$$\boxed{\begin{array}{c} X \\ R(X) \\ X \text{ P[coll. } -\alpha\text{-tul]} \end{array}}$$

    where R is obtained from the CN of the NP

To reduce condition X P[coll, +α-tul] further, CR. Pred[coll, +α-tul] is formulated as in (36).

(36) CR.Pred[coll,+α-tul]

Triggering   S

configurations   /   \

γ⊆γ̄∈Con$_K$:   X   P[coll, +α-PM(tul)]

where X is a non-individual discourse referent
and P is a predicate which is VP or a
λ-abstracted one

Operations: (a) Get rid of PM(tul) from α.

(b) Introduce a new condition **sub-entailed by
P(Q)** into Con$_K$.

(c) Introduce a new condition [$_S$ X Q] into Con$_K$.

Condition **sub-entailed by P(Q)** is verified in a model M iff there is at least
one embedding function f such that f(P) sub-entails f(Q) in M. Condition [$_S$ X
Q] is further reduced into a duplex condition by the rule of distributivity
expansion since Q is distributive.[8] Now, DRS (35) is reduced into (37) which is
finally reduced into (38).

(37)
$$
\begin{array}{c}
X \\
R(X) \\
X\ P[coll,+\alpha] \\
\text{sub-entailed by P (Q)} \\
X\ Q
\end{array}
$$

(38)
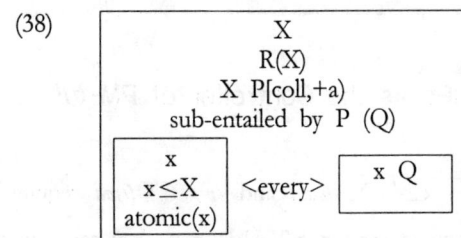
$$
\begin{array}{c}
X \\
R(X) \\
X\ P[coll,+a) \\
\text{sub-entailed by P (Q)}
\end{array}
$$

$$
\boxed{\begin{array}{c} x \\ x \leq X \\ atomic(x) \end{array}} \quad \text{<every>} \quad \boxed{x\ Q}
$$

When the predicate of a sentence with PM-*tul* is distributive, the sub-entailment of the predicate is the same as the predicate itself. Therefore, the sub-entailed predicate is redundant. In this case, PM-tul is just deleted when the condition to be reduced is well-formed. (I ignore the pragmatic information assigned to α by PM-tul.) For example, sentence (39) is reduced into DRS (41) via DRS (40).

(39) John-kwa Bill-i   cam -ul   konhi -tul ca-ko-iss-ta.
      and   NOM sleep Acc soundly PM be sleeping
      'John and Bill are sleeping soundly.'

(40)

$$
\boxed{\begin{array}{c}
X,y,z \\
\text{John } (y) \\
\text{Bill } (z) \\
X = y \oplus z \\
\text{X-ka cam-ul konhi-tul ca-ko-iss-ta}
\end{array}}
$$

(41)

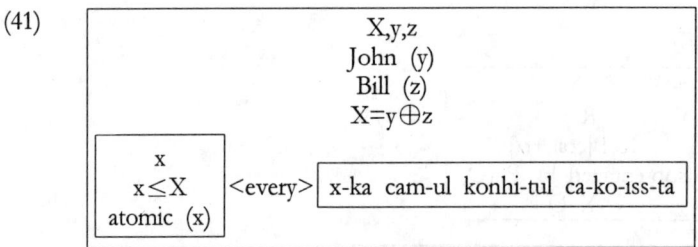

5.3.3. Quantificational NPs as the Controller of PM-*tul*

Some Korean NPs such as *kak CN*, *NP-mata* and *enu CN-(i)na* require a distributive predicate as I have shown in section 5.2. However, they can control

PM-*tul* as in (41).

(41)   a.   kak haksayng-i cam-ul konhi-tul   ca-ko-iss-ta.
            every student NOM sleep ACC soundly be sleeping
            'Every student is sleeping soundly.'

       b.   haksayng-mata cam-ul konhi-tul ca-ko-iss-ta.
            'Every student is sleeping soundly.'

       c.   enu haksayng -ina cam-ul konhi-tul ca-ko-iss-ta.
            'Every student is sleeping soundly.'

If such NPs are reduced by the DR construction rule for quantificational NPs of Kamp and Reyle's system in the way that they are reduced into a duplex condition, an unacceptable condition is inevitably produced. For example, sentence (41)a should be reduced into DRS (42). The condition *x-i cam-ul konhi-tul ca-ko-iss-ta* is unacceptable since the controller of *konhi-tul* is x which is not a non-individual discourse referent.

(42)

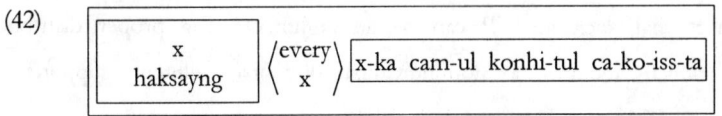

Now, it is clear that these NPs must introduce a non-individual discourse referent for sentences in (41) to be reduced properly with keeping intact the DR construction rule for a predicate with PM-*tul* in it. In my approach where a quantificational NP also introduces a non-individual discourse referent, sentences in (41) do not pose any problems. For instance, sentence (41)a is processed into DRS (44) via DRS (43).

(43)

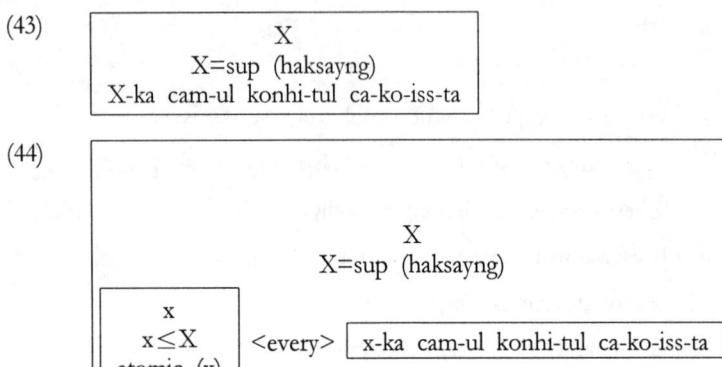

(44)

5.4. Conclusion

In this chapter, I showed that even an NP which requires a distributive predicate must introduce a non-individual discourse referent by investigating some characteristics of Korean quantifiers, the distributivity induced by Korean particle *-ssik*, and the sub-entailment requirement of a predicate with PM *-tul* in it. The fact that such an NP can be an argument of a proper distributive predicate which requires a non-individual discourse referent supports my approach and is against Kamp and Reyle's.

Notes to Chapter 5

1. Recall that according to Roberts (1987), the rule of thumb to determine whether or not an NP introduces a non-individual discourse referent is whether or not the NP denotes a group entity. She does not regards as a test for groupness whether or not an NP can be followed by a collective predicate. See Chapter 2 for further information.

2. Professor James Yoon, Byongkwon Kim and Kang-hyuk Lee also agree the judgments on the acceptability of sentences in (6).

3. For more information on the characteristics of Korean determiners, see J.Lee (1991).

4. Choe (1987) extensively deals with the semantics of -ssik which he categorizes into anti-quantifiers. Gil, D. (1988, 1990) and Cho and Morgan (1989) also deal with the problems concerning Korean particle -ssik.

5. Choe (1987) defines the distributivity as the number dependance between two or more arguments of a predicate. See Chapter 3 of Choe (1987) for further reference.

6. See Chapter 3 for further discussion on "sub-entailments."

7. I will not discuss here what the pragmatic function is. See. H. Lee (1992), chapter 5.

8. Recall that the predicate P has some "distributive" sub-entailments. That is, the predicate Q sub-entailed by P must be distributive.

Chapter 6. Conclusion

In this study, I have tried to construct a new NP semantics system by arguing for the hypothesis that *every* NP introduces a discourse referent of an appropriate type. I follow other assumptions of Discourse Representation Theory such that (i) anaphoric pronouns are bound variables, (ii) quantifiers introduced by quantificational determiner or quantificational adverbials can bind more than one variable simultaneously, and (iii) free variables are bound by the existential quantifier provided by Existential Closure (or Default Existential Generalization).

To achieve my goal, I compared my approach mainly with Kamp and Reyle (1990)'s and Roberts' who maintain that a non-quantificational NP introduces an individual or a non-individual discourse referent based on its semantic number and a quantificational NP introduces a pair of DRSs connected by the quantifier of the NP. In the antecedent DRS (the first DRS of the pair), an individual discourse referent is introduced. Actually, this position has been held by the majority of linguists and philosophers who have been interested in natural language quantification. I call their approach non-unified one toward distributivity because it treats the distributivity in sentence (1) and sentence (2) differently. The distributivity in sentence (1) is captured by the distributivity expansion which applies to a non-individual discourse referent and the distributivity in sentence (2) which is captured by way of quantification.

(1)   John and Mary wore blue jeans today.

(2)   Every student wore blue jeans today.

In Chapter 2, I have specified the system of the non-unified approaches proposed by Kamp and Reyle (1990) and Roberts (1987). Then, I have pointed out some fundamental problems of their approaches. Here, I was mainly concerned with two problems:

(A) A quantificational NP is also an indefinite NP. If we admit that a quantificational NP introduces a pair of DRSs, we have to modify the assumption that an indefinite introduces a (individual or non-individual) discourse referent in the way that an indefinite non-quantification NP introduces a (individual or non-individual) discourse referent. However, it is impossible or at best very difficult to provide a set of reliable criteria to classify an NP into individual-denoting (or non-quantificational) or into quantificational.

(B) Non-unified approaches cannot explain the following set of data even when we admit into the system some pragmatic accommodations such as abstraction, summation, and other operations proposed in Kamp and Reyle (1990) and Roberts (1987).

(i)   [Every son of John]$_i$ contributed money to buy a diamond ring for their$_i$ mother.

(ii)   Most students gathered in the hall.

(iii)   "Many students lifted a piano" reads as

a. Many students as a group lifted a piano.

b. Many students lifted a piano, individually.

(iv)   "Most farmers who own a donkey beat it" reads as for most farmers who own a donkey, they beat every donkey they own.

In Chapter 3, I have specified my alternative which I call a unified approach since it deals with the distributivity in sentences (1) and (2) in the same way such that the distributivity is the result of distributivity expansion. I also call it a non-quantificational approach toward distributivity since distributivity is not directly captured by quantification. The system of my approach comprises the following set of assumptions:

(A)   A semantically singular NP is translated into an individual variable. In DRT terms, such an NP introduces an individual discourse referent.

(B)   A semantically non-singular NP is translated into a non-individual variable. In DRT terms, it introduces a non-individual discourse referent.

(C)   A quantifier can bind more than one variable simultaneously (unselective binding).

(D)   Only the existential quantifier and the universal quantifier are the quantifiers of my system. The existential quantifier is introduced by Default Existential Generalization (Existential Closure) and the universal quantifier is introduced by the rule of distributivity expansion.

(E)   A natural language determiner marks the size or the cardinality of the i-sum which is denoted by an NP with the determiner.

I have shown, in this Chapter, that my approach can solve the problems raised by a non-unified approach without proposing ad hoc conditions. Here, I have also tried to restrict the pragmatic accommodations as much as possible. I have specified the semantics of various NPs in my approach. In addition, I have shown that the source of the distributivity must be the predicate in predicate-argument structure but not the argument.

Chapters 4 and 5 are about further empirical evidence for my approach. In Chapter 4 I have dealt with the fact that sentence (3) and (4) have the readings of (5) and (6), respectively. These phenomena are named "asymmetric quantification" by Rooth (1987) and "proportion problem" by Kadmon (1987, 1990).

(3)   Most farmers who own a donkey beat it.

(4)   Many students who drive a Ford hate it.

(5)   For most farmers who own a donkey, they beat every donkey they own.

(6)   For many students who drive a Ford, they hate every Ford they drive.

If the unselective binding hypothesis is correct, sentences (3) and (4) should read as (7) and (8), instead.

(7)   For most farmers who own a donkey, they beat most donkeys they own.

(8)   For many students who drive a Ford, they hate many Fords they drive.

Kamp and Reyle solved this problem by complicating the semantics in a way to incorporate the quantification over the equivalent set. To do this, they had to introduce a new notion of "principal discourse referent" into their system. But they could not explain why a certain discourse referent must be chosen as the principal discourse referent. Further, they still need some mechanism to explain the asymmetric quantification in sentence (9).

(9)   Some students who drive a Ford hate it.

(10)   For some students who drive a Ford, they hate every Ford they drive.

I have shown that my approach augmented with some rules for complex NPs with relative clauses (which are also needed in Kamp and Reyle's system) can explain the above data without stipulating the principal discourse referent and thus without complicating semantics unnecessarily.

Chapter 5 has been about what I call a "proper distributive predicate" which requires a non-atomic individual as its argument. For example, a Korean predicate which contains a pragmatic morpheme -tul (PM-tul) requires a non-atomic individual as its argument. Sentence (11) is not acceptable while sentence (12) is.

(11)   #John-i   ppali -tul   o-ess-ta.
        Nom quickly PM-tul came
        'John came quickly.'

(12)   John-kwa Bill-i   ppali   -tul   o-ess-ta.
        and   Nom quickly PM-tul came
        'John and Bill came quickly.'

However, *kak*-CN '*every*-CN' which requires a distributive predicate can combine with a proper distributive predicate. Sentence (13) is acceptable but sentence (14) is not. Sentence (15) is perfectly good.

(13) kak haksayng -i   o-ess-ta.
     every student Nom   came
     'Every student came.'

(14) #kak haksayng -i   mohi-ess-ta.
      every student Nom   gathered
     'Every student gathered.'

(15) kak haksayng -i   ppali -tul   o-ess-ta.
     every student Nom quickly PM-tul came
     'Every student came quickly.'

This result undermines the assumption taken up by an non-unified approach that an NP which is required to be followed by a distributive predicate must be translated into an individual variable. Rather, the result confirms that such an NP may (or must) be translated into a non-individual discourse referent. This is additional evidence for my approach over non-unified ones.

I have shown in this study that any approach toward the NP semantics which treats quantificational NPs differently from non-quantificational ones must be replaced by a theory which treats every NP as introducing an individual or a non-individual discourse referent on a DRS (in other words, it is translated into a variable of individual or non-individual type).

참고 문헌

김민수 (1981), 『國語意味論』, 서울: 일조각.

심재기 (1982), 『國語語彙論』, 서울: 집문당.

심재기, 이기용, 이정민 (1984), 『意味論序說』, 서울: 집문당.

이기용 (1974), 「몬태규 문법의 특성」, 『語學研究』, 10:2, pp.26-36.

_____ (1985), 『On Montague Grammar』, 서울: 한신문화사.

_____ (1998 a), 『언어와 세계―형식의미론』, 서울: 태학사.

_____ (1998 b), 『시제와 양상―가능세계 의미론』, 서울: 태학사.

_____ (1998 c), 『상황과 정보―상황의미론』, 서울: 태학사.

이익환 (1984), 『現代意味論』, 대우재단 학술총서, 서울: 민음사.

_____ (1985), 『意味論 槪論』, 서울: 한신문화사.

이장송 (1995), 『Distributivity and Quantification in Discourse Representation Theory』, 서울: 한국문화사

Aoun, Joseph, Norbert Hornstein, and Dominique Sportiche (1981), "Aspects of Wide Scope Quantification," *Journal of Linguistic Research* 1: 67-95.

Asher, Nicholas (1991), *Reference to Abstract Objects in English: A Philosophical Semantics for Natural Language Metaphysics*, manuscript, Department of Philosophy and The Center for Cognitive Science, University of Texas at Austin.

Bartsch, R. (1973), "The Semantics and Syntax of Number and Numbers," in J. Kimball (ed.), *Syntax and semantics* 2, Seminar Press, New York.

Bach, Emon (1981), "On Time, Tense, and Aspect: An essay in English Metaphysics," in Peter Cole (ed.), *Radical Pragmatics*, Academic Press, New York.

Bach, Emon & Barbara Partee (1980), "Anaphora and Semantic Structure," in Jody Kreman & A.E. Ojeda (eds.), *Papers from the Parasession on Pronouns and Anaphora*, Chicago Linguistic Society, Chicago.

Bartsch, Renate (1973), "The Semantics and Syntax of Number and Numbers," in John P. Kimball (ed.), *Syntax and Semantics* 2, Seminar Press, New York.

Barwise, Jon (1979), "On Branching Quantifiers in English," *Journal of Philosophic Logic* 8: 47-80.

Barwise, Jon (1985), "A model of the treatment of anaphora in situation semantics," *CSLI Working Paper* #1, Stanford University.

Barwise, Jon (1987), "Noun Phrases, Generalized Quantifiers, and Anaphora," in P.

Gardenfors (ed.), *Generalized Quantifiers: Linguistic and Logical Approaches*, Dordrecht, Reidel.

Barwise, Jon & Robin Cooper (1981), "Generalized Quantifiers and Natural Language," *Linguistics and Philosophy* 4: 159-219.

Buerle, Rainer & Urs Egli (1985), "Anapher, Nominalphrase und Eselssaetze," in *Arbeitspapiere des Sonderforschungsbereichs* 99, Konstanz.

Beatie, James (1788), *The Theory of Language*, reprinted (1968), Menston, The Scholar Press.

Bennett, Michael R. (1974), *Some Extensions of a Montague Fragment of English*, Ph.D. dissertation, UCLA.

Blau, Ulrich (1981), "Collective Objects," *Theoretical Linguistics* 8: 101-130.

Bunt, H.C. (1979), "Ensembles and the Formal Semantic Properties of Mass Terms," in Francis J. Pelletier (ed.), *Mass Terms: Some Philosophical Problems*, Reidel, Dordrecht.

Carlson, Gregory N. (1977), *Reference to Kinds in English*, Ph.D. dissertation, University of Massachusetts, Amherst. Reproduced (1977) by the Indiana University Linguistics Club.

Carlson, Gregory (1982), "Logical form: types of evidence," *Linguistics and Philosophy* 6: 295-318.

Carlson, Lauri (1980), "Plural Quantification," manuscript, MIT.

Chierchia, Gennaro (1984), *Topics in the Syntax and Semantics of Infinitives and Gerunds*, Ph.D. dissertation, University of Massachusetts, Amherst.

Chierchia, Gennaro (1988), "Dynamic Generalized Quantifiers and Donkey Anaphora," in M, Krifka ed., *Genericity in Natural Language SNS* - Bericht 88-42, University of Tbingen, W. Germany.

Chierchia, Gennaro & Mats Rooth (1984), "Configurational Notions in Discourse Representation Theory," in Charles Jones & Peter Sells (eds.), *Proceedings of NELS* 14, Graduate Linguistics Student Association, University of Massachusetts, Amherst.

Chierchia, Gennaro & Sally McConnel-Ginet (1990), *Meaning and Grammar-An Introduction to Semantics*, the MIT Press, Cambridge, Massachusetts.

Choe, Jae-woong (1987), *Anti-Quantifiers and A Theory of Distributivity*, Ph.D. dissertation, University of Massachusetts, Amherst.

Choi, H. B. (1929), *Wuli Malpon* ('Grammar of Our Language'), Chungum-sa Pub. Co., Seoul.

Chomsky, Noam (1980), "On Binding," *Linguistic Inquiry* 11: 1-46.

Chomsky, Noam (1981), *Lectures on Government and Binding.* The Pisa Lectures, Foris, Dordrecht.

Cooper, Robin (1979), "The interpretation of Pronouns," in Frank Henry & Helmut S. Schnelle (eds.), *Syntax and Semantics*, Vol. 10: Selections from the Third Groningen Round Table, Academic Press, New York.

Cooper, Robin (1983), *Quantification and Syntactic Theory*, Reidel, Dordrecht.

Cooper, Robin & Terence Parsons (1976), "Montague Grammar, Generative Semantics and interpretive Semantics," in Barbara H. Partee (ed.), *Montague Grammar*, Academic Press, New York.

Dougherty, Ray C. (1969), "An Interpretive Theory of Pronominal Reference," *Foundations of Language* 5: 488-519.

Dougherty, Ray C. (1970), "A Grammar of Coordinate Conjoined Structures: I," *Language* 46: 850-898.

Dowty, David R. (1986), "Collective Predicates, Distributive Predicates, and All," *ESCOL* 1986, 97-115.

Dowty, David R., & Belinda Brodie (1984), "The Semantics of "Floated" Quantifiers in a Transformationless Grammar," in Mark Cobler, Susannah MacKaye, & Michael Westcoat (eds.), *Proceedings of WCCFL* III, The Stanford Linguistics Association, Stanford University, 75-90.

Dowty, David, R., Robert E. Wall, & Stanley Peters (1981), *Introduction to Montague Semantics*, Reidel, Dordrecht.

Evans, Gareth (1977), "Pronouns, quantifiers and relative clauses (I)," *Canadian Journal of Philosophy*, 7.

Evans, Gareth (1980), "Pronouns," *Linguistic Inquiry* 11: 337-362.

Farkas, Donka F., & Yoko Sugioka (1983), "Restrictive If/When Clauses," *Linguistics and Philosophy* 6: 225-258.

Fiengo, Roberts, & Howard Lasnik (1973), "The Logical Structure of Reciprocal Sentences in English," *Foundations of Language* 12: 1-47.

Fodor, Janet, & Ivan Sag (1982), "Referential and Quantificational Indefinites," *Linguistics and Philosophy* 5: 355-398.

Frey, Werner, & Hans Kamp (1986), "Plural Anaphora and Plural Determiners," manuscript, University of Texas, Austin.

Gazdar, Gerald (1980), "A cross-categorial semantics for coordination," *Linguistics and Philosophy* 3: 407-409.

Gazdar, Gerald, Ewan Klein, Geoffrey Pullum, and Ivan Sag (1985), *Generalized Phrase Structure Grammar*, Blackwell.

Geach, Peter T. (1962), *Reference and Generality*, Cornell University Press, Ithaca.

Gil, David (1987), "Definiteness, Noun Phrase Configurationality, and the Count-Mass Distinction," in Eric J. Reuland and Alice terMeulen (eds.), *The

Representation of (In)definiteness, The MIT Press, Cambridge, Massachusetts.

Gillon, Brendan (1987), "The Readings of Plural Noun Phrases in English," *Linguistics and Philosophy* 10: 199-219.

Gillon, Brendan (1990), "Plural Noun Phrases and Their Readings: A Reply to Lasersohn," *Linguistics and Philosophy* 13: 477-485.

Gertzer, G., (1978), *Universal Algebra*, 2nd edition, Springer, New York.

Green, Georgia M. (1981), "Pragmatics and syntactic description," in *Studies in the Linguistic Sciences*, 11(1), 27-38, Department of linguistics, University of Illinois, Urbana, IL.

Green, Georgia M. (1982), "Linguistics and the pragmatics of language use," *Poetics*, 11, 45-76.

Green, Georgia M. (1989), *Pragmatics and Natural Language Understanding*, Lawrence Erlbaum Associates, Publishers, Hillsdale, New Jersey.

Grice, H.P. (1967), "Logic and conversation," William James Lectures, Harvard, published in Donald Davidson & Gilbert Harman (eds.), *The Logic of Grammar*, 1976.

Groenendijk, Jeroen, & Martin Stokhof (1989), "Dynamic Predicate Logic," manuscript, University of Amsterdam.

Grosz, B. J., Joshi, A. K., and Weinstein, S. (1983), "Providing a unified account of definite noun phrase in discourse," in *Proceedings of the 9th International Joint Conference on Artificial Intelligence*, Cambridge, Massachusetts.

Hak, Isabelle (1984), "Indirect Binding," *Linguistic Inquiry* 15: 185-224.

Hausser, Roland (1974), *Quantification in an Extended Montague Grammar*, Ph.D. dissertation, University of Texas, Austin.

Heim, Irene (1982), *The Semantics of Definite and Indefinite Noun Phrases*, Ph.D. dissertation, University of Massachusetts, Amherst.

Heim, Irene (1990), "E-type Pronouns and Donkey Anaphora," *Linguistics and Philosophy* 13.

Heim, I., H. Lasnik & R. May (1991), "Reciprocity and Plurality," *Linguistic Inquiry*, Vol. 22: 63-101.

Higginbotham, James (1983), "Logical Form, Binding, and Nominals," *Linguistic Inquiry* 14: 395-420.

Hinrichs, Erhard (1985), *A Compositional Semantics for Aktionsarten and NP Reference in English*, Ph.D. dissertation, The Ohio State University.

Hinrichs, Erhard (1986), "Temporal Anaphora in Discourses of English," *Linguistics and Philosophy* 9: 63-82.

Hintikka, Jaako (1974), "Quantifiers vs. Quantification Theory," *Linguistic Inquiry* 5: 153-177.

Hoeksema, Jack (1983), "Plurality and Conjunction," in Alice G.B. terMeulen (ed.), *Studies in Modeltheoretic Semantics*, Foris, Dordrecht.

Hong, K.S. (1990), "Subjecthood Test in Korean," ms..

Jackendoff, Ray S. (1977), *X′ Syntax: A Study of Phrase Structure*, MIT Press, Cambridge, Massachusetts.

Jackendoff, Ray S. (1983), *Semantics and Cognition*, The MIT Press, Cambridge, Massachusetts.

Janssen, Theo M.V. (1984), "Individual concepts are useful," in Fred Landman & Frank Veltman (eds.), *Varieties of Formal Semantics*, Foris, Dordrecht.

Kadmon, Nirit (1985), "The Discourse Representation of Noun Phrases with Numeral Determiners," in Stephen Berman, Jae-Woong Choe & Joyce McDonough (eds.), *Proceedings of NELS* 15, Graduate Linguistic Student Association, University of Massachusetts, Amherst.

Kadmon, Nirit (1987), *On Unique and Non-Unique Reference and Asymmetric Quantification*, Ph.D. dissertation, University of Massachusetts, reproduced by the GLSA, Linguistics Dept., University of Massachusetts, Amherst.

Kadmon, Nirit (1990), "Uniqueness," *Linguistics and Philosophy* 13: 273-324.

Kamp, Hans (1981), "A Theory of Truth and Semantic Representation," in Jeroen Groenendijk, Theo M,V. Janssen & Martin Stokhof (eds.), *Formal Methods in the Study of Language*, Vol. I, Mathematische Centrum, Amsterdam, reprinted in Goenendijk, Janssen & Martin Stokhof (eds.), (1984) Truth, Interpretation and Information, Foris, Dordrecht.

Kamp, Hans (1986), SID without Time, manuscript, University of Texas.

Kamp, Hans & U. Reyle (1990), From Discourse to Logic: An Introduction to Modeltheoretic Semantics of Natural Language, Formal Logic and Discourse Representation Theory, manuscript.

Karttunen, Lauri (1976), "Discourse referents," in James D. McCawley (ed.), Syntax and Semantics 7: Notes from the linguistic Underground, Academic Press, New York.

Karttunen, Lauri (1977), "Syntax and semantics of questions," *Linguistics and philosophy* 1: 3-44.

Keenan, Edward L. & Leonard M. Faltz (1985), *Boolean Semantics of Natural Language*, Dordrecht, Reidel.

Keenan, Edward L & Y. Stavi, (1986), "A Semantic Characterization of natural Language Determiners," *Linguistics and Philosophy* 9: 259-326.

Kempson, Ruth, & Annabelle Cormack (1981), "Ambiguity and Quantification," *Linguistics and Philosophy* 4: 259-309.

Kratzer, Angelika (1989), "Stage-Level and Individual-Level Predicates," in Bach, Kratzer, and Partee, eds., *Papers on Quantification*, NSF Report, University of Massachusetts, Amherst.

Krifka, Manfred (1991), "How to Get Rid of Group, Using DRT: A Case for Discourse-Oriented Semantics," *Texas Linguistic Forum* 32: Discourse 72-109.

Kuh, Hakan (1986), "Plural Copying in Korean," *Harvard Studies in Korean Linguistics*, 239-250, Harvard University, Cambridge, Massachusetts.

Ladusaw, William A. (1979), *Polarity Sensitivity as Inherent Scope Relations*, Ph.D. dissertation, University of Texas, Austin, reprinted (1980), Indiana University Linguistics Club.

Ladusaw, William A. (1982), "Semantic Constraints on the English Partitive Construction," in Daniel P. Flickinger, Marlys Macken, & Nancy Wiegand (eds.), *Proceedings of WCCFL* I, The Stanford Linguistics Association, Stanford University.

Landman, Fred (1986), "Towards a Theory of Information," *GRASS* 6, Foris, Dordrecht.

Landman, Fred (1986), "Pegs and Alecs," in F.Landman, *Towards a Theory of Information: The Status of Partial Objects in Semantics*, Dordrecht, Foris.

Landman, Fred (1989), "Groups, I," *Linguistics and Philosophy* 12: 559-605.

Landman, Fred (1991), *Structures for Semantics*, Kluwer Academic Press, Dordrecht.

Langendoen, D. Terance (1978), "The Logic of Reciprocity," *Linguistic Inquiry* 9: 177-197.

Lasersohn, Peter (1988), *A Semantics for Groups and Events*, Ph.D. dissertation, The Ohio State university.

Lasersohn, Peter (1990), "Group Action and Spatio-Temporal Proximity," *Linguistics and Philosophy* 13, 179-206.

Lasnik, Howard (1976), "Remarks on coreference," *Linguistic Analysis* 2: 1-22.

Lasnik, Howard (1980), "On two recent treatments of disjoint reference," *Journal of Linguistic Research* 1: 48-58.

Lee, Han-gyu (1992), *The Pragmatics and Syntax of Pragmatic Morphemes in Korean*, Ph.D. dissertation, University of Illinois at Urban-Champaign, Urbana.

Lee, Ik-Whan (1979), *Korean Particles, Complements, and Questions: A Montague Grammar Approach*, Ph.D. dissertation, University of Texas at Austin.

Lee, Ki-Yong (1974), *The Treatment of Some English Constructions in Montague Grammar*, Ph.D. dissertation, University of Texas at Austin.

Lewis, David (1975), "Adverbs of quantification," in Edward L. Keenan (ed.), *Formal Semantics of Natural Language*, Cambridge University Press.

Lewis, David (1979), "Score-keeping in a language game," in Rainer Bauerle, Urs

Egli, & Arnim von Stechow (eds.), *Semantics from a Different Point of View*, Springer, Berlin.

Link, Godehard (1983), "The Logical Analysis of Plurals and mass Terms: A Lattice-theoretic approach," in Rainer Bauerle, Christoph Schwarze, and Arnim von Stechow (eds.), *Meaning, Use, and Interpretation of Language*, de Gruyter, Berlin.

Link, Godehard (1984), "Hydras: On the Logic of Relative Clause Constructions with Multiple Heads," in Fred Landman & Frank Veldman (eds.), *Varieties of Formal Semantics*, Foris, Dordrecht, 245-257.

Link, Godehard (1987), "Generalized Quantifiers and plurals," in Peter Gardenfors (ed.), *Generalized Quantifiers*, Reidel Publishing Company, 151-180.

Link, Godehard (to appear), "Plural," in Dieter Wunderlich & Arnim von Stechow (eds.), *Handbook of Semantics*.

Loenning, Jan-Tore (1989), Some Aspects of the Logic of Plural Noun Phrases, *COSMOS-Report* 11, Dept. of Mathematics, University of Oslo.

Lyons, John (1977), *Semantics*, Vol I & II, Cambridge University Press.

May, Robert (1977), *The Grammar of Quantification*, Ph.D. dissertation, MIT.

May, Robert (1985), *Logical Form: Its Structure and derivation*, MIT Press, Cambridge, Massachusetts.

Massey, Gerald J. (1976), "Tom, Dick, Harry, and All the King? men," *American Philosophical Quarterly* 13: 89-107.

Montague, Richard (1970), "Universal Grammar," *Theoria* 36: 373-398.

Montague, Richard (1973), "The Proper Treatment of Quantification in Ordinary English," in Jaakko Hintikka, Julius Moravcsik, & Patrick Suppes, (eds.), *Approaches to Natural Language: Proceedings of the 1970 Stanford Workshop on Grammar and Semantics*, Reidel, Dordrecht, reprinted in Thomason (1974).

Morgan, Jerry L. (1973), *Presupposition and the representation of meaning: Prolegomena*, Ph.D. dissertation, University of Chicago, Chicago, IL.

Morgan, Jerry L. (1975), "Some interactions of syntax and pragmatics," in P. Cole & J. Morgan (eds.), *Syntax and Semantics*, vol. 3: Speech Acts (pp. 289-304), Academic Press, New York.

Morgan. Jerry L. (1981), "Discourse theory and the independence of sentence grammar," in D. Tannen (ed.), *Georgetown University Roundtable on Language and Linguistics* 1981: Analyzing discourse: Text and talk (pp> 176-204), Georgetown Press, Washington D.C..

Neale, Stephen (1990), *Descriptions*, The MIT Press, Cambridge, Massachusetts.

Partee, Barbara H. (1984), "Nominal and Temporal Anaphora," *Linguistics and Philosophy* 7: 243-286.

Partee, Barbara H. & Emmon Bach (1981), "Quantification, Pronouns, and VP Anaphora," in Jeroen Groendijk, Theo M. V. Janssen & Martin Stokhof (eds.), *Formal Methods in the Study of Language, Vol. I, Mathematische Centrum*, Amsterdam. Reprinted in Groenendijk, Janssen & Stokhof (eds.), (1984) Truth, Interpretation and Information. Foris, Dordrecht.

Partee, Barbara H., Emon Bach and Angelika Kratzer (1987), *Quantification: A Cross-Linguistic Investigation*, NSF Proposal.

Partee, Barbara H. & Mats Rooth (1983), "Generalized conjunction and type ambiguity," in Rainer Bauerle, Christoph Schwarze, and Arnim von Stechow (eds.), *Meaning, Use and Interpretation of Language*, de Gryter, Berlin.

Partee, B. H., A. terMeulen and R.E. Wall (1990), *Mathematical methods in Linguistics*, Kluwer Academic Publishers, Dordrecht.

Quine, W.V.O. (1960), *Word and Object*, The MIT Press, Cambridge.

Quirk, R., S. Greenbaum, G. Leech and J. Svartik (1985), *A Comprehensive grammar of the English Language*, Longman, New York.

Reichenbach, Hans (1947), *Elements of Symbolic Logic*, University of California Press, Berkeley.

Reinhart, Tanya (1983), "Coreference and bound anaphora: A restatement of the anaphora questions," *Linguistics and Philosophy* 6: 47-88.

Reyle, Uwe (1991), *DRT: Nominal Anaphora and Tenses*, Ms, The Third European Summer School in Language, Logic and Information, Universität des Saarlandes, Saarbrüchen, August 12-23, 1991.

Roberts, Craige (1987), *Modal Subordination, Anaphora, and Distributivity*, Ph.D. dissertation, University of Massachusetts, Amherst.

Root, Rebecca (1986), *The Semantics of Anaphora in Discourse*, Ph.D. dissertation, University of Texas, Austin.

Rooth, Mats (1986), "NP Interpretation in Montague Grammar, File Change Semantics, and Situation Semantics," manuscript, CSLI, Stanford University.

Rooth, Mats & Barbara H. Partee (1982), "Conjunction, type ambiguity, and wide scope or," in Daniel P. Flickinger, Marlys Macken, & Nancy Wiegand (eds.), *Proceedings of WCCFL* I, The Stanford Linguistics Association, Stanford University.

Russell, B. (1905), "On Denoting," *Mind* 14.

Scha, Remko (1981), "Distributive, Collective and Cumulative Quantification," in Jeoren Groenendijk, Theo M. V. Janssen & Martin Stokhof (eds.), Formal Methods in the Study of Language, Vol.I, Mathematische Centrum, Amsterdam. Reprinted in Groenendijk, Janssen & Stokhof (eds.), (1984) *Truth, Interpretation and Information*, Foris, Dordrecht.

Schwarzschild, Roger (1990), "Against Groups," in M. Stokhof & F. Torenvliet (eds.), *Proceedings of the 7th Amsterdam Colloquium*, ITLI, University of Amsterdam.

Schwarzschild, Roger (1991), *On the Meaning of Definite Plural Noun Phrases*, Ph.D. dissertation, University of Massechusetts, Amherst.

Sells, Peter (1985), "On the Nature of 'Logophoricity'," Annie Zaenen (ed.), *Studies in Grammatical Theory and Discourse Structure*, Vol. II: Logophoricity and Bound Anaphora, CSLI, Stanford.

Sidner, C.L. (1981), "Focusing for interpretation of pronouns," *Computational Linguistics* 7(4): 217-231.

Stalnaker, Robert (1979), "Assertion," in Peter Cole (ed.), *Syntax and Semantics* 9, Academic Press, New York.

Tarski, Alfred (1952), "The Semantic Concept of Truth," in Linsky, ed. (1952), pp. 13-47.

Thomason, Richmond H. (1974), *Formal Philosophy: Selected Papers of Richard Montague*, Yale University Press, New Haven.

Thomason, Richmond H. (1980), "A Model Theory for Propositional Attitudes," *Linguistics and Philosophy* 4: 47-70.

Ullman, Stephen (1962), *Semantics: An Introduction to the Science of Meaning*, Oxford: Basil Blackwell.

van Benthem, Johan (1983), "Determiners and logic," *Linguistics and Philosophy* 6: 447-478.

van Benthem, Johan (1986), *Essays in Logical Semantics*, Kluwer Academic Press, Dordrecht.

van Eijk, Jan (1983), "Discourse Representation Theory and Plurality," in Alice terMeulen (ed.), *Studies in Modeltheoretic Semantics*, Foris, Dordrecht.

Webber, Bonnie (1978), *A Formal Approach to Discourse Anaphora*, Technical Report 3736, Bolt, Beranek and Newman, Inc., Ph.D. dissertation.

Webber, Bonnie (1983), "So What Can We Talk About Now?" in Michael Brady, & Robert C. Berwick (eds.), *Computational Models of discourse*, The MIT Press, Cambridge, Massachusetts.

Wierzbicka, Anna (1980), *Lingua Mentalis: The semantics of Natural Language*, Academic Press, Sydney.

Williams, Edwin S. (1980), "Predication," *Linguistic Inquiry* 11: 203-238.

찾아보기

담화표상이론

이장송 지음

1999년 5월 3일 인쇄
1999년 5월 15일 발행

발행인: 김진수
발행처: 한국문화사
133-112 서울시 성동구 성수 1가 2동 13-156
전화 • 02) 464-7708, 3409-4488
팩스 • 02) 499-0846
등록번호 제2-1276호

값18,000원

ISBN   89 - 7735 - 618 - 0